ecpr PRESS

I0095961

Theorising Decentralisation

Comparative evidence from sub-national Switzerland

Sean Mueller

ecpr PRESS

© Sean Mueller 2015

First published by the ECPR Press in 2015

Cover: View of Swiss Cantonal Tree in Leicester Square, London © dade72/Shutterstock.com

The ECPR Press is the publishing imprint of the European Consortium for Political Research (ECPR), a scholarly association, which supports and encourages the training, research and cross-national co-operation of political scientists in institutions throughout Europe and beyond.

ECPR Press
Harbour House
Hythe Quay
Colchester
CO2 8JF
United Kingdom

All rights reserved. No part of this book may be reprinted or reproduced or utilised in any form or by any electronic, mechanical, or other means, now known or hereafter invented, including photocopying and recording, or in any information storage or retrieval system, without permission in writing from the publishers.

Typeset by Lapiz Digital Services

Printed and bound by Lightning Source

British Library Cataloguing in Publication Data

A catalogue record for this book is available from the British Library

ISBN: 978-1-78552-12-9-4
PDF ISBN: 978-1-78552-140-9
EPUB ISBN: 978-1-78552-1-41-6
KINDLE ISBN: 978-1-78552-14-2-3

www.ecpr.eu/ecprpress

ECPR Press Series Editors
Dario Castiglione (University of Exeter)
Peter Kennealy (European University Institute)
Alexandra Segerberg (Stockholm University)

More Monographs from ECPR Press

Conditional Democracy: The Contemporary Debate on Political Reform in Chinese Universities
(ISBN: 9781907301698) Emilie Frenkiel

Consultative Committees in the European Union: No Vote – No Influence?
(ISBN: 9781910259429) Diana Panke, Christoph Hönnige and Julia Gollub

Democratic Reform and Consolidation: The Cases of Mexico and Turkey
(ISBN: 9781907301674) Evren Celik Wiltse

Politicisation, Issue Salience and Consumer Policies of the European Commission
(ISBN: 9781785521270) Christian Rauh

Please visit www.ecpr.eu/ecprpress for information about new publications.

Contents

List of Figures and Tables

Figures

Note: Some figures are available in colour, *see* http://press.ecpr.eu/resources.asp

Tables

Abbreviations

BDP	*Bürgerlich-Demokratische Partei*	Democratic Citizens' Party
CC	(*Kantonsverfassung/Constitution Cantonale*)	Cantonal Constitution
CVP	*Christlichdemokratische Volkspartei*	Christian-Democratic Party
FC	(*Bundesverfassung/Constitution Fédérale*)	Federal Constitution
FDP	*Freisinnig-Demokratische Partei*	Liberal Party
LG	(*Gemeinde/Commune*)	Local Government
LGA	(*Gemeindeverband/Association des communes*)	Local Government Association
MCP	(*Landrat, Grossrat, Conseiller* etc.)	Member of Cantonal Parliament
SP	*Sozialdemokratische Partei*	Socialist Party
SVP	*Schweizerische Volkspartei*	Swiss People's Party

The 26 Swiss Cantons

AG	Aargau		NW	Nidwalden
AI	Appenzell Inner-Rhodes		OW	Obwalden
AR	Appenzell Outer-Rhodes		SG	St. Gall
BE	Berne		SH	Schaffhausen
BL	Basel-Countryside		SO	Solothurn
BS	Basel-City		SZ	Schwyz
FR	Fribourg		TG	Thurgau
GE	Geneva		TI	Ticino
GL	Glarus		UR	Uri
GR	Grisons		VD	Vaud
JU	Jura		VS	Valais
LU	Lucerne		ZG	Zug
NE	Neuchâtel		ZH	Zurich

Preface

This book, which draws on my PhD thesis defended at the University of Kent in May 2013, has four inspirational sources. The first is Adrian Vatter's *Kantonale Demokratien* (2002), a systematic comparison of the 26 Swiss cantons as political systems in their own right; the second is Michael Burgess' *Comparative Federalism* (2006), a conceptual exegesis of federalism from historical, philosophical and comparative perspectives. Together, they have made me realise that what is still missing is a systematic comparison and explanation of federalism *within* the Swiss cantons. Due to my fascination with anything Anglophone I had chosen Michael Burgess as my first supervisor at Kent, while Adrian Vatter later became the external examiner. I thank them for their support, wisdom and critiques both during and after my PhD studies.

The third inspiration comes from Robert Putnam's *Making Democracy Work* (1993), after whose cross-regional methodology I decided to model my mixed-methods research design. I had the pleasure to rely on that book to introduce BA students at Kent to the intricacies of comparative politics, between 2009 and 2012. The fourth and final inspiration came from Christopher Hughes' *A History of the Cantons*, an unfortunately never finished collection of essays on each Swiss canton's peculiar path to modernity. In that sense my aim was to contribute to a better understanding of federalism through studying the Swiss cantons and explaining centralisation and decentralisation within them. The legacy of Christopher Hughes continues to live on in the form of the *Centre for Swiss Politics*, also based at Kent, whose Director Paolo Dardanelli was my second supervisor. I thank him for the many interesting and challenging discussions on Swiss politics, Swiss federalism and, of course, the Swiss cantons.

Lidija Basta Fleiner has been a key motivational force to undertake my PhD studies in the first place, both indirectly through letting me work with her and directly through repeatedly reminding me to do so. Marie-Louise Burgess at the *Centre for Federal Studies* I thank for helping me procure financial support from the *James Madison Trust*, and for including me in the organisation of several summer schools in Canterbury. The same goes for my colleague, flatmate and friend, Sören Keil, now at Canterbury Christchurch University. I thank Stefan Rossbach and Francis Pritchard for having entrusted me with seminar teaching at Kent right from the beginning. The convenor of the comparative politics module, Ed Morgan-Jones, provided many key references, recommendations and critical questions on my methodological proceedings. Matt Loveless I thank for assistance with quantitative techniques and for organising an ESRC workshop on conceptualising causality. All other participants of the Comparative Politics research group, as well as all my PhD colleagues at Kent, I thank for having listened to earlier drafts. Thomas Fleiner, Nenad Stojanovic, Daniel Bochsler, Clive Church, Hans-Peter Schaub, Wolf Linder and Andreas Ladner

I thank for feedback and data on the Swiss, cantonal and/or local aspects of this book. I twice applied for a doctoral grant from the Swiss National Science Foundation and, although unsuccessful, three anonymous reviewers provided extremely useful feedback. The same was the case as regards the ECPR's two peer reviewers.

The idea of travelling to all the cantons came to me while chatting to childhood friends in Glarus. I have received logistical support in Fribourg, Berne, Basel, Zofingen and Chur: thank you Jonas and Rolf & Reni for lending me your car and thank you Bashkim and Sabrina, Kian, Bianca and Takeo and Felix for hosting me on various occasions. My 54 interview partners across Switzerland I thank for having received me and talked to me so openly about whatever I felt was interesting. These hours were enjoyable lessons in politics, law, history and economy from the local through the cantonal to the national – and sometimes even the global – level. The Federal Office for Statistics, numerous cantonal associations and political parties, as well as all cantonal and local authorities that have fed me with otherwise unavailable material, I proudly thank for making Switzerland such a wonderful, because open, accessible and modest country to study.

I thank Olivier Meuwly for his reflections on the political history of Vaud and also, together with Barbara Studer Immenhauser, for the helpful literature suggestions. Oscar Mazzoleni and Philippe Koch I thank for the enthusiasm they shared with me in resurrecting the Federalism & Territorial Politics working group of the Swiss Political Science Association. The UK PSA, the Swiss Embassy in London and the Swiss National Science Foundation I thank for travel grants to attend conferences and summer schools in Edinburgh, Belfast, London, Brussels, Basel, Lucerne, Lugano, and Venice at which parts of, or offshoots from, my research were presented, or where I have received further training.

I am grateful to Alexander Arens for preparing the map of cantonal decentralisation (Figure 4.10) and the following persons and organisations for permissions to reprint, and help in translating into English, a number of figures: Marco Zanoli (Figure 6.2); Paul Messerli, Hans-Rudolf Egli, and the *Geographische Rundschau* (Figure 6.3); Andreas Meyerhans, the *Historischer Verein Schwyz* and *Chronos* (Figure 6.4); André Rüegsegger and August Mächler of the Canton of Schwyz (Figure 6.5); Barbara Stolba and Christian Kleeb of the NZZ (Figure 6.6); and Walter Frizzoni and Sandra Fritschi of the Canton of Grisons (Figure 6.7). Samuel P. Bisig gave a critical lecture on the full PhD manuscript while Ildi Clarke thoroughly proofread and indexed the final book manuscript, for which many thanks are due. All remaining errors and inaccuracies are my sole responsibility, of course.

I am also indebted to my father: his constant source of critical thinking and rigorous parsimony, even after he passed away on that sunny October morning in 2010; my mother: restless, hardworking and dedicated as I have strived to be; my sister: creative, thoughtful and profound as I wish this thesis to be; and my wife Natia: the constant, constructive and caring support without which both my working and this thesis would have been entirely impossible. The sense of progressive patriotism developed over the course of this research is a result both of the critical distance imparted to me as child of my parents and of looking at Switzerland from the outside. If I studied the Swiss cantons while at Kent, then with the double intention of learning more about my fatherland (literally) and how best to conceive of, measure and explain territorial differences and similarities across political systems. I dedicate this book to my father.

Sean Mueller
Berne, May 2015

Non è questo 'l terren ch'i' toccai pria?
Non è questo il mio nido
Ove nudrito fui sí dolcemente?

Non è questa la patria in ch'io mi fido,
Madre benigna et pia,
Che copre l'un et l'altro mio parente?

Petrarch, 'Italia mia' (1344)*

---

*   'Is not this the ground that I first touched? Is not this my nest, where I was so sweetly nurtured? Is not this the homeland in which I trust; the benign, devout mother that covers both my parents?', translation from *The Institute for the Study of Western Civilization*, Cupertino CA. Available online: http://www.westernciv.com/greatminds/petrarch/petrarchmiaitalia.shtml (last accessed 15 January 2015).

Introduction

Why are some political systems more centralised than others? In Europe as much as elsewhere, a trend of the past decades has been to decentralise, regionalise, or federalise (Burgess 2012; Keating 2013; Schakel *et al.* 2015). However, why political systems have once centralised or continue to do so is equally, if not even more relevant – for before one can *de*centralise, there needs to *be* a centre in the first place. And yet attempts to systematically define, measure and explain centralisation are rare (*see* however Kollman 2013), not least because the concept itself is contested. Accordingly, this book has five research goals.

Research goals

The five research goals this monograph aims to achieve are the following:

1. Reconceptualise centralisation to define its meaning and distinguish its dimensions.
2. Develop a theoretical framework from which testable hypotheses can be drawn.
3. Measure centralisation in a both internally and externally valid and reliable way.
4. Explain centralisation using both quantitative and qualitative methods.
5. Collect and combine data on the 26 Swiss cantons as the comparative template for both measurement and explanation.

1. *Concept.* More than 30 years ago, Jim Bulpitt (1983: 34) wrote that the concept of 'centralisation needs to be repaired, not written off'. This book attempts to provide exactly this. More particularly, centralisation is argued to consist of three distinct dimensions. This builds on existing scholarship but also takes it one step further. Comparative politics has traditionally focused either on the *policy*-dimension of vertical power sharing, such as the ratio of money raised or spent by lower-level entities (e.g. Rodden 2004); or on the *polity*-dimension, such as constitutional autonomy and sub-national veto rights (e.g. Watts 2008). This is all very relevant, but insufficient if we want to understand how political power is really organised and exercised territorially. That is why I add a third dimension composed of *political actors and processes*. Such an enlargement of our understanding of (de)centralisation is necessary since the three dimensions – policy, polity and politics – can be complementary or contradictory (Piattoni 2010). They are complementary in a confederal political system, where most functions are exercised sub-nationally, where regions retain residual powers and veto rights over national decision, and where political parties and elections, too, are primarily organised in a confederal manner (Duchacek 1987: 160; Forsyth 1981: 1). But the three dimensions are contradictory in a system like the European Union, where

some functions have been Europeanised, whose budget consists of bottom-up contributions, where the Member States remain the masters of the treaties, where supra-national elections are often second-order, but where lobbying, in turn, is rather centralised (Hix and Høyland 2011; Hooghe and Marks 2001). Being aware of centralisation's three dimensions is key to understanding how they interact, what causes them, and what effect they have on the whole and on actual decision making.

2. *Theory*. The second step in every attempt to generate scientific knowledge is theorising (Munck 2010: 10). Numerous efforts to explain (de)centralisation have already been undertaken, so the goal here is not to add yet another set of potential causes, but rather to integrate alternative approaches into a coherent framework. That framework, presented in Chapter Two, consists of both socio-cultural and structural conditions that enable/obstruct political decisions on more/less centralisation. The reason for this integration is that *societal* approaches (e.g. Livingston 1956; Erk 2008) explain why in a context of territorial diversity federalism is an appropriate remedy for conflict, but not why or when exactly actors choose how much centralisation. Explanations focusing on *actors* (e.g. Riker 1964; Alonso 2012), in turn, fail to appreciate the importance of cleavages, territorial identity and political culture, treating them as exogenous to their theory. Others, finally, disregard both societal diversity and actors, either because they are animated by assumptions of *optimal unit size* (e.g. Tiebout 1956; Alesina and Spolaore 2003) or because they are convinced of the primacy of *political culture* (e.g. Duchacek 1987; Elazar 1995–1999). Thus, after a systematic enquiry into three traditional approaches to explaining (de)centralisation, I develop a single, integrated theoretical framework. In that framework I hypothesise the causal influence of a 'federal' political culture and a conservative political ideology next to, rather than in isolation from, structural factors such as population size, area and distance.

3. *Measurement*. To test the hypotheses derived from that integrated theoretical framework built around centralisation so repaired, we must find a solution for the fact that while 'centralization is relatively simple to define, it is complex to measure' (Blondel 1995: 229). Surveying a range of literatures from fields as diverse as federalism, regionalism, local government studies, party politics, political geography, International Relations, and state formation helps in that endeavour. In fact, each (sub)discipline has focused on different indicators of one of the three dimensions of centralisation. For example, the party politics literature measures centralisation within parties through candidate selection (Janda 1980; Detterbeck and Hepburn 2010); fiscal federalism, among other things, looks at the ratio of lower-level staff salaries from total public salaries (Chhibber and Kollman 2004: 234); and local government scholars like Page (1991) and Tarrow (1974, 1977) have long argued that local influence over higher-level politics can be captured through the existence of double mandates, e.g. a mayor who is also a national MP (in French: *cumul des mandats*).

4. *Explanation*. The fourth research goal of this book is to explain centralisation. That means empirically identifying 'the causal circumstances that

brought it about' (Little 1998: 160) and involves an assessment of both regularity (if x, then y) and process (through z) (Gerring 2007: 97; Collier 2011). I will combine quantitative and qualitative methods in a 'nested analysis' (Lieberman 2005), for while the former increase our confidence in external validity and help in dealing with multicausality, the latter's strengths are internal validity and context sensitivity. Finally, an explanation of political phenomena also has to reveal the way in which actual political decisions are taken, for actors alone are able to act. This calls for a specific kind of empirical evidence to be provided (*see* Tarrow 1995), namely interviews with individuals involved in such processes and data on parliamentary debates and government reports to assess motivations and to gain insights into the impact of ideology and political culture on political behaviour.

5. *Empirics.* The fifth and final goal then is purely instrumental – but no less ambitious. It consists in collecting the necessary data on *all* the Swiss cantons to both measure and explain centralisation. But instead of studying national-regional or national-local relations, I study local governments *as part of* their region, that is centralisation *within* the 26 cantons as largely independent and fairly similar political systems. There are two reasons why choosing a single country and, of all places, such a small one as Switzerland, is a suitable way to go:

- First, there is a theoretical puzzle. Every scholar of comparative politics adduces Switzerland as one of the most decentralised, 'most federal' case (e.g. Elazar 1987). But even the quickest of all glances beneath the national level reveals that some of Switzerland's 26 cantons are themselves very centralised, while in others the local trumps the cantonal level in terms of policy-making, the way political actors are organised, or where residual powers lie institutionally (Horber-Papazian and Jacot-Descombes 2014; Fiechter 2010; Rühli 2012). This creates many interesting questions, for example: how is it possible that regional centralisation cohabits with national non-centralisation? What factors explain the former, which ones the latter, or are the same causal processes at work for both? If so, to what extent do rivalling national-level frameworks for explaining territorial governance – relying, respectively, on societal heterogeneity, political culture, party-politics, or size – travel 'downwards'? Which ones work best or, if complementary, how can they be combined? Exactly why are the French-speaking cantons more centralised? Has it got to do with political culture, path dependency, or both? And is that true even when controlling for area, population size and/or topography? But then what about differences *within* the group of French-speaking cantons, and where does that leave political ideologies and actors?
- Second, and following on from that cross-cantonal variation, there is methodological convenience. The Swiss cantons are numerous enough to allow for statistical tests to detect representative covariation, but also similar enough to safely assume that several background variables (e.g. stability, wealth and trust in politics, or a shared history and 'civic' understanding of nationhood) are controlled for (Lijphart 2002: 14).

This matters because two problems continue to haunt comparative federalism and territorial politics: On the one hand, only so many countries are federal, so there are not enough cases to comprehensively test a theory, while there are too many variables for a small-N comparison to be validly made (Lijphart 1971 and 1975). On the other hand, if the selection criteria are sufficiently 'stretched' (Sartori 1970) – say, by speaking of 'regional authority' (Hooghe *et al.* 2008 and 2010) instead of federalism – the number of cases conveniently rises, but only to lead to the second problem: lack of internal validity (*see* Przeworski and Teune 1970; Blalock 1982; Peters 1998; Brady and Collier 2004). One way out of this dilemma of 'too many variables, not enough cases' vs. 'concept stretching' (Geddes 2007) is precisely a sub-national comparison, understood here not as a within-case, but as a cross-case comparison. Thus OLS regression analyses are strengthened by the fact that Local Governments (LGs) have the same basic meaning across all 26 polities; studying four cantons in-depth then allows me to trace the actual causal process to where decisions are taken: by political parties, the government, in parliament, through lobbying, and/or by the electorate. In sum, although the empirical emphasis is on Switzerland and the Swiss cantons, the overall goal remains to conceptualise, theorise, measure and explain (de)centralisation *in general*.

In terms of terminology, 'centralisation' and 'decentralisation' are henceforth treated as ideal-type endpoints on a continuum called '(de)centralisation'. I will use the latter expression to refer to the general phenomenon and the former two for specific instances of it. For the Swiss cantons, I will speak of 'cantonal decentralisation' throughout, unless when specifically referring to 'the centralised cantons'. But why would one want to study (de)centralisation in the first place?

Why studying (de)centralisation matters

Decentralisation is widely advocated as a means to foster legitimacy, stimulate more equitable growth, enhance policy efficiency and increase democratic accountability; it is even made a key element of 'good governance' in general. The World Bank, for example, published an extensive review of projects worth 80 billion USD that contain a decentralisation component, showing when and how decentralisation stimulates local participation and sustainable growth (Mansuri and Rao 2012: 2). The worldwide development and cooperation community is flooded with such working papers on 'best practices' and 'lessons learned', sponsored by both bilateral and multilateral donors (e.g. BMZ 2008; Dabla-Norris and Wade 2002; UN-HABITAT 2009; Litvack and Seddon 1999; Kauzya 2005; MacDougall 2001). In Western Europe, 'regionalisation' has also been well under way for the past 40 years (*see* Putnam 1993; Jeffery 1996; Keating 1998; Loughlin 2001a; Dardanelli 2005). Even the archetype of nation-state centralisation, France, has embarked on reforms in that direction (Hoffmann 1959; Nordlinger 1965; Ashford

1978; Gourevitch 1980; Ammon *et al*. 1996; Loughlin and Seiler 2001). In short, because decentralisation is meant to be good, we need to know more about it.

But if most of these developments, and particularly the case of France, are driven mainly by considerations for efficiency, other sub-state entities more dramatically aspire for outright independence, like Scotland, Flanders, at least two Spanish regions or the infamous 'Padania' (Giordano 2000, 2001; Giordano and Roller 2004; Moreno *et al*. 1998; Murphy 2002; McDonnell 2006), in the long run, and try their best to attract European Union funding (Hooghe and Marks 2001; Mathias 2004; O'Dowd *et al*. 2003; Sykes and Shaw 2008), in the medium term. A similar wave of enthusiasm has swept across 'local self-government', defined in the European Charter of Local-Self-Government (1985, Art. 3.1) as 'the right and the ability of local authorities, within the limits of the law, to regulate and manage a substantial share of public affairs under their own responsibility and in the interests of the local population'. So even the local dimension is increasingly analysed using terms such as 'local state' (Cockburn 1977), 'local governance' (Denters and Rose 2005) or 'new localism' (Pratchett 2004; *see also* Pierre 1990; Le Galès 1995 and 2002; Gurr and King 1987; Greenwood and Stewart 1986; Gourevitch 1977; Goldsmith 1995, 2006). Centralisation is thus increasingly questioned, both as regards its redistributive function at the national level (Loughlin 2007b; Loughlin and Delcamp 2003; Pasquier 2005; Greer 2006a, 2006b; Toonen and van der Meer 2006) and within the EU (Burgess 2000; Majone 2006; McKay 2001; Bartolini 2004), for example by the UK.

However, as much as decentralism, localism and regionalism are related phenomena, 'centralisation' has only rarely been addressed in a conceptually consistent, theoretically grounded and empirically sustained way. Speaking of (de)centralisation as a continuum implies a change in perspective, away from local or regional autonomy to a focus on the encompassing political system. But what is the benchmark model, what are types of centralisation, dimensions to be included, and how do they relate to each other and to both its causes and effects? Treisman (2007) goes some way towards comprehensiveness, but constricts himself to effects; Bulpitt (1983), on the other hand, convincingly relates 'territorial systems analysis' (federalism) to decentralisation, but applies his framework to the UK only. Theoretical and conceptual questions thus often remain unanswered, also because, as de Tocqueville (2010 [1835]: 143) already observed, 'centralisation is a word repeated constantly today, and, in general, no one tries to clarify its meaning'.

In sum, studying (de)centralisation matters because it touches aspects vital for the legitimacy of political systems (e.g. forms and extent of local participation, territorial accountability, and transparent decision-making) and the efficiency with which they deliver public services (keywords here are fiscal equivalence, subsidiarity and 'the optimal scale'; Piattoni 2010: 33). Nevertheless, what is missing is a convincing account of why some actors in some systems chose a different degree of (de)centralisation than other actors in other contexts. To be able to start such an enquiry it is, first of all, necessary to provide a working definition of (de)centralisation.

What studying (de)centralisation contributes to

At its very core, (de)centralisation captures the degree to which political power (and not simply 'authority', as for Hooghe *et al.* 2008) is wielded by one government in relation to other governments on a territorially smaller/larger scale (Smith 1985: 1). Power is, of course, a fundamental attribute of political systems. Hence, every political system, indeed every social system that uses territory as a structural element for its hierarchy (Sack 1986; *see also* Saltman 2002; Kolers 2009; Delaney 2005; Edney 1974), is characterised by more or less centralisation, regardless of the actual level at which it is situated. The EU can be described as more centralised in one policy area than in another (Hooghe and Marks 2001), and less centralised before 1992/3 than after (Hix and Høyland 2011). Regional political systems, too, can be more or less centralised: in the United States, for example, one then talks about 'second-order devolution' (Bowman and Kearney 2011; *see also* Krueger and Bernick 2009). Thus, key to a proper understanding of (de)centralisation is the relationship between power and territory (Bulpitt 1983; Johnston 2001; Teschke 2006). For the sake of convenience, let us then stipulate that *a system is centralised if all political power is organised, located and exercised in and by the centre, while the less this is the case, the more there is decentralisation.*

The relations between the Swiss cantons and 'their' local government are exactly of this very same nature: power, territory and more or less autonomy for one or the other level. Swiss federalism thus enables a wonderful cross-sectional comparison that holds key attributes constant. And even if unearthing data on cantonal-local relations in Switzerland also contributes to another debate that has gained prominence in recent times, that about the role of local governments in federal states (Steytler 2009; Gamper and Palermo 2011), my purpose is *not* to explain Swiss federalism as such. The contextual goal, rather, is to make a specific contribution to the literature on Swiss politics and answer the question: Why are some cantons more centralised than others? This type of explanation is, for Hall (2013: 21), 'historically specific', i.e. 'one that provides a full account of the causal factors leading up to that outcome with some indication of their relative importance'. The standard answers given in the existing literature are political culture and history, but what is lacking is 'a theory' that specifically explains the impact of culture and history on political agency as well as the causal mechanisms that then link agency to cantonal decentralisation (Little 1998).

However, and more importantly, beyond the Swiss case a second type of explanation I want to provide is 'theory-oriented' (Hall 2013: 21). In order to do this convincingly, validly and reliably, my logically prior goal in this book is to provide a conceptual clarification of what I want to explain (the dependent variable) and relate this to a set of testable expectations (hypotheses) on the causal impact of independent variables. In trying to arrive at a single explanation for (de)centralisation I thus wish to make a theoretical contribution to the literature on comparative territorial politics, which I understand to include federal, regional and local government studies as well as theories of state formation and EU integration. But can an explanation of (de)centralisation with the Swiss cantons really be generalised to other, national political systems? Yes, for given certain assumptions, sub-national conclusions do apply to a larger universe of stable, democratic political systems of a size sufficiently large to warrant representative institutions (such as a parliament and a government) and organisations (chiefly parties and interest groups). I will return to that question at the end of this book, once the empirical evidence has been provided and the theoretical framework refined (*see* Chapter Eight).

Structure of the book

To come up with such a theoretical framework in the first place and firmly anchor it in the field of comparative territorial politics, Chapter One discusses several literatures that a) make a contribution to understanding the concept of (de)centralisation; b) propose theories to explain different degrees thereof; or that c) have already dealt with Swiss cantonal-local relations. I will draw on scholarship from various disciplines in addition to political science (especially political geography, macro-sociology and history) because they, too, have provided valuable insights into how the relationship between power and territory can or ought to be conceptualised. I do not wish to construct a 'science of territory' or 'territorology' (Brighenti 2010) but build a more solid conceptual ground for (de)centralisation than has commonly been the case (Maass 1959): to answer why (de)centralisation happens one must have a clear idea of what it *is* in the first place.

I then re-conceptualise (de)centralisation as being both multi-dimensional, that is with a polity-, policy- and politics-dimension, as well as continuous (Chapter Two). In comparing the merits of different perspectives to explaining (de)centralisation, I show why a novel approach is needed. The question that animates that chapter is the following: if we were able to characterise every political system in the world, past and present, as to its degree of (de)centralisation, then why would we see what we would see? This is indeed *the* question. Traditionally, answers have come from either a structuralist or agency-premised camp. An example for the latter is provided by the UK case, where devolution is argued to have taken place in 1997 because Labour was losing ground in Scotland (e.g. Bogdanor 2001; Hopkin 2009; Hough and Jeffery 2006; Alonso 2012). As an example for the former type of explanation, the US federation may be mentioned: there are 50 States today because from the original 13 former British colonies, the American Commonwealth has expanded westwards with federalism as the only way to bring about the benefits of a republic in such a large territory (e.g. Calhoun 2003 [1851], *The Federalist Papers* 1787–88; *see also* Huntington 1959). So devolution as party-political calculus in the one, federalism as the result of structural determinism in the other case? Or rather, did not Westminster (also) devolve powers because its centralist 'internal colonialism' (Hechter 1975) needed adaptation for the same reasons as outlined above, i.e. regional nationalism? And is not the US still federal thanks (also) to the decentralised nature of its political parties (Riker 1964)? In the place of such a rigid dichotomy I will propose an integrated theoretical framework of why (de)centralisation comes about, arguing that political actors rationally opt for more/less (de)centralisation influenced by both socio-cultural and structural factors. Mine thus falls in the middle of the mentioned two extreme types of approaches, because my theory spells out why and how certain conditions (size, political culture, diversity and socio-economics) influence which political actors (parties and the electorate) in making what kinds of decisions.

Chapter Three, on the case study design, introduces the Swiss cases and presents the research design used to then test that theory. The four chapters that follow are empirical and devoted to causality, which I consider to be twofold: 'difference making' and 'mechanistic' (Williamson 2009). Difference making refers to *regularities* and *covariation*, which are best detected using statistical analysis. Therefore, Chapter Four elaborates a continuous measure of cantonal decentralisation and applies it to all 26 cantons. I will use both existing databases and novel empirical data to combine 16 indicators into a single ranking. This index corresponds to the dependent variable in the quantitative analysis undertaken in Chapter Five (N = 26), which concludes with a regression model to 'predict' cantonal decentralisation using area, political culture and the strength of left-wing parties. Data for all the main variables used in these two chapters, dependent as well as independent, are listed in the Data Appendix.

The next two empirical chapters serve to uncover the *mechanistic* dimension of causality. I will rely on four cantons as case studies: Vaud, Berne, Schwyz and Grisons. These four are chosen as 'onliers' in the final regression model in Chapter Five, that is, they are all well 'predicted' by the theory (*see* Chapter Three for full discussion). Chapter Six provides an analytical narrative of the history of cantonal polity building leading to present degrees of decentralisation in each of the four cantons. I will highlight how exactly the causal factors identified in the quantitative analysis have come to impact on political decisions. Chapter Seven observes contemporary policy-making in these four cantons to provide a context-specific understanding of (de)centralisation in each case. The huge differences so discovered, which range from top-down inter-executive centralisation in Vaud to intra-cantonal federalism in Grisons, confirm that knowing degrees of decentralisation/centralisation matters for a better understanding of political processes.

The empirical-analytical part of this book ends with comparative reflections on both types of findings, quantitative and qualitative (Chapter Eight). After systematically comparing the results of within-case process tracing, an explanatory typology covering all 26 polities is developed. Then, stepping outside the cantonal box, the evidence from sub-national Switzerland serves to corroborate and refine the general theory of (de)centralisation. Undoubtedly, cantonal decentralisation is important because it matters for Swiss federalism, politics and society. But in answering the 'why'-question for this bounded context, *general* lessons can be drawn about motivations, constraints and opportunities for (territorial) institutional choice as well.

The book concludes by answering the main research question posed above: why are some political systems more centralised than others? It ends by drawing three lessons for further studies: that (de)centralisation is best understood (and measured) as having three dimensions; that each dimension as well their aggregate are continuous and bounded, respectively, by ideal-type points at both ends (for the dimensions) and each corner (for the three-dimensional aggregate); and that it is the interaction of political culture, area and political agency that determines degrees of (de)centralisation.

Chapter One

Existing Insights

This chapter reviews the existing literature on (de)centralisation, in general, as well as studies that have dealt with cantonal-local relations in Switzerland. The first section highlights the fundamental ambivalence inherent in the notion of (de)centralisation: is it a process, a status, both, or neither? Reviewing the existing literature helps in defining the key dependent variable of this book: (de)centralisation as a 'static' ascription of political systems. I propose a continuum ranging from fully centralised to confederal political systems. The second section briefly reviews the three main approaches to explaining (de)centralisation: socio-cultural, structural and political. The goal is to show that while the first two highlight the *conditions* under which (de)centralisation is more or less likely, only the last one offers a causal *process* in which political decisions are actually made. The third section of this chapter analyses existing studies of intra-cantonal decentralisation in Switzerland. The purpose there is to highlight the advantage of moving to the sub-national level in the search for explanations, in general, and the need to better understand why there is such a wide cross-cantonal variation, in particular.

Definitions

Before embarking on explaining cantonal decentralisation, it is necessary to muster the requisite vocabulary. At first sight, 'centralisation' seems to be one of the few concepts in political science that are *not* 'essentially contested' (*see* Heywood 2000). Its use is ubiquitous, ranging from EU studies and federalism to political sociology, public administration and geography (Peter 1928; Rezazadeh 1961; Slater 1989; Kochen and Deutsch 1973; Grodzins 1963). And yet, precise definitions of centralisation are rare. *The Oxford Concise Dictionary of Politics* (McLean and McMillan 2009), for example, makes no mention of it at all. As pointed out by Bulpitt (1983: 20), centralisation's 'place in life has been to act as a "fall guy" for the far more popular idea of decentralisation.' It is therefore defined only implicitly and *ex negativo*. However, the problem with this ontological assumption is that it is far from clear what exactly centralisation's opposite is: is it *decentralisation* as 'both reversing the concentration of administration at a single centre and conferring powers of local government' (Smith 1985: 1; *see also* Polsby 1979: 2); *federalism* as the ultimate form of 'non-centralisation' (Elazar 1987: 34); *regionalisation* as creating multiple, i.e. regional centres (Keating 1998: 113); *localisation* as in the 'displacement of state forms, functions and activities to bodies operating at a local scale' (Somerville 2004: 146); or *multi-centralism* as in Stein Rokkan's 'multi-centre territories' (Flora *et al.* 1999: 176; *see also* Mitchell 1997: 11)? A concept with so many opposites runs the risk of not having a core itself.

In the political science literature containing territorial analyses, centralisation as 'the residual part of the [ideal type decentralisation-centralisation] dichotomy' (Bulpitt 1983: 19) is most often simply omitted. At best, it is subsumed within modernisation (e.g. 'the sheer growth in central government'; Sharpe 1979: 13; *see also* Poggi 1978); the formation of 'those centralized institutions generally called "states"' (Mann 1997: 112); or as part of a wider cleavage structure: the 'nation-state in its centralized form [...] contested by one or some of its peripheries' (Mény and Wright 1985: 6; *see also* Lipset and Rokkan 1990 [1967] and Paasi 2002: 197). More recently, the concept's role as a 'fall guy' has been extended to international relations (e.g. globalisation as a challenge to the 'autocentric national economy', for Brenner 1998: 14; *see also* Vollaard 2009a: 43) and EU-studies (the European Commission and Parliament as 'autonomous centres of political power in Europe', for Keating 2009b: 43; *see also* Mitchell 1997: 11; Mamadouh 2001: 434).

What, then, is centralisation? Centralisation is elusive because it involves an assessment of 'a condition *or* a trend in an areal hierarchy of power' (Fesler 1968: 370; emphasis added). In other words, (de)centralisation can refer both to a *process* and to a *situation* of (de)centralisation. However, the former only makes sense if understood as moving from a situation at t to a situation at $t+1$ (temporal comparison); comparing existing nation-states in terms of their static degree of centralisation invariably involves a spatial comparison. At its core, (de)centralisation is therefore a situation. It is possible to heuristically use all of centralisation's opposites to define this core: if non-centralisation means there never *was* a centre in the first place; decentralisation, that power is taken *away* from the centre; and multi-centralisation, that we have *many* (regional or local) centres, then centralisation can only mean that a) there *is* a centre, b) there is just *one* centre and that c) this one centre is indeed *central*, in the sense of retaining all or at least most of the political power.

This definition of the centralisation of political systems moves beyond a definition of centralisation as 'the location of key decision-making functions in the capital city' (Bulpitt 1983: 20). It entails a Weberian ideal-type that is 'beyond the range of any real political system. Total decentralization would require the withering away of the state, whereas total centralization would imperil the state's capacity to perform its functions' (Fesler 1968: 371). But the merit of this ideal-type definition of full centralisation is that it relates territory to power in three basic, intuitive ways:

- *Place* refers to the location of power on the territory: exactly where is the centre? Asking for place makes sense only if the underlying assumption is brought forward: 'that the location of decision-making affects [...] the nature of decision-making' (Bulpitt 1983: 32). If location had no influence on politics, we would not need to be concerned with it here.[1]

---

1. I do not go as far as to assume that centralisation, as the *location* of power in the centre, is 'automatically' bad (Bulpitt 1983: 33), but simply assume an effect, without normatively qualifying it.

Centralisation therefore means that power resides *in* the centre – that we have 'centrality', for Vollaard (2009a, 2009b) (*see also* Gottmann 1952, 1969; Scott 1996; Amin 2004).

- *Space*, on the other hand, alludes to how '[p]olitical boundaries represent one major way in which people seek to organize space for their use. Territorial boundaries [...] sort people out in space so as to minimize conflict and aggression and organize competition and cooperation' (Elazar 1999: 877). Here, the question is: exactly what kind of centre are we talking about – a national, regional, or local centre? In any case, centralisation means that power extends *from* the centre over the whole territory: it 'radiates out from an identifiable central point, with a reach that appears almost effortless' (Allen 2004: 19; *see also* Honey 1976 and Lapid 1999). This element is also captured by the concept of 'jurisdiction' (Fesler 1968: 170; *see also* Brenner *et al.* 2003; Töpperwien 2004; Park 2008).

- *Hierarchy*, finally, refers to the relation between different power centres that are territorially conceived: exactly what kind of relationship exists between the national and regional centres, or between regional and local centres? This introduces a qualitative distinction on top of the gradual scale: on the one side, federalism's core element is 'constitutionally entrenched' sub-national autonomy, which results in 'mutual interdependence' (Burgess 2006a: 2; *see also* Bowie and Friedrich 1954; Vile 1961; Anderson 2008; Beramendi 2009). Centralisation, on the other side, ensues in a clear 'geographical hierarchy' (Smith 1985: 1), where several local or regional centres are subordinate to a single, national centre. Ideally, the centre 'imposes a principle of order [and] acts as a dominator' (Thoenig 2008: 285; *see also* Ansell 2004; Braun 1997; Gottmann 1980).

It was an International Relations scholar who noted that 'the distinctive feature of the modern system of rule is that it has differentiated its subject collectivity into territorially defined, fixed and mutually exclusive enclaves of legitimate dominion' (Ruggie 1993: 151). This is true for inter- as well as intra-state relations (Jones 1999; Larkins 2009; Nettl 1968; Newman 1999; Strayer 1971; Tilly 1975). Place ('fixed'), space ('territorially defined'), and hierarchy forms the backbone also of two further concepts, which, unlike centralisation, have received extensive treatment in the literature: federalism and decentralisation. Discussing these two helps defining the endpoints of the (de)centralisation continuum, as is done next.

The endpoints of the continuum

At the most general level, territory 'underpins the state as a principle of domination and control; and it structures the system of representation and participation within it' (Keating 1998: 1; *see also* Walker 1984; Forsberg 1996; Rokkan and Urwin 1982). If centralisation expresses one form of relationship between territory and power (a single centre from which power radiates both outwards and downwards), federalism expresses another. Indeed, federal studies are replete with discussions of centralisation because '[n]o government has ever been called federal that has been organized on any but the territorial basis' (Livingston 1956: 2–3). I regard federalism as territorial by definition. For Burgess (2006b: 103), too, '[t]erritoriality is firmly integrated in the mainstream literature on federalism'; federal theory consequently studies 'the territorial distribution of power' (Duchacek 1987: 12). Quite often centralisation and federalism are regarded as antonyms, but even in a non-federal state at least some decentralisation and even in a federation at least some centralisation, will necessarily occur (Hesse 1962; Friedrich 1968; Lluch 2012). There simply 'are no totally centralized states in which all governmental authority is concentrated in the headquarters of national government agencies' (Smith 1985: preface; *see also* Blondel 1995: 229, and Fleiner and Basta Fleiner 2000: 17). Nevertheless, a brief discussion of four federal scholars highlights the different ways in which centralisation can be defined.

Elazar's *Exploring Federalism* starts off with the distinction that a federal constitutional framework involves 'non-centralization on contractual basis', whereas decentralisation would be 'a matter of grace, not right' (1987: 35). Elazar also stipulates that 'in a non-centralized political system, power is so diffused that it cannot legitimately be centralized or concentrated without breaking the structure and spirit of the constitution' (1976: 13). If a federal state were to move in the direction of more centralisation it would, therefore, at one point cease being a federation– but when exactly is left open. On the other hand, in federations power is not just decentralised, but really non-centralised. For Elazar, clearly federalism and centralisation are mutually exclusive and polar opposites.

This understanding is in line with earlier literature. Wheare's 'federal principle' stipulated that a federation is defined as:

> [...] an association of states so organized that powers are divided between a general government which in certain matters – for example, the making of treaties and the coining of money – is independent of the governments of the associated states, and, on the other hand, state governments which in certain matters are, in their turn, independent of the general government. This involves, as a necessary consequence, that general and regional governments both operate *directly* upon the people; each citizen is subject to two governments. (Wheare 1963: 2; original emphasis)

Both territory and power reappear in this definition. As with centralisation, their triple connection can be made explicit as *place* (one plus 13 centres, at the time of the founding of the US), *space* ('general' vs. regional) and (the absence of) *hierarchy*, i.e. 'mutual independence'. However, Wheare adopts a legal-constitutional approach; hence the federal principle is 'embodied in the modern *Constitution* of the United States' (1963: 10); it is because 'there is a difference between the two *constitutions*' that South Africa, where 'the regional governments are subordinate to the general government', is not a federation (1963: 13); and 'it is clear that the principle upon which the Swiss *Constitution* is drawn up' does follow the federal principle (1963: 17; all emphases added). Wheare may thus very well caution that 'it is not sufficient to look at constitutions only. What matters just as much is the practice of government', and that

> [t]he test which I apply for federal government is then simply this. Does a system of government embody predominantly a division of powers between general and regional authorities, each of which, in its own sphere, is co-ordinate with the others and independent of them? [...] What determines the issue is the working of the system. (Wheare 1963: 33)

However, he fails to operationalise this complementary element beyond legal analysis. Where he gives examples, the discussion of the 'workings of the system' does not move beyond the non-use of constitutional prerogatives by 'constitutional convention' (for Canada; 1963: 19); impressionistic 'intervention[s] of the general government in the affairs of the regional governments' (for Argentina; 1963: 22); or the use of 'financial powers [...] to bring the state finance under the control of the general government' (for Weimar Germany; 1963: 24). Finally, one of the main reasons why Wheare does *not* treat the USSR 'as an example of the working of federal government' is – once more – 'the full powers conferred by Article 14 of the *Constitution* upon the All-Union Government' (1963: 26; emphasis added), and not so much the 'practice of government'. I shall return to this legal dimension of (de)centralisation when discussing the literature relating to the Swiss cantons.

Situated between Elazar's very broad discussion of 'various kinds of federal arrangements' (Elazar 1999: 881) and Wheare's 'narrowness' (Burgess 2006a: 29) are two further scholars, Riker (1964, 1969, 1975) and Livingston (1952, 1956). They mirror the divide between structuralist and rational choice approaches (*see* Stoker and Marsh 2010: 3), with Riker trying to detect federations without federalism (such as the USSR) and Livingston going the opposite way in his search for federalism beyond federations (King 1982). Livingston (1956: 5) insists on societal factors as not just shaping, but indeed 'demanding' federal institutions: it is 'social diversities that produce federalism'. Wherever we find the former, the latter seemingly automatically follows. For Riker (1964: 16), on the other hand, such a perspective amounts to 'bypassing the act of bargaining' – and thereby 'bypassing the political' in political science – which, according to him, has led to the creation of a federation in the very first place.

Both Riker and Livingston, then, argue against the reductionist view offered by focusing on federal constitutions alone. By implication, they also argue against unduly extending the notion of federalism to non-state phenomena. But their common refutation of 'the lawyers' distortion' (Riker 1964: 51) of the federal picture leads them in opposite directions. For Riker, 'the decentralized party system is the main protector of the integrity of states' (1964: 100). Later scholars have built on his legacy. Political parties, 'even if their ideology is nonterritorial and their goals and links supranational', still direct 'their pressure [...] at territorial authorities and institutions' (Duchacek 1987: 51). Actors rationally choose to create and/or maintain a certain territorial structure because it serves them well (Hopkin 2009; *see also* Chandler 1987; Hrbek 2004; Hadley *et al*. 1989; Scharpf 1995). For Livingston, on the other hand, federalism means a) 'diversities in the society' which are b) 'grouped territorially' (Livingston 1956: 56). The only way then to accommodate territorial diversity is through federal institutions. For the purpose of explaining federations, 'uncodified social structures remain indispensable to analyses of how political systems function' (Erk 2003: 54). Hence, what is social structure for the one, is political agency for the other: the key to understanding territorial politics. I will return to both authors when discussing determinants of (de)centralisation more specifically. Both approaches contribute to our understanding of (de)centralisation, emphasising how centralisation and federalism are *not* mutually exclusive and how degrees of (de)centralisation can change over space and time.

A final contribution from federal studies comes from Preston King, who makes a 'useful', even if not 'widely observed' (1982: 75) distinction: 'We shall take it that federalism is some or several varieties of political philosophy or ideology, and that federation is some type of political institution' (1982:75). This uncouples ideology from institutions and is a useful distinction because it allows distinguishing *norms* from *facts*. One should therefore not mistake a country's self-declaration as a federation as (sufficient) proof of its being federal (*see* Livingston 1956: 2). King also marvellously draws a line from Bakunin's socialist anarchism ('decentralist federalism'; 1982: 41) to *The Federalist Papers'* adaptation of Jean Bodin and Thomas Hobbes for the North-American context ('centralist federalism'; 1982: 29). Federalists have at times even advocated both centralism and decentralism at the same time, e.g. Friedrich (1968) in speaking of federalism as a contract.[2]

In sum, a federation may be either 'centralized' or 'peripheralized' (Riker 1964: 6). The most peripheralised federation is a confederation, in which the periphery always 'overawes' the centre (Riker 1964: 6; also Hughes 1963; Forsyth 1981). For Hueglin and Fenna (2006: 34) confederations are 'more than alliances or leagues', because even there at least some legislative, administrative and/or fiscal functions are centralised. But since the 'locus of sovereignty' remains with the member states, 'confederal arrangements leave the central government dependent on the member states for revenue and with little scope for making domestic policy' (2006: 34). They thus agree with Duchacek (1987: 160) who stated that '[i]n a union of states a permanent common machinery is not endowed with any significant central coercive device and tax-collecting powers'. Also, members of a confederation do not 'lose their identity as states' (Forsyth 1981: 1), since they 'raise themselves

---

2. This ultimately leads to Althusius' (1995 [1614]: I/1) view of politics as 'the art of associating men for the purpose of establishing, cultivating and conserving social life among them' (*see* Hueglin 1998: 6). Note that Proudhon sees in a federal constitution the only way to 'trouver l'équilibre entre deux éléments contraires, l'Autorité et la Liberté' (Proudhon 1863: 75), and not just the *territorial* dimensions of national vs. regional (and/or local).

by contract to the threshold of being one state' (Forsyth 1981: 2) without however crossing that bar. In intergovernmental relations terms, confederalism remains at the horizontal level, ranging from (unilateral) policy emulation through ad hoc coordination and co-decision procedures to (policy-specific) supra-governmentalism (Bolleyer 2009: 19). I shall return to confederalism as ideology when discussing arrangements between Swiss local governments to impede the centralisation of a specific task at the cantonal level (*see* Horber-Papazian 2006). For now, it suffices to accept confederal decentralisation as the ideal-type opposite to full centralisation.

In terms of terminology, then, federal studies alert us to the fact that 'the characterization of federation as a degree of decentralization equally involves characterizing it as a degree of centralization. The one is inversely proportional to the other; each in this sense may be converted into the other' (King 1982: 126). In other words, '[c]entralization and decentralization are best regarded as opposite tendencies on a single continuum [...]. It should be possible to compare individual political or administrative systems by noting their relative positions on the continuum' (Fesler 1968: 371). Accepting this inverse proportionality, I replicate King's distinction between federalism and federation for centralism/decentralism as *ideologies* and centralised/decentralised states as their desired empirical *outcomes*. The following *convention* thus guides this book:

A. The suffix '-ism' signifies a philosophical or ideological (Burgess 2006b: 103) dimension of territorial politics: federalism, confederalism, centralism, decentralism, regionalism and localism.
B. A *confederation* is an ideal-type arrangement of institutions embodying confederalism.
C. A *centralised state* is an ideal-type arrangement of institutions embodying centralism; a *decentralised state* an arrangement falling short of B.
D. As attributes of political systems at any governmental level, the epithets *decentralised* and *centralised* will be used.
E. The term *political system* pre-supposes territory, people and government (Weber 1992 [1919]: 6) i.e. a set of political institutions with the capacity to make collectively binding decisions upon a territorially defined society.

The continuum along which any type of political system (letter E) can be placed therefore ranges from confederal to centralised political systems, both of which are ideal-types. I use the epithets (letter D) to avoid confusion both with political systems at the nation-state level (where the continuum ranges from a centralised state to a confederation – B and C) and ideology (A). Armed in this way, it is possible to express the goal of this book as trying to explain centralisation through cantonal decentralisation, i.e. the specific degrees of (de)centralisation present in one particular set of regional political systems: the Swiss cantons. I now turn to a second body of literature that distinguishes between types of decentralisation to show how they help in determining degrees of it.

Types and degrees of decentralisation

A second sub-discipline in the territorial politics literature places the unitary centralised state at the heart of its attention. Here, decentralisation is conventionally divided into three types. This distinction originates in public administration (Hutchcroft 2001: 27) and is here drawn from Rossi (1999; but *see also* Rhodes 1981: 37). It introduces three new terms:

1. *De-concentration*, where 'selected functions are taken over by the field offices of central state hierarchy' (Rossi 1999: 17).
2. *Delegation*, where 'responsibilities are transferred to regional or national, and usually semiautonomous governmental units' (Rossi 1999: 17).
3. *Devolution*, which refers to 'the transfer of certain powers and resources to legitimate local governments such as partial states, provinces, districts or municipalities who are obligated to act based on national policies' (Rossi 1999: 18).

This threefold classification is in part a response to the criticism levelled by Fesler (1965: 537):

> Our languages dichotomize 'centralization' and 'decentralization', a peculiarity that easily converts to a polarization and antithesis that poorly serve political science. We appear to have neither a term that embraces the full continuum between the two poles, nor a term that specifies the middle range where centralizing and decentralizing tendencies are substantially in balance.

So the three terms bring us closer to conceptually capture at least parts of this 'middle range' in the territorial dimension of politics (Smith 1985; also Duchacek 1987). They express different types of decentralisation, operating in different dimensions of politics. I briefly discuss each type in turn.

De-concentration, to start with, is a simple locational matter. It is institutionalist in the minimal sense of place. Power remains at the centre in all but form – only some of its agents have moved out into 'the country' (Bulpitt 2009: 68) or, as the French would put it, '*sur le terrain*' (Garrish 1986: 54). De-concentration means an 'intra-organizational transfer of particular functions and workloads from the central government to its regional or local offices. The capital retains the major level of authority over the content of policies' (Hutchcroft 2001: 30).

The French state has long been regarded as 'the most centralised' in the Western world (Loughlin and Seiler 2001: 191). The little of decentralisation that there was, until the 1980s, consisted in a mere de-concentration of oversight functions, embodied in the departmental and later regional prefect. The size of the French *départements* at the time of their creation in 1790 'was determined by the distance covered in a day's horse ride to reach its principal city. [...] Napoleon retained the departmental structure, but instituted the system of prefects to ensure central control of his territory' (Loughlin and Seiler 2001: 196). The case of the Swiss canton of Vaud, discussed more extensively later on, will show to what extent this idea has travelled across borders. The institution of the prefect in particular

[...] is there to bear responsibility for application of national programs in his area, and he is expected to bring to his task a broader, more sensitive appreciation of the character of that area than any highly specialized functional agent can be expected to have. (Fesler 1965: 560)

The prefect is appointed by the centre and heads the various field services, i.e. the areal branches of national ministries (Loughlin 2007a: 116). The model has been exported to other countries – hence their denomination as 'Napoleonic countries': France, Belgium, Luxembourg, Spain, Portugal, Italy and Greece (Hesse and Sharpe 1991).[3] However, by the 21st century Belgium has become a federation, Spain a 'regionalised state' (Swenden 2006: 11–12), and Italy has been erratically moving in the same direction (Putnam 1993; Keating and Wilson 2010). Portugal rejected such regionalisation in a referendum held in 1998 (Loughlin 2001b: 268), whereas Greece chose a middle-way, retaining its 51 prefects but having them popularly elected since 1994 (Loughlin 2001c: 277–278). In Luxembourg, a 'district commissioner' is appointed by the central government for each of the three 'administrative districts' (Hendriks 2001: 177). Acting as a 'hierarchical intermediary between the central government and municipal authorities', Luxembourg can thus be said to best 'approach the ideal type of the centralized unitary state' (Hendriks 2001: 177–178).

Prefects are also found in Scandinavia. Bjørnå and Jenssen (2006: 328) argue that the Swedish and Norwegian prefects 'visualize shifts between political values of centralization, decentralization and re-centralization', as the institution has undergone some major changes in the last 40 years. Danish prefects are less powerful, but equally effective in supervising municipalities. They conclude their analysis on a very positive note:

The office of the prefect seems a useful 'instrument' to ensure equality [...]. [Prefects] are placed locally and hold information and authority that gives them a unique position as a link between the central and local government; they are contributing to cohesion and coordination [...]. We do not think the prefectures will vanish from the administrative scene as they constitute a system of supervision and control that is easy to operate and they have proved capable of working efficiently and smoothly [...]. (2006: 328)

It will be interesting to see how the Swiss prefects perform *their* functions – indeed, what their functions are in the first place and what differences exist across cantons and time. I will discuss some literature on this question in the last section of this chapter; for now, let us move on to the second type of decentralisation, delegation.

---

3. Loughlin (2001a: 11) places Luxembourg within the 'Germanic' (alongside Germany, Austria and The Netherlands) and only the other six countries mentioned here into the 'Napoleonic state tradition'. This may be true for the purpose of his study, which is on subnational democracy; the analysis (Hendriks 2001) conducted in the same edited volume confirms, however, that as regards the territorial dimension, Luxembourg clearly belongs to the Napoleonic tradition.

Delegation, as it is understood here, goes a small but significant step further than de-concentration. To location (i.e. mere geographical displacement of supervision) it adds space, retaining however the clear hierarchy embedded in centralisation. The spatial component so introduced is called 'jurisdiction', because it best expresses the areal scope of authority (Skelcher 2005: 91). But why should we speak of jurisdiction instead of sovereignty? The problem with using the term sovereignty is ontological. It is generally accepted that 'the state unit confronts us, as it were, in its physical, corporeal capacity: as an expanse of territory' (Herz 1957: 474). The modern state is a territorial state. But 'systems of rule need not be territorial at all', or at least not 'territorially fixed' (Ruggie 1993: 149; *see also* Penrose 2002: 283; Sack 1986; Bancroft 2000: 53; and Kratochwil 1986: 29–30). Fleiner (2002: 114) explains how sovereignty has often been regarded 'as arising from a 'Big Bang', out of which emerged the legal system, the state, the constitution-making power, legitimacy and court jurisdiction'. In this perception, power and jurisdiction appear indivisible: 'A state without sovereignty cannot exist' (2002: 114).

But to understand the territorial distribution of power *within* a state it is necessary to conceptually separate the two (*see* Nettl 1968). To equate territory with sovereignty obscures the fact that 'territory and function are linked in complex ways' (Keating 1998: 3), as when the state 'defines territories both for the purposes of public policy and as the basis for representation' (1998: 7). Delegation, then, is the first *qualitative* step in view of creating regional or local governments as spaces for public policy, representation and identity. It is through 'jurisdictional integrity' that we can understand this outcome best: in this term, jurisdiction 'delimits the spatial domain within which the body has authority to act in relation to a policy domain', while integrity expresses the 'democratic relationship between the governmental body and the citizenry it serves' (Skelcher 2005: 92–93). Delegation therefore is different from de-concentration on two accounts: it gives authority to a new territorial entity (space) and it allows for a direct link to the citizenry within this area. This matters because we can already now anticipate that, for example, the double legitimacy of mayors elected to a national or regional parliament might help strengthen local autonomy.

A further distinction is that between 'administrative' and 'fiscal decentralisation' (Watts 2008: 173; also Furniss 1974). Falleti (2005: 329) defines administrative decentralisation as a 'set of policies that transfer the administration and delivery of social services such as education, health, social welfare, or housing to subnational governments'. Fiscal decentralisation, in turn, 'refers to the set of policies designed to increase the revenues or fiscal autonomy of subnational governments' (2005: 329). In both instances, the transfer is 'downward', yet the 'type of authority' (2005: 329) so delegated is different. The problem with both definitions is that decentralisation is understood as a policy, obscuring the fact that countries might decentralise but still end up being highly centralised – especially so in Latin-America (Montero and Samuels 2004: 3). Decentralisation policies are defined as making the political system more decentralised, by delegating fiscal or administrative capacities, or both. For the purposes of this book, and to separate process from outcome and policy from politics and policy, fiscal decentralisation simply captures a situation in which lower-level entities enjoy at least some jurisdiction in fiscal matters (e.g. tax-raising powers, the ability to borrow, expenditure autonomy etc.), while administrative decentralisation captures the extent to which they have their own bureaucracy (*see* Musgrave 1965; Dafflon 1992b; Bird and Tarasov 2004; Rodden 2002, 2003 and 2006).

Falleti (2005: 329) additionally mentions 'political decentralisation' as 'designed to devolve political authority or electoral capacities to sub-national actors'. Again, this is a policy-understanding and different from my static use of (de)centralisation. Moreover, the expression is misleading on at least three accounts. First, *all* delegation is political, otherwise what is delegated would not be related to the capacity to make collectively binding decisions (the political system) and ought to be labelled 'privatisation'. Second, the notion simplifies and hence obscures the distinctive quality of what is at stake: the 'creation of subnational legislative assemblies' or 'constitutional reforms that strengthen the political autonomy of subnational governments' (Falleti 2005: 329) can hardly be said to be of equal importance to raising user charges for waste disposal or have local governments provide certain services under central supervision or not. Third, the predictive capacity of 'political decentralisation' is circular. Even Falleti (2005: 329) is aware of its tautological consequences: 'political decentralization, by the definition provided previously, should almost invariably increase the degree of autonomy of subnational officials from the center'. In her own words (2005: 329): 'constitutional reforms that strengthen the political autonomy of subnational governments' lead to an increase in '... the degree of autonomy of subnational officials from the center!' The structural arrangements political decentralisation intends to capture are better summarised by devolution, the third type of decentralisation.

Devolution is distinguished from the other two forms of decentralisation on two accounts: it potentially involves all three domains of state activity, i.e. administrative, financial *and* legislative powers (Watts 2008: 172–174), and at the receiving end of these powers are *governments*, i.e. 'general-purpose, elected political bodies' (Keating 1998: 113). Like de-concentration and delegation, devolution involves *place* as (re)location. Like delegation, it involves *space* as territorially defined jurisdiction. But unlike either, devolution creates a *new hierarchy*. The reasons for all three may be the same: efficiency, for example, is often introduced as a 'reason for the devolution of power to sub-central government units' (Kay 2005: 547; *see also* Blondel 1995: 232). But from observing the process in the UK, another 'major reason for the decision of the Labour leadership to implement a scheme of devolution in Scotland and Wales was the growing nationalist threat in Scotland and Wales' (Gamble 2006: 26). I will return to causes of (de)centralisation in the next section. For now, it suffices to introduce the term 'regionalism', an ideology or movement advocating the 'symbolic content' of regional space as a 'social, economic and political construction' (Keating 1998: 7; *see also* Sharpe 1993: 1; Loughlin 2000: 12; Jeffery 2000; and Swenden 2006: 14).

One particular feature of such regions is that often, amongst many other things, they are now in control of *their* local governments – they are, at the same time, in the 'middle' of the state hierarchy and at the apex of their own territorial hierarchy. For Scottish local governments, '[d]evolution has offered an opportunity to reconnect with (new) central governments' (Jeffery 2006: 63), while regionalism in Spain has 'created a framework in which local government has a secondary role compared to that attributed to ACs [Autonomous Communities]. […] the condition of local governments will depend heavily on the intergovernmental style of each AC and the extent decentralization will be used within ACs' (Carrillo 1997: 63). Thus, at least in these examples, regionalism means place (regional centrality), space (the region), *and* a new hierarchy (between regional and local governments next to that between national and regional governments). This brings me to consider the literature dealing with sub-national governments and the relations between them.

Of regional and local governments

Every state is divided into smaller areas. Even Luxembourg, the archetype of unitary centralism, is divided into two *régions naturelles*, four *circonscriptions électorales*, three *districts administratifs*, twelve *cantons* and 105 *communes*.[4] Germany on the other hand, the EU's largest country, is divided into 16 *Länder*, of which five are further divided into 39 *Regierungsbezirke*; then 429 *Kreise;* and, at the local level, a total of 1,457 *Verwaltungsgemeinschaften* and 12,379 *Gemeinden*.[5] In theory, each layer of Luxembourg and Germany could be called a governmental level. But government means more than simply a) *any* area with b) *some* functions. To visualise the state as a pyramid, in Figure 1.1, is another heuristic device, similar to space, place and hierarchy: as the number of units decreases, their respective area increases.

Henceforth, the term 'state level' shall be taken to encompass three generic notions: the national government of which there is always only one in a state, and regional and local governments of which there are always two or more. Only with reference to Figure 1.1 does it make sense to speak of vertical (downward or upward, i.e. national-regional, regional-local and national-local) and horizontal (inter-regional and inter-local) relations. In some countries, 'region' denotes a specific set of institutions, for example the regional governments in Italy since the reforms in the late 1940s and early 1970s (Keating and Wilson 2010; Putnam 1993; on Italy as a 'congeries of regions', *see* Elazar 1987: 76). In other countries, the term is altogether absent from the legal-political discourse: the only regions

---

4.   *See* 'Portail des Statistiques – Grand-Duché du Luxembourg', Territoire, tables 'Superficie des cantons et communes' and 'Evolution du nombre des communes', at http://www.statistiques. public.lu (last accessed 7 March 2015).

5.   In EU terminology, the first three correspond to NUTS (*Nomenclature des Unités territoriales statistiques*) regions level 1, 2 and 3 and the latter two to 'Local Administrative Units' (LAU) level 1 and 2, respectively (Eurostat 2009: 149).

Figure 1.1: Three generic state levels

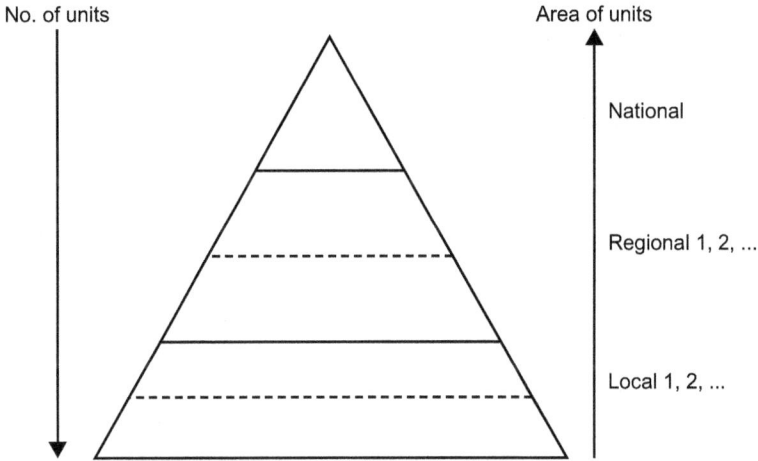

Switzerland knows are for statistical purposes,[6] although the term is used *within* some cantons (e.g. in Berne and Grisons; *see also* Mueller and Dardanelli 2012). A third set of countries asymmetrically recognises 'nationalities and regions', e.g. Spain (Giordano and Roller 2004). Finally, there can be two or more regional levels, e.g. the German *Länder*, *Regierungsbezirke* and *Kreise*, and/or two or more local levels, e.g. the *Verwaltungsgemeinschaften* and *Gemeinden* (*see also* Hooghe *et al.* 2008: 112).

The spatial extension of one of these multiple jurisdictions is regional if its area is, on average, smaller than the national, but larger than the local level. A jurisdiction is local if it has, on average, the smallest extension, but is closest to an individual person, be it a resident or a citizen. Finally, the national level denotes the uppermost stratum inside the state; the adjective will be used synonymously to 'central', in unitary states and 'federal', in federations. 'National', 'regional' and 'local' are *generic* terms.[7] In Switzerland, the *particularly* national is known as the federal; the regional as the cantonal; and the local as the communal or municipal level. Whenever speaking of this country, I shall use these terms interchangeably.

---

6. The EU through NUTS divides Switzerland into seven 'regions at level 2': CH01 Région lémanique, CH02 Espace Mittelland, CH03 Nordwestschweiz, CH04 Zürich, CH05 Ostschweiz, CH06 Zentralschweiz and CH07 Ticino (Eurostat 2009: 153). These correspond to the domestic – and equally purely statistical – *Grossregionen* (*grandes régions, grandi regioni*) and comprise, respectively, the cantons (or, in NUTS: 'regions at level 3') GE, VD, VS; BE, FR, JU, NE, SO; AG, BS, BL; ZH; AR, AI, GL, GR, SG, SH, TG; LU, NW, OW, SZ, UR, ZG; and TI (BFS 2012).

It has already been defined that regional governments refer to 'general-purpose, elected political bodies, with their own functions and powers' on a regional scale (Keating 1998: 113). Local government, on the other hand, denotes the presence of the same governmental structures but this time at the local level, i.e.:

> [...] the organized sum of the political *institutions* which function in a given *locality* to provide the bundle of governmental *services* and activities which can be manipulated locally to serve local needs in light of the local value system. (Elazar 1966: 169; emphasis added)

For the purpose of this book, three cumulative attributes define local governments: they are a) multi-purpose organisations, b) local in character and extension and c) embodied with direct, popular legitimacy (Stewart 1983: 13; *see also* Sharpe 1970: 171 and Ostrom 1990). However, one danger to which Fesler (1965: 537) alerts is over-simplification:

> [...] to homologize metropolis and village as 'local governments,' primitive areas and highly civilized areas as 'states' or 'provinces,' and prosperous areas and endemically depressed areas as 'regions' is likely to obscure as much as enlighten our discourses on general patterns of decentralization.

Nevertheless, at this definitional level one should opt for simple, abstract categories, so that the subsequent empirical analysis can establish the exact content of these 'conceptual containers' (Sartori 1970). Only simple definitions enable complex comparisons. Therefore, any government that is sub-regional is automatically local, as long as the institutions serve multiple purposes, are imbued with at least some popular legitimacy, *and* fulfil at least some public tasks in their area.

Now the definitional hurdle is cleared we can move on to review actual studies of central-local relations. The literature is divided because in federal states local governments are at the mercy of their regional governments, whereas in unitary states the primary relation is national-local. What is more, regional studies have developed as a distinctive sub-branch without giving the place of local governments within these regions adequate space. So we have studies of local governments in unitary states (e.g. Baldersheim and Rose 2010; Chandler 2009; Clark 1984; Clark 1974; Fleurke and Willemse 2004; Humes 1991; John 2001; King and Pierre 1990; Maass 1959; Page and Goldsmith 1987; Page 1991; Rhodes 1981; Sharpe 1970; Stewart 1983; Garrish 1986) that do not speak to studies of local government within the regions of federations. The latter are quite a

---

7.   Both 'national' and 'regional' are spatial categories and mean no offense to either regions that consider themselves historic, ethnic and/or linguistic 'nations' (e.g. Scotland; *see* Jeffrey 2008: 555 n.2) or states forming 'bicommunal societies' (e.g. Cyprus), 'multinational federations' (e.g. India; *see* Burgess and Pinder 2007), or 'plurinational democracies' (e.g. Spain; *see* Requejo 2005).

recent addition (e.g. Steytler 2009; Gamper and Palermo 2011), but already Elazar (1966: 164) stated that 'in a strictly legal sense it must be understood that all local governments in the United States are creatures of their respective states'. The common law country saw this principle expressed as 'Dillon's Rule', after Ohio Judge John Foster Dillon, according to whom local governments are 'the mere tenants at will of their legislature' (quoted in Marbach *et al.* 2006: 154). Local governments, in the US,

> [...] owe their origin to, and derive their powers and rights wholly from, the [State] legislature. It breathes into them the breath of life, without which they cannot exist. As it creates, so may it destroy. If it may destroy, it may abridge and control. (Marbach *et al.* 2006: 154)

In unitary states, local governments are subject to the national level alone. In the pre-devolution UK, for example, the structure resembled a 'patchwork', where the centre 'determines by statute the functional responsibilities of local authorities, as well as the money that local governments have available to discharge their delegated functions' (Sutcliffe 2007: 259). National control *is* 'central control' (Rhodes 1981). A study of local governments in Switzerland, on the other hand, mirrors the US situation: Swiss municipalities are equally 'creatures of their respective states', i.e. the cantons. Students of local government in the US generally summarise their work into 'state-local relations'; Bowman and Kearney (2011: 564) note that

> [...] there is extensive interstate variance in local discretionary powers, based on state constitutional and statutory law, court decisions and particularly on the presence and strength of state-adopted home rule provisions.

Other prominent examples from this literature include Berman and Martin (1988), Berman (2009), Krueger and Bernick (2009), Zimmerman (1994, 2010). Stephens (1974) and Stephens and Wikstrom (2000) conceptualise their object as 'state decentralization'; Richardson *et al.* (2003) and Krane *et al.* (2001) prefer 'municipal home rule'. Apart from the brief chapter by Magin and Eder (2008), Germany has not, so far, received the same kind of attention as the US in terms of regional-local relations. Regional-local relations in federations other than the US are clearly underdeveloped.

On the other hand, regional studies (e.g. Brusis 2002, 2003; Bradbury 2006, 2010; Fargion *et al.* 2006; Hepburn 2011; Jeffery 2000, 2008; Kay 2005; Keating 1998, 2003, 2004, 2008; Loughlin 2000; Sharpe 1993; Tarrow 1974) analyse the degree, nature, past and future development of regional authority as opposed to the national level, but not with regards to 'their' local governments. This 'new wave of regionalism' started in the late 1980s and drew its inspiration mainly from processes of 'economic restructuring; globalization; the transformation of the nation state; and above all by European integration' (Keating 2003: 261). A recent special issue of *Regional and Federal Studies* on regional authority, for example, found huge varieties across the OECD (Hooghe *et al.* 2008), and I will return to this when discussing the conceptualisation of (de)centralisation in the next chapter. What is missing is an equally admirable effort at developing a 'local authority index'.

In sum, the area of local-regional governmental relations occupies a niche between local, regional and federal government studies. For some countries (the US, Germany), this niche has partly been filled. Before considering how the Swiss literature on cantonal-communal relations has imported some, but not all of the theoretical contributions, I briefly review the three most prominent approaches to explaining (de)centralisation. This prepares the ground for the theoretical framework presented in Chapter Two.

Explanations

Approaches to explaining (de)centralisation can be divided into three groups: socio-cultural, structural in a narrow sense and political. The first two are structural in a wider sense (the 'super-structure'), the last actor-centred. Each approach figures prominently in a different sub-set of the territorial politics literature. At first sight, they attempt to explain slightly different objects: 'federalism', 'territorial governance' and 'devolution', respectively. Nevertheless, they can be read as rival explanations: is (de)centralisation caused by societal diversity, by size, or by (electoral) politics instead? Merely reviewing the three approaches at this stage lays the ground for the theoretical framework presented in the next chapter. I discuss the three approaches in turn.

The socio-cultural approach

Two strands within federal studies argue that federalism is caused by 'society'. The first is *sociological federalism* (Livingston 1952, 1956; Erk 2003, 2008), the epithet suggesting its origins in societal (Parsons 1967), system (Easton 1965 and 1968 [1953]) and 'congruence' analysis (Eckstein and Gurr 1975; Eckstein, 1980). The second is *covenantal federalism* (Elazar 1995–1999; Kincaid 1982; *see also* Moots 2009), in turn adapting general political culture approaches (*see* Inglehart 1977 and 1988; Almond and Verba 1965; Jackman and Miller 1996; Wildavsky 1987; Pye 1968) to the study of federations. In simplified form, their respective propositions read as follows:

1. *Federalism is caused by societal diversity:* by implication, a larger number of societal cleavages – linguistic, religious and/or ethnic – make a decentralised 'institutional architecture' (Treisman 2007) more likely.
2. *Federalism is caused by a political culture of subsidiarity:* Duchacek (1987: 344), for example, suggests that a 'tendency or habit of thinking primarily in local (territorial) initiative and responsibility' makes federalism more likely – although his examples include English county councils.

Both strands assume culture and society to drive politics. Values, ideas, beliefs, habits, customs, symbols, traditions of behaviour and attitudinal predispositions to action are responsible for 'different social, economic and political outcomes' (Lane and Ersson 2005: 3). Further, because '[p]olitical culture is the property of a collectivity – nation, region, class, ethnic community, formal organization, party, or whatever. Individuals have beliefs, values and attitudes but they do not have cultures' (Elkins and Simeon 1979: 129), and consequently, political culture can only mean the aggregate of individual values, i.e. the *dominance* of certain attitudes, values, ideas etc. over others. Hence, *federal* political culture describes 'the extent to which the political attitudes and beliefs of a population reflect attachment to key values associated with federalism' (Brown 2013: 298; *see also* Cole and Kincaid 2006). Societal diversity, in turn, centres not on aggregate but *individual* differences, because 'ethnicity is best understood as an ordering principle [...] to differentiate one individual from another based upon specific traits' (Albert 2012: 71). It is only through 'diversity' that we move to the collective level, where societal diversity is understood as the relative size, type and number of ethnic/linguistic/religious groups *within* a given society. But how do diversity and/or political culture translate into federal structures?

Within sociological federalism – that branch of federal studies that uses *societal differences* as explanatory variables – the most elaborate is 'the theory of congruence between ethno-linguistic social structure and political institutions', advanced by Jan Erk (2003: 50). Building on Livingston's (1952, 1956) idea of a 'federal society', his premise is that 'uncodified social structures remain indispensable to analyses of how political systems function' (Erk 2003: 54). Unfortunately, the 'theory' proposed by Erk is little more than a different way of looking at federalism. Instead of offering a set of logical explanations, i.e. causal mechanisms bounded by precisely identifiable scope conditions linking ethnic diversity to federalism, all that the article (2003: 64) establishes is co-variation between language groups (as a measure of ethnic diversity) and their 'public spaces' (as a measure of federalism). In Erk's (2008: 11) later work, the causal mechanisms are spelled out more clearly through two intervening variables: 'ethno-linguistic social structure [...] influences and delimits political choices' made by political *actors*, who then decide on public *policies*, which in the long run lead to the postulated congruence between the social and institutional structures. Erk and Koning (2010: 355), finally, postulate 'that institutions change to reach a better fit with the underlying structural base. The direction for institutional change in federal systems with territorially based linguistic heterogeneity is decentralizing, for homogeneous ones the direction is centralizing'. Political actors have here disappeared at the expense of interest groups (2010: 356), which organise along linguistic lines because they not only want to effect institutional, but also policy-specific change, of which the former then is simply a side effect (2010: 357). Let me briefly turn towards some empirical evidence before moving on to political culture.

Every major quantitative study of (de)centralisation has tested for the influence of ethnic diversity. But the evidence is inconclusive: some find a positive and significant correlation with the 'Regional Authority Index' (RAI; Hooghe *et al.* 2008 and 2010), fiscal decentralisation (Panizza 1999, Stegarescu 2005) and federalism (Lijphart 1999); some a negative correlation with fiscal decentralisation (Arzaghi and Henderson 2005; Treisman 2006; Timofeev 2003); and others, no significant effect on either federalism (Arzaghi and Henderson 2005) or fiscal decentralisation (Wallis and Oates 1998). Apart from differences in measurement, results obviously also depend on case selection (Geddes 2007). Moreover, critics of the sociological approach are right in pointing out that '[f]ederalism is not necessarily a response to ethnic diversity, and, indeed, many of the best-known examples of federal government are in states whose populations are mono-ethnic, or almost so' (Coakley 2005: 291; *see also* Amoretti and Bermeo 2004). What is more, ethnic diversity may be so strong as to bring about the very demise of the political system – see the creation of Belgium in 1830 instead of a Dutch-Belgian federation, or the successor states of the Yugoslav Federation. So federalism

> can quarantine ethnic conflict but at the same time it also provides territorial minorities with a voice in the politics of the centre. [...] the self-rule that federalism brings strengthens the resource base of regional minorities [...] and thus reduces the cost of secession. (Erk and Swenden 2010: 12; *see also* Murphy 1989)

In other words, while the societal diversity-argument may make a normative point for federalism, it needs to be supplemented to be able to explain degrees of (de)centralisation. One such supplement is political culture, which I regard as an answer to the question of when exactly societal diversity causes decentralisation and when not. This brings me to review the second causal contribution of federal studies.

A second strand within socio-cultural federalism argues that *political culture*, i.e. deeply entrenched expectations (Kavanagh 1972) and 'a particular pattern of orientations to political action' (Almond 1956: 396), form the background against which (de)centralisation is chosen. For Duchacek (1987: 341), a 'federal political culture' is defined by 'a set of orientations toward the federal political system and attitudes toward the role of self (in the federal case, the component units as well as the individuals) in the system'. An indication of what that means is 'that a local, provincial, or regional habit (if discovered and proven) of looking for guidance to the national capital and not questioning its directives constitutes *prima facie* evidence of a unitary rather than a federal political tradition' (1987: 343). Because of the importance of political culture for federalism, most studies of it at the sub-national level have focused either on the US (e.g. King 1994; Lieske 1993; Miller 1991; Morgan and Watson 1991) or Canada (e.g. Simeon and Elkins 1974 and Henderson 2004).

But where, in turn, does political culture come from? As with societal diversity, history plays a decisive role. Studies have found that former Portuguese and Spanish colonies tend to be most fiscally centralised (Treisman 2006) and that having inherited the French legal system has a positive effect (Arzaghi and Henderson 2005), but civil law origins produce a negative effect (Stegarescu 2005) on centralisation. Burgess (2009: 8) takes the concept of 'federal political culture' further than Duchacek (1987) by reading into it a general 'recommendation and (sometimes) active promotion of support for federation or some form of federal arrangement that falls short of full federation'. His advice is somehow followed by Stegarescu (2005), who finds that Catholic countries tend to be more fiscally centralised than non-Catholics ones: according to him, 'Catholic doctrine is seen to be more hierarchical and interventionist than Protestantism, which stresses individual responsibility instead' (2005: 22).[8] Religion, obviously a crude measure of political culture, brings me to consider Elazar's (1995–99) *covenant*.

A 'covenantal process of state formation' is characterised by 'the deliberate coming together of equals to establish a mutually useful governmental framework within which all can function on an equal basis, usually defined by a pact' (Elazar 1997: 239). Once achieved, these precise 'patterns of political culture' (1997: 240) remain embedded, so that 'preexisting political cultures influence the choice of models and the institutions to operationalise them' (1997: 240). However, Elazar also warns that 'since the antecedents of both culture and institutions go back to "time immemorial", that is, before recorded history, we cannot say much about cause and effect but must think of the two as functions of each other' (1997: 248–9). For Elazar, federalism is unthinkable without proper cultural foundations. He specifically adduces Switzerland as founded 'on the twin pillars of a federal political culture and a strong religious tradition' (Elazar 1993: 12). In a cross-national comparison, Elazar concludes that '[t]oday, the Swiss are probably the most federal people in the world in terms of their political culture', precisely because they have 'internalized the proper combination of individual autonomy and commitment to group effort, which is essential for successful federal arrangements' (1993: 12; *see also* Burgess 2006: 54, on Switzerland's 'distinct federal political culture'). Moreover, because of its frequent popular votes, Switzerland offers a unique opportunity to directly observe – and precisely measure – such support for autonomy, federalism, and hence lesser or greater centralisation. I will present such a measure in Chapter Four, but now turn to a second approach to explaining (de)centralisation.

---

8. Even a cursory look at the 'Swiss case' would however disprove this: in 1847, the Catholic (and rural) cantons fought to maintain the confederal structure while the Protestant (and urban, pre-industrial) cantons eventually achieved a significant centralisation.

The structural approach

A different explanation of (de)centralisation, altogether, is provided by the structural approach. There are three causal factors at play here: area, distance, and population size. Each one figures prominently, but not exclusively in a different strand of the academic literature:

1. In fiscal federalism, one variant of *the fiscal decentralisation theorem* argues that the greater the area, the more likely policy preferences will vary (e.g. Ebel and Yilmaz 2002). Hence, only decentralisation can achieve the optimal balance between costs (lower through proximity) and benefits (higher through economies of scale) – de Vries (2000: 203) calls this 'the fantasy of the appropriate scale'.
2. In political (macro)sociology, Stein Rokkan's *centre-periphery* paradigm argues that decentralisation increases to the extent that peripheries are able to resist the centre's attempt at economic, military-administrative and cultural system building – which is more likely to be the case in distant, inaccessible regions with strong cities of their own (Rokkan and Urwin 1983: 15; *see also* Tarrow 2004).
3. In the literature on state (re)structuring, Hooghe and Marks (2013) provide evidence that decentralisation is mainly driven by *population size*. Therefore, 'the larger the country, the more decentralized its government, whether federal or not' (Dahl and Tufte 1973: 37).

One problem common to all three arguments is a lack of theoretical *process-specification*. Economists fail to convincingly show why exactly a certain governmental structure is adopted. Their argument only makes sense if we assume that there is a) perfect information available to b) rationally thinking and acting political actors c) interested in the 'greater good' and d) able to calculate the 'proper' scale e) for each public policy (*see* Tiebout 1956: 419). Hooghe and Marks (2013: 197) equally conclude that '[t]he causal mechanism by which population affects government structure, soft information, depends on the benefit of dialogue in producing public policy', admitting however that there is still 'much to learn about' this mechanism (2013: 197). Finally, a 'polycephalic' structure is characteristic of the European city-belt (Rokkan and Urwin 1983: 36), but the specification of when, how and why exactly a centre becomes 'the political response' (1983: 179) remains open. Nevertheless, the general structural argument is powerful and backed up with evidence, as I now show by discussing the merits of each strand in turn.

Fiscal federalism is probably the most scientific branch in federal studies, owing to the precise nature of its variables. Its view on politics is as being demand-driven: citizens' preferences for both a specific quality and quantity of public policies determine politics. Based on this assumption, Treisman (2007: 58) summarises the underlying logic of achieving administrative efficiency as follows:

[…] when public goods and services have different optimal scales of provision, increasing the number of tiers and creating units of different size at the different levels make it possible to provide a diverse portfolio of public goods more cost-effectively.

In political systems extending over only a small area – say, Luxembourg (2,600 km^2) or Liechtenstein (160 km^2) (*see* World Factbook 2012) – there is thus little reason to decentralise. The 'optimal scale' for the provision of most services is likely to be the national level, if not beyond. The opposite is the case for larger political systems (Hooghe and Marks 2013), where decentralisation alone guarantees the same efficiency. Therefore, area is the prime explanatory variable in a purely fiscal take on (de)centralisation, and the empirical evidence presented is indeed compelling: Treisman (2006), Panizza (1999), Arzaghi and Henderson (2005), Stegarescu (2005), Garrett and Rodden (2003) and Rühli (2012) all find negative correlation coefficients for area and either political or fiscal centralisation. Wallis and Oates (1988) and Hooghe and Marks (2013) find no significant effect, although in both studies the sign points in the hypothesised direction. Only Timofeev (2003: 31) finds a positive and significant effect in his study of Russian regions, but is sceptical of his own results. Overall, regional authority, federalism and fiscal decentralisation all tend to be higher in larger countries.

No wonder then that Alesina and Spolaore (2003: 137) regard 'decentralization [within nation-states] as an intermediate organization form in between the maze of overlapping jurisdictions on the one extreme and the one-level-of-government-does-it-all on the opposite extreme'. In other words, 'in the absence of transaction costs or economies of scale, one would not need' the national level at all (2003: 138). It would mean going too far to claim that states *only* exist because they are able a) to 'internalise' spillover effects arising from the provision of some services while simultaneously b) ensuring that economies of scale are obtained in the provision of others (2003: 140). What matters here is that a – in theory limited – series of policy-specific trade-offs 'across jurisdictions as a result of both differentials in preferences and cost differentials' (Oates 1999: 1122) determines the overall degree of (de)centralisation. However, these differentials are not solely dependent on area, but also on topography and population size, two variables discussed next.

Stein Rokkan's *centre-periphery model* (Flora *et al.* 1999) best shows the importance of topography. Mann (1997 [1984]) also explains the history of Western Europe as the attempt by peripheries to become themselves centres (*see also* Sidgwick 1903 and Dyson 1980). One of the paradoxes in that process is that centre building occurred first at the edges of the former Roman Empire (Swenden 2006: 23). For Lipset and Rokkan (1990 [1967]), the territorial dimension is one of two fundamental political cleavages (on its revival, *see* de Winter *et al.* 2006). A periphery is the first element in a spatial archetype in which the periphery is subordinate to the authority of the centre. Within this archetype, the centre represents the seat of authority and the periphery those geographical locations at the furthest distance from the centre, but still within the territory controlled from the latter. (Rokkan and Urwin 1983: 2)

The degree of (de)centralisation then, is the result of the 'politicization of peripheral predicaments', that is dependent on the 'strength and vitality of region-specific political mobilization and the scope of the territorial/group demands laid at the door of the political centre' (Rokkan and Urwin 1983: 121) and the interaction of this with the type of central response. This latter condition can range from granting full independence through – possibly asymmetrical – regional authority and cultural autonomy to full integration (1983: 141; Piattoni 2010: 40; *see also* Tarlton 1965 and Agranoff 1999). The merit of Rokkan and Urwin's analysis (1983) is that they provide a conceptual framework for systematically mapping centre building and accompanying peripheral resistance:

> Typically, a centre controls the bulk of the transactions among the holders of resources across a territory; it tends to be closer than any alternative site to the resource-rich areas within the territory; and it is able to dominate the communication flow through the territorial diffusion of a standard language and through its control of a set of institutions for consultation and direction. (1983: 14)

For each of the three dimensions of centre building – cultural, economic and military-administrative – there are two reciprocal power relationships (1983: 14). So to linguistic, religious and/or ideological standardisation, there are potentially opposed efforts at maintaining a distinctive identity in literature, faith and/or the media; administrative subordination and elite alliances may meet, indeed provoke, violent resistance/war; and top-down monetarisation and incorporation in exchange networks may have to compete with attempts at autarky and the persistence of alternative markets (1983: 15). These processes can be reinforcing or contradicting (1983: 16). To take two contemporary examples, contrast the (economic) integration into the EU's Single Market with the success of populist right-wing parties in 'defence' of their (cultural-political) nation (e.g. UKIP, Lega Nord, FPÖ and BZÖ; *see* Pelinka 2002); or compare the maintenance of a distinct Church, local government and legal system in Scotland since 1707 (Keating 2009a: 18) with today's economic dependence on the English South-East. Returning to the centre-periphery framework and its theoretical implications, clearly what matters most is the structural factor of *distance*, because it

> [...] has always set limits to empire-building: the longer the distance from the centre to areas of recent conquest, the greater the need for relay points of command in the provinces and the greater the risk that these will become the nuclei of independent centre formation. Similarly for systems of cultural

communication via script, the greater the distance between the core area and the outlying mission field, the greater the likelihood of 'noise' and distortion in the message flow. (Rokkan and Urwin 1983: 16)

That distance from the core area matters seems to be confirmed by a casual glance at contemporary asymmetrical federal political systems. Regional authority is higher in Scotland than in Wales (Edinburgh–London: 640 km; Cardiff–London: 240 km); highest in the 'special regions' of Italy (Trieste/Aosta/Palermo–Rome: 680–930 km by land); and higher for the Basque Country and Navarre (Bilbao/Pamplona–Madrid: 400–430 km) than for any other Spanish 'autonomous community'.[9] So it is distance *in combination with* area that matters (Arzaghi and Henderson 2005: 1179). However, none of the existing quantitative studies of (de)centralisation have tested for distance explicitly. Some assume, for the sake of model building, that policy preferences are constant across national territory (Arzaghi and Henderson 2005: 1156 n.9). Alesina and Spolaore (2003: 33), on the other hand, take the exact opposite position when they equate ideological with geographical (i.e. territorial) distance. But even they admit that this 'imperfect correlation between geographical and ideological distance' distorts '[m]any good insights' (2003: 222).

One such insight appears when accepting that not only absolute measures of distance (i.e. area) matter, but also the latter's *relative* importance. Topography, 'the arrangement of the natural and artificial physical features of an area' (Oxford Dictionary of English 2005), is as important, and possibly more important, than either distance or even area itself. Or, in the words of the centre-periphery paradigm: 'topography, as it were, can be married to typology' (Rokkan and Urwin 1983: 21). High mountains may cut off and shield an otherwise close and exposed area, leaving it with more autonomy (even independence, e.g. Andorra) than adjacent but more exposed territories; the sea may increase the military capacity to resist/reverse centre-building (e.g. Ireland); and abundance of natural resources (e.g. water) and access to trade routes (Switzerland) may lessen economic dependence on outside centres. Indeed, the premise that distance leads to 'spatial decay' in public service provision is turned on its head by Cox (1979) and other observers of US inner cities, where often the *real* decay takes place as richer citizens move into the suburbs. Mobility clearly needs to be factored into the equation if location is to matter.

Both the areal and distal hypotheses boil down to the idea of federalism as management of size (Burgess 2006), and of *population size* more particularly. Size is an equally potent correlate of (de)centralisation as is area: it significantly and positively affects regional authority (Hooghe and Marks 2013), fiscal decentralisation (Arzaghi and Henderson 2005) and federalism (Lijphart 1999: 251) in different countries as well as fiscal decentralisation in the US States (Wallis and Oates 1988) and the Swiss cantons (Rühli 2012). Only Stegarescu (2005)

---

9.   Region-specific authority scores for 2006, obtained from the website of one of the RAI-authors, Arjan Schakel, at http://www.arjanschakel.nl/regauth_dat.html ('Region Scores' dataset, last accessed 13 May 2012). Distances calculated using Google Maps, http://maps.google.co.uk.

finds a negative effect; Treisman (2006), Panizza (1999) and Garrett and Rodden (2003) find no effect at all. But when Hooghe and Marks (2013) rerun Stegarescu's sample with *their* measure of the dependent variable, they do find a positive and significant effect, as they also do for Panizza's sample. And so population size competes with area over which factor explains most of the variance. But why would that be so? In political geography, it is observed that

> urban growth [...] arises on crossroads, natural or manmade and proceeds owing to its function of centrality, developing as a 'hub'. At a preliminary stage the city tries to set itself up as a crossroads for exchanges, either at a breaking point of transport, such as a seaport, a river confluence, or a portage between inland waterways, or at the contact of contiguous but different economic regions. The beginnings are therefore linked *not* with the centrality in the original territory but rather with a peripheral position likely to attract the confluence of trade routes. (Gottmann 1973: 152; emphasis added)

As postulated by the literature on metropolitan government and urban areas, local autonomy is also a function of 'social and economic' resources available locally (Clark 1974: 30–31; *see also* Chattopadhyay 2011: 21–22). Together with area and distance, cities call for an even greater policy mix: not just 'irrigation versus snow removal' (Clark 1974: 29) in the plains as opposed to mountainous regions, but often a wholly *different* set of public goods, e.g. care for the homeless, nightlife regulation, public transport, 'new' minorities, unemployed, green spaces, a service-economy, childcare etc. in *addition* to basic services like water and garbage disposal (*see* della Santa 1996). Demands for these arise not because of location or distance, but are man-made.

Nevertheless, quantitative findings on this aspect of size are mixed. General urbanisation is found to have a *negative* effect on fiscal decentralisation by both Stegarescu (2005) and Timofeev (2003). Wallis and Oates (1988: 22), however, conclude the exact opposite: urbanisation has a *positive* influence on fiscal decentralisation. A demographic dominance of the capital city – not the same as general urbanisation – works against federalism but has no significant effect on fiscal decentralisation for Arzaghi and Henderson (2005); and population density is negatively correlated with fiscal decentralisation in the Russian regions (Timofeev 2003: 32). Timofeev (2003: 32) also finds a *positive* correlation between urban/rural homogeneity and expenditure decentralisation. In other words: the fewer the cities, the more decentralised the political system, which runs against his hypothesis that power is devolved to where most people have different policy tastes and the idea of polycephality, which assumed many cities were needed to cause decentralisation. Table 1.1 summarises the quantitative evidence of the seven cross-sectional explanatory studies of (de)centralisation discussed thus far. I now turn to the political approach, which provides a third set of theoretically argued and empirically backed up explanations.

Table 1.1: General determinants of (de)centralisation

Analysis	Hooghe and Marks (2013)	Treisman (2006)	Panizza (1999)	Arzaghi and Henderson (2005)		Wallis and Oates (1988)	Stegarescu (2005)	Timofeev (2003)
Dependent Variable	*Reg. authority*	*fiscal dec.*	*fiscal dec.*	*fiscal dec.*	*federalism*	*fiscal dec.*	*fiscal dec.*	*fiscal dec.*
Affluence/income/GDP	Positive	positive	positive	positive	positive	no effect (+)	positive	positive (2001)
Area	no effect (+)	positive	positive	positive	positive	no effect (+)	positive	negative (2001)
Capital city dominancy	–	–	–	negative	no effect (-)	–	–	negative
Catholic	–	–	–	–	–	–	negative	–
Civil law origin	–	–	–	–	–	–	positive	–
Democracy	Positive	no effect (+)	positive	–	–	–	–	–
Ethnic heterogeneity	Positive	negative	positive	negative	no effect (+)	no effect (+/-)	positive	negative (1996)
Former colony of ESP or P	–	negative	–	–	–	–	–	–
French law	–	–	–	negative	no effect (-)	–	–	–
Growth rate	–	–	–	–	–	–	negative	–
Left government	–	–	–	–	–	–	positive	–
Population density	–	–	–	–	–	–	–	negative
Population size	Positive	no effect	–	positive	positive	positive	negative	–
Regional disparity	–	–	–	–	–	–	positive	–
Regional parties	Positive	–	–	–	–	–	–	–
Urbanisation	–	–	–	–	–	positive	negative	negative (1996)
*Sample size (*sub-national)*	*39*	*58–64*	*54–57*	*45*	*43*	*48**	*23*	*66–69**

Note: Cells indicate direction of significant results in regression analyses; 'no effect' = no significant effect found (direction of relationship); '-' = not tested.

The political approach

A third approach to explaining (de)centralisation catapults political actors to the centre-stage. Type and degree of (de)centralisation now primarily depend on the rational choice of individual policy-makers. This causal mechanism comes in two variants:

1. *Political ideology*: institutional choice is driven by principles. The political left, in particular, is said to act in favour of centralism to guarantee equality, enhance state interventionism and redistribute income (de Vries 2000: 199). This is diametrically opposed to the idea of a minimal (central) state and free-market competition, values cherished on the right (e.g. Hayek 2011 [1960]).

2. *Elite bargain*: institutional choice is driven by interests. Political actors bargain with each other to pool some of their resources, e.g. defence and trade, but retain others, e.g. education and culture (Riker 1964). Bargaining takes place 'between prospective national leaders and officials of constituent governments (Riker 1964: 11). Both structural constraints and socio-cultural determinism largely disappear here in favour of 'a plan of local [i.e. regional] governments to retain autonomy when creating a central government for defence or expansionist purposes' (Riker 1969: 138; *see also* Grodzins 1967; Swenden and Maddens 2009; Detterbeck and Hepburn 2010).

As with the two previous approaches, the arguments of each sub-strand are linked to each other. Both emphasise political actors and downplay the structural context. Hayek (2011 [1960]: 380) is probably the most powerful *ideologue* to advocate decentralisation in the name of liberty:

> While it has always been characteristic of those favouring an increase in governmental powers to support maximum concentration of these powers, those mainly concerned with individual liberty have generally advocated decentralization. [...] It is usually the authoritarian planner who, in the interest of uniformity, governmental efficiency and administrative convenience, supports the centralist tendencies and in this receives the strong support of poorer majorities, who wish to be able to tap the resources of the wealthier regions.

Hayek not only defends the 'liberty of the wealthier regions, which would be subjected to expropriation from the poorer ones' (Alesina and Spolaore 2003: 142), but also claims that 'competition between local authorities' provides an 'opportunity for experimentation with alternative methods which will secure most of the advantages of free growth' (Hayek 2011 [1960]: 380; *see also* Miller 2010: 12–13). But does the liberal right really favour decentralisation and the progressive left centralisation? The actual evidence is mixed.

Alonso (2012: 89) shows that in Spain (in the 1990s), Belgium (2003) and in the UK (2005) significantly more *citizens* in the 'pro-periphery' camp placed themselves on the right. However, when analysing party manifestos of nation-wide *parties* for the same period, she finds that at least in Spain and the UK there is a significant correlation between favouring decentralisation and the left (2012: 79). Stegarescu (2005: 23), who hypothesised 'that progressive governments are more concerned with equity considerations and therefore favour state control and stronger centralization', finds that the higher the fraction of seats retained by left-wing governmental parties in the national parliament, the *higher* expenditure decentralisation (2005: 25). When regressing on tax decentralisation, left governments barely make a difference: the coefficients are negative, as expected, but fail to reach statistical significance (2005: 25). Finally, Steunenberg and Mol (1997) provide an explanation according to which, on the one hand, tax centralisation increases with GDP but is independent of government composition because 'taxes are rigidly institutionalised' and cannot easily be changed (1997: 248–50). Public expenditure, on the other hand, does vary with ideology: 'left-wing or "progressive" governments are much more concerned with equity considerations of publicly provided goods and services than "conservative" governments, they generally favour "state control" and therefore centralization of public production' (1997: 250). Using a dummy variable to code the presence of parties left of the median parties in each country, they find that, indeed, having a progressive government (coalition) has led to a 2.2 per cent increase in central expenditure in Belgium, France, Germany and the UK (1950–90, N = 154; 1997: 251–2). Moreover, for the UK they also find a positive and significant relationship between a progressive government and central taxation (1997: 251–2 – this can be explained by the ease with which majoritarian governments can change even 'rigidly institutionalised' rules).

This mixed evidence can partly be explained if we regard political parties not only as monistically ideological and genuinely altruistic, but also as strategically opportunistic and programmatically flexible actors. Parties in general and politicians in particular, also cause (de)centralisation for reasons other than ideological commitment. Or, more cynically: ideologies are themselves driven by *interests* (Burgess 1993: 104). Building loosely on Riker (1964 and 1969), Alonso (2012) provides the most recent and exhaustive study of the influence of what she calls 'electoral geography' and 'peripheral threats' on the decision of governmental parties to not only promise, but actually deliver devolution. First of all, she treats the centre-periphery dichotomy like any other issue dimension along which parties (and voters) place themselves (2012: 25). The distinction between national and local/regional parties, then, is not so much based on what they advocate as on the electoral arenas in which they compete. Voters pragmatically – and sometimes strategically – chose 'the party that is closest to their interest' (2012: 39). Secondly, in their strategic moves along the centre-periphery axis to maximise such votes, parties are constrained by their credibility only. This credibility is, in turn, severely restricted as long as the state remains unitary, for state-wide parties cannot simultaneously claim to advocate regional autonomy but not implement it, once in government. Peripheral parties, on the other hand, do not face such constraints and 'can strategize [...] without raising suspicions of opportunism, unreliability and/or irresponsibility' (2012: 45).

Devolution happens when a 'peripheral threat' appears, that is electoral success of one or more peripheral parties in a region with 'systemic' as well as a 'partisan electoral relevance' (Alonso 2010: 13). Losing votes to state-wide party B in a small region with correspondingly few seats in the national parliament will not induce the same kind of reaction in party A as losses to regionalists in Andalusia, Lombardy, Flanders or the English South-East (Alonso 2012: 101–2). Therefore, '[n]ational parties with a geographical concentration of the vote' in regions where regional parties are on the rise, and/or parties with prospects of establishing governmental 'regional strongholds', are opposed to maintaining centralisation (Alonso 2010: 10).

Similar attempts to rationally explain decentralisation are provided by Sorens (2009), O'Neill (2003), Meguid (2008) and Kollman (2013). Sorens (2009: 256) distinguishes between 'central government office seeking' and 'regional government office seeking'. Applied to the UK, the rise of the SNP would at least partially explain why Labour – despite a redistributive and egalitarian ideology – devolved power to Scotland (but less so in Wales, hence an asymmetrical solution): to gain regional office (e.g. Hopkin 2009). However, in a fully rational world the Conservatives would outbid Labour in granting Scotland independence, since a) they are a marginal force there anyway and b) it would reduce the total number of Westminster seats by mostly Labour-held Scottish seats.[10] Nevertheless, in March 2012 David Cameron vowed to 'fight for the UK with everything we've got',[11] although he then agreed on a referendum on Scottish independence that eventually failed in September 2014. Either electoral strategy is not all there is to it, or the benefits are not always clear (e.g. because of the costs to the Conservatives if they fail to defend the Union), or some party leaders have not yet understood how to capitalise on the issue.

For O'Neill (2003: 1071), this kind of 'theory linking decentralization to the electoral considerations of political parties' still positively and dramatically differs from both the structural and socio-cultural approach considered above. But as I argue in the next chapter, the three should be regarded as complementary, not contradictory (*see also* Montero and Samuels 2004: 34). Electoral calculations only explain one part of the story. Political actors might not only be interested to gain office at *both* levels (Alonso 2012: 52), but also act out of a historical-ideological commitment to unity (e.g. the Conservatives in Spain), in reaction to socio-linguistic pressures (Belgium), or because the kind of policy they pursue requires a certain degree of (de)centralisation (UK). The merit of a partisan logic of (de)centralisation, however, is attention to timing (Meguid 2008: 5) and splits between parties (Alonso 2010: 5). Hooghe and Marks also find a significant and

---

10. A point made by Charlie Jeffery at the 2012 Annual Conference of the UK Political Science Association in Belfast, 3–5 April, in the panel on 'Devolution in the UK: Process, Prospects and Pitfalls'.

11. Andrew Black: 'Prime Minister David Cameron in Union 'fight' pledge', *BBC News*, 23 March 2012, at http://www.bbc.co.uk/news/uk-scotland-scotland-politics-17475300 (last accessed 18 October 2012).

positive correlation between regional authority in 39 democracies and the strength of regionalist parties, that is, parties with an 'exclusively regional electoral base' (2013: 30).

O'Neill (2003) finds a similar correlation in Latin America between strong local bases within presidential parties and support for decentralising reforms. Her 'puzzle: how to reconcile politicians' drive to increase their power with a series of centrally orchestrated decentralizing reforms' (2003: 1087) is resolved through a double bargain. A first bargain involves parties and voters: 'A party distributes political and fiscal power to the arenas in which their political allies seem most likely to gain control' (2003: 1087). Parties, no matter if peripheral or state-wide, rationally seek to maximise their votes and gain governmental office (Alonso 2012). A second bargain takes place within the party, between the national and sub-national elite: 'decentralization varies in degree and form as a function of the interests and location of the 'party brokers' – the political leaders who exert the most influence over political careers' (Montero and Samuels 2004: 23). For Argentina, Eaton and Dickovick (2004: 108) show how president Menem has 'used his considerable partisan powers to build support for re-centralizing changes that were resisted by the governors. [...] a series of closed-door meetings between himself and exclusively Peronist governors [allowed him] to purchase [their] support'. In other words, devolution is indeed just one of many electoral strategies available (Alonso 2012), the activation of which depends on the place and strength of regionalist parties (Fearon and van Houten 2002: 14).

This concludes my review of explanatory studies on (de)centralisation. I now turn to the question of how studies of cantonal-local relations in Switzerland have dealt with this particular aspect.

Cantonal-local relations in Switzerland

In Switzerland, the relations of local governments with their canton have not yet been systematically studied from a political science perspective. This gap becomes apparent by comparing Vatter (2002), who explicitly (2002: 22–23) does *not* address cantonal decentralisation as a dependent variable in his study of cantonal politics, with Ladner (1991), who, in turn, does *not* address cantonal politics as an independent variable in his study of local politics. Although the Swiss cantons are important 'building blocks' of Swiss politics (Müller 1987; *see also* Siegfried 1948) and although federalism is a key principle of this polity (e.g. Vatter 2006a: 98; *see also* Nüssli 1985 and Frey 1977), decentralisation *within* the cantons has not received the attention it deserves (*see also* Vatter 2006b and 2014; Ladner and Steiner 2005; Urio 1986).

The few studies that do exist of local autonomy *or* cantonal structures by and large mirror the general literature. By far the most widely shared observation is that the francophone cantons are internally more centralised than the German-speaking ones because they are 'more French' (e.g. Giacometti 1941 and 1952; Meylan 1972; Meyer 1978; Grodecki 2007; Horber-Papazian 2004 and 2006). Many elements – historical, structural, ideological – flow into this argument, but essentially it is one of political culture, built over centuries of political socialisation, direct influence from France (through TV, radio, newspapers and literature) and ensuing different policy preferences (Freitag 2006: 134). Eugster *et al.* (2001), for example, have argued that the 'significant Latin-German gap in the demand for government provided social insurance' (2001: F416) is related to language as 'a medium by which attitudes, values and beliefs are transmitted from one generation to the next. Language is central to the spreading of beliefs and norms and determines an individual's social identity' (2001: F415). But a similar effect remains to be shown empirically for cantonal decentralisation.

A second set of explanatory factors relates to size (e.g. Geser 1981 and 1996; Meylan *et al.* 1972; Fleiner-Gerster 1992; Fiechter 2010). Ladner (1994) finds local autonomy to be highest in middle-sized communes, which tend to be found in larger cantons, and which, thereby, have a polycephalous city-structure (Rokkan and Urwin 1983; Flora *et al.* 1999). Finally, if societal diversity is a cause of federalism at the national level (e.g. de Reynold 1982: 9), then linguistic and/or religious diversity could reasonably be expected to have a similar, i.e. a decentralising influence at the cantonal level. But no study has yet compared this systematically.

In sum, despite the import of general theories into Swiss literature, there are surprisingly few academic studies that have systematically tested any one, let alone all three types of causes of (de)centralisation. This might be an unfortunate consequence of the so widely held, almost axiomatic belief that 'Frenchness' matters most. Interestingly enough, two of those rare studies that do compare cantonal decentralisation are rather recent: both Fiechter (2010) and Rühli (2012) study, amongst many other things, the extent to which communal autonomy depends on a series of cantonal factors. Table 1.2 lists their main findings.

Rühli (2012: 74) relies on a mixture of structural and cultural factors. Cantonal area and the median Local Government (LG) population per canton together explain 21 per cent of the variation. If a categorical variable for 'Latin culture' (cantons where French or Italian is spoken) and another for 'mountain cantons' is included, the model explains 48 per cent. Area and LG population size have a positive, Latin and mountains a negative effect on the local share of total public expenditure, i.e. on expenditure decentralisation (2012: 177). Fiechter (2010) on the other hand tests for predictors of four different 'facets of local autonomy': legal, political, economic and social (2010: 45). His main hypothesis combines structure (local size) with cantonal belonging (2010: 48). At the level of cantons the following are tested: the 'degree of institutional freedom', or legal local autonomy (2010: 67); expenditure decentralisation and administrative decentralisation (2010: 78); and the results from the 2005 survey among local secretaries on 'perceived local autonomy' (2010: 96). He does not combine them into a single index and relies on bivariate correlations alone. While the number of LGs consistently fails to be significantly related to local autonomy/cantonal decentralisation, francophone cantons have significantly lower legal local autonomy, less administrative decentralisation as well as lower degrees of perceived local autonomy; both median and mean local population only matter for legal autonomy. By and large, this confirms both Rühli's findings and previous assumptions.

Table 1.2: Common predictors of Swiss local autonomy

Variables	Rühli (2012)		Fiechter (2010)		
Dependent variable	*Expenditure decentralis.*	*Legal local autonomy*	*Expenditure decentralis.*	*Administrative decentralis.*	*Perceived autonomy*
Cantonal area	Positive	–	–	–	–
Median LG population	Positive	Positive	no effect (+)	no effect (+)	no effect (+)
Latin language	Negative	Negative	no effect (-)	Negative	Negative
Mountain cantons	Negative	–	–	–	–
Mean LG population	–	Positive	no effect (-)	no effect (-)	no effect (-)
Number of LGs	–	no effect (-)	no effect (+)	no effect (-)	no effect (-)
Sample size	26		25 *(no Basel-City)*		26

Note: Cells indicate direction of significant results in OLS regression (Rühli) and bivariate correlation (Fiechter); 'no effect' = no significant effect (direction of relationship); '-' = not tested.

However, neither of these two studies tests for political factors, both are centred more on local autonomy than cantonal centralisation and, most crucially, neither provides an answer as to *why exactly* the seven 'Latin' cantons are more centralised. The best study in terms of analysing the political factors enabling communes to influence cantonal politics is Horber-Papazian (2004), but her evidence draws on six cantons only. All other studies of local governments either offer an extensively legal treatment of local autonomy in general (Nawiasky 1946; Thürer 1946; Althaus 1949; Zwahlen 1968; Jagmetti 1972; Fleiner-Gerster 1992; Braaker 2000; Bapst 2000; Tanquerel and Bellanger 2007; Meyer 1978) and/or are confined to a single canton (e.g. Langhard 1977, Albonico 1979, Fortunato 1974 and Fetz 2009 for Grisons; Luchsinger 1941, Heer 1944, Winteler 1961 and Kronenberg 2011 for Glarus; Niederer 1956 for Valais; Pestalozzi 1973, Schellenberg 1975 and Bütikofer 1950 for Zurich; Raith 1984 for Basel-City; Schaltegger 1952 for Thurgau; Fagagnini 1974 and Glaus 1984 for St. Gall; Fleiner 1986a for Lucerne; Friedrich *et al.* 1998 for Schaffhausen; Friedrich 1999 for Berne; Kennel 1989 and Huwyler 2009 for Schwyz; Mermoud 2005 for Vaud; Reiser 1998 for Geneva; and Dafflon 1992a for Fribourg).

Gasser (1943, 1952 and 1976), Frenkel (1993) and Barber (1974 and 1988) treat communes in a historical, participatory and libertarian perspective while Geser's (1981, 1996, 1997a and 1997b) is a sociological understanding of the internal workings of Swiss communes (*see also* Debarbieux and Rudaz 2008; Weinberg 1983). Horber-Papazian and Soguel (1996) outline recent reforms while Geser (2004) and Horber-Papazian (2006) describe Swiss communes in general. Finally, there are several studies that prepare or analyse territorial reform in individual cantons (e.g. Ladner and Fiechter 2008 for Vaud; Steiner *et al*. 2010 for Uri; Dafflon and Tòth 2003 for Fribourg; Pacella and Mazzoleni 2010 for Ticino; Schmitt 2002 for Valais; Fivaz and Schwarz 1999 as well as Wernli 2005 for Aargau; and Ecoplan 2009 for Berne), but while some of them attempt to draw comparisons with other cantons, coverage is far from complete. In sum, whereas the literature on Swiss federalism studies the cantons within the encompassing federation, the issue of local governments as 'creatures of their states' (to paraphrase Elazar 1966: 164) has not received the same kind of attention in political science.

Conclusion

Reviewing several literatures, in this chapter, has first of all helped to define (de)centralisation as a basic attribute of political systems. I have staked the ideal-type endpoints of the (de)centralisation continuum through centralisation at one end and confederal political systems at the other. The three types of decentralisation discussed in this chapter – devolution, delegation and de-concentration – will form the basis of a tri-dimensional conceptualisation of (de)centralisation itself in Chapter Two.

It was also shown how three approaches to explaining (de)centralisation can be deduced from disparate fields (socio-cultural and fiscal federalism, territorial governance and state restructuring) in the general literature and how they have so far been applied. The conclusion from this exercise is that each approach has its merits, but also its deficiencies, so there is a need to integrate them into a single framework. This, too, will be undertaken in Chapter Two.

Finally, discussing the Swiss literature has revealed a gap when it comes to applying comparative theories of (de)centralisation to the Swiss cantons. Apart from two very recent studies (Rühli 2012 and Fiechter 2010), this object lacks the kind of attention it deserves. What has therefore emerged is the need to a) systematically compare types and degrees of decentralisation across *all* cantons by b) drawing on *theoretical* reflections developed elsewhere. In other words, why exactly are the French-speaking cantons the most centralised? Has it to do with political culture, political agency, ideology, history, or both? And is that true even when controlling for area, population size and/or topography? What about differences within the group of German-speaking or among French-speaking cantons? So that the answers to these questions can then be linked back to the general debate, a sound and solid methodology is necessary. To present and explain that method will be the purpose of Chapter Four.

Chapter Two

Concept and Theory

In order to systematically compare and explain cantonal decentralisation, a theoretical framework is needed. This has to serve three purposes, as formulated authoritatively by Müller and Strøm (1999: 11) for the analysis of party behaviour:

> First, [a conceptual framework] should allow us analytically to describe different party objectives and relationships between them. Second, it should contain operationalizable terms that we can apply to concrete situations in which party leaders make their critical choices. Third, it should lend itself to more formal theoretical efforts by scholars who set themselves such goals.

My goal includes this last one: it aims to be a theoretical, and not simply a conceptual framework. The first three sections in this chapter 'repair' (de)centralisation by distinguishing between a polity-, a policy- and a politics-dimension. The theoretical approaches to studying (de)centralisation reviewed in Chapter One are then integrated into a single model, in the fourth section. The hypotheses derived from that model will subsequently be tested empirically.

'Concept repairing'

'Centralisation needs to be repaired, not written off', wrote Jim Bulpitt (1983: 34) almost 30 years ago. What he meant by that was that a 'more plausible and fruitful definition would help' and that 'The concept also needs to be unpacked' (1983: 34). Almost 30 years later, Jonathan Bradbury and Peter John (2010: 295) guest-edited a special issue of *Government and Opposition* 'to explore [...] the significance for contemporary scholarship' of Bulpitt's landmark study of territorial politics in the UK. However at this moment, two divides hamper scientific progress in this area: one conceptual, the other methodological.

The *conceptual divide* relates to the fact that when explaining (de)centralisation, different scholars speak of different things, hence they employ a different measure – most often their own. Hooghe and Marks (2013), for instance, oppose their measurement of 'regional authority' (*see also* Hooghe *et al.* 2008 and 2010) to that employed in five other studies: two measure federalism (Lijphart 1999 and Arzaghi and Henderson 2005), two others fiscal decentralisation (Panizza 1999 and Stegarescu 2005) and one 'political decentralisation' (Brancati 2006). The list is nearly endless: Alonso (2010 and 2012), testing an 'electoral geography' theory, speaks of 'political devolution', by which she refers to Falleti's (2005 and 2010) 'political decentralisation', while Wallis and Oates (1988) regress on 'fiscal concentration'. Naturally, lack of agreement on the dependent variable contributes to confusion around explaining it. Moreover, categorical variables (e.g. Lijphart 1999; Brancati 2006; Hooghe and Marks 2013) find themselves opposed to continuous variables, depending on whether 'degrees of federalism' or of fiscal decentralisation are operationalised. What is (de)centralisation and how can we measure it?

The *methodological divide* appears when observing that each of the three approaches tests its claims differently. Structural and socio-cultural approaches lend themselves more easily to quantitative analysis, due to the interval-nature of key independent variables (km^2 or the proportion of ethnic groups; e.g. Fearon 2003: 204; *see also* Selway 2011 and Ordeshook and Shvetsova 1994). Micro-level approaches, in turn, study a single or a small number of cases, because techniques to measure partisanship and electoral strategies are either cumbersome, and therefore hard to apply to a larger number of cases (*see* Blatter and Blume 2008; Levy 2008); or such measures are crude and hence fail to capture what is a fairly sophisticated process: time- and context-specific political decisions on centralisation as a reaction to, or in anticipation of, electoral losses in a specific region (Alonso 2012). But causality is twofold: to understand *regularity*, cross-case data is needed; to understand *process*, within-case study insights (Bennett 2002; Ragin 1987). Both are comparative and one ought to combine the two techniques in an effort to extract the best of each, which is what I shall attempt in the empirical part of this book (*see also* Chapter Three). For now, suffice it to say that only a middle-range theory is able to cover both dimensions of causality.

So what exactly is it that, in political science as much as in politics, makes decentralisation rival with democracy over the status of a 'concept that no political theory, ideology or movement can afford to eschew' (Smith 1982: 137)? After all, thinkers as distinguished as Aristotle, Plato, Bullinger, Althusius, Hobbes, Tocqueville, Montesquieu, J. S. Mill, Victor Hugo, John Locke, Leibniz, Hamilton, Jay, Madison, Th. Jefferson and Calhoun (Scott 2011; Baker 2000; Riley 1976) have discussed local, regional and federal alternatives to centralisation. One of the reasons for centralisation's prominence may be what lies at its heart – territory, power and the relation between the two – also lies at the heart of Western Europe's most successful political export product ever: the nation-state. It is primarily for reasons of 'identification and defence' that the nation-state 'confronts us, as it were, in its physical, corporeal capacity: as an expanse of territory' (Herz 1957: 474). There is something primordial, intrinsically instinctive hidden beneath territory (Ardrey 1975 [1966]). Nevertheless, while 'centralization is relatively simple to define, it is complex to measure' (Blondel 1995: 229).

Chapter One has identified the ideal-type end-points of the centralisation-decentralisation continuum as fully centralised political systems at one end and decentralised political systems at the other. This assumes a one-dimensional space. But my argument in this section is that each of the existing measures of (de)centralisation has focused on a different dimension and that they can most usefully be aggregated into the three-dimensional conceptualisation shown in Figure 2.1.

This three-dimensional conceptualisation of (de)centralisation borrows from two sources. The first is the idea of political systems as delineating those institutions, actors and processes that possess the capacity to issue decisions binding upon a territorially fixed collectivity (Easton 1965; Weber 1992 [1919]). The second is Multi-Level Governance, a field in which Piattoni (2010: 22) similarly observes that one 'almost inevitably ends up analysing all three aspects of state-society interactions: political mobilization, policy-making and state structuring' or, in other words: politics, policy and polity (2010: 18). The following discussion aims to show why this is important for our understanding of (de)centralisation.

Every political system aggregates inputs/demands and produces outputs (policies). Responsible for aggregation and production are political actors (politics) embedded in their institutional structures (polity). Understanding the political space in this way delineates my ontological position on human beings as essentially rational, but constrained in their actual choice of decisions by structural factors such as – in this order – their political culture, political institutions and the extent to which they are informed about and understand both the feasibility and most likely consequences of their choices. To the extent that human beings engage in political decisions, they are categorised as political actors and can conveniently be sub-divided into five groups according to the intensity of this engagement: the electorate (that part of 'the people' that actually turns out to vote whenever occasion arises), officials (those holding a political office), political parties (comprising most, if not all, of the members of the second group, plus other party members), civil servants (bureaucrats and other public employees) and interest groups. Naturally there may be some overlap, e.g. a local councillor who is also a party member and who regularly goes to the polls. Different actors matter for different dimensions, as I show next.

Figure 2.1: Three-dimensional conceptualisation of (de)centralisation

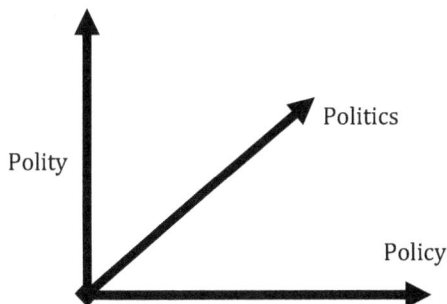

Existing measures

Accepting, for the moment, that there are three dimensions to (de)centralisation, how have they been measured? And how can they be integrated into a single index? The politics-dimension is the most underconceptualised, hence I will discuss it in the next section. Here, I discuss existing measures, starting with the policy-dimension, which is the most prominent one currently employed in the literature, and then move on to discuss the polity-dimension. After reviewing these existing measures I show how a politics-measure could be developed. The actual measurement of politics-decentralisation will be undertaken in Chapter Four, where I apply all three measures to the Swiss cantons.

Policy-(de)centralisation

A first aspect of local or regional autonomy relates to public functions and their vertical distribution: the larger the proportion of decisions taken by central authorities from all decisions by public bodies in a system, the more centralised it is (Blondel 1995: 229). In my terminology, this captures the policy-dimension of (de)centralisation because the idea is to capture the role that the territorial variable plays for systemic outputs. There are three ways to measure the distribution of powers defined as functions in this dimension.

A legal approach distinguishes between 'exclusive', 'concurrent', 'residual' and 'implied powers' (e.g. Boeckenfoerde *et al.* 2007: 35–36). These concepts attribute the primary or sole responsibility to carry out certain tasks to one or several of the governmental levels defined in Chapter One (i.e. national, regional, local). Ronald Watts equally distinguishes between the 'the *scope of jurisdiction* exercised by each level of government, and the *degree of autonomy* or freedom from control by other levels of government with which a particular government performs the tasks assigned to it' (Watts 1996: 65–65; original emphasis). To determine 'legislative decentralisation', he assesses the 'formal allocation by the constitution of legislative powers to each level of government' (1996: 66), to which might be added policy-specific, ordinary legislation and adjudication as key sources for measurement, as well as 'the extent to which each field of jurisdiction is exclusively assigned to one level of government, concurrent or shared.' (1996: 66)

A political economy approach (e.g. Ebel and Yilmaz 2002: 4) on the other hand centres on 'the share of subnational governments in total government spending or revenue', arguing however that 'the existence of elected local council, locally approved budget, local governments' borrowing power, capacity of local governments to collect taxes' would also need to be taken into account (2002: 5). Rodden (2004: 484) equally cautions that 'it is difficult to know what to make of expenditure decentralization data without additional data on the regulatory framework for subnational finance'. Even using only own-source revenue 'overestimates the extent of subnational revenue autonomy. [...] the central government may nevertheless maintain the power to set the rate and the base, leaving the subnational governments as mere collectors of centrally determined taxes' (2004: 484). What really matters, then, is 'the share of total tax revenues over which subnational governments possess full autonomy to set their own tax rates and their own rates and base' (2004: 484). But since both these measures are positively and significantly correlated with expenditure decentralisation (2004: 487), one might still, in the absence of reliable data, prefer to use the latter.

A public administration approach, finally, proposes to look at bureaucracy more narrowly. Treisman (2002: 13) calls this focus 'on how administrative resources are distributed across tiers of government' an instance of 'personnel decentralization'. Hence, '[t]he greater the share of administrative personnel employed at lower tiers, the greater is *personnel decentralization*' (2002: 13 original emphasis). A more refined measure used by Chhibber and Kollman (2004: 234) relates to 'the proportion of total governmental wages attributed to the central government' employees. Thus, administrative decentralisation is assessed either through the share of local staff from total public staff or by determining the share of local salaries from total public salaries.

While certainly of value, these measures alone are hardly able to express complex concepts such as autonomy, influence, or centralisation *tout court*. Rodden (2004: 492) concludes his review of existing policy-measures by stating that '[s]tudies of normative fiscal federalism and American constitutional theories of dual federalism have cast a long shadow', meaning that the prominence given to fiscal and legal indicators is not justified. Indeed, the main alternative has been to measure the institutional dimension, to which I turn next.

Polity-(de)centralisation

A second aspect of local or regional autonomy pertains to the number and size of units. How many sub-national entities a system has, how big they are, and where they are located in relation to the centre may matter for the vertical distribution of power (Rokkan and Urwin 1983: 7). This pertains to the institutional or polity-dimension of (de)centralisation. Freitag and Vatter (2008: 278), for example, propose a measure of decentralisation that takes 'the average number of persons per municipality in a canton, thus covering the administrative fragmentation with regard to the number of local authorities in a given canton'. The double problem with this measure is that while it captures the demographic distribution, the assumption that bigger municipalities have more autonomy must not necessarily be true.[1] Second, this distribution is likely to be influenced by territorial reforms or the general demographic development (Magin and Eder 2008: 204). Reforms may or may not change the vertical distribution of power, and they may or may not strengthen local autonomy.

A different indicator of the actual authority of subnational polities is the 'Regional Authority Index' (RAI) developed by Hooghe *et al.* (2008 and 2010). Disaggregating regional authority into 'self-rule' and 'shared rule' and then each

---

1.   As an assumption, it requires testing, which is what I will do in Chapter Four.

dimension into four further sub-dimensions allows them to quantify regional authority across 42 countries between 1950 and 2006 (2008: 112). Their eight dimensions are as follows (2008: 115):

1. Institutional depth: The extent to which a regional government is autonomous rather than deconcentrated [coded from 0 to 3].
2. Policy scope: The range of policies for which a regional government is responsible [0–4].
3. Fiscal autonomy: The extent to which a regional government can independently tax its population [0–4].
4. Representation: The extent to which a regional government is endowed with an independent legislature and executive [0–4].
5. Law making: The extent to which regional representatives co-determine national legislation [0–2].
6. Executive control: The extent to which a regional government co-determines national policy in intergovernmental meetings [0–2].
7. Fiscal control: The extent to which regional representatives co-determine the distribution of national tax revenues [0–2].
8. Constitutional reform: The extent to which regional representatives co-determine constitutional change [0–3].

Indicators 2 and 3 are classic policy-measures. Indicators 1 and 4 on the other hand capture institutional expressions of autonomy and measure whether a subnational government possesses 'a non-deconcentrated, general-purpose, administration not subject to central government veto' (Hooghe *et al.* 2008: 124) and whether regional executive *and* legislative bodies are directly elected (2008: 129). Indicators 5 to 8 mirror this distinction at the national level: institutionally, by asking 'whether regions, *qua* regions, are represented in a chamber of the national legislature, whether regional representatives constitute a majority in that chamber, and whether the regionally constituted chamber has authority to veto ordinary legislation' (2008: 131, original emphasis) and assessing the frequency and institutional weight of intergovernmental meetings (2008: 133); and policy-wise, by asking for the extent of regional involvement in national fiscal policy and constitutional change. In sum, the policy dimension is disaggregated into four sub-dimensions and four other sub-dimensions are added to measure the institutional, polity-dimension of (de)centralisation.

This institutional dimension depicts earlier attempts, chief among them Lijphart's (1999: 188–9) 'fivefold classification' of 'degrees of federalism and decentralization'. His index is based on five sub-indices (1999: 3–4):

1. Unitary and centralized government versus federal and decentralized government.
2. Concentration of legislative power in a unicameral legislature versus division of legislative power between two equally strong but differently constituted houses.
3. Flexible constitutions that can be amended by simple majorities versus rigid constitutions that can be changed only by extraordinary majorities.

4. Systems in which legislatures have the final word on the constitutionality of their own legislation versus systems in which laws are subject to a judicial review of their constitutionality by supreme or constitutional courts.
5. Central banks that are dependent on the executive versus independent central banks.

But whereas Hooghe *et al.*'s (2008: 116) eight dimensions are reliably shown both to relate to each other and cluster along the two stipulated dimensions of shared rule and self-rule, Taagepera (2003: 11–12) fails to find similar empirical evidence for Lijphart's five dimensions; only bicameralism (indicator 2) and federalism (indicator 1) are modestly correlated and all correlations are driven by Australia, Canada, Switzerland, the US and Germany (Taagepera 2003: 12). Too many other, non-territorial elements weaken this index.

A final proposal to measure the institutional dimension of (de)centralisation is made by Arzaghi and Henderson (2005: 1158). Their index 'varies from zero to four, with higher values meaning a greater degree of institutional regional autonomy.' It assigns country scores as follows:

(1) official federal versus unitary government structure, (2) election of a regional executive, (3) election of a local executive, (4) ability of the center to suspend lower levels of government or to override their decisions, (5) no, limited, or full revenue raising authority of lower levels governments, and (6) revenue sharing. Items (1)–(4) take a value of either 0 or 4; items (5) and (6) take values of 0, 2, or 4. [...] The federalism index is a simple average of the scores. (2005: 1178–8)

Correlating this index with the more conventional methods of gauging fiscal centralisation (for them, 'the share of the central government in total government current consumption') shows a moderately strong correlation (2005: 1160). The two dimensions are related, but remain distinct. Hooghe and Marks (2013) equally provide evidence that *their* measure (the RAI) and fiscal decentralisation (in that case tax decentralisation, *see* Stegarescu 2005) are not sufficiently correlated that the two could be directly substitutable, but correlated enough to complement each other (*see also* Schakel 2008 for the validation of the RAI onto Lijphart 1999, Arzaghi and Henderson 2005 and five other indices).

At this stage, the stipulation that the policy- and polity-dimension of (de)centralisation are interrelated but not equivalent must thus be taken as a strong assumption, not a verified fact. It is possible to compare one way of measuring (de)centralisation (e.g. fiscal decentralisation) with another (e.g. the RAI), as Schakel (2008: 166) does. But rather than trying to find the single best measure, I argue that it makes more sense to disaggregate (de)centralisation into three dimensions first, measure each dimension separately, and then combine them into a single index. This is what I will do for the Swiss cantons in Chapter Four. However, there is yet no measure of the politics-dimension of (de)centralisation, although political science is in clear need of one, as I discuss next.

The politics-dimension

A final element of (de)centralisation, then, has to do with political actors, process and territorial mobilisation (Piattoni 2010: 36). I call this aspect of (de)centralisation the *politics*-dimension, which is the most under-conceptualised. To the best of my knowledge, no study has ever compared the vertical organisation of political parties, the share of local representatives, *and* the territorial dimensions of the electoral systems across political systems. I first discuss the need for a politics-measure before presenting possible elements thereof.

The need for a politics-measure

An empirical-analytical understanding of politics (Schreyer and Schwarzmeier 2000: 16), itself a precondition to any comparative exercise, aims to explain both formal and real structures of societal power. 'Rule' (*Herrschaft*, for Max Weber 1992 [1919]) and 'authority' (Hooghe *et al.* 2008) form two interlocked aspects of political power. If the task is to 'construct clear comparative typologies to describe how political-administrative systems (complex amalgams of structures of authority *and structures of power*) are territorially organized and reorganized' (Hutchcroft 2001: 28; emphasis added), then something has been lacking so far. To fully comprehend this point we need to briefly step back.

My understanding of a political system is based on the theory developed by David Easton (1968 [1953] and 1965), adapted, however, toward the school of historical '(new) institutionalism', for which institutions are 'the formal or informal procedures, routines, norms and conventions embedded in the organizational structure of the polity' (Hall and Taylor 1996: 938; *see also* Broschek 2011; Mayntz and Scharpf 1995; Peters 1999; Thelen 1999; Lavander 2010). Politics then refers to the 'players' playing the actual game of 'authoritative allocation of values for a society' (Easton 1968 [1953]: 134): political parties, associations, trade unions and pressure groups (Schmidt 2004: 537; *see also* Scharpf 1997). Institutions represent 'a single, even if important, instance' of political research (Easton 1968 [1953], 115), but only 'an understanding of who has power and how it is used helps us to understand how social policy is formed and executed' (Easton 1968: 143). For Easton, political analysis can neither be confined to 'the state', nor to 'power' exclusively. The former is an object too narrow, the latter too broad, once it becomes accepted that 'the authoritative allocation of values' can take place also *outside* state structures, as the advocates of Multi-Level Governance also famously claim. Nevertheless, such value allocation always operates with *political* power only. The idea of a political system bridges the gap between the state and political power. Empirically, then, it is political actors in general and parties in particular that link society and system, territory and interests: 'Political parties, even when committed to transterritorial creeds, are usually organized to reflect or manipulate the interests of electoral (territorial) districts' (Duchacek 1987: 3).

(De)centralisation, as was discussed above, results in a hierarchical, top-down perspective of the political system (Smith 1985). We have already followed Fesler's

(1965: 548) advice that 'looking at the problem properly implies a continuum between the poles of centralization and decentralization'. But if '[d]ecentralization of a combined political-administrative character, such as devolution to subnational democratic governments, has political features' (Fesler 1965: 550), then one must also look in the political arena for indicators of its type and degree. However, in the wider territorial politics literature there long existed

> a division between those who study public administration and administrative law on the one hand, and those who study political parties, public opinion, electoral behavior, and legislative institutions and processes, on the other. (Fesler 1965: 553)

And yet it is perfectly 'conceivable that decentralist legislative and political portions of the system make almost irrelevant the centralist qualities of the administrative portion of the system' (1965: 554). Belgium, for example, is legally and administratively a federation, although political party organisation and electoral competition have become confederal (Detterbeck and Hepburn 2010).

The lesson to be learned from all this is that one must take into account the *whole* political system for determining its degree of (de)centralisation. This is also true for the opposite tendency, as when 'a substantial decentralization of the bureaucratic apparatus [is] offset by continued centralization of the party apparatus' (Fesler 1965: 555). The 'power to determine and revise the pattern, structure and resources of the local governments within their jurisdiction' (Humes 1991: 183) is, in that perspective, eminently political. Thus, 'territorial politics should never be restricted to the description of legal texts and the levels that are formalized' (Thoenig 2008: 282), that is to the polity- or policy-dimensions alone. Laws may be the starting point, but it is politics that matters.

This point is taken up by Hutchcroft (2001), whose efforts centre on developing 'two distinct continua', one for 'administrative' and one for 'political' decentralisation (2001: 28), and on analysing 'the complex interplay of these two spheres' (2001: 33). The administrative continuum however moves barely beyond what I have already established as definitions of the three sub-types of decentralisation (de-concentration, delegation and devolution). It is his conception of 'political decentralisation' that is innovative in that it explicitly measures 'a range of local *and* national political factors' (Hutchcroft 2001: 34; original emphasis). It is in this sense that (de)centralisation is 'multi-dimensional' (Vollaard 2009a: 99), and we should measure its additional components as well as the polity- and policy-dimensions.

Admittedly, '[p]ower is a complex phenomenon and its distribution difficult to measure' (Fesler 1965: 537). My focus is on politics, that is the actor- and process-related dimension of political power (Pennings *et al.* 1999: 35). For democratic political systems, this dimension of (de)centralisation can analytically be separated into direct and indirect local representation; actors of central supervision, typically the prefects; political party organisation; and the territoriality of electoral systems (and direct democracy, if existent). I discuss each component in turn.

Local representation and central supervision

The first two questions that can be asked of a political system is whether 'local executives [are] appointed by the center or elected by popular vote' and whether there are 'effective mechanisms for popular participation at the local level' (Hutchcroft 2001: 34). Arguing that centralisation is lessened in the presence of local participation corresponds to federal theory, where 'self-rule' (Elazar 1987) stands for the right to organise and staff one's own institutions 'for purposes of local autonomy and the preservation of specific identities and interests' (Burgess 2006a: 136). Such participation is therefore inversely connected to centralism: the higher local participation, the higher local legitimacy, and the less the centre's grip on local power. In this 'formal' perspective, local autonomy *is* decentralisation (Fleurke and Willemse 2004: 525). But representation at the central level is equally crucial. With any division of powers, integration is a necessary remedy to avoid fragmentation (Neidhart 2002: 268). Page's (1991) thoughts are useful in this regard as he distinguishes between direct and indirect representation.

Indirect representation refers to the double tenure of mandates across governmental layers, e.g. a mayor who is also an MP or even a Minister, known in French as *cumul des mandats* (Page 1991: 60). Page (1991: 57) notes that the problem with such 'political localism' is that whether or not MPs have once served, or are still serving, as local and/or regional councillors may simply be irrelevant. Past tenure wrongly assumes that earlier affiliation would lead to present sympathies; an assumption which 'confuses past environment with current motivation' (1991: 59). And precisely because the *cumul des mandats* is such a French peculiarity, we would instead need 'indicators of the degree to which national political careers are built up through mobilization of local political support' (1991: 62). This leads him to advocate some sort of 'contextualised comparison' (Locke and Thelen 1995), whereby patronage in Italy and clientelism in Spain are regarded as conceptual equivalents to the *cumul des mandats* (*see also* Goldsmith 1990: 21).

Local representation can also take place *directly*, through informal access to subnational authorities (Page 1991: 6). Local actors such as mayors, clerks, local councillors etc. can 'use their political authority as local representatives' (1991: 5) not in the parliament or executive but through lobbying. In a 'clientelistic/ patronage model' of local government autonomy, for example in France or Italy (*see* Tarrow 1977), 'the primary duty of local politicians is to deliver specific public goods and services to these constituents and to see that the interests of their community are well represented and protected, especially at higher levels of government.' (Goldsmith 1990: 21) To the extent that such channels permeate the political system, it becomes more 'parochial' and decentralised in its outlook (Duchacek 1987). Access to the central arena takes place collectively through corporate lobbying (Page 1991, 43; *see also* Piattoni 2014). Thus, the existence of one or several Local Government Associations (Page 1991: 45), their coverage and internal unity (1991: 47), the type of authority the group can exert over its members (binding or consultative; 1991: 50), and the observed impact of the association on national politics seem to be good measures of such 'indirect political localism' (1991: 50). In sum, whether local officials are elected locally, whether the local electorate has other means to participate in local affairs and the extent to which local representatives lobby directly or indirectly at the centre are indicators not only of democracy, but also of (the politics-dimension) of (de)centralisation.

Finally, actors of supervision need to be included, too. It is debatable whether prefects, the archetype of central supervision in the French model (e.g. Garrish 1986: 1), act not also as representatives of their region or *département* at the centre. Theoretically, it may well be the case that prefects further *decentralise* a political system by non-centralising decisions in the capital. Since currently in a number of Swiss cantons prefects still exist (Bochsler *et al.* 2004), I will try to capture this by distinguishing appointed from elected prefects. I contend that the latter provide for bottom-up influence, and so are more decentralist than appointed ones. As appointed central representatives, they are instinctively associated with centralisation, i.e. a 'central state official whose duties include the supervision of local government actions' (Page 1991: 28). A complement to such supervision is district representation, which also exists in some Swiss cantons (districts are situated between the local and cantonal governments). This adds a dimension of non-centralisation, in Elazar's (1987) terms, as it can hardly be said to be a function of cantonal oversight under any circumstance, all the less so if directly elected by the people of the district. This aspect, however, relates to measurement, which I undertake only in *Chapter Four*. I now turn to a second component of politics-(de)centralisation: political parties.

Federal parties and party federalism

A second aspect of democratic politics concerns political parties. The literature assumes that the procedure for the selection of candidates and the degree of (de)centralisation correlate (Deschouwer 2006; Katz and Mair 1994; Crotty 1968; Duverger 1959 [1951]; Panebianco 1988; Moon and Bratberg 2010). In Rodden's (2004: 488) words,

> it is important to assess the relationship between the central and subnational electoral arenas. For instance, the slate of candidates competing in local elections might be chosen by central [national] government party officials. At the other end of a spectrum, state [regional] or local officials might play a key role in selecting candidates for central government elections.

Hutchcroft's (2001: 36) last two indicators equally address whether 'political parties [are] organized along national or local/regional lines, and what is their level of internal cohesion' – a party-political dimension; and in how far 'administrative structures [are] insulated from party patronage' (2001: 36). This latter issue can largely be ruled out by narrowing the scope conditions of the conceptual framework to liberal democracies (Tarrow 2010). But the territorial dimension of party-political organisation promises to be revealing, for the following reason.

Parties are essential to the workings of democracy (e.g. van Biezen 2003; Müller and Strøm 1999). The idea that a party's strategy and behaviour are determined by federalism inheres with Thorlakson's (2007) *institutional approach to party organisation.* The realisation of a federal design in a state creates 'multiple arenas of competition' (2007: 73), each with different offices at stake and with distinct policies to make. Thorlakson argues that

> [...] decentralization gives parties and voters both incentive and opportunity to mobilize and respond to locally defined issues, leading to the development of 'unique' party systems at the state [regional] level, with fewer competitive linkages to the federal [national] arena. (2007: 71)

Parties turn federal to the extent that the overarching polity embodies federalism. By that, they 'bring together what institutions divide' (Bogdanor 1988: 85). However, other authors reverse the causal connection (Watts 2006). Approaching, in turn, the federal design of a state from the perspective of political parties, Riker (1964) saw in the territorial structure of a party system the only reliable indicator of how centralised or 'peripheralized' a federal polity really was. His *party-political approach to federalism* reads as follows:

> The federal relationship is centralized according to the degree to which the parties organized to operate the central [national] government control the parties organized to operate the constituent [regional] governments. (1964: 129)

For Riker, then, a polity is federal to the extent that parties embody federalism. Both Riker's and Thorlakson's inferences may hold true; indeed, they can be seen as complementary. Their emphasis on the relationship between party system and federal system may be different, but both make valuable contributions toward understanding the importance of territory for politics. Any 'non-centralised' system (Elazar 1987: 34) is then operated by parties competing on multiple levels and exhibiting at least two (or *n*, for *n* relevant levels) 'cores' (Deschouwer 2003). If the formal, constitutional division of authority across different territorial scales matches the real, actor-related distribution of power, a polity is truly 'multilevel' (Benz 2009). In his later writings on federalism, Riker (1969: 139) brings this assumption to the point:

> [T]he essence of local autonomy has little to do with whether or not the central constitution grants particular rights to local officials but has very much to do with whether or not local officials are elected by or are in some other way responsive to local citizens.

In other words, unless policy- and polity-(de)centralisation are accompanied by the creation (and subsequent maintenance) of respective electoral arenas, autonomy as the 'lung' of federalism remains all but symbolic. On the other hand, once a political system is moving in the direction of more decentralised decision-making structures, parties follow and adapt to 'peripheral' (e.g. regional or local) issues at stake – ideologically as well as organisationally: parties themselves become 'multilevel organizations' (Deschouwer 2006).

Thus, the 'ideal federal party [...] exists at all levels – national, regional and local – and fields candidates at all levels' (Filippov *et al.* 2004: 192; *see also* Epstein

1967: 32). What this means for the measurement of (de)centralisation is clear: to take the 'vertical organisation' of political parties as a second component in the politics-dimension, next to actors of local representation and central supervision.

The party politics literature offers various aspects of party organisation one could focus on to gauge their internal degree of (de)centralisation. Kenneth Janda (1980: 108), in what is both the oldest and most extensive attempt at measuring the territoriality within parties, operationalises the 'centralization of power as the location and distribution of effective decision-making authority within the party' amidst eight variables. The problem with half of them is that they measure party democracy more than party federalism. This is especially true for variable no. 2 ('Selecting the National Leader', 1980: 110), where decentralisation equals a 'democratic' and centralisation an 'oligarchic' method of leader selection; but also for variable no. 8 ('Leadership Concentration', 1980: 117), where Janda himself admits that 'it does not necessarily follow that power is more centralized in a party with few leaders rather than many' (1980: 116). The assumption for both is that centralisation involves as few as one person only, whereas decentralisation is only possible with 'diffused' centres of power. But we should restrict the notion of (de)centralisation to its *territorial* dimensions alone, and not mix it with personal, democratic elements of party organisation. After all, a party with one (even self-perpetuating) leader may nevertheless be organisationally decentralised. Variable no. 7 ('Administering Discipline', 1980: 116) relates more to party behaviour and variable no. 6 ('Controlling Communications', 1980: 114–115) to party strategy, but not so much to party organisation.

Only the four variables on the 'Nationalization of Structure' (from 0 = 'local organizations are [...] the only discernible structural element in the party' to 9 = 'there are only national organs'; 1980: 109), 'Selecting Parliamentary Candidates' (from 1 = 'Nominations are determined locally by vote of party supporters' to 9 = 'Selection is determined by a national committee or party council'; 1980: 111), 'Allocating Funds' (from 0 = 'Responsibility for collecting and allocating funds is diffused throughout the party' and 1 = 'Funds are collected and allocated primarily by local organizations' to 6 = 'Funds are collected primarily by the national organization'; 1980: 112) and 'Formulating Policy' (from 0 = 'Responsibility for formulating policy is diffused throughout the party' and 2 = 'Local party organizations enact policy resolutions' to 7 = 'Major policy positions are determined and announced by the party leader or a small subgroup of the national committee'; 1980: 113) really capture the territorial dimension.

Thorlakson (2007, 2009, 2010), with a different empirical context in mind, is also concerned with the 'vertical integration' of parties. This notion indicates a slight normative twist: 'Integrated parties and centralized party systems prevent the centrifugal disintegration of federations' and 'entice sub-national parties to remain loyal to the broader federal party' (Thorlakson 2010: 2). She proposes, firstly, five indicators of *vertical integration*, which all relate to 'organizational linkages, interdependence and cooperation' (Thorlakson 2009: 161) between the national and the regional level:

[1] upward resource and service provision (upward vertical integration), [2] downward resource and service provision (downward vertical integration), [3] cooperation, [4] the range of policy distance between the state and federal party (left-right difference) and [5] the extent to which the subnational party perceives the federal party to be the same party with the same goals and interests (shared goals). (Thorlakson 2010: 8)

Indicators no. 1 and 2 measure the same principle from two different angles, the difference to variable 3 being only that here 'endorsements or public appearances on the campaign trail' are counted in addition to resource sharing. And indicators no. 4 and 5 really pertain more to 'party system congruence', that is 'the similarity of party systems across jurisdictions' (Thorlakson 2007: 69), or the 'ideological distance between the state and federal parties (Thorlakson 2010: 9). A second dimension of party territoriality is *influence*, which 'refers to the degree to which the state party organization is an important force in the federal party structure' (Thorlakson 2009: 162). Such bottom-up influence is classified 'as low (1), moderate (2) or high (3) according to the way in which the party structure provides for representation of state party organizations in the overall party governance structure' (2009: 162). Here, then, is one clear 'parallel' (Epstein 1967: 32) to the idea of shared-rule in federal states: direct representation of lower level entities qua territoriality. Finally, as a third dimension of vertical party organisation, Thorlakson (2010: 9) develops a composite index of *subnational party autonomy*, which is

[...] constructed from survey questions that ask respondents to use a Likert scale to rate the extent to which the federal [national] party organization has influenced [...] [1] the content of party policy programme, [2] the choice of candidates for state and [3] federal elections, [4] the choice of state party leader and [5] voting behaviour in the state parliament. (2010: 9)

This builds on a previous effort (Thorlakson 2009: 163), which was, however, less fine-tuned. Now, '[p]arty policy programme' and 'choice of candidates for federal election' correspond to Janda's (1980) 'formulating policy' and 'selecting parliamentary candidates', whereas 'choice of state party leader' and 'voting behaviour' modify Janda's 'selection of national leader' and 'administering discipline', respectively. However, Thorlakson adds an indicator of choice of *regional* candidates, not included in Janda's dataset.

The most concise measurement to date is that of Elodie Fabre (2008, 2011). She proposes to measure the territorial dimension of party organisation along two dimensions: 'integration of regional parties' *in* (Fabre 2008: 319) and 'autonomy of regional party branches' *from* the central party (2008: 321). Fabre thus essentially adopts Thorlakson's (2009: 161–162) three dimensions: 'vertical integration', 'influence' and 'autonomy', but collapses them into just two – as Thorlakson later (2010) did herself. These two dimensions are now called 'level of involvement of regional subunits in central party organs' and 'level of autonomy of regional sub-units' (Fabre 2011: 346). She operationalises them into ten variables, each coded nominally from 0 to 4 (2011: 347):

[For the level of involvement] (1) the selection of the leader of the state-wide party, (2) the composition of the central party executive, (3) the selection of candidates for state-wide parliamentary elections, (4) the formulation of party programmes for state-wide parliamentary elections and (5) the process to amend the party constitution [...] [For the level of autonomy] (6) the ability of regional party branches to organize themselves [...], (7) the selection of regional party leaders, (8) the selection of candidates for regional elections, (9) the adoption of regional election programmes, and (10) the financial autonomy of the regional branches [...].

In the empirical section, I will exclusively rely on the way parties select their candidates for cantonal parliamentary elections as an indicator of party (de)centralisation. The latter could, of course, be more reliably estimated by drawing on more – or even all – of the proposed indicators; especially financing and the formulation of programmes would seem promising. Restricting myself to candidate-selection as the essential function of political parties has however the merit of data availability (party statutes) and external validity. On this, I follow Schattschneider (1942: 64): 'The nature of the nominating procedure determines the nature of the party; he who can make nominations is the owner of the party. It is therefore one of the best points at which to observe the distribution of power within the party.' All three authors just discussed have measured party (de)centralisation taking the selection of parliamentary candidates into account, which testifies to its key role. This leaves us with the third and final aspect of politics-(de)centralisation.

The territoriality of electoral systems

The territorial dimension of a political system, and of parties as political actors within that system, are assumed to be interdependent. The particular organisation of a party and the particular organisation of government are 'parallel' (Epstein 1967: 32). Parties 'both shape processes of decentralization and federalism and need to respond to political imperatives induced by the territorial structure of a state.' (Hopkin and van Houten 2009: 131) The most prominent of these imperatives is the electoral system: 'Votes are the currency of democratic politics, but their use and value depend on the rules by which other goods may be purchased' (Müller and Strøm 1999: 21). On specifically territorial rules, Hutchcroft (2001: 35) questions whether, and to what degree, 'the electoral system provide[s] for representation of local or regional interests in the national legislature'. There are two extreme points:

A system of proportional representation (P.R.) in which the entire country is a single district provides no formal scope for representation of local or regional interests. [...] A single-member district plurality electoral system, on the other hand, provides considerable potential for representation of local and regional interests. (Hutchcroft 2001: 35–36)

Rodden (2004: 492) builds this observation into a continuum: starting with the 'centralised unitary states' (Swenden 2006) of Israel (and The Netherlands; *see* PARLINE 2012), in which the whole country forms one single constituency for parliamentary elections; moving on to the UK, where the whole territory is divided into 650 'local' single-member constituencies; to Switzerland, where the 26 cantons form the 'regional' constituencies for elections to the National Council (and even autonomously decide on the electoral rules for the Council of States, *see* Knapp 1986: 35); and ending with the German *Bundesrat*, the members of which are appointed by the 16 *Landesregierungen*. In that sense, the number and size of constituencies for legislative elections in a political system is the final indicator of its (de)centralisation. I will apply this and the other aspects and dimension of (de)centralisation to the Swiss cantons in Chapter Four and now present my theoretical framework.

Theoretical framework

The model

My explanatory model is displayed in Figure 2.2. It is to be read in conjunction with conceptualising (de)centralisation as tri-dimensional and my ontological conviction that middle-range theories best capture reality. Reading causality backwards, I argue (de)centralisation to be the direct result of decisions by political actors (*agency*). Institutional design, actor organisation and policy output are purposive, not accidental. The first proposition, therefore, is that the actors responsible for deciding on the political system – political and bureaucratic elite, electorate, interest groups – rationally chose system properties that lie closest to their interests.

The balance between these sets of actors is different for each system, leaving more or less room for 'objective' (technocratic) or 'subjective' (partisan or ideological) decision-making. Both types of influences matter, as brought out so clearly by the political approach to centralisation for partisanship and by fiscal federalism for structure. While a causal connection between ideology and centralisation may very well exist, it is context that specifies the direction of the influence (Hooghe and Marks 2001; Calhoun 2003 [1851]; Riker 1964; Burgess 1993).

It is thus no accident that political actors occupy the visual centre in this model. I additionally distinguish pre-, post- and parliamentary phases and incremental from more fundamental institutional reforms. In the semi-direct democracy of Switzerland, for example, 'grand coalition' governments initiate, the bureaucracy prepares, parties debate in parliament under lobbying influence from vested interests, and the electorate has the last say. 'Policy-specific change' reflects the *courant normal*, 'general reforms' refer to 'critical junctures' as 'brief phases of institutional flux' (Capoccia and Kelemen 2007: 341) in which 'the structural (that is, economic, cultural, ideological, organizational) influences on political action are significantly relaxed for a relatively short period' (2007: 343).

However, elite bargaining alone focuses too much on the institutional – and especially electoral – dimension of (de)centralisation, an ideological explanation fails to take into account party and electoral systems, and both neglect the cultural-historical dimensions of politics. After all, language *is* a powerful

Figure 2.2: Explanatory model

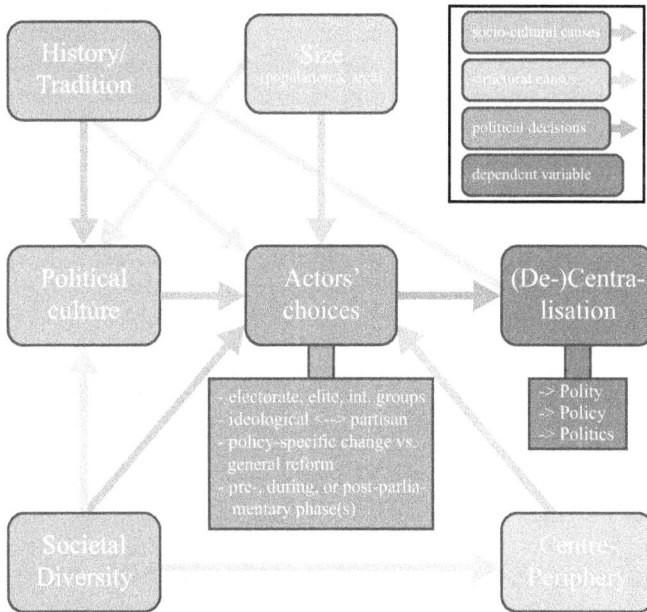

Note: This figure is also available in colour, *see* http://press.ecpr.eu/resources.asp.

mobilisation device, as shown by a sociological approach; and economic inequality, distance and regional patriotism often *trigger* regional autonomy movements in the first place, as shown by a structural approach. But political approaches fail to specify the impact of area, size, distance, diversity or culture on ideology and bargains. My second proposition, therefore, is that *context matters* (*see also* Falleti and Lynch 2009). It constrains actors' choices to more or less realistic (=feasible) proposals. As Montero and Samuels (2004: 34; emphasis omitted) state it: 'historical-institutional and socio-economic legacies matter'. Intertwined into that idea is the observation that (de)centralisation in itself is not a goal, but 'a by-product' (Hooghe and Marks 2001: 75) of dividing the burden, responsibility and costs of public service delivery across different levels of governments.

Indeed, context can 'constrain individual choice or affect individual strategies, but also […] affect the articulation of interests, and particularly the articulation of collective interests' (Thelen 2002: 92). In some areas, when it comes to (de)centralisation there is only very little ideological politics, but many interest group- or political party-specific goals; in other areas, e.g. defence, an ideology of neutrality or nationalism may be all-embracing. In moments that for their extra-ordinariness can be labelled critical junctures (Thelen 2002: 97), actors have the opportunity to develop grand theories or visions about the future territorial structure of their system. These windows of opportunity arise because the traditional territorial structures are questioned from within, e.g. through peripheral nationalism or economic decline/rise, or from the outside, e.g. through EU-funding being made conditional on setting up regional structures (Hooghe and Marks 2001: 92). If in those exceptional moments anything goes, 'normal politics' is conditioned by both socio-culture and structure (Capoccia and Ziblatt 2010: 943).

Under *socio-cultural causes* I understand, firstly, political culture: deep-seated values and beliefs, customs, and ways of doing things, as outlined by the covenantal approach to federalism. These are, in turn, influenced by historical tradition, hence political systems are centralised to the degree that the political actors responsible for decision-making *generally* favour a centralised political structure. Actors are *also* driven by attitudes, values, tradition and regularised patterns of behaviour, which have been inherited through a history of, for example, catholic colonialism (e.g. Latin America), protestant individualism (parts of Germany and Switzerland) or common law localism (the US).

Secondly, societal diversity *may* matter for explaining (de)centralisation. Diversity is in itself not a reason for more or less (de)centralisation, but presents a potential that can be activated by the elite (Baldersheim and Rose 2010: 13). Societal structures *antedate* actor's choices, because 'ethno-linguistic fault-lines are too deep to be mere products of elite manipulation' (Erk 2008: 11). The hierarchy of cleavages thus understood – class in one, language in another and religion in a third context – is equally dependent on manipulation (Lijphart 1979). For example, while religion was one of the main causal factors of the 1847 civil war in Switzerland, it is class that dominates Australian society (Erk and Koning 2010: 365). The potential for cleavage activation increases to the extent that a) '[t]astes for public goods and services [...] vary across ethnic groups' (Treisman 2006: 293; *see also* Oates 1972 and Alesina *et al.* 1999: 1251) and that b) we have a 'federal society', a term which Livingston (1952: 85) used synonymously with societies in which differences are 'grouped territorially' (*see also* Panizza 1999: 110; Duchacek 1987: 94; and Stein 1968: 729).

Structural causes, in turn, are further divided into (absolute) size and (relative) centre-periphery. Size includes both area and population. On size, the argument flows from large areas to 'spillovers across jurisdictions', to 'market failures', to decentralisation as offsetting these failures (Panizza 1999: 106; *see also* Oates 1999: 1135). Why would, as Treisman (2006: 319) asks, 'efficiency [...] tend to win the day'? Local/regional demands for decentralisation are more powerful in larger political systems because a) a large area increases the likelihood for territorially bounded variation in policy preferences, b) such variation facilitates articulation, mobilisation and active lobbying for decentralisation (politics) *and* c) the logic of liberal democracy demands that governmental structures (polity) sooner, rather than later, pass the legitimacy test. The same is true for population size (Taagepera 2003: 17; Gottmann 1973: 112): the longer it takes to bring information and people back and forth, the more likely a task will be delegated in full, especially if 'soft information' is required (Hooghe and Marks 2013).

On topography, my discussion of the centre-periphery paradigm (Rokkan and Urwin 1983) has shown that within established liberal democratic systems a) the *accessibility* of the periphery for the centre to 'penetrate' economically, socially and administratively and b) the distance between *settlements* matter for determining a more or less of (de)centralisation. This is because 'empty space', which by definition is uninhabited (e.g. desert or rain forest; Gottmann 1973: 112), does not generate the kind of demands for 'differential treatment' (Clark 1974: 29) postulated by fiscal federalism. Therefore, in the empirical section I will propose a measure of distance that directly takes into account the time of a journey from the remotest area to the capital city (*see also* Clark 1974: 29).

In sum, while culture is the property of societies, structure is largely independent of it and related to space more generally. In the words of Robert Sack (1983: 60–61), socio-cultural conditions express a 'social definition of territory', whereas structural conditions express a 'territorial definition of social relationships'. Together, they condition political agency. Two other considerations could be wealth and democracy itself. The latter I exclude from my theory because I assume it to be constant. All the studies mentioned so far found either a negative or no effect for both affluence/income/per capita GDP and democracy/democratisation on centralisation. Growth rates on the other hand are positively correlated with centralisation (Stegarescu 2005) – a sign that as the economy grows, it is primarily the central state that assumes new redistributive and welfare functions. Stegarescu (2005) also finds a positive correlation between regional disparity and fiscal decentralisation – suggesting that richer regions are more successful in pushing for devolution than poorer ones. I will use per capita GDP as a control variable, in Chapter Five.

Assumptions and hypotheses

The model presented can be used to explain a situation of centralisation under two cumulative conditions (*see also* Ylvisaker 1959: 27–29 and Clark 1974: 22):

a. A political system with at least two layers, e.g. national and regional or regional and local.
b. Liberal democracy, including free and fair electoral competition, rule of law and a commitment to non-violence.

Again, my aim is not to explain the (non)formation of federations (e.g. Deutsch *et al.* 1968 [1957]) but degrees of (de)centralisation once the system is in place. Also, I largely disregard levels of democracy (Panizza 1999: 123), macro-economic development (Falleti 2010) and violence (Brancati 2006) as explanatory factors, holding them constant through restricting my scope conditions.

My model allows two hypothetical predictions. Take it that in system A, the area is large, people live scattered all around, with no single dominant centre but many 'regional centres', and values of diversity/competition triumph over those of equality/uniformity. We would expect the political system to be most decentralised. In fact, this is exactly the case of canton Grisons, where politicians, citizens and interest groups prefer to maintain the local structures and only cost-intensive public policies like infrastructure and police are centralised at canton-level. Culturally sensitive policies like education are centrally funded but with extensive local autonomy in the implementation phase: communes autonomously decide in what language instruction takes place, also because society is tri-lingual, and it takes a long time to reach the capital from the most distant regions, high up in the mountains.

On the other hand, imagine system B, which is the exact opposite of system A: extended over a small and compact area, with people concentrated in a single economically dominant centre practically spanning the whole territory, and values of equality/uniformity triumphing over those of diversity/competition. Here we would expect an extreme case of centralisation – and this is exactly the case of both Geneva and Basel-City. In Geneva, the city both antedates and dominates the surrounding 44 communes. The high density (1,500 inhabitants/km2) makes different regulations across the 45 entities redundant, while central regulation enhances the constitutionally mandated and culturally propagated principle of equality. Basel-City, deprived of its surrounding countryside since 1833, has not even judged it necessary to maintain a separate city administration: its 'local' affairs are directly managed by the canton. Even more so than Geneva, Basel-City *is* the city even in name; in both cantons, no societal diversity, rivalling city or peripheral region exist to claim local autonomy. Table 2.1 shows all 16 logically possible combinations of the four independent variables.

We can confidently expect the space for 'subjective' decisions by political actors on centralisation to be restricted when all four conditions converge towards one end of the continuum, i.e. a small area, monocephalic city-structure, unitary political culture and a homogeneous society (e.g. Luxembourg). We can also be confident if the contextual balance is clearly tipped into one direction, say if in a *small* area a heterogeneous society is found, federal political culture and polycephalic structures (e.g. Switzerland), or if in a *large* area the society is homogeneous, the political culture unitary and the city-structure monocephalic (e.g. France). But it is less clear what political actors will decide when the scores are even, e.g. a federal political culture in a heterogeneous society, spread over a small area with a monocephalic structure. I leave scrutiny of this middle ground to the empirical analysis. The next chapter describes the methodology.

Table 2.1: Predictive grid

Societal Diversity	Political Culture	Size and Centre-Periphery Structure			
		Small area and/or population		Large area and/or population	
		Monocephalic	Polycephalic	Monocephalic	Polycephalic
Homogeneous	Unitary	**Most centralised**	Rather centralised	Rather centralised	?
	Federal	Rather centralised	?	?	Rather decentralised
Heterogeneous	Unitary	Rather centralised	?	?	Rather decentralised
	Federal	?	Rather decentralised	Rather decentralised	**Most decentralised**

Chapter Three

Case Study Design

Why are some countries more centralised than others? Twenty years ago, Robert Putnam (1993: 3) compared the Italian regions in order to answer a similarly universal question: 'Why do some democratic governments succeed and others fail?' While his study combined an interest in democracy *as such* with 'the subtleties of Italian life' (1993: xii), mine aspires to a similar matching of general theories of (de)centralisation with Swiss intricacies. Drawing inferences about a general phenomenon – power, democracy, (de)centralisation – based on detailed knowledge of just a single country is one of the basic methods of comparative politics. However, the following analysis is also a cross-case, or 'large-N', *and* a within-case, or 'small-N', analysis, where N refers to the number of cases (Landman 2008: 26).[1] After a short and contextual section, I present the research design used in this book over the subsequent chapters.

The 'Swiss case': Cantons and communes

Normally, Switzerland alone could only partially serve comparative purposes. The main reason for this deficiency is the uniqueness of many of its political elements, let alone their interaction. The country combines some of the rarest attributes of political systems worldwide (Linder 1999; Papadopoulos 1991; Lehmbruch 1993; Elazar 2001):

- A collegial federal executive of seven councillors, voted into power by parliament but not removable during four years, acting both as head of state and head of government.
- A perfectly symmetric bicameralism in terms of powers, but diametrically opposed as regards each chamber's electoral logic (proportional to cantonal population vs. cantonal equality).
- Extensive direct-democratic elements, both *ex ante* (popular initiative) and *ex post* (mandatory and optional referendum), fully binding the authorities, plus the absence of a constitutional court.
- A free-list electoral system combining party-lists with candidate preferences enabling multipartism (effective number of parliamentary

---

1. The expressions small- and large-N are imprecise. The way I understand them is that 'small' refers to any number of 2+ cases that are still suitable for qualitative, i.e. context-specific analysis. While 'large' is usually used for survey-data or electoral analyses, where the number of (individual) respondents typically reaches several thousands, I also regard N=26 as large-N because I apply regression analysis.

parties after the 2011 federal elections: 5.57; Mueller and Dardanelli 2013).

- A foreign policy of strict neutrality, not only practised since 1515, externally accepted since 1648 and 'guaranteed' since 1815 but also publicly cherished and made an element of national identity at least since World War I (Riklin 1992).

How could one control for all, or at least some, of these factors in explaining Swiss federalism – i.e. exceptionally low degrees of centralisation – in a cross-national comparison? And yet every student of federalism and/or the European Union as 'multilevel governance' agrees that the 'Swiss case' has to be included somehow, in his or her study (*see* Bolleyer 2009: 213; also Bache and Flinders 2004; Piattoni 2010; Zürn *et al.* 2010). But rather than giving up on the inherent non-comparability of the Swiss case, we *can* learn something about Swiss federalism – by comparing the Swiss cantons.

More importantly, causal inferences can be drawn by conveniently testing hypotheses derived from a theoretical framework: *all* 26 cantonal entities exhibit a directly elected collegial executive; they *all* provide binding direct-democratic channels of decision-making (Stutzer 1999), subject to the same federal law; they *all* practice some form of electoral proportionality; and *none* has a foreign policy as it is commonly understood. As is known since J. S. Mill, having similar values on potential independent variables means being able to exclude them from a causal explanation of different outcomes (known as 'method of difference'; *see* Van Evera 1997). In other words, what the Italian regions were for Putnam (1993) are the Swiss cantons for me: a comparative template to measure and explain (de)centralisation (*see also* Gerring 2007: 139). To understand why this is possible, further contextual information needs to be provided.

On 1 April 2012, Switzerland was divided into 26 cantons, 139 districts and 2,485 communes (BFS 2012). The distribution of communes is uneven: in Base-City and Glarus there are only three, in Berne 382 and in Vaud 326 communes. 18 cantons have districts, again from only three in Jura and Appenzell Outer-Rhodes to twelve in Zurich and 13 in Valais. Except for Schwyz, where districts have the capacity to raise their own taxes, all districts are statistical entities, administrative areas, judicial circles and/or constituencies for cantonal parliamentary elections (Rühli 2012: 38). Communes, on the other hand, have tax-raising capacities in all 26 cantons (Horber-Papazian 2006; Horber-Papazian and Jacot-Desombes 2012), while the cantons themselves enjoy wide-ranging powers, from education and police to social care and infrastructure (Germann and Weibel 1986; Delley and Auer 1986; Buser 2004; Fleiner 2000; Allemann 1977; Kirchgässner and Guptara 2006; Kölz 2004; Reinhardt 2008).

Historically, the Swiss Confederation has grown from a defence alliance among the cantons in Central Switzerland (Uri, Schwyz, Obwalden/Nidwalden) to a network of 'mutual assistance' pacts between the rural *Landkantone* (the original three plus Glarus, Zug and Appenzell Inner- and Outer-Rhodes) and the city-dominated *Stadtkantone* (Zurich, Berne, Lucerne, Fribourg, Solothurn, Basel and Schaffhausen). Between the early 16th and the end of the 18th century 'the XXIII

Stände' (from 'estates': the Confederation was, with the exception of bilingual Fribourg and several subject territories, a German-speaking polity) centralised only the bare minimum of powers at the confederal level (Würgler 2008). Or not even the minimum, for the absence of a (con)federal army facilitated the French invasion of 1798 and subsequent occupation, which was to last for 15 years. After the hyper-centralisation imposed by the French Directorate, the system returned to its confederal nature in 1815, but nine 'liberated' areas were added as cantonal members of the polity with the same rights and duties (Table 3.1).

In 1848, the step from a confederation to a federation was taken after a brief – and 'very civil' (Remak 1993) – civil war between Catholic-rural and Protestant-urban cantons (Bonjour 1948). The Federal Constitution (*Bundesverfassung*, FC) has been amended numerous times since then but was fully revised only in 1874 and 1999, when an article was inserted that 'guarantees' local autonomy (Art. 50.1). However, local autonomy continues to be exclusively determined by cantonal legislation (Braaker 2000), even if politically the position of Swiss communes is exceptionally strong. On aggregate, communes collected 23 per cent of all public revenue in 2010, as opposed to 42 per cent by the cantons and 35 per cent by the Confederation (EFV 2012). Local money is used mainly to finance education, social security and administrative costs. Table 3.2 lists the expenditures of Swiss cantons and communes for 2010 and 2009, respectively, the most recent years for which verified data are available. Communes outspend the cantons in four out of ten domains: more than fourfold for housing, threefold for environment protection, twofold for leisure/culture/religion, and minimally in defence matters – and this despite the fact that total cantonal expenditures have risen by 1.6 billion CHF between 2009 and 2010 (EFV 2012).

Each canton has its own constitution, its own directly elected parliament, and its own directly elected collegial government (Lutz and Strohmann 1998). They also have their own party systems (Ladner 2004). Swiss political parties are themselves aggregations of cantonal sections (Thorlakson 2009), and with a few exceptions, cantonal parties have autonomous local sections (Ladner 1991; Klöti and Kübler 2004). In the past, cantonal governments have functioned as 'gatekeepers' between LGs and the federal level, except for minor tasks such as in defence, where federal law mandates communes to maintain air raid shelters (Thürer 1986). Although this has changed due to the increasingly trans-local and trans-cantonal nature of public policy, e.g. transport and the accompanying 'metropolitanisation' of cities (Bassand 2004; *see also* Ladner 2007; Kübler and Schwab 2007; Steiner 2003; Leresche 1992; Leresche and Joye 1993; Perritaz 2003; Blöchliger 2005), communes, however much autonomous, remain a subordinate part of their canton.

Nevertheless, as Steinberg (1976: 57; original emphasis) observes, '[t]he basic unit of Swiss politics, and the key to understanding them, is the *Gemeinde* or commune. [...] the community of free citizens has always been understood as the lawful "sovereign"'. Neidhart (2002: 260–261) also speaks of Switzerland as a 'political pyramid' where all layers are more or less autonomous (*selbstständig*), due to 'own powers and own money', and where 'the municipality is the base and fundament' (*see also* Baker 1993 and Geser *et al.* 1996). There are in fact five different types of communes: political, school, citizens' (*Bürgergemeinden*)

Table 3.1: Overview of the Swiss cantons

Canton	Capital city	Year of accession	Area [km²]	Population (2010)	LGs (2012)	Districts (2012)	Official Language
ZH	**Zürich**	**1351**	**1,729**	**1,373,068**	**171**	**12**	**German**
BE	**Bern**	**1353**	**5,959**	**979,802**	**382**	**10**	**G + F**
LU	**Luzern**	**1332**	**1,494**	**377,610**	**87**	**5**	**German**
UR	**Altdorf**	**1291**	**1,077**	**35,422**	**20**	**–**	**German**
SZ	**Schwyz**	**1291**	**908**	**146,730**	**30**	**6**	**German**
OW*	**Sarnen**	**1291**	**491**	**35,585**	**7**	**–**	**German**
NW*	**Stans**	**1291**	**276**	**41,024**	**11**	**–**	**German**
GL	**Glarus**	**1352**	**685**	**38,608**	**3**	**–**	**German**
ZG	**Zug**	**1352**	**239**	**113,105**	**11**	**–**	**German**
FR	**Fribourg**	**1481**	**1,671**	**278,493**	**165**	**7**	**F + G**
SO	**Solothurn**	**1481**	**791**	**255,284**	**120**	**10**	**German**
BS*	**Basel**	**1501**	**37**	**184,950**	**3**	**–**	**German**
BL*	**Liestal**	**1501**	**518**	**274,404**	**86**	**5**	**German**
SH	**Schaffhausen**	**1501**	**299**	**76,356**	**27**	**6**	**German**
AR*	**Herisau**	**1513**	**243**	**53,017**	**20**	**3**	**German**
AI*	**Appenzell**	**1513**	**173**	**15,688**	**6**	**–**	**German**
SG	St. Gallen	1803	2,026	478,907	85	8	German
GR	Chur	1803	7,105	192,621	176	11	G + I + R
AG	Aarau	1803	1,404	611,466	219	11	German
TG	Frauenfeld	1803	991	248,444	80	5	German
TI	Bellinzona	1803	2,813	333,753	147	8	Italian
VD	Lausanne	1803	3,212	713,281	326	10	French
VS	Sion	1814	5,225	312,684	141	13	F + G
NE	Neuchâtel	1814	803	172,085	53	6	French
GE	Genève	1814	282	457,715	45	–	French
JU	Delémont	1979	839	70,032	64	3	French
CH	Bern	1848	41,285	7,870,134	2,485	139	G + F + I

Note: LGs = Local Governments (communes/municipalities), F = French, G = German, I = Italian, and R = Romansh. Romansh is a 'national' but not an 'official language' of Switzerland (Art. 4 and 70.1 FC 1999). Cantons in bold = 'The Old XIII', *half-cantons.

Table 3.2: Aggregate expenditures by Swiss cantons and communes (2009/10)

Purpose	Public expenditures [1,000 CHF]			
	Cantons (2010)		Communes (2009)	
1. General administrative costs	8,961,599	12%	7,073,423	17%
2. Defence	225,009	0.3%	227,176	1%
3. Public order and security	6,016,159	8%	2,330,072	5%
4. Economic affairs	11,067,741	15%	6,134,260	14%
5. Environment protection	1,118,673	1%	3,198,106	8%
6. Housing and public buildings	205,083	0.3%	920,697	2%
7. Health	9,690,977	13%	1,439,655	3%
8. Leisure, culture, religion	1,611,785	2%	2,951,417	7%
9. Education	20,867,983	28%	10,805,354	25%
10. Social security	14,995,455	20%	7,454,715	18%
Total	74,760,464	100%	42,534,874	100%

Source: EFV 2012, tables GFS.1312.05 (p. 90) and GFS.1313.05 (p. 93).

and welfare communes as well as local corporations (Rühli 2012: 33). Except for the first, these are all single-purpose local authorities – 'Type II' for Hooghe and Marks (2003: 236). One could also add the 'church communes' (*Kirchgemeinden*). The political or 'residents' commune' (*Einwohnergemeinde*) was introduced in Switzerland only in 1798/99 (Meylan *et al.* 1972: 21). Especially in the German-speaking cantons the single-purpose entities continue to perform important functions, e.g. primary schools, welfare in Glarus before 2006 (Kronenberg 2011), alpine pasture in Grisons, naturalisation in St. Gall or forest management in Ticino (Rühli 2012: 35). Because the political commune – henceforth simply commune, LG or municipality – is by far the most important local entity, and the only one that is present in all the 26 cantons (Fiechter 2010: 13), I shall focus on the relations between them and 'their' canton alone, in this book. It is important to add that *a priori* there is no legal distinction between the smallest commune, Corippo TI with 15 inhabitants (in 2010), and the largest city, Zurich with 371,000 inhabitants (Ladner 2009: 337, and BFS 2012). This concludes my short introduction to the multi-layered political system of Switzerland.

Research design

There are four aspects to my research design. Two of these are rather common, although *combining* a cross-sectional analysis with case-study research has only recently become embraced more widely. A 'nested analysis' uses the results from the quantitative analysis to guide the selection of case studies. Finally, the whole comparison is situated at the sub-national level, using the Swiss cantons as units of observation. In other words, the way I choose to test my theory is through a sub-national comparison mixing large-N/cross-case with the small-N/within-case logic. The rationale for this is the overarching desire to establish causation as confidently as possible: together, these four elements help to measure my concepts reliably and accurately (Adcock and Collier 2001); compare across space without 'over-stretching' them (Sartori 1970: 57); establish regularity and co-variation (Brady 2008); and 'trace' the causal mechanisms leading to more or less cantonal decentralisation (Collier 2011; Bennett 2008). I will discuss each element of my research design with its ensuing benefit in turn.

Cross-case comparison and regularity

Firstly, the basic idea of comparative politics (and indeed of the very act of comparing) is that it allows the uncovering of similarities and differences. A comparison of a large enough number of cases permits a statistical inference which is able to estimate how much of the variation in the dependent variable can be predicted. Multiple regression analysis helps solve a key problem of social sciences, multicausality, by 'basing estimates of the relationships only on the unique variation and covariation of the variables.' (Franzese 2006: 38) In other words, regression analysis distils the variation that can mathematically be attributed to a single independent variable from that which is due to other factors. (There are also statistical ways to deal with two other problems, context-conditionality and endogeneity, e.g. by modelling an interaction term or resorting to instrumental variables (Franzese 2006: 47 and 64). To deal with these two, however, I will use process-tracing, discussed below.)

The strengths of the quantitative method lie not in its complexity, but in its simplicity. Gerring (2007: 97) lists the four main advantages of the 'cross-case' method as being better able to test hypotheses (rather than generate them), providing external validity (usually at the expense of internal validity), focusing on causal effects (but not mechanisms) and operating with a broad range of propositions (rather than the 'thick description' factors emphasised in case study research; *see* Geertz 1973). In other words, statistical models provide a measure of association that, even if not itself a proof of causality and depending both on its strength and level of significance, nevertheless constitutes a first step toward causality. Statistics highlights the effect of the model that is tested and estimates the probability that this effect has occurred by chance, i.e. the likelihood that it would occur again if we had information on the 'population' (Gerring 2007: 95), and not just a sample thereof.

In this book, an ambivalent relationship exists that can never be fully resolved for sub-national studies (see below). Because my sample of 26 cases is at the same time the population, i.e. it covers *all* 26 Swiss cantons, I am effectively operating with a 'census'. Conventional probability tests are thus circular: the probability that the resulting association might obtain on the population is by definition 1, i.e. sure to occur because derived from it in the first place. Nevertheless, if the Swiss cantons are taken as proxies for political systems as such, generalisations beyond the Swiss case are possible, and here levels of probability matter once more. Freitag and Vatter (2008: 273–4) have justified this use: 'a comparative analysis of the Swiss cantons [...] suggests itself because the sub-national units vary considerably in terms of the autonomy of their local authorities', so there is sufficient variation in the *explanandum*. Hence, to make descriptive inferences, levels of significance can be disregarded; to make causal inferences, in turn, they must be taken into account (King *et al.* 1994: 34; *see also* Achen 1982).

In comparing the Swiss cantons, the other two standard assumptions of comparative politics are also met: due to Swiss federalism, the Swiss cantons are independent from each other and yet sufficiently similar to be compared (unit independence and homogeneity, respectively; *see* Landman 2008). In terms of external validity, then, there is nothing in the way of assimilating a comparison of 26 Swiss cantons theoretically (even if not empirically, of course) to a comparison of, say, the 27 EU Member States. In fact, a sub-national comparison possesses at least one key advantage over common cross-sectional analyses that operate at the nation-state level: internal validity. But even if strong and significant, all that measures of association indicate is the strength and direction of a relationship. Real world phenomena are of course much more complex than any mathematical model can possibly capture. To be sure(r) that it is really those factors that a regression analysis identifies as driving (de)centralisation, we first of all need careful measures. Moving the comparison to the sub-national helps in this attempt.

Sub-national level and internal validity

Before a quantitative analysis can be undertaken, all the variables need to be measured accurately, that is their operationalisation has to proceed in a comprehensive, consistent, reliable, and internally valid way (Putnam 1993: 64). This task is made easier in a comparison of *different* units at the sub-national level of the *same* country, for two reasons. On the one hand, it permits variation on the dependent variable (decentralisation within Swiss cantons) without having to control for too many other, potential causal factors (*see also* Vatter 2002, 2003; Vatter and Freitag 2002, 2007; Bochsler 2009). If there is variation as to the degree of cantonal decentralisation – and there is – then it cannot be because of the level of democracy, governmental stability or affluence, all of which are all relatively similar across the 26 cases. In that sense, any sub-national comparison resembles a most-similar-systems research design (MSSD).

On the other hand, comparing at the sub-national level reduces the number of assumptions that have to be made in order for comparison to take place in the first place. The Federal Constitution mandates all 26 cantons to have popularly amendable, 'democratic' constitutions (*see* Schmitt 2012: 151) and all cantons have the same kind of local governments with their autonomy guaranteed by federal law and minimally (i.e. constitutionally) defined in more or less the same way (Horber-Papazian 2006). Therefore, municipalities, political parties, tax autonomy, constitutional guarantees, parliaments, governments, public functions etc. are not only conceptually, but also empirically equivalent across all 26 cases (with the only exception of the municipality of Basel-city, which has delegated its entire administration to the canton – it still exists, but only on paper; *see* Raith

1984). And yet, for all these similarities, cantons vary enormously in their size, economic structure, progressiveness, and linguistic and religious diversity. A sub-national comparison, in Switzerland at least, is therefore *also* a most-different-systems research design (MDSD).

In sum, a sub-national setting is the perfect environment for multi-variable comparisons because one can 'establish control over potential explanatory variables' (Snyder 2001: 95) while still 'meaningfully capture' (Adcock and Collier 2001: 530) the hypothesised cause/effect variables we are really interested in, i.e. that between structure, agency and cantonal decentralisation.

Case studies and causality

But even a quantitative analysis at the sub-national level would fail to resolve the problem that correlation does not equal causation. Multiple regression analysis fulfils the primary purpose of testing the theoretical model, thereby increasing our confidence that it captures the causal mechanisms leading to (de)centralisation. The sub-national level makes for internal validity and reliable data (often from the same national source). But even both together cannot fully get us there: correlation is not causation. This is so because

> There is no such thing as pure social causation from macro-state to macro-state; instead, hypotheses about social causal mechanisms must be constructed on the basis of an account of the 'microfoundations' of the processes that are postulated. Individuals choosing in the context of structured circumstances of choice are the engine of social change. [...] The central focus is 'agency' [...]. Social entities and structures – institutions, ideologies, technological revolutions, communications and transportation systems – all these exercise causal powers through the effects that they have on individual choices, preferences, beliefs, etc. (Little 1998: 161)

The causal power of a hypothesis, therefore, comes to play only when linking macro- to micro-events, which is what my theoretical framework has accounted for in modelling the influence of structure on (de)centralisation through political agency. Moreover, statistical tests are adequate in discerning 'direct generic causal connections', but 'to identify a causal relation between two kinds of events or conditions, we need to identify the typical causal mechanisms through which the first kind brings about the second kind.' (Little 1998: 164) Only case-study research allows for a more convincing separation of necessary vs. sufficient variables (Dion 1998) by 'tracing' (George and Bennett 2005) the causal mechanisms. Little (1998: 174) provides the best description of the case study approach:

> The researcher examines specific conjunctions of factors and outcomes and attempts to draw causal analysis and inference in these particular cases. And in most cases we can understand this approach as an effort to uncover the microfoundations of the phenomenon in question.

Gerring (2007: 94) accurately defines a case study 'as the intensive study of a single case for the purpose of understanding a larger class of cases (a population).' (*See also* Eckstein 2000 and Vromen 2010) The third element of my methodology, therefore, studies four cantons in-depth and employs a 'structured and focused' comparison (George and Bennett 2005) to uncover the micro-foundations behind cantonal decentralisation. The four cantons studied are 'diverse cases' in that they exhibit the full variation on the dependent variable *and* different constellations of independent variables (Gerring 2007: 98): an egalitarian political culture in Vaud (one of the most centralised cantons), a strong federal political culture in Schwyz, territorial fragmentation with no real centre in Grisons (the most decentralised canton), and strong left-wing parties in Berne. Studying each canton in-depth permits '*typological* theorizing – where different combinations of variables are assumed to have effects on an outcome that vary across types' (Gerring 2007: 98, original emphasis; *see also* Collier *et al.* 2008).

Four is also an ideal number to study in-depth while still comparing across cases. All that a 'structured and focused' comparison (George and Bennett 2005) asks is to employ the same logic ('structure') when selecting the qualitative material, and to remain 'focused' on the overall idea, which is to understand why these cantons are as centralised as they are. Case studies are not only alternative but also supplementary to quantitative techniques: 'Case studies, if well-constructed, allow one to peer into the box of causality to the intermediate causes lying between some cause and its purported effect' (Gerring 2004: 348), which is about the only thing that regression analysis cannot offer. The fourth and final element in my methodology provides a justification of why and how the case-study evidence will have to speak to the results of the quantitative analysis.

Nested analysis and model testing

Once the 'quantitative bones' of causality are strong enough (Chapters Four and Five), the analysis can move to the 'qualitative flesh' (Tarrow 1995: 473). Complementing the cross-case with the within-case logic, I follow Tarrow's (1995: 474) methodological advice that

> Whenever possible, we should use qualitative data to interpret quantitative findings, to get inside the processes underlying decision outcomes, and to investigate the reasons for the tipping points in historical time-series. We should also try to use different kinds of evidence together and in sequence and look for ways of triangulating different measures on the same research problem.

The 'different kinds of evidence' comprise, for the quantitative section, official statistical data, national referenda results and individual-level surveys; for the case studies, historical studies, official constitutional debates, policy documents, and governmental recommendations. Both kinds of data are supplemented by 46 interviews (more than 55 hours in total) conducted over summer 2011 with cantonal, local and political party-representatives in each of the 26 cantons. Information gathered from interviews is qualitative in that it provides 'deep' knowledge into cantonal developments and debates; it is quantitative in that by covering the same organisation in all cantons (the cantonal departments responsible for local affairs and LGAs) coverage approximates the broad scope of the statistical method (*see* Leech 2002; Rubin and Rubin 1995).

In all this, the key to uncover the theoretical micro-foundations is a focus on institutional reforms and surrounding debates in cantonal parliaments, as well as on policy initiatives and papers put forth by cantonal governments and other actors. So, wherever possible, interview partners were asked to reflect about ongoing reform processes, both general (e.g. the district reform in Grisons) and policy-specific (e.g. the police reform in Vaud). Such reflections, when granted, allow a rare look behind appearances into the actual motivations, interests and ideas of political actors (*see* Erk 2008: 14–16, for a similar approach).

The cases selected for in-depth study are thus 'nested' because, as defined by Lieberman (2005: 435–6), my method 'combines the statistical analysis of a large sample of cases with the in-depth investigation of one or more of the cases contained within the large sample'. Provided the quantitative model is robust, case-study analysis can be confined to 'model-testing'. For this to work, the selected cases must be on the line of fit, i.e. well explained by the model. Opening up four cases for qualitative study also allows making sure a core weakness of statistics does not 'infect' the final causal assessment: spuriousness. This works because the structure of a nested analysis is strictly hierarchical, whereby

> the regression analysis determines the explanatory power of a model, the causal effects of the independent variables, and their statistical significance. The residuals of the cases provide the basis for case selection. The inferential goal of the qualitative analysis is to discern whether the significant independent variables are linked to the dependent variable through causal mechanisms. (Rohlfing 2008: 1493)

In other words, the purpose of the case studies is to show the independent variables 'in action', identifying instances and providing evidence of a different kind as to their effect on cantonal decentralisation.

To sum up, my fourfold methodology – an initial cross-case comparison at the sub-national level, then four 'diverse' cases 'nested' within this analysis – allows me to systematically, validly *and* reliably test my theory. As already stated above, the Swiss case lends itself perfectly to such an exercise because determining the powers of LGs is one of the few exclusive competencies left with each of the 26 cantons (e.g. Bapst 2000; Geser 2004; Meylan 1986). In other words, cantonal decentralisation is *a priori* purely dependent on cantonal politics, with only minimal federal interference (e.g. Thürer 1986). This, in turn, enables measuring decentralisation within the Swiss cantons independently from one another, a step I take next.

Chapter Four

Measuring Cantonal Decentralisation

This chapter first discusses existing measures of cantonal decentralisation, which, as I will argue, only capture either the policy- or the polity-dimension. I next develop a new measure to capture the politics-dimension (*see also* Mueller 2011). To my knowledge, no study has ever *systematically* measured the vertical organisation of political parties, the share of local representatives, *and* the territorial dimension of democratic processes (elections and referenda) across *all* 26 cantons, let alone explained all this. It is here that the first contribution to the empirical originality of this book lies. The three measures are integrated into a final index of cantonal decentralisation in section three of this chapter.

Existing measures

Many authors writing on cantonal-local relations mention a variation across cantons, but only a few have set out to systematically measure it. Neidhart (2002: 264), for example, speaks of 'different degrees of cantonal centralisation', but does not provide a measure. Studies that provide innovative measures of local autonomy (e.g. Fiechter 2010), on the other hand, do not make the linkage to cantonal decentralisation, that is they try to generalise to the Swiss level, thus bypassing the cantonal level. But exactly how decentralised are the Swiss cantons? What types of decentralisation are prevalent in some, which ones in other cantons: mere administrative de-concentration, fiscal or legislative delegation, statutory devolution, and/or federal-type guarantees entrenched in cantonal constitutions? How large is the overall cross-sectional variation that I aim to explain (in Chapters Five and Six) using the theoretical framework presented (in Chapter Two)?

Existing measures either relate to the legal framework (Giacometti 1941; Fiechter 2010; Grodecki 2007), to fiscal indicators (e.g. BADAC; Freitag and Vatter 2008), or to a kind of expert perception of local autonomy by communal clerks (Ladner 1991, 2005, and 2009). This last measure comes closest to the notion of an actor-related dimension of cantonal decentralisation, but is still insufficient to fully grasp, more particularly, the *political* dimension of the division of territorial power. The oldest measure relates to polity, hence I discuss this one first.

The polity-dimension

Historically, a Swiss municipality is

> not just one administrative institution amongst many others, but a political
> institution, that is a public collectivity organised democratically and with a

general purpose. [...] It forms the first level of the institutional architecture of Switzerland, below the federal and cantonal levels.' (Moor 2007: 9)[1]

Steinberg (1976: 57) also observes that '[n]owhere is the basic sovereignty of the people more obvious and direct than in the *Gemeinde*, the basic unit of the Swiss political community.' Whether 'residual powers' – a federal concept captured by the notion of 'subsidiarity' (Burgess 2006a: 167) – are ascribed to the local level is, thus, a first indicator of the degree of territorial division of power in the Swiss cantons. The historical evolution of Switzerland and a general underdevelopment of Swiss political science until quite recently (*see* Linder 1996) explain why there are three measures of the legal-institutional dimension of cantonal decentralisation, only one or two of the policy- but none of the politics-dimension.

Giacometti was the first to regard the Swiss cantons as 'unitary' (*unitaristische*) political systems, which, 'to a higher or lower degree, exhibit a territorial division, a so-called decentralisation' (1941: 69). To him, cantons are 'exponentiated self-governing entities' (1941: 28) and municipalities 'collective authorities of residents within the state' (1941: 71). While cantons are at least 'fake states' (*unechte Staaten*; 1941: 30), the very existence of municipalities is through cantonal law alone (1941: 71). The difference between cantons' position in the Swiss federation and that of the municipalities within their canton is thus subtle, but clearly discernible nevertheless:

> Cantons represent an organic aggregation of municipalities, as does the Confederation of cantons. The difference between the architecture of the federation and that of the cantons lies in the absence of the contractual instance for the latter, because, historically speaking, the municipalities do not appear as the creators of the cantons in the same way as the cantons do in relation to the Confederation. (1941: 71)

Therefore, all that municipalities can achieve is to have their powers separated into as little 'delegated rule' as necessary and as much 'self-rule' as possible (1941: 74). Local 'autonomy' thus appears as the mere absence of cantonal 'administrative discretion' (*Ermessenskontrolle*, 1941: 75). Table 4.1 sorts the – at that time – 25 cantons into three groups, which Giacometti (1941: 77) saw as embodying different constellations of delegated and self-rule – that is, their degree of local autonomy and hence decentralisation. Because it was part of Berne for so long, we can safely add Jura to the middle group.

Meyer calls these a 'Zurich', a 'Berne', and a 'Geneva group', respectively, named after the dominant 'model canton' (1978: 92). However, this classification is purely based on the legal grounds of autonomy, not on 'factual autonomy' (de Spindler 1998: 85). That is, we find a very extensive local autonomy in the Zurich group, while municipalities in the Geneva group serve mainly as 'decentralised

---

1. This and all subsequent translations are mine.

Table 4.1: Local autonomy according to Giacometti (1941)

Large local autonomy (N = 11)	Medium local autonomy (N = 9/10)	Small local autonomy (N = 5)
ZH, SZ, OW and NW, GL, ZG, AI and AR, GR, AG, TG	BE, LU, UR, SO, BS and BL, SH, SG, TI (+JU)	GE, VD, NE, FR, VS
'Zurich Group'	'Berne Group'	'Geneva Group'

executors' for cantonal (and federal) policies (Meyer 1978: 93). In the middle group, centred on Berne, more local duties fall into the category of delegated tasks than in the Zurich group; however, self-rule is still more extensive than in the Geneva group (Meyer 1978: 93). In all this, local autonomy is a mere *consequence* of cantonal law: 'local autonomy means the capacity of the commune with regards to some of its task to make certain choices or take certain initiatives and, the case being, to have them prevail even if opposed by the cantonal authorities' (Meylan *et al.* 1972: 52). In short, the three groups are established based on the degree of cantonal control; cantonal decentralisation begins where central control ends.

This logic, like others in the field of Swiss local government studies (Meyer 1978: 48), corresponds strongly to a premise borrowed from the German 'theory of the state', where

> it is evident that centralization and decentralization, generally considered as forms of State organization with reference to territorial division, must be understood as two types of legal orders. [...] Only a juristic theory can provide the answer to the question as to the nature of centralization and decentralization. (Kelsen 1961: 303–4)

Decentralisation then appears as the sole, legal *raison d'être* of Swiss municipalities (Meyer 1978: 4). They are, on the one hand, more than de-concentrated elements of the state, unlike prefects, which 'represent the cantonal government' (e.g. Art. 93.2(a) CC BE) and which are thus examples of 'administrative decentralisation' (Giacometti 1941: 69). Swiss municipalities are, on the other hand, still far from achieving the degree of constitutional autonomy that cantons enjoy in the Swiss federation.

This point is taken up by Fiechter (2010) in his study of Swiss LGs, however only as part of a much wider approach to measuring local autonomy. He develops an index of 'legal autonomy', which consists of two components. The first measures the degree to which the existence and autonomy of municipalities is guaranteed beyond Art. 50.1 FC (Fiechter 2010: 63; *see also* Grodecki 2007). On a six-point scale, a canton scores high if 'local autonomy' is mentioned in the cantonal constitution and the cantonal law on communes; if municipalities are listed by name in both; and if communes are protected from forced mergers (Fiechter 2010: 63; *see also* Kennel 1989). A second component measures the degree to which municipalities are free to choose their own organisation (Fiechter 2010: 65): on a six-point scale, a canton scores high if legal prescriptions for the type and number of members of the local executive are absent and if municipalities can choose between a local parliament and a citizens' assembly (2010: 65). The first is called 'existence and autonomy guarantee', the second 'organisational freedom'.

The two indices are positively correlated, but the correlation is weak and insignificant (Pearson' r = .369, p = .063). Neither of the two correlates with Giacometti's three groups,[2] cautioning us not to combine the three indices into a single, combined measure. A means comparison – more adequate for ordinal variables such as these – further shows that while cantons in the Geneva group consistently score lowest on both dimensions, there is no significant difference between the Berne and Zurich groups – in fact, the mean values for both indices are *lower* in the Zurich group.

Both Giacometti's categorisation and Fiechter's two indices highlight an enormous variation across Swiss cantons. In some cantons, LGs not only enjoy significant levels of autonomy, but are even named in the CC. The existence of each individual commune is thus constitutionally entrenched. This fact has led some observers to speak of the 'internal federalism' of Swiss cantons (Linder 1999: 156), indeed of 'communal federalism' (*Gemeindeföderalismus*; Schweizer 1981). For Neidhart (2002: 264), too, a canton is 'a small federation' (*Föderation im Kleinen*), and even Giacometti (1941) at one point speaks of the 'cooperative structure' (*genossenschaftlicher Aufbau*) of the cantons. Finally, until today, Switzerland is 'probably the only country in the world having also municipal nationality' (Basta Fleiner 2000: 80) and one where residual powers belong not just to the cantons, but also to the communes (Ladner 1994: 68). Moreover, municipalities are perceived as important political structures as such (Horber-Papazian 2004; Ladner 1991): sources of prestige and support (Moor 2007), first entry-point for citizens when dealing with public issues (Meylan 1972), and staffed by a separate 'communal elite' (Neidhart 2002: 262).

However, even if both Giacometti and Fiechter are cognisant of these facts, their measures fail to validly capture this general importance. The 'problem' is that LGs and their autonomy are constitutionally recognised in all cantons, so they resemble the position of the cantons in the Swiss Confederation. But they also have to implement cantonal and federal policies, depend on funds and subsidies, and are subject to administrative control – so they resemble decentralised, at times (e.g. for federal elections; Grodecki 2007) even de-concentrated entities. It is therefore not enough to measure their relative importance through 'legal' autonomy. A third component, really a different method of data gathering, must be added to such a Whearean perspective on territorial power. This real-life component is provided by surveys among local secretaries.

The Swiss National Science Foundation has supported a total of five surveys among local secretaries (*Gemeindeschreiber*), in the years 1988, 1994, 1998, 2005

---

2. Cronbach's Alpha for the three measures is a low .572 (N = 26), if we code the Zurich group members as 2, the Berne ones at 1, and the Geneva ones at 0. My thanks to Erica Zaiser for pointing this out to me.

and 2009. In 1994, 2005, and 2009, questions on local autonomy were included. The most important one asks secretaries to rate their municipality on a scale from 1 ('no autonomy') to 10 ('very high autonomy'). Ladner (1994: 80) reports the findings from the 1994 survey, but since raw data is available (GSB 1994, 2005 and 2009), we can make our own calculations. Correlating the three datasets results in significant Pearson's r coefficients of between .703 and .775 – in other words the three indicators can safely be built into a single measure of perceived decentralisation simply by averaging the three cantonal aggregates. That leaves us with the most decentralised cantons Zug, Obwalden, Thurgau and Appenzell Outer-Rhodes on the right and the most centralised cantons Geneva, Neuchâtel and Jura on the left of Figure 4.1. The mean value is 5, while a standard deviation (*SD*) of .78 indicates that cantons vary quite considerably on this dimension of locally perceived decentralisation.[3]

This index and Giacometti's three groups (incl. Jura in the Berne group) are highly correlated.[4] The same is not the case with Fiechter's (2010) two indices of organisational freedom and existence guarantee – neither individually, in parallel, nor combined. I will therefore omit his two indices from my further measurement of the polity-dimension and focus on Giacometti's categorisation and locally perceived decentralisation only.

In combining Giacometti's (1941) three groups with data from the surveys among local secretaries, we must be clear about the theoretical relationship between these indicators. Goertz (2006: 108) also averts that 'how we conceptualize a phenomenon has deep and intimate links with basic-level causal theories.' Both the legal and the perceived components are relevant to the idea of polity-decentralisation: Zurich for example, which constitutionally provides for extensive local autonomy, is more decentralised than Geneva, where communes mainly serve as 'decentralised' executors (Meyer 1978: 93). It must come as no surprise, then, that local secretaries in Geneva have consistently ranked their autonomy as the lowest, compared with all other cantons. If for Giacometti (1941) cantonal decentralisation begins where central control *ends*, then it is only consistent with the idea of a separate polity-dimension of decentralisation to regard the level of perceived local autonomy as the *start* of it. Perceptions matter, because it is (also) based on these that politics often works in actual practice. The two are different takes on the same idea, i.e. freedom from cantonal interference in basic, institutional matters, but one must not be a condition of the other. Two further examples clarify this view: who is to say that Valais is centralised? Giacometti places it in the (most centralised) Geneva group, but its average score in the local surveys is sixth highest. The same is true for Schwyz: Giacometti places it in the (most decentralised) Zurich group, but its average score in the local surveys

---

3. N (GSB$_{1994}$) = 1,549; N (GSB$_{2005}$) = 2,003; N (GSB$_{2009}$) = 1,317 (*see also* Data Appendix).

4. Cronbach's alpha for the four measures, 'Giacometti Index', 'GSB$_{1994}$', 'GSB$_{2005}$' and 'GSB$_{2009}$', is a high .885 (N = 26).

Figure 4.1: Index of perceived decentralisation (1994, 2005 and 2009)

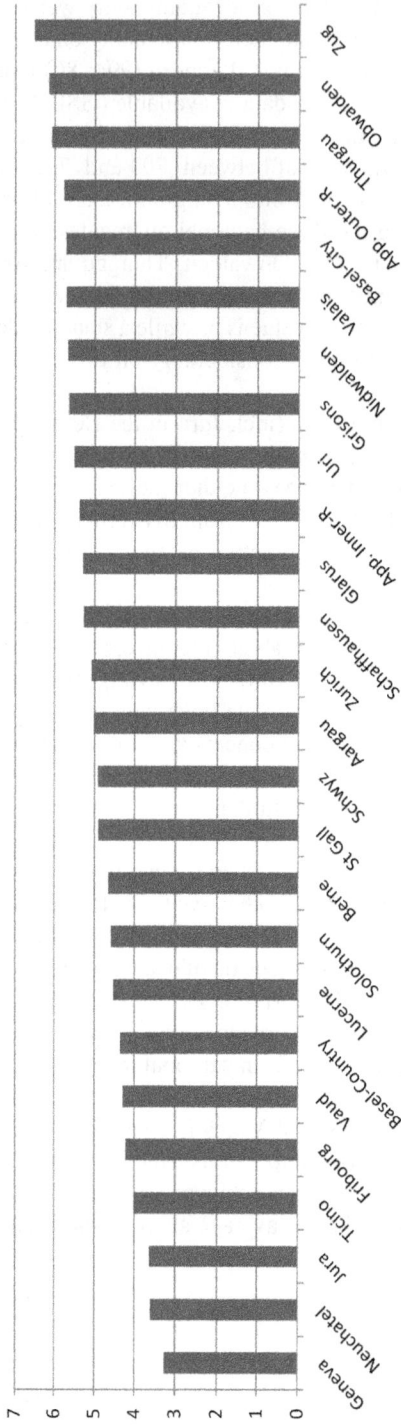

is just below average. If time difference between the two measures (1941 vs. 1994/2005/2009) was to explain these discrepancies, then why not so for other cantons?

Rather than multiplying the perceived values with a code for group belonging, I think it best to average the standardised values of each. I thus develop the following *composite measure of polity-decentralisation*:

1. A canton is coded 0 for membership in the Geneva group, 1 for the Berne group, and 2 for the Zurich group. This results in the *Giacometti-Index of legal decentralisation*.
2. The mean cantonal values on local autonomy from the 1994, the 2005 and the 2009 surveys are averaged, resulting in an *index of locally perceived decentralisation*.
3. To arrive at a combined measure of polity-decentralisation, I take it that a canton is decentralised in its polity-dimension if it is decentralised *either* in its legal *or* in its locally perceived dimension. Therefore, I *average* the standardised values of the indices calculated in steps 1 and 2.

Figure 4.2 ranks the Swiss cantons by their degree of polity-decentralisation, taking into account both legal and locally perceived decentralisation. Geneva, Neuchâtel, Fribourg and Vaud are by far the most centralised, and Zug, Obwalden and Thurgau the most decentralised cantons in this first dimension of overall cantonal decentralisation.

The advantage of combining the two is to arrive at a first general picture of cantonal decentralisation; however, only as regards the legal framework and the local perception of its actual operation. The delivery of public services provides the link between the two, so I now move on to cantonal policy-decentralisation.

The policy-dimension

A policy-oriented view of the Swiss cantons emphasises their individualist, democratic element over the collective, territorial one. The basis of this assumption – and the ensuing measure of cantonal decentralisation – is Art. 51.1 FC, which says that '[e]ach Canton shall adopt a democratic constitution. This requires the approval of the People and must be capable of being revised if the majority of those eligible to vote so request'. This is interpreted to mean two things. First, that the content of any CC should be based on rule of law and the direct election of cantonal authorities and, second, that all revisions of the CC must be approved by a majority of citizens – and by it only (Delley and Auer 1986: 86). Both result in the primacy of (individual) liberty over (territorial) federalism. In fact, most CCs provide for a *lower* threshold to be amended, asking typically only for a majority of people actually taking part in the vote (Forster 2000: 137). To ask for a higher threshold would violate federal law: any type of qualified majority is in contradiction with federal law and therefore 'unconstitutional' (Fleiner 2000: 112).

Admitting that the democratic principle must prevail over the territorial principle at all times, the Swiss cantons nevertheless exhibit a wide variation

Figure 4.2: Polity-decentralisation across the Swiss cantons

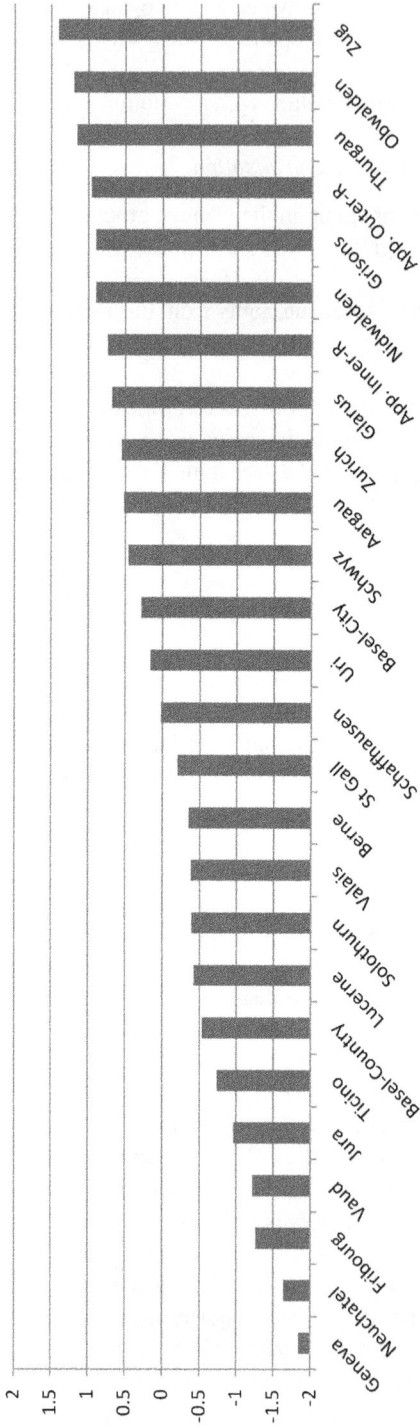

in what exactly the duties of local communities are. After having discussed decentralisation from a legal-institutional perspective, we are now in a better position to understand how this ensues in a measure from a fiscal or policy-oriented perspective. Two primary measures are commonly employed: *expenditure decentralisation*, either in general terms (e.g. Rühli 2012: 177) or as the ratio of local from total public expenditure only for administrative duties (BADAC 2012), or *revenue decentralisation*, again either generally or confined to tax revenue (e.g. Freitag and Vatter 2008: 281). In other words, if Swiss LGs are (also) the executors of the cantonal (and federal) will, this must be discernible from their prime activities: spending money, both across a range of policies and for administrative duties specifically. From the *administrative* side of decentralisation studies (e.g. Horber-Papazian 2006) we are, thirdly, reminded that measuring the average number of local staff across the 26 cantons provides one with the day-to-day importance of LGs (Bochsler *et al.* 2004: 113). The share of local staff's wages from the total public wages in a canton rounds up the picture on policy-decentralisation. I will now present data for each of the three elements of policy-decentralisation: expenditure, revenue, and administrative decentralisation; all provided by BADAC, the BFS, and the EFV.[5]

To begin with, *general* revenue and expenditure decentralisation in the Swiss cantons are highly and positively correlated (Pearson's r = .866, p < .001; *see Figure 4.3*). On average, however, expenditure achieves a much greater degree of decentralisation than revenue: the mean value for the former is a high 42.1 per cent, while for the latter it is a low 27.2 per cent. Expenditures also span a wider range (*SD* = 12.09) than revenues (*SD* = 7.98). Basel-City is a special case because, as already stated, the municipal administration of the city of Basel is entirely run by the cantonal authorities, a fact which somewhat distorts the picture since the other two municipalities in this half-canton are very small. Nevertheless, since this 'exception' is valid for both the expenditure and the revenue side, I average the two measures into a single *index of fiscal decentralisation*.

A more particular indicator of expenditure decentralisation taps the local share of expenditure for administration only. BADAC provides annual data for the years from 1997 to 2003. All seven measures strongly correlate[6] and can thus be averaged into a single *index of administrative decentralisation*, shown in Figure 4.4. This index is, in turn, highly and positively correlated both with revenue (Pearson's r = .763, p < .001) and expenditure decentralisation (r = .743, p < .001). Finally, an even more sophisticated approach measures both the local share of total public *staff* and the local share of total public *salaries* per canton. The two correlate very strongly and positively (Pearson's r = .941, p < .001;

---

5.   In the BADAC database I specifically draw on Tables Csi2.21d (administrative expenditures; 1997–2003), Csi3.12a (local staff; 2008) and Csi10.41d (local expenditures; 2008). Special thanks to Merlina Bajic, BFS/Sektion Unternehmensstruktur, for providing me with the latest data on the 'Business Census' (BZ 2008) via email in June 2012.

6.   Cronbach's alpha for all seven items = .988; N = 26

Figure 4.3: Cantonal expenditure by revenue decentralisation

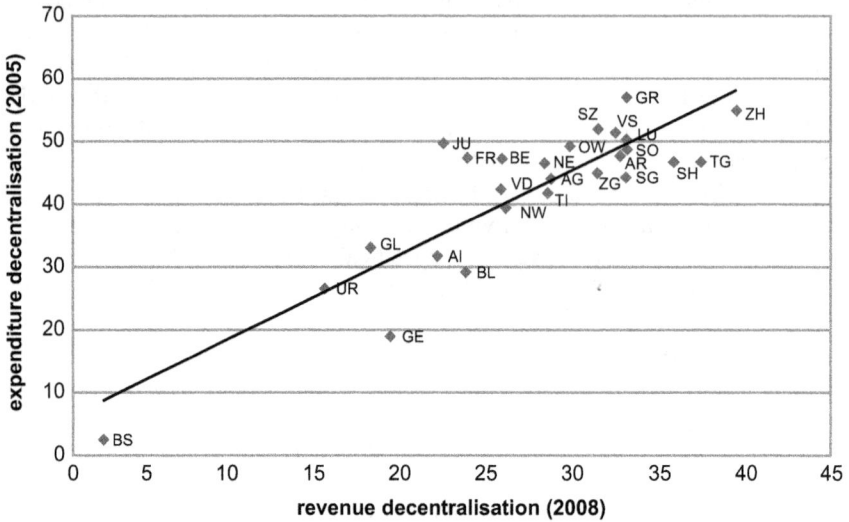

see Figure 4.5), so that I again average them into a single *index of personnel decentralisation* (adopted from Treisman 2002).

Stemming from a belief that a canton is only decentralised in its policy-dimension if it scores high on *all* these fiscal, administrative and personnel indices, I develop the following *composite measure of policy-decentralisation*:

1. General revenue and general expenditure decentralisation are 'substitutable' (Goertz 2006: 108), so I average their respective values into an *index of fiscal decentralisation*.
2. The values arrived at by calculating the local share of total public expenditures for administration only (average from 1997 to 2003) I take as an *index of administrative decentralisation*.
3. Local staff and local staff salaries are equally substitutable, so I again average these measures into an *index of personnel decentralisation*.
4. To arrive at a combined measure I take it that a canton is decentralised in its policy-dimension if, and only if, it is decentralised in its fiscal, personnel *and* administrative dimension contemporaneously. Therefore, I *multiply* the indices calculated in steps 1, 2 and 3. There is no need to standardise their values at this stage as all are expressed in percentages.

In other words, an integrated measure of policy-decentralisation can only be the product of fiscal, personnel and administrative decentralisation. Simply averaging the values of fiscal and personnel decentralisation would mean that they are substitutable: that a canton is decentralised if it is *either* marked by fiscal *or* by personnel decentralisation. But fiscal decentralisation can easily be offset by administrative centralisation, in the same way that personnel centralisation can

Figure 4.4: Index of administrative decentralisation

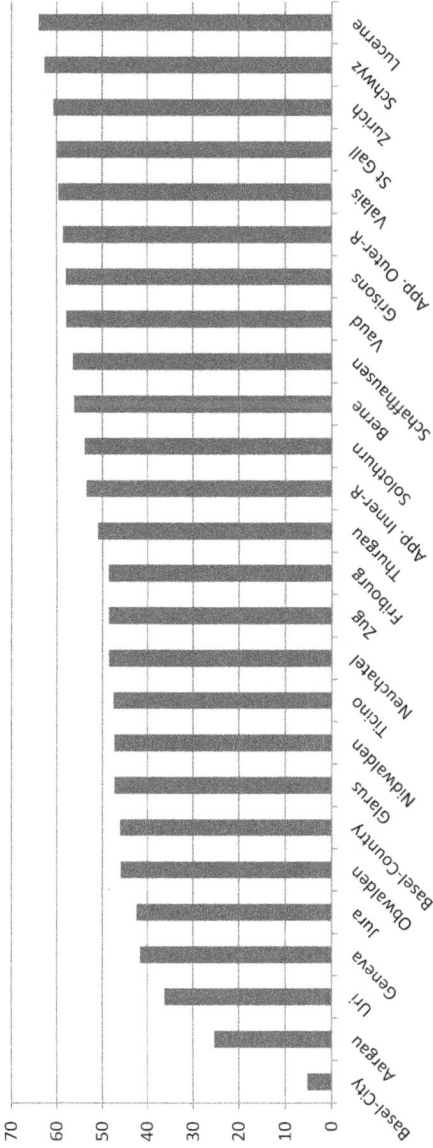

Figure 4.5: Cantonal salary by staff decentralisation

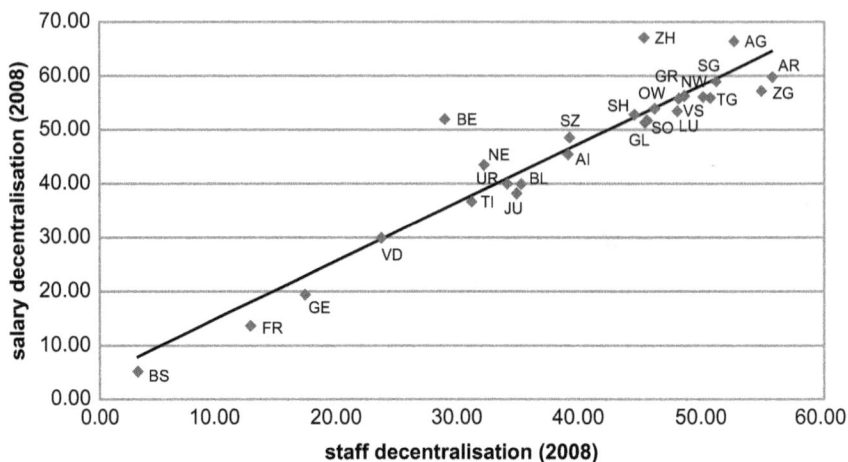

easily be offset by fiscal decentralisation. All three components are necessary and together they are jointly sufficient conditions (Goertz 2006: 115) for policy decentralisation. Figure 4.6 ranks the Swiss cantons by their degree of policy-decentralisation.[7] The most centralised cantons on this second dimension of cantonal decentralisation are placed to the left, the most decentralised ones to the right.

A different measure is again developed by Fiechter (2010: 67), who speaks of the 'political autonomy' of Swiss LGs. Measuring the cantonal-local ratio of public expenditures serves him to count the policy areas in which the local share exceeds 50 per cent (2010: 70). The result is that in Schaffhausen, Zurich and Grisons, municipalities account for more than 50 per cent of public spending in six policy areas; in Thurgau, they do so in five, and in a further seven cantons (Schwyz, Solothurn, St. Gall, Valais, Neuchâtel, Berne and Vaud), they do so in four areas (2010: 72). Only in Basel-City do municipalities spend less than 50 per cent in all six fields – indeed, they hardly spend 3 per cent on average (2010: 70). Slightly less centralised are Uri, Geneva and Basel-Countryside (more than 50 per cent local spending in one area) and Glarus, Appenzell Inner-Rhodes, Fribourg and Jura (more than 50 per cent local spending in two areas) (2010: 70).

However, his measure is problematic on three accounts. First, it assumes the comparability of policy fields as diverse as public security, housing, traffic and finances (*see also* Treisman 2002; Riker 1964). Second, the cut-off point of 50 per cent may seem to make sense at first sight, but lacks theoretical justification. What

---

7. Cronbach's alpha for fiscal, personnel and administrative decentralisation is .831; if run with the five sub-indicators individually, it is .907 (both times N = 26; *see also* Figure 4.8: Concept-Structure of Cantonal Decentralisation).

Figure 4.6: Policy-decentralisation in the Swiss cantons

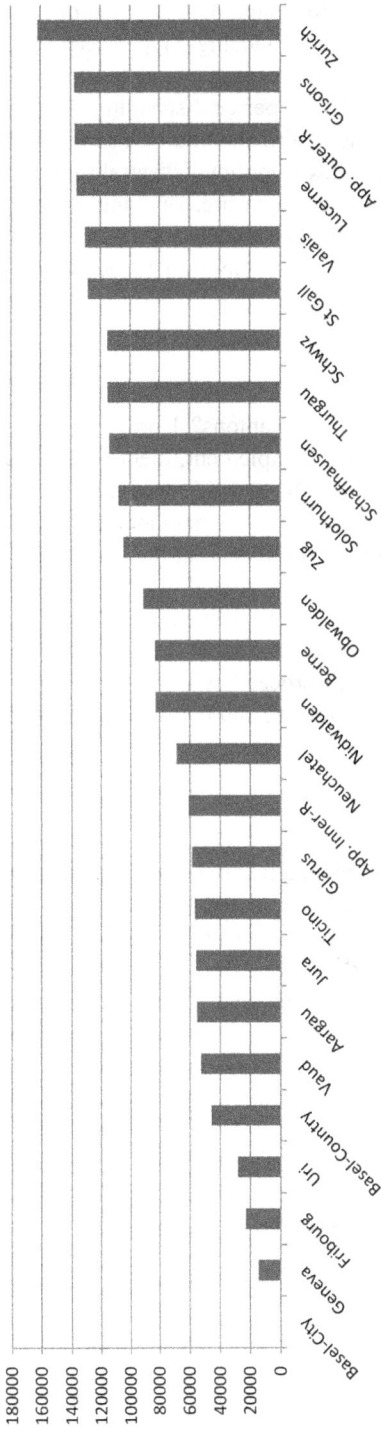

is the difference between LGs in Geneva financing 49.6 per cent of environment and planning policies and LGs in Thurgau financing 51 per cent of transport? Or between LGs in Glarus spending 49.6 per cent of social welfare and those in Schaffhausen 51.8 per cent? Or between 51.8 per cent spending for education in Grisons but only 48.7 per cent in Lucerne? Third and finally, his overall results are largely correlated with my composite index of policy-decentralisation,[8] yet mine seems a more objective and, therefore, valid measure. Drawing on several years and ways to calculate is also more reliable. This concludes my review of existing measures of cantonal decentralisation. I now move on to develop a politics-measure of cantonal decentralisation.

The politics-dimension[9]

How *politically* decentralised are the Swiss cantons? I propose not to replace existing measures but to add to, and thus complement, them with a measure of the politics-dimension. It is theory that ought to guide method (Pennings *et al.* 1999: 8), and that is why the main reason for this methodological innovation stems from my theoretical interest in decentralisation in the Swiss cantons as an attribute of *political* systems. As I have already argued in Chapter Two, for such systems three dimensions are worth examining: political institutions as 'polity', output as 'policy' and political processes and actors as 'politics' (Neidhart 2002: 20). Due to the lack of prior elaboration, I proceed deductively and first measure regionalism and localism, then party federalism, and finally electoral systems and direct democracy.

Intra-cantonal regionalism

Both ontological assumptions about cantonal territorial organisation mentioned so far, i.e. the 'cantons as unitary states' (Giacometti 1941) and 'internal federalism' (Linder 1999), centre on the local dimension only ('bottom-up'). My perspective, however, is on the cantons as political systems. Supervision and intermediate levels are essential in this 'top-down' perspective. However, no comparative study of the Swiss cantons has ever systematically discussed the prime institutions of cantonal supervision, the prefects, other than *en passant*. When prefects *are* discussed, then only in a legal, public administration or single-canton perspective (e.g. Emery 1986; Altenburger 1988; Meylan 1994; Schwoerer 1998; Schmitt 2002; *see also* Gassmann and Mueller 2011). This may be so because their role is thought to be rather irrelevant. But such intra-cantonal 'regionalism' (Neidhart 2002: 268–269) is itself a phenomenon to be measured, and its causes and effects

---

8.   Cronbach's Alpha for his measure and policy-centralisation's three components (fiscal, personnel and administrative centralisation) is a good .778 (N = 26).

9.   For an earlier version of this section, *see* Mueller (2011); for an elaboration on intra-cantonal shared rule, *see* Mueller (2014).

to be studied, rather than simply ignoring its existence. In any case, the wider literature discussed in Chapter One has it that prefects not only embody oversight and tutelage over lower-level powers, but also that they provide at least some input from below:

> The prefect is there to bear responsibility for application of national programs in his area, and he is expected to bring to his task a broader, more sensitive appreciation of the character of that area than any highly specialized functional agent can be expected to have. His concern is the total area and the total national activity in relation to that area. (Fesler 1965: 560)

Does this apply also to cantonal prefects? We can only say, at this stage, that given the rather limited number of staff in the prefectures in *all* cantons, and the scarcity of literature on them, they seem to be of minor importance and perform mainly a role of informational linkages between the cantonal centre and LGs (Meylan *et al.* 1972). In terms of operationalisation, I associate both popular election and other forms of direct participation as indicating more *de*centralisation. I thus modify Hutchcroft's (2001) advice into one of *district appointments vs. district elections*, and code cantonal political systems as set out in Table 4.2. That is, I regard the existence and type of district assemblies and prefects as a first component of politics-decentralisation.

Both elements tap 'regionalism' within the Swiss cantons (*see also* Mueller and Dardanelli 2012). Districts capture the degree of representative regionalisation: bottom-up legitimated district structures in Grisons, Schwyz, Berne and Valais make a canton a *regionalist* canton, whereas to possess no locally appointed or direct-democratic/elected district assembly makes the canton a simple two-level polity. Locally appointed district assemblies exist only in Valais (*Conseil de district*; Art. 66 CC Valais) and, since recently, in Berne (*Regionalkonferenz*). The 'prefects'-variable captures the degree of administrative regionalisation by determining the presence/absence and constitutional origins of prefects. A canton with centrally appointed prefects is more centralist than a canton with regionally elected or no prefects. The reason for coding cantons with locally appointed district assemblies as more *decentralised* than those with no such assemblies, but cantons

Table 4.2: Coding scheme for district assemblies and cantonal prefects

District assemblies	Prefects		
	None	Elected	Appointed
Elected/direct	4: GR and SZ	3: –	2: –
Locally appointed (delegates)	3: –	2: BE and VS	1: –
None	2: GL, GE, NE, JU, BS, AI, AR, OW, NW, SH, TI, UR, ZG, BL, TG and SG	1: AG, FR and ZH	0: SO, LU and VD

Note: Figures in the cells indicate the degree of cantonal decentralisation (author coding).

with centrally appointed prefects as more *centralised* than those with elected prefects, is that prefects are, almost by definition, 'administrative resources of the state dedicated to supervising' LGs (Zimmerman 1994: 8). Popular election may attenuate central supervision and provide for bottom-up inputs, but a prefect remains the agent of the central (i.e. cantonal, in Switzerland) government; this is why even cantons with elected prefects (Aargau, Fribourg, Zurich) are coded as being more centralised than cantons with no prefect at all, unless a locally appointed district assembly is there to counterweigh such centralisation (as in Berne and Valais).

Intra-cantonal localism

A second element of politics-decentralisation points to the direct and indirect influence local officials have over cantonal political processes. Is the presence of local councillors in the cantonal legislature an indicator of decentralisation? It certainly is an indicator of 'representation and defence of communal interests', for Meylan *et al.* (1972: 279–81). Delley and Auer (1986: 94) also observe that

> the parliaments of the *Landsgemeinde* cantons, especially in Appenzell Inner-Rhodes, resemble diets where periodically the local and cantonal executives gather and [...] the parliament of Grisons is that of a federal canton [*un Canton fédératif*] which in terms of its cultural, linguistic and confessional diversity resembles a small [version of the Swiss] Confederation.

The problem with the double-tenure of local and cantonal office is, of course, to know whether that has any relevance (Page 1991: 57). That Members of the Cantonal Parliament (MCPs) have once served, or are still serving, as local councillors does not necessarily indicate that their 'primary loyalty' (Stein 1968) lies with the local rather than the cantonal level. Page (1991: 59) argues that previous tenure wrongly assumes that past affiliation leads to present sympathies – an assumption that 'confuses past environment with current motivation'. I will thus restrict my further discussion to MCPs both temporally, i.e. to MCPs who are at the same time holding local office, and functionally, i.e. to mayors only. Such mayor MCPs matter, at least potentially, for decentralisation, and it is better to measure their presence and then systematically assess their effect in a later step, rather than dismiss them at this early stage. Moreover, and at least for Switzerland, some evidence already exists.

Horber-Papazian (2004: 54) reports that at the national level, mayor MPs managed to insert the already mentioned article protecting local autonomy into the new FC of 1999. For Bogdanor (1988: 84), 'the main element of unification between the federal parliament and the cantons is secured not through the second chamber, but by means of the *cumul des mandats*.' Neidhart (2002: 269) equally draws attention to the fact that personal contacts between cantonal and local officials are an important element in Swiss politics, and posits that 'local officials' (*Gemeindefunktionäre*) constitute one of the most influential groups in cantonal parliaments. Besides, if the *cumul des mandats* really is such a French peculiarity, as Page (1991) argues, one would expect more of it in the French-speaking cantons. Whether this is true (and meaningful) can again only be confirmed if, as an observable implication, we encounter a higher percentage of mayor MCPs in the *Romandie* (the French-speaking area of Switzerland to the West) as opposed to the *Deutschschweiz* (German speaking parts) and/or the Italian parts (Ticino and the South of Grisons).

But current, systematic and reliable data are scarce. Meylan *et al.* (1978: 281) mention that in 1950 one third of MCPs in Vaud were also local officials, not specifying how many were mayors. Horber-Papazian (2004: 54) reports their share in the cantonal parliaments only for Fribourg (29 per cent), Vaud (24 per cent), Valais (22 per cent), Neuchâtel (17 per cent), Jura (10 per cent) and Geneva (9 per cent). Already within this group of French-speaking cantons, then, there is a three-fold ratio between the most and the least 'localist' cantonal parliament. Rühli (2012: 57) has most recently surveyed all cantons to find out the share of mayor MCPs. His findings are largely consistent with those reported here, the only difference being that I have mostly relied on official 'declarations of interest' published for each MCP and have not asked cantonal experts, as he did, so mine is a more valid way to measure *cumuls des mandats*.[10] Adding to the degree of intra-cantonal regionalism, I thus count the *number of Members of Cantonal Parliament (MCPs) that are at the same time mayors* as my second indicator of the politics-dimension of decentralisation. Table 4.3 presents the absolute number of such 'mayor MCPs' (first column). Percentages in the second column indicate the share of mayor MCPs of all MCPs (LMCP1), percentages in the third column indicate the share of mayor MCPs per total number of LGs (LMCP2) and the last column averages the previous two.

All cantons except Uri and Basel-City have at least one mayor sitting in their parliament. But while in Thurgau mayors account for a fifth in the whole chamber, in seven cantons they barely constitute two, and in 14 other cantons between 5 and 10 per cent of the chamber. In two cantons, finally, mayor MCPs make for between 15 and 17 per cent of the total number of MCPs. This first relative weight matters because with it the likelihood to sit prominently in key committees (e.g. finance or legal affairs) increases. This indicator can thus be regarded as capturing two potentials: first, the higher the number of mayor MCPs, the greater the chances to form issue-specific coalitions uniting different political parties. Second, the efficiency to speak on behalf of communes rises the more MCPs there are defending the local cause. The 'voice of the communes' is less likely to be heard (or to be well received) if always the same two or three mayor MCPs admonish it, than when 26 MCPs take turns in doing so.

---

10. The declarations of interests by MCPs are obligatory but no checks on their accuracy or completeness is carried out. However, because MCPs have to fill them in by themselves, the possibility that somebody would 'forget' to mention his mayoral office could be taken as *prima facie* evidence that for him/her local affiliation does not matter – hence, not to count this is indeed more valid than 'objective' measures, such as outside observation by cantonal experts.

Table 4.3: Cumul des mandats *in cantonal parliaments*

Canton	Mayor MCPs	LMCP1	LMCP2	LMCP3
GL	3	5.00%	100.00%	52.5%
AI	5	10.20%	83.33%	46.77%
TG	26	20.00%	32.50%	26.25%
AR	7	10.77%	35.00%	22.88%
LU	16	9.41%	18.18%	13.8%
GR	20	16.67%	10.53%	13.6%
SH	5	6.25%	18.52%	12.38%
FR	16	14.55%	9.52%	10.92%
BL	8	8.89%	9.30%	9.1%
AG	19	9.50%	8.30%	9.07%
SO	11	7.64%	8.80%	8.22%
OW	1	1.82%	14.29%	8.05%
TI	8	8.89%	4.42%	6.65%
ZH	11	6.11%	6.43%	6.27%
VD	15	10.00%	4.00%	6.17%
VS	8	6.15%	5.59%	5.87%
NW	1	1.67%	9.09%	5.38%
BE	14	7.00%	3.57%	5.29%
ZG	1	1.25%	9.09%	5.17%
JU	3	5.00%	4.69%	4.84%
SZ	2	2.00%	6.67%	4.33%
SG	4	2.22%	4.65%	3.44%
NE	2	1.74%	3.77%	2.76%
GE	1	1.00%	2.22%	1.61%
BS	0	0%	0%	0%
UR	0	0%	0%	0%

Note: Mayors include a Stadtpräsident, Landammann, Gemeindeammann, Stadtammann, Gemeindepräsident, Präsident des Gemeinderates (BE and LU), Bezirkshauptmann (AI), syndic (VD and FR), président du Conseil communal (NE), président de commune (VS), maire (JU and GE) and sindaco (TI). Own calculations based on websites and e-mail correspondence [February 2011]. Data sorted by last column.

A second indicator that can easily be calculated relates the number of mayor MCPs to the total number of LGs in a canton (LMCP2). The figure reaches 100 per cent in Glarus, where since January 2011 all three mayors have sat in the *Landrat*. Appenzell Inner-Rhodes obtains a share of 83 per cent, but the only other two cantons with very high scores are Appenzell Outer-Rhodes and Thurgau. If LMCP1 captures *efficiency* likelihood, LMCP2 captures *representativeness*.

To combine both indicators using the mean obscures high values on either, but every other way would result in a significant loss of information. LMCP3 thus shows the four leaders (Glarus, Appenzell Inner-Rhodes, Thurgau and Appenzell Outer-Rhodes) in terms of the potential of LGs both to a) efficiently influence the proceedings within a cantonal parliament with b) a high degree of outside representativeness. In these cantons, municipalities are clearly better positioned to do this and political decentralisation on this aspect is, therefore, higher than in Basel-City, Uri, Geneva or Neuchâtel.

Direct representation can also find expression in specifically designed, 'territorial' second chambers, embodying shared-rule (Fleiner 2000). However, none of the cantons has a second chamber. What we find, instead, in some cantons are quotas providing for regional/local representation. I additionally code the presence of *territorial quotas*, i.e. a fixed number of seats in either the cantonal executive or the legislative for specific territories, as indicative of such decentralisation. The two can be separated because in the Swiss cantons, both branches – and sometimes even the judicial branch – are elected by popular vote, necessitating an electoral system properly speaking (Shugart 2005).

The only cantons that *explicitly* provide territorial quotas are Valais and Berne. In Valais, of the five cantonal executive seats, only two are actually elected over the whole canton; of the other three, one each must come from one of the three regions, which are aggregations of (contiguous) districts (Art. 52 CC VS). One region comprises a German-speaking majority of residents, also known as *Oberwallis*. In Berne, a similar provision exists, but this time for executive *and* parliamentary elections (Arts. 73 and 84 CC BE). The 'Bernese Jura' mentioned in both articles is the region comprising the three French-speaking districts of Berne. I code the presence of territorial quotas at 2, and add the scores for legislative and executive elections: 4 for Berne, 2 for Valais and 0 for all other cantons.

Finally, localism can find its way into cantonal processes also through *lobbying*. Although many associations exist and their usefulness can be debated, especially in small cantons (*see* Geser 1981), for the present purpose, I follow Page (1991, 43–50) and code a canton from 0 (centralised) to 4 (decentralised), taking into account the existence of one or more cantonal Local Government Associations (LGAs). Column A in Table 4.4 lists them by name; followed by their degree of institutionalisation, a functioning website indicating a permanent and professional structure (B); whether the LGA statutes are publicly available, indicating a legal personality (C); as well as the existence of a special group in the cantonal parliament to represent and lobby for local interests (D), e.g. the 'Club des Communes' in Fribourg. I then add the scores for each aspect.

In sum, the presence of prefects is taken to indicate centralisation, all the more so if no accountability via regional elections is provided. Only two cantons, Berne and Valais, provide for explicit territorial quotas. Mayors holding parliamentary office on the cantonal level, on the other hand, indicate a decentralisation of politics, all the more so if backed up by a strong LGA outside and a special 'communal group' inside the cantonal parliament. Next to localism and regionalism so measured, a third important aspect relates to political party organisation, to which I turn next.

Table 4.4: Direct localism in the Swiss cantons

	A: Local Government Association	B	C	D	Total
BE	Verband Bernischer Gemeinden	1	1	1	4
FR	Association des communes fribourgeoises / Freiburger Gemeindeverband	1	1	1	4
SO	Verband Solothurner Einwohnergemeinden	1	1	1	4
GE	Association des communes genevoises	1	1	0.5	3.5
VD	Union des communes vaudoises	1	1	0.5	3.5
ZH	Gemeindepräsidentenverband des Kantons ZH	1	1	0.5	3.5
LU	Verband Luzerner Gemeinden	1	1	0.25	3.25
BL	Verband der GemeindepräsidentInnen BL	1	1	0	3
VS	Comité de la Fédération des communes valaisannes / Verband der Walliser Gemeinden	1	1	0	3
GR	Interessengemeinschaft Kleingemeinden GR	0	0	1*	3
	Verband Bündnerischer Bürgergemeinden	0	0		
JU	Association jurassienne des communes	0	0		
	Associations de maires dans le district de Delémont	0	0	0	3
	Ass. de maires dans le dist. des Franches-Montagnes	0	0		
NE	Association des communes neuchâteloises	1	1	0	3
SZ	Verband Schwyzer Gemeinden und Bezirke	1	1	0	3
TG	Verband Thurgauer Gemeinden	1	1	0	3
TI	Associazione dei comuni urbani Ticinesi	0	0	0.5	3
	Associazione comuni e regioni montagne ticinesi	0.5	0		
UR	Urner Gemeindeverband	1	0	0.5	2.5
AG	Gemeindeammänner-Vereinigung des Kantons AG	1	0	0	2
SG	Vereinigung St. Galler GemeindepräsidentInnen	1	0	0	2
SH	Gemeindepräsidentenkonferenz des Kantons SH	0	0	0.25	1.25
AI	Hauptleutekonferenz des Kantons AI	0	0	0	1
AR	Gemeindepräsidentenkonferenz des Kantons AR	0	0	0	1
NW	Gemeindepräsidentenkonferenz des Kantons NW	0	0	0	1
OW	Gemeindepräsidentenkonferenz des Kantons OW	0	0	0	1
ZG	Gemeindepräsidentenkonferenz des Kantons ZG	0	0	0	1
BS	(*none*)	0	0	0	0
GL	(*none*)	0	0	0	0
Total	28 cantonal LGAs	15.5	12	7	62.5

Note: A: name, if existent (coded as 1), of the cantonal LG association; B: functioning website (coded as 1) or special URL (.5); C: association statutes publicly available; D: intra-parliamentary group (coded as 1), permanent committee (.5), or special/extraordinary committee on LG affairs (.25); * planned at time of data gathering [February 2011]. Sorted by last column

Cantonal 'party federalism'

The recruitment function of political parties is highlighted in Switzerland – and, by extension, in the Swiss cantons – due to the generally very extensive channels for direct democracy. Issue-based debates are thus largely removed from party politics, which make measures of policy formulating (Janda 1980), party system congruence (Thorlakson 2007), or election programmes (Fabre 2011) questionable as to their relevance for capturing the essential functions of cantonal parties. The 'anatomy of parties' (Sartori 2005 [1976]: 66) is therefore best measured through assessing candidate selection procedures, for it is here that Swiss parties really function as *political* parties. It would also be methodologically redundant to include measures of leadership concentration (Janda 1980) or even of cantonal or local leader selection (Fabre 2011): *all* cantonal parties have local branches (or neighbourhood sections, in Basel-City), *all* provide for internal democracy, and *each* level is more or less left its own sphere of action ('stratarchy', for Carty 2004).

This, and the theoretical reasons elaborated earlier on, lead me to focus on candidate-selection, i.e. the extent to which the cantonal level dominates the selection procedure or how much autonomy local/district parties have in nominating candidates. I thus posit that if all or most of the political parties in a canton *select the candidates for cantonal parliamentary elections* at the *cantonal* level, the canton is centralised; if all or most of them select these candidates *locally*, a system is decentralised. I only look at the four 'national' parties SP, CVP, FDP and SVP to ensure comparability: apart from Appenzell Inner-Rhodes, where neither SP[11] nor FDP exist, all of those four exist in all the cantons; in Valais, they even exist in a French- and in a German-speaking version, making for a total of 106 cantonal parties. Adapted from Fabre (2011), the cantonal score is determined by the average of the party scores, which I code as follows:

- 0 = Candidate selection done entirely at cantonal level with no formalised regional or local inputs (=centralised organisation).
- 1 = Candidate selection done at cantonal level with some (e.g. consultative or indirect) regional or local input.
- 2 = District-level nominations subject to cantonal-level approval, or done by a special electoral commission with local and cantonal representatives.
- 3 = Local nominations subject to cantonal-level approval, or district-level nominations not subject to cantonal-level approval.
- 4 = Candidate selection done entirely at local level, or local nominations subject only to district-level approval (=confederal organisation).

The maximum value per canton is 4, indicating that all candidate-selection for cantonal parliamentary elections is localised. The minimum value is 0, which would mean a fully cantonalised candidate selection procedure for all four – or eight, in Valais, or two, in Appenzell Inner-Rhodes – cantonal political parties.

---

11. An SP was founded in Appenzell Inner-Rhodes only in summer 2012 (NZZ of 20 August 2012, p. 12).

Table 4.5 displays the body or level responsible for candidate selection for each party in each canton, as well as the average scores per canton. Ranking is by cantonal score, with the most decentralised cantons at the top, the most centralised ones at the bottom.

Elections

The process-aspect of the politics-dimension, finally, is best captured by operationalising the territoriality of the electoral system and, for Switzerland, that of direct-democratic instruments. On the first, I code a canton as 4 if the constituencies perfectly correspond to the municipalities, indicating a complete localisation of elections: by design, communes will have one of 'their' representatives in the cantonal parliament. At the other end of the scale, I code a canton as 0 if the whole territory is just one constituency, as in Geneva and Ticino, where no guarantee for territorial representation is built into the electoral system.[12] Table 4.6 shows this *index of electoral decentralisation*.

The use of special electoral districts I code as 1: they provide at least some territorial dimension to parliamentary elections. The use of administrative districts on the other hand I code as 2: to territorial distinctiveness is now added a certain sense of regional identity, fostered and perpetuated by administrative structures, e.g. the court system in Aargau (Rühli 2012: 38). This makes for more decentralisation than mere special electoral districts. Finally, the use of 'historic' regions (the *Kreise* in Grisons) as well the splitting up of administrative districts into smaller constituencies (in Basel-Countryside and Zurich) I code as 3: not fully localised, but more so than using simple administrative districts as constituencies.

Direct democracy

The very final dimension of cantonal politics-decentralisation concerns direct democracy. This element may be peculiar to Switzerland, but other polities also know such instruments; even in the EU the 'Citizen Initiative' has recently been added to strengthen the democratic legitimacy of the polity. For the Swiss cantons, Fiechter (2010: 76) lists how, in several cantons, LGs have the possibility to amend the cantonal constitution, propose a new cantonal law, and/or challenge a legal, fiscal or 'otherwise important' decision by the cantonal parliament. The first two options are summarised as 'communal initiative', the last one as 'communal referendum' (*see also* Schmitt and Gassmann 2005: xvii).

In most cases, either potentiality is exercised by the local executive; however, communes are usually free to decide who within them can demand the instrument. Only if the cities of Zurich or Winterthur alone challenge a cantonal decision must this be decided by their local parliaments. In Obwalden, even individual members

---

12. Although, at least, in Ticino informal provisions within the parties exist; many thanks to Oscar Mazzoleni and Nenad Stojanovic for pointing this out to me.

Table 4.5: Cantonal party decentralisation

Canton	SP	FDP	CVP	SVP	AVRG
SZ	(not mentioned)	(not mentioned)	Orts- and Bezirksparteien	General assembly 'positioning'	4.0
OW	(missing)	(not mentioned)	(missing)	General assembly 'positioning'	4.0
NW	(missing)	(not mentioned)	(missing)	General assembly 'positioning'	4.0
GL	Cantonal coordination	Cantonal coordination	Cantonal coordination	Cantonal coordination	4.0
AI	n.a.	n.a.	(not mentioned)	(missing)	4.0
GR	(not mentioned)	(not mentioned)	Kreisparteien	(not mentioned)	4.0
ZG	(not mentioned)	(not mentioned)	(not mentioned)	Members assembly on list apparentements	3.8
UR	(not mentioned)	(not mentioned)	Ortsparteien	Electoral committee	3.5
SO	Bezirks- or Amteiparteien	Ortspartei → Bezirks- or Amteiparteien	Amteiparteien	Ortsparteien → Amteiparteien	3.5
VS-d	Sektionen → Parteikongress	(not mentioned)	(not mentioned)	Bezirkssektionen	3.5
JU	Fédérations de districts → (cantonal) Congrès	(missing)	(missing)	(not mentioned)	3.5
LU	Amtsparteien	Wahlkreisverbände	Amtsparteien	Amtsparteien	3.3
AR	Delegates assembly 'positioning'	Ortsparteien → delegates assembly	(not mentioned)	Executive Committee → electoral commission	3.3
AG	Sektionen → Bezirksparteien	Bezirksparteien	Bezirksparteien	Bezirksparteitag	3.3
VS-f	Fédérations de districts	Association du district/régionale (=séctions and groupements locaux of the constituency)	(not mentioned)	Séctions de district	3.3
FR	Fédérations de districts	(missing)	Regionalparteien	Bezirkssektionen	3.0
SG	Kreisparteien	Regionalparteien	Regionalparteien	Kreisparteien	3.0
TG	Bezirksparteien	Bezirksparteien	Ort- and Bezirksparteien	Bezirksparteien	3.0

Table 4.5 (continued)

Canton	SP	FDP	CVP	SVP	AVRG
VD	Assemblée générale de la Régionale (=constituency)	(missing)	Séctions locales, grouped by constituency; assemblée générale for apparentements	Séctions de districts	3.0
ZH	Bezirksparteien propose	Bezirksparteien propose	Bezirksparteien	General assembly 'positioning'	2.8
BE	Regionalverbände	Kreisparteien	Cantonal delegates	Sektionen → Wahlkreisverbände	2.8
BL	Nomination: Sektionen, Approval: cantonal delegates	Wahlkreisparteien	Parteitag	(not mentioned)	2.8
SH	Bezirkswahlparteitage (=Sektionen of constituency)	Parteitag	Orts- and Bezirksparteien	Kreisparteien (consisting of Sektionen, meets 2 years before elections)	2.8
NE	Comité de région	Districts and séctions	(missing)	Assemblée générale; but séctions with 'total autonomy'	2.7
TI	Congresso (=cantonal)	Assemblea dei rappresentanti (district level, of local mayors) → Comitato Cantonale	Comitato cantonale (=district delegates and other members)	District sections → comitato cantonale	1.5
BS	Delegates assembly (Sektionen represented)	Parteitag	Parteiversammlung	General assembly 'positioning'	1.3
GE	Assemblée générale extraordinaire	Commission des listes and assemblée des délégués	Assemblée des délégués	Assemblée générale	0.5

Notes: '(not mentioned)' = not mentioned in cantonal party statute, so local/regional section competent by default; '(missing)' = information missing (as of 26 Feb 2011), '→' = the act of proposing candidates to another body or level; Ortsparteien, Sektionen and séctions = local level parties; Bezirksparteien, Bezirkssektionen, Amteiparteien, Amtsparteien, (Wahl-) Kreisparteien, Fédérations de districts, Regionalverbände and Regionalparteien = regional/district-level parties; 'VS-f' and 'VS-d' = French-speaking and German-speaking parts of Canton Valais, respectively. If candidate selection is not mentioned in the cantonal party statute, I assume that the local level has sole responsibility ('residual powers').

Table 4.6: Cantonal electoral decentralisation

Canton	No. and name of constituencies	Score
UR	24 Gemeinden	4
SZ	30 Gemeinden	4
OW	7 Gemeinden	4
NW	11 Gemeinden	4
GL	3 Gemeinden	4
ZG	11 Gemeinden	4
BS	5 Wahlkreise	4
AR	20 Gemeinden	4
AI	6 Bezirke *(=LGs)*	4
ZH	18 Wahlkreise	3
BL	12 Wahlkreise	3
GR	39 Kreise	3
FR	8 Wahlkreise/cercle électoraux	2
SO	5 Amteien	2
AG	11 Bezirke	2
TG	5 Bezirke	2
VS	14 Wahlkreise/cercles électoraux	2
NE	6 districts	2
JU	3 circonscriptions	2
BE	9 Wahlkreise/cercles électoraux	1
LU	6 Wahlkreise	1
SH	6 Wahlkreise	1
SG	8 Wahlkreise	1
VD	13 arrondissements	1
TI	1 *(cantonal territory)*	0
GE	1 *(cantonal territory)*	0
Average score		**2.5**

of the local executive can file a *Volksmotion*. In all but two cases the procedure ends with a binding popular vote regardless of what the cantonal parliament says, that is the cantonal electorate has the final say; in Zurich, the communal initiative only ensues in a popular vote if a majority of MCPs are supportive, and the same in Obwalden for both instruments. Table 4.7 lists the type, requirements and only ever usages to date of such local power over cantonal politics.

In all this, communes do not have to act through bilateral negotiations or 'second chambers'. Instead, they can directly influence cantonal policy-making, all but bypassing the cantonal authorities. However, their veto is suspensive and

Table 4.7: Overview of direct-democratic decentralisation

Canton	Type	Bearer	Requirements	Usage	Legal Basis
Communal initiative					
NW	leg. & fiscal	local executive	1 LG	–	Arts. 54.4 & 55.4 CC NW
ZH	leg. & const.	local executive	1 LG & majority of MCPs	2006/11	Arts. 23, 24.b & 31.1 CC ZH
BL	leg. & const.	local executive	5 LGs	–	Art. 49 CC BL
JU	leg. & const.	local executive	8 LGs	–	Art. 75.1 CC JU
SO	leg. & const.	local executive	10 LGs	**2009**	Art. 30.3 CC SO
GR	constitutional	local executive	1/7 of all LGs	–	Art. 12.1 CC GR
	legislative	local executive	1/8 of all LGs	–	Art. 12.2 CC GR
TI	legislative	local executive	1/5 of all LGs	**2005/10**	Art. 41.1 CC TI
OW	leg. & fiscal	every member of local executive	1 local councillor & majority of MCPs	2011	Art. 61.2 CC OW
Communal referendum					
NW	leg. & fiscal	local executive	1 LG	–	Arts. 54.4 & 55.4 CC NW
TI	leg. & fiscal	local executive	1/5 of all LGs	–	Art. 42 CC TI
BL	legislative	local executive	5 LGs	–	Arts. 31.2 & 49.1(b) CC BL
JU	leg. & fiscal	local executive	8 LGs	**2008/09**	Art. 78 CC JU
GR	leg. & fiscal	local executive	1/10 of all LGs	–	Art. 17.1 CC GR
SO	leg. & fiscal	local executive	5 LGs	2004	Art. 36 CC SO
ZH	leg. & fiscal	local executive	12 LGs	–	Arts. 33.2(b) & 33.4 CC ZH
		local parliament	Zurich city or Winterthur	**2008/10**	
OW	leg. & fiscal	every member of local executive	1 local councillor & majority of MCPs	–	Art. 61.2 CC OW
LU	leg. & fiscal	local executive	1/4 of all LGs	–	Art. 25 CC LU

Note: bold = successful usages; Source: Fiechter (2010) and own compilation based on media and official websites (see footnotes 13 to 15).

their proposal material for discussion only, because the electorate has the final say and no 'double majority' of citizens and LGs, as on the federal level for citizens and cantons, is required. Nationally, the referendum 'has become the most common weapon with which to challenge the authorities. […] it hangs, like the sword of Damocles, as a permanent threat above the political process' (Trechsel and Kriesi 1996: 192). But what is the situation at the cantonal level?

Communal referenda have been successful in two out of three attempts thus far. In Jura, it was used for the first time in May 2008, when 17 (out of then 83) LGs called for a popular vote on a new framework law for water (Gassmann 2009). But in the ensuing vote, 54 per cent of citizens rejected the new law. In Zurich, the *Gemeindereferendum* was used for the first time in December 2010, when the city parliament of Zurich challenged a new fiscal law. The electorate then narrowly rejected the law on 17 June 2012: although 111 LGs (out of 185, i.e. 60 per cent) and 154,075 citizens accepted it, since only a popular majority was required the 43,441 no-votes from within the city of Zurich were enough to tip the final score against the law: 154,982 citizens said no. Unsuccessful was the LGA of Solothurn, who coordinated a referendum in which 33 LGs (out of 126) challenged the repartition of user charges for issuing new passports as 'unfair'. In the popular vote of 16 May 2004, however, more than 60 per cent agreed with the new directive.[13]

Communal initiatives, on the other hand, have failed twice out of the only four times in which they have ever been attempted, and even the two successes are only partial. In Obwalden, all seven municipalities recently petitioned the canton to rethink the shifting of additional health care costs downwards. But because the cantonal parliament flatly rejected the *Volksmotion*, no popular vote took place. In Zurich, in 2006, 42 LG executives demanded a stop to the further extension of Zurich Airport by modifying the respective legislative act. The cantonal parliament accepted the motion by 100:64, but a popular vote took place because it was demanded by a parliamentary minority. On 27 November 2011, 58 per cent of the electorate rejected the communal initiative.[14]

The only two successful examples of communal initiatives are indirect. The first comes from Ticino, where in 2005 17 municipalities demanded a modification of the repartition of water charges between communes and canton. Eventually, 59 other communes supported the initiative. The cantonal government rejected the demand but proposed to modify the law on fiscal equalisation, which was what everything was really about. After the cantonal parliament accepted an indirect counter-proposal with 60:16, the initiative was withdrawn in October 2010.

---

13. On Jura, information at 'Les Jurassiens font barrage à la loi sur la gestion des eaux', at http://www.aqueduc.info/Les-Jurassiens-font-barrage-a-la;, results at http://w3.jura.ch/votation/m-votat.htm. On Zurich, information and results both at http://www.statistik.zh.ch/internet/justiz_inneres/statistik/de/wahlen_abstimmungen/abstimmungsarchiv.html and for Solothurn at http://www.so.ch/staatskanzlei/politische-rechte/archiv-wahlen-abstimmungen/2004 (all last accessed 7 March 2015).

14. On Obwalden, *see* '*Volksmotion der Obwaldner Gemeinden abgeblitzt*', Schweizer Radio DRS, 29 September 2011, at http://www.drs.ch/www/de/drs/nachrichten/regional/zentralschweiz/296993.volksmotion-der-obwaldner-gemeinden-abgeblitzt.html. On Zurich, information and results at http://www.statistik.zh.ch/internet/justiz_inneres/statistik/de/wahlen_abstimmungen/abstimmungsarchiv.html (last accessed 7 March 2015).

Without a popular vote, the initiative was thus successful in reorganising the water charges in a way that would get mountain communes a bigger share of 'their' water. A similarly indirect success took place in Solothurn: in May 2009, the cantonal LGA launched a legislative initiative, signed up for by 86 LGs, to more than double the contribution of the canton towards teachers' salaries, from 25 to 55 per cent. As in Ticino, the initiative was withdrawn after the cantonal government agreed to a reform of the fiscal equalisation scheme.[15] In sum, although few in number, direct-democratic instruments have had an effect in at least four cases: two on water, one on taxes, one on schools – but all to do with money and within the last four years. Where does all this leave us for measuring cantonal decentralisation?

In order to take this variety into account, it is best to start deductively. Initiatives are 'worth more' than referenda, for they are positive instruments in view of enacting new legislation, while referenda are purely reactive. Rather than coding cantons simply through a dummy variable on whether they provide for local shared rule or not, as Fiechter (2010: 78) proposes, and instead of calculating the share of LGs required per total LGs, as Schmitt and Gassmann (2005: xix) advocate, I proceed in ordinal steps. Cantons thus score highest (4) on my *index of direct-democratic decentralisation* if LGs have the power *both* to propose cantonal constitutional provisions *and* veto cantonal ordinary legislation (as in Solothurn, Basel-Countryside, Grisons and Jura), or if the right can be exercised by as few as one single (private or 'communal') voter, at the *Landsgemeinde* of Glarus and Appenzell Inner-Rhodes.[16] They score 3 if the constitutional initiative is replaced with a *legislative* initiative, meaning that LGs are restricted in what they can initiate (as in Ticino). Cantons score 1 if LGs possess only one instrument, i.e. they can either launch a legislative initiative (as in Nidwalden) *or* veto cantonal laws (as in Lucerne). Finally, since in Zurich the local initiative must be endorsed by parliament first, this is not a real initiative but rather a half-initiative, while the right to challenge cantonal acts is perfectly established and, as for Zurich and Winterthur, a single city may call for it. This certainly makes for a more localised direct-democratic system than in Nidwalden or Lucerne, but less than in Ticino, where local initiatives result in cantonal votes anyway. I thus code Zurich 2, together with Obwalden, and all other cantons 0.

---

15. On Ticino, *see 'Iniziativa elaborata per la ripartizione dei canoni d'acqua tra Cantone, commune e patriziati – Rapporto del Gruppo lavoro'*, 24 June/11 November 2005, at http://www4.ti.ch/fileadmin/DFE/DR-UE/politica/Osservazioni_Iniziativa_canoni_acqua.pdf, and *'Passa la modifica della Legge sulla perequazione finanziaria'*, Ticino online, 18 October 2010, at http://www.tio.ch/Ticino/Politica/News/592417/Passa-la-modifica-della-Legge-sulla-perequazione-finanziaria/Scrivi. On Solothurn, http://www.vseg.ch/gemeindeinitiative and 'Rückzug der Gemeindeinitiative', DRS 1 Regionaljoural Aargau Solothurn, 29 April 2010, at http://www.drs1.ch/www/de/drs1/sendungen/regionaljournal-aargau-solothurn/2744.bt10134072.html (all last accessed 17 September 2012).

16. It is very common for mayors to speak on the behalf of 'their' municipality, explicitly or implicitly by being announced as 'the president of the municipality XY'; *see* Mueller 2007.

A composite index of politics-decentralisation

Thus far, I have discussed and measured seven distinctive aspects of the politics-dimension of cantonal decentralisation: regionalism (district assemblies and prefects), *cumul des mandats* (mayor MCPs), territorial quotas (for the legislative and executive branch), the strength of LGAs, party decentralisation (as regards candidate selection for cantonal parliament elections), the number and size of constituencies and direct democracy (communal referendum and initiative). Values for each canton are listed in the Data Appendix.

How can these seven measures now be combined into a single, composite measure? A scale-analysis reveals that overall correlation is rather low,[17] so there is either more than one dimension inherent in the dataset or some measures point into a different direction. Goertz (2006) advises that concept formation should correspond to concept measurement as closely as possible. Thinking in terms of a 'substitutability continuum' (2006: 45), the question then is whether one or several of these measures are indispensable to politics-decentralisation, and whether some of them can substitute for some other aspects. In other words, can party decentralisation *compensate* for lack of indirect local representation? Or is politics decentralised only if *both* candidate-selection is localised *and* indirect local representation high? The answer is a mixture of both, as the first factor analysis presented in Table 4.8 reveals.[18]

In this analysis, and using .35 as the threshold (*see* Vatter 2002: 399), a first component is positively correlated mainly to localised constituencies, the extent of regionalism and party decentralisation, but negatively correlated to the strength of LGAs. In other words: where LGs are ensured representation through localised constituencies, regionalism and/or party decentralisation, LGAs can afford to be weak, so the latter compensates for the absence of the former

Table 4.8: Two factor analyses for cantonal politics-decentralisation

Measure	Three-Components Solution			Single-Component Solution
	1	2	3	
LG constituencies	0.794	0.293	−0.281	0.832
Regionalism	0.727	−0.081	0.195	0.371
Strength of LGAs	−0.640	−0.085	0.574	−0.709
Direct democracy	−0.116	0.818	−0.069	0.457
Mayor MCPs	0.159	0.750	−0.204	0.654
Party decentralisation	0.493	0.619	0.120	0.677
Territorial quotas	0.054	−0.107	0.884	−0.366

---

17. Cronbach's alpha = .123 (seven items).

18. Principal component analysis, rotation using the Varimax Kaiser Normalisation method (converged in five iterations). Bartlett's Test of Sphericity: $X^2 = 39.793$ (p < .01).

three elements. This component explains 37 per cent of the variance. A second component correlates strongly with the extent of direct democracy, direct local representation both in relation to MCPs within parliament and LGs outside of it, and again party decentralisation. This component explains another 18 per cent of the overall variance. A third component finally, explaining 15 per cent of the variance, is positively correlated with territorial quotas and the strength of LGAs only.

However, notably party decentralisation loads onto two components, and for some measures the correlation is negative with some, but positive with other components. Due to a lack of prior empirical assessments on what each measure actually means, and to facilitate the later quantitative analysis, I rely on a simple regression analysis to combine the seven indicators into a composite index. We currently lack data on the voting behaviour of (mayor and non-mayor) MCPs to fully assess whether their presence really works along the lines hypothesised here. In the expert survey conducted by Rühli (2012: 56), local influence is reported to be high in *all* cantons, regardless of the number or share of mayor MCPs. Nevertheless, communes perceive their influence to be highest when they can delegate a member of a permanent or project-specific working group, not when working through 'their' representatives in the cantonal parliament (2012: 176) where they have to compete with party interests, but the likelihood to sit in these groups rises in proportion to the number of mayor MCPs.

Relying on the result of a factor analysis that searches for a single factor only is equivalent to calculating cantonal politics-decentralisation as a function of these seven measures (last column in Table 4.8). Figure 4.7 thus ranks the Swiss cantons by their degree of politics-decentralisation. Glarus and Appenzell Inner-Rhodes are politically the most decentralised cantons, the *Landsgemeinde* providing a direct voice for individual citizens (and municipalities), with a high share of mayor MCPs (at least in relation to the number of LGs) and each commune being guaranteed a seat in the cantonal parliament by design of the electoral system. They are followed by the other small German-speaking cantons and Grisons. Geneva and Ticino, where the canton forms the only constituency, but also Berne and Fribourg with elected prefects, district constituencies and strong LGAs, as well as Lucerne and Valais with appointed prefects, are among the most centralised cantons on this dimension. It is now time to bring the three measures back together again.

Final index of cantonal decentralisation

In developing a politics-measure of cantonal decentralisation, the second section of this chapter has filled a gap in the study of (de)centralisation in general, and of cantonal-local relations in particular. Existing general analyses, discussed in Chapters One and Two, have only rarely taken the politics-dimension into account when studying the territorial organisation of political systems. At best, aspects of it have been studied in the respective sub-fields, e.g. party decentralisation

Figure 4.7: Politics-decentralisation in the Swiss cantons

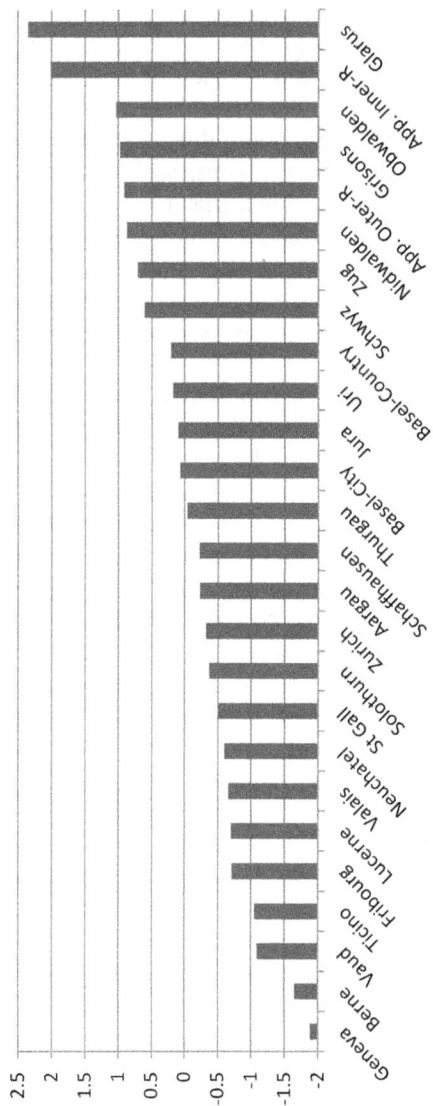

in party politics (Fabre 2011; Thorlakson 2010; Janda 1980). Studies of cantonal decentralisation in Switzerland, on the other hand, not only avoid the term decentralisation, but in so doing focus on the local (e.g. Rühli 2012 and Fiechter 2010) level exclusively, rather than adopting a holistic view on 'cantonal democracies' (Vatter 2002) and centring on the *relations* between the two levels which, for example, includes the role of prefects.

I have discussed seven aspects of cantonal *politics* as regards its territorial organisation. A first set of factors pertains to elections: in some cantons the whole canton forms a single constituency (Geneva, Ticino), whereas in others the municipalities are, by design, guaranteed a seat in the cantonal parliament (e.g. in Glarus). I then measured the position of prefects and district assemblies, special quotas to protect territorially grouped minorities (in Berne and Valais), and the organisation of cantonal political parties in view of candidate selection. Another important dimension of politics is the way and degree to which Local Governments are represented and how they lobby for their interests through special associations and even parliamentary groups, such as the 'Club des Communes' in the Fribourg parliament. Switzerland being a semi-direct democracy, the way in which LGs *qua* LGs have a chance to partake in cantonal politics is the third important element of politics-decentralisation. The fact that Zurich introduced this element in 2004, and that in several other cantons such instruments have also *and* only quite recently been used, attests to the veracity of this proposition.

Conventional indicators of cantonal decentralisation, on the other hand, cover the legal-constitutional or the fiscal, personnel and administrative sides of it. The scope of local autonomy directly links with Watts' (2008: 172) *polity*-focus on the 'scope of jurisdiction' and 'degree of autonomy' as well as Burgess' (2006a) 'constitutional entrenchment'. Keeping with Wheare's (1963) own advice that legal norms alone do not suffice to establish a polity's territorial character, a more realistic picture of decentralisation is provided by looking at the *policy*-dimension: what is spent/raised by which level and how are policies administered? However, none of the existing indices measures the politics-dimension, except maybe for the surveys of cantonal secretaries. Figure 4.8 shows the full structure of cantonal decentralisation conceptualised and measured through these three dimensions.

Clearly distinguishing between the three dimensions enables me to now aggregate them into a single index. I took it that (de)centralisation is a political system-attribute. As such, it pertains to all of its three dimensions: institutions as legally codified and subjectively perceived; the financing and implementation of public policies; and political actors such as parties, mayors and LGAs, as well as democratic processes such as elections and communal referenda and initiatives. But how should the three dimensions be aggregated and, more importantly still, is the assumption of three dimensions really supported by the empirical data? To answer that last question, I have run a factor analysis with all the 12 indicators of cantonal decentralisation. The result is that yes, there are three dimensions, but they are obviously not as neat and tight as assumed. Table 4.9 lists the three

Figure 4.8: Concept-structure of cantonal decentralisation

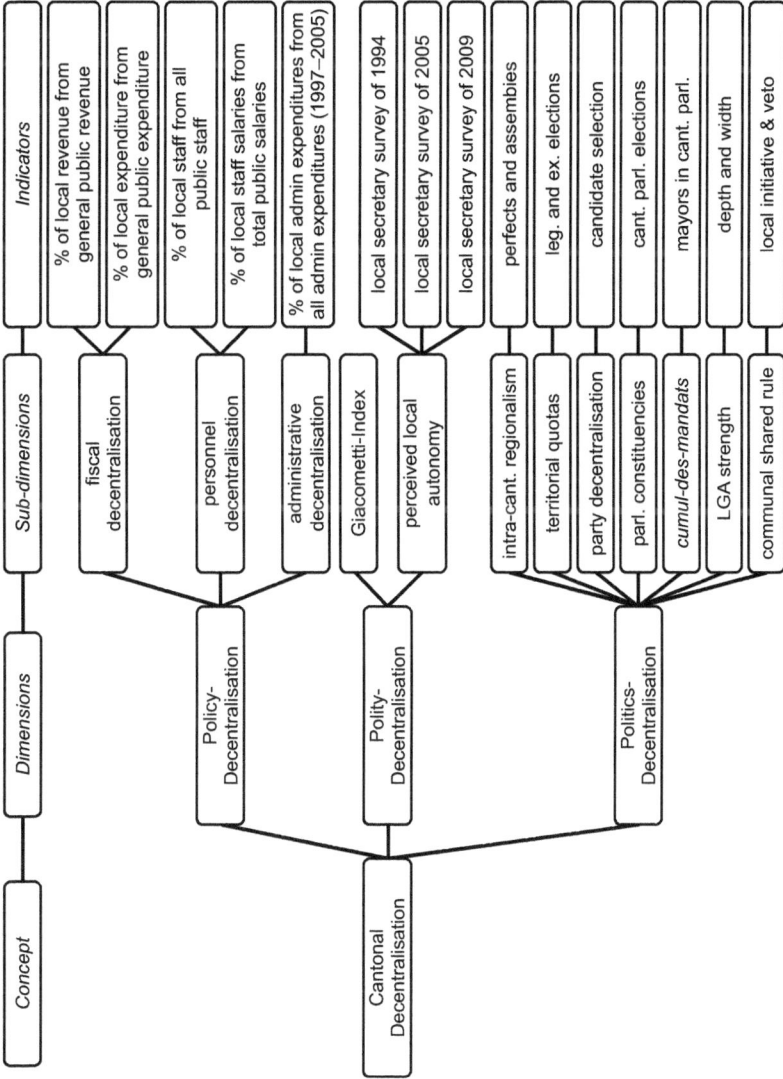

Table 4.9: Factor analysis for cantonal decentralisation

Indicators	Components		
	1	2	3
DV1: fiscal decentralisation (2005/2008)	−.085	.936	−.092
DV2: personnel decentralisation (2008)	.407	.792	.079
DV3: administrative decentralisation (1997–2003)	−.213	.863	.012
DV4: Giacometti-index	.747	.298	.353
DV5: perceived LG autonomy (1994, 2005 and 2009)	.885	.173	−.069
DV6: regionalism index (2011)	.478	.003	−.102
DV7: types of territorial quotas (2011)	−.080	.219	−.551
DV8: party decentralisation (2011)	.507	.614	.292
DV9: constituency index	.824	−.084	.274
DV10: Mayor MCPs (2011)	.249	.168	.696
DV11: strength of LG associations (2011)	−.768	.331	−.258
DV12: direct-democratic decentralisation (2011)	−.095	.127	.827

components that result from that test:[19] While the first two components match perfectly onto the *policy-* and *polity-*dimensions of (de)centralisation, the same cannot be said of the indicators for politics-decentralisation. Only indicators 7, 10 and 12 clearly load onto a different component.

Nevertheless, a reliability test of the three standardised dimensions as calculated in the first two sections of this chapter reveals a sufficiently large commonality.[20] Accordingly, Figure 4.9 ranks the 26 Swiss cantons by their degree of overall decentralisation calculated as the arithmetic mean of its three (standardised) dimensions.[21]

The ranking displayed in Figure 4.9 contains a basic confirmation of, but also a few surprises that seem to go against, the standard wisdom on cantonal-local relations in Switzerland. Confirming such wisdom are the positions of the

19. Principal component analysis, rotation using the Varimax Kaiser Normalisation method (converged in four iterations). Bartlett's Test of Sphericity: X^2 = 162.665 (p < .01).

20. Cronbach's alpha = .688 (three items). Especially politics- and polity-decentralisation are strongly correlated (Pearson's r = .721, p < .01). The correlation between polity- and policy-decentralisation is .439 (p < .05), that between policy- and politics-decentralisation .119 (p = .564).

21. Alternatively, I have run a factor analysis as in Table 4.9, where it was specified that only one component should be extracted. The regression-based factor scores from this are basically the same as those presented in Figure 4.9 (Pearson's r = .966, p < .01). Nor do the results of all subsequent analyses change if these factor scores are used in place of the much more intuitive and transparent aggregate.

Figure 4.9: Swiss cantons by their degree of decentralisation

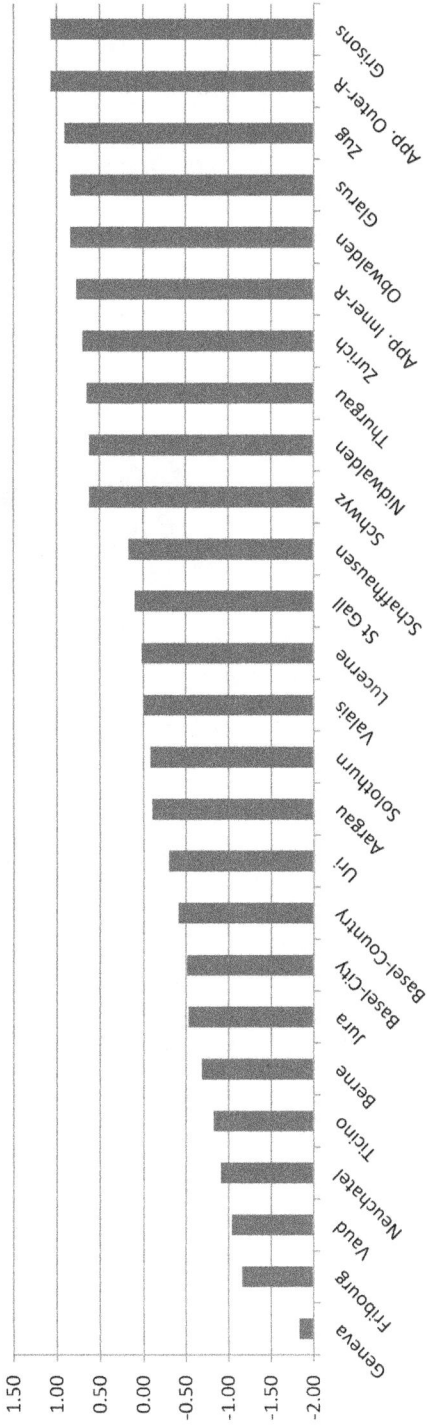

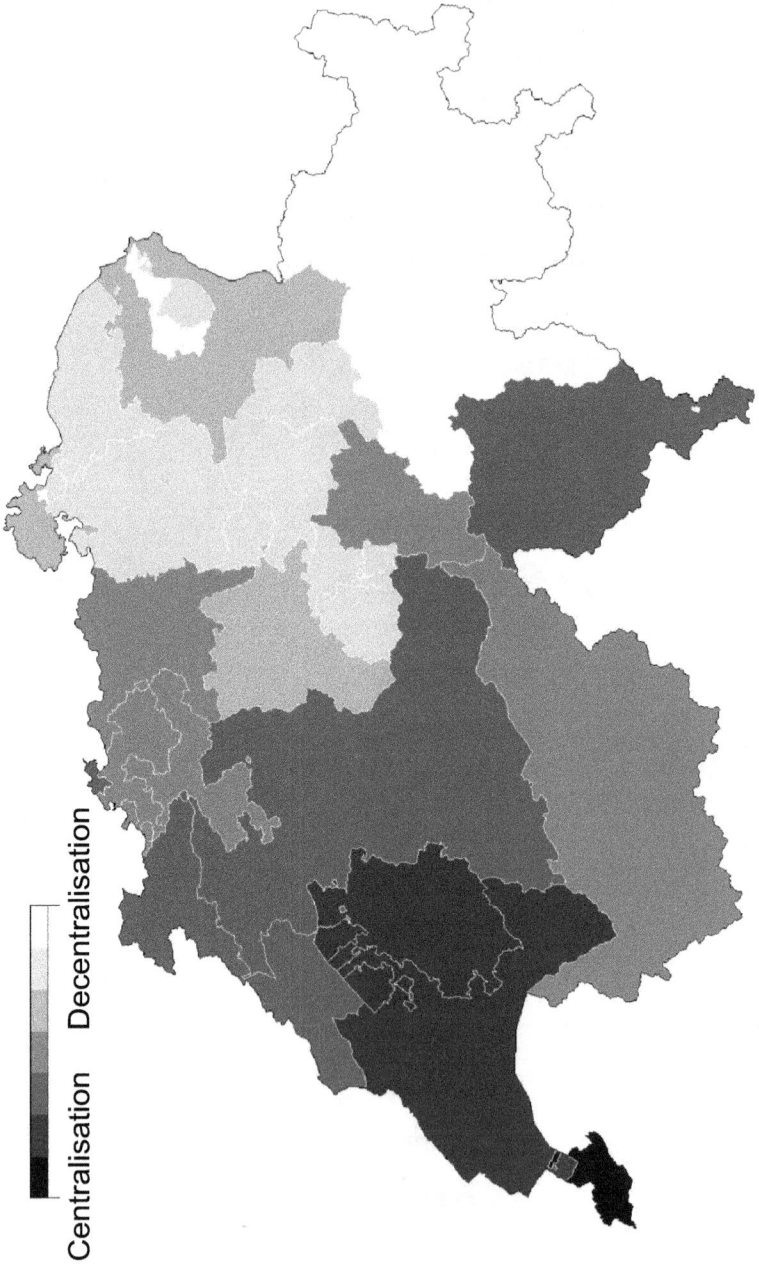

Figure 4.10: A map of cantonal decentralisation

French-speaking cantons Geneva, Fribourg, Vaud, Neuchâtel, as well as Ticino (among the most centralised) and that of Grisons and many small, rural and German-speaking cantons (Appenzell Outer-Rhodes, Zug, Glarus, Obwalden, Appenzell Inner-Rhodes, Nidwalden and Schwyz) which appear to be among the most decentralised cantons. What may be surprising, however, is how far on the centralised side Berne is ranked – and that this canton is situated next to its neighbour and former integral part, Jura, which yet again confirms conventional wisdom. Intuitively, Basel-City on the other hand, should appear to be much more centralised than it is ranked here – however, its middle places on both the politics- and the polity-ranking drag it into the centre here, still below the mean and more centralised than Basel-Countryside.

Figure 4.10 maps these patterns geographically, highlighting the increase in decentralisation if moving from the very West of Switzerland (the French-speaking cantons) to the very East (Grisons). This again confirms conventional wisdom dating back to, at least, Giacometti (1941).

Conclusion

This chapter has measured the degree of overall decentralisation in all 26 Swiss cantons. I have not only included several conventional measures and indicators but also developed a new index to capture the politics-dimension of cantonal decentralisation. The ensuing final index is thus based on a broad range of variables, both temporal (1941–2011) and with regard to the type of data (fiscal, legal and political). The external validity of this index is very high, given that all existing measures of cantonal decentralisation are included within it. Nevertheless, what this index additionally shows is how interrelated both the legal and fiscal dimensions are with politics. Two patterns have emerged: a categorical difference between the 'Latin'- and the German-speaking cantons (categorical because the distinction appears in all three component indices), and a gradual difference within the German-speaking group. To validly and systematically answer why both differences occur, I now proceed to quantitatively test the theoretical model presented in Chapter Two, using this final index as my dependent variable throughout the next chapter.

Chapter Five

Predicting Cantonal Decentralisation

This chapter takes the first step towards explaining cantonal decentralisation: a cross-sectional quantitative analysis marks the beginning of my nested research design. The main instruments employed are correlation analysis and means comparison, illustrated through scatter and box plots. In building linear regression models I rely on the ordinary least square technique. To enrich this exercise, I occasionally draw on my original dataset of 46 interviews in all 26 cantons. Some of these comments have been instrumental in generating causal hypotheses, and it is now possible to verify their accuracy in the form of (statistical) regularity. The dependent variable is measured using the final index of Chapter Four. The overall model tested is the one described in Chapter Two, from which eight case-specific hypotheses can be derived (Table 5.1).

The first section operationalises the independent variables, taking full profit of the sub-national setting to which they all apply. Each hypothesis is then tested individually, and each approach separately, before I conclude with a linear regression model that integrates all three approaches. This allows me to compare each approach with the other two, and all three, with the integrated model to judge which one best explains cantonal decentralisation as conceptualised and measured in this book. This final model then guides the selection of cases studied in more detail over the subsequent two chapters.

Determinants of cantonal decentralisation

Socio-cultural indicators

The problem with societal diversity is that it can mean anything from the number and types of cleavages to ethnic, linguistic and/or religious groups, their degree of polarisation and/or politicisation, 'cultural distance', etc. (Stoll 2008). If operationalisation entails 'the elaboration of a suitable measurement methodology, which focuses squarely on the link between the concept being measured and the measures being proposed' (Munck 2010: 19), tapping societal diversity as a 'latent variable' (Stoll 2008) entails two related problems: validity and reliability (Jackman 2008: 120).

To be *valid*, the measure must capture what the concept proposes to. I therefore restrict the operational definition of societal diversity to linguistic and religious diversity only. This choice emanates from the main scope condition of the sociological theory of federalism (Erk 2008): that societal differences be 'territorially grouped' (Livingston 1952: 85). In Switzerland, only the catholic vs. protestant and the linguistic 'cleavages' have ever been territorial (Linder 2010).

Table 5.1: Case-specific hypotheses

A. Socio-Cultural Hypotheses	
H1:	Cantons with territorially grouped *linguistic and/or religious diversity* are less centralised than cantons with a more homogeneous population.
H2:	The more prevalent a culture of subsidiarity (*federal political culture*), the less centralised a canton.
B. Structural Hypotheses	
H3:	Cantons extending over a smaller *area* are more centralised than those extending over a larger area.
H4:	Less *populous* cantons are more centralised than more populous systems.
H5:	Cantons with one dominant city (*monocephalic*) are more centralised than those with multiple such cities (*polycephalic*).
H6:	A canton will be more centralised the lower the average journey time (*distance*) from the border to the cantonal capital.
C. Political Hypotheses	
H7:	The more *politically left* a cantonal society, the more centralised the canton.
H8:	The less and the weaker *communal patriotism*, the more centralised a canton.

Reliability is ensured through the sub-national setting: to actually measure such diversity within the different cantons, I use the same census data provided by the Swiss Federal Office for Statistics (BFS). Finally, we need information both on the size and type of linguistic and religious *groups*, because the theory tested is not concerned with the number of cleavages as such, but with 'ethnic' identity generated by them (Stoll 2008).

Traditionally, societal diversity has been measured as ethnic, linguistic, and/ or religious diversity, *assuming* that a) ethnicities are territorially grouped and that b) 'native language marks ethnicity' (Fearon 2003: 210). Treisman's measure of 'ethnic division' uses 'the share of the population that spoke a language other than the official language at home' as an indicator (2006: 297), although he earlier (2006: 292) conceptualised these groups as having to be 'territorially compact'. The operationalisation does not account for his conceptualisation – nor does his other measure, the ethnolinguistic fractionalisation index compiled by Soviet geographers in the 1960s.[1] And while he deplores that 'since no comprehensive, cross-national accounting of which cultural cleavages were politically salient in different periods exists, this was the best alternative available' (2006: 298), nothing is said about the territoriality of ethnic groups (Christin and Hug 2006).

For Switzerland, the principle of territoriality is directly enshrined into the constitutional foundation: '*cuius regio, eius lingua*' means that cantons (and even

---

1.   Fractionalisation is defined as $1 - 1/\Sigma gi2$, where g denotes the share of ethnic group i (Fearon 2003: 208).

Table 5.2: Cantonal linguistic and religious diversity

Religious diversity	Linguistic diversity		
	Monolingual	Bilingual	Trilingual
Monoconfessional	ZH, LU, UR, SZ, OW, NW, ZG, SO, BS and BL, SH, AR, AI, TG, TI, VD, NE, GE and JU	BE, FR, VS	–
Biconfessional	GL, SG, AG	–	GR

municipalities) define their own official language(s) (Fleiner 1986b). Thus, the only way to operationalise linguistic diversity is to use the official language(s) of the canton as an indicator. This makes for three categories: one trilingual (Grisons), three bilingual (Fribourg, Valais and Berne) and 22 monolingual (one Italian-, four French- and 17 German-speaking) cantons. Religious diversity, I equally measure categorically, coding as biconfessional cantons those that in 1850 had equally strong Catholic and Protestant population shares, with each group territorially concentrated in separate parts of the canton. Four cantons fall into this category: St. Gall, Grisons, Aargau and Glarus; all other cantons are monoconfessional. The reason for taking 1850 as the reference year is, on the one hand, to account for the lagged effect of religious diversity on the political system (Stoll 2008: 1449). On the other hand, religion has undergone major transformations in the past years; atheists for example are the second largest 'religious' group in Basel-City. The resulting classification of cantons as mono-, bi- and tri-lingual as well as mono- and bi-confessional is displayed in Table 5.2. It makes little sense to apply a continuous measure for religious and linguistic diversity because their distribution is clearly bi-modal.[2]

The overwhelming majority of cantons (19 of 26) belong to the upper left cell: one canton, one religion, one language. In passing, one key success of Swiss federalism may thus be noted: crosscutting cleavages (Linder 2010: 29), for even this biggest group quickly disintegrates if divided according to *which* language is spoken and *which* religion is practised: German and Protestantism in Zurich, Basel-City and Basel-Countryside, Schaffhausen, Appenzell Outer-Rhodes and Thurgau; German and Catholicism in Lucerne, Uri, Schwyz, Obwalden and Nidwalden, Zug, Solothurn and Appenzell Inner-Rhodes; French and Protestantism in Neuchâtel and Vaud; French and both religions (but not territorially grouped) in Geneva; French and Catholicism in Jura;[3] and Italian and Catholicism in Ticino. Equally so for the three bilingual cantons: Berne was and still is predominantly protestant, Fribourg and Valais are both catholic. However, all three biconfessional cantons are German-speaking. For lack of more cases, I will make use of a simple dummy variable [*SocDiv*] to measure societal diversity: 1 if a canton is either bilingual

---

2.   I thank Matt Loveless for this advice.

3.   Jura only became a canton in 1979, but is coded here as if it had become a canton already in 1850.

but monoconfessional (Berne, Fribourg, Valais), biconfessional but monolingual (Glarus, St. Gall, Aargau), or trilingual and biconfessional (Grisons); and 0 for all the other 19 cantons.

Indicators for political culture

Under a federal political culture I understand positive orientations towards the overall federation and the autonomy of component units (Duchacek 1987), respect for minorities (Burgess 2006a), and public policy preferences in line with the subsidiarity principle (Burgess 2009) – in sum, a general preference for local solutions (Elazar 1993). For Switzerland, political culture has usually been measured through the language variable. The problem with this is that the measure might supplant the concept, i.e. one ends up attributing a preference for centralism to language as such, and not to the political culture or history hidden beneath or conveyed through it.

For Switzerland in particular, the simplified statement 'Frenchness = centralism' dates back to Giacometti (1941 and 1952). It was then adopted by Meyer (1978) and Grodecki (2007) (see Fiechter 2010: 49). Horber-Papazian also relies on the already mentioned survey among local secretaries (Ladner 1994 and 2008) to stipulate that 'belonging to the historically more centralist cantons, the French-speaking municipalities' have less autonomy (Horber-Papazian 2006: 243). To keep up with this tradition, I use language as one – but not the only – measure of political culture. The measure comes in three variants. One is to measure 'Frenchness' categorically: 19 predominantly German-speaking cantons (incl. Grisons), Berne with a small francophone minority, cantons with a strong and territorially concentrated German-speaking minority (Valais and Fribourg), and 'pure' francophone cantons (Geneva, Vaud, Neuchâtel, Jura), plus the Italian-speaking Ticino. A continuous measure (e.g. Gruner 1977) would fail to express the bi-modal structure of cantonal distribution along this variable. A kind of ordinal option is proposed by Rühli (2012: 177), who codes Geneva, Jura, Neuchâtel, Ticino and Vaud as 1; Valais and Fribourg as .65; Berne as .1 and the other 18 cantons (the 'base category' when it comes to linear regression) as 0. I will rely on this measure [Latin1] but also, to facilitate cross-group comparisons by having more equally staffed groups, on a simple dummy variable [Latin2], coding the seven 'Latin' cantons (Fribourg, Ticino, Vaud, Valais, Neuchâtel, Geneva and Jura) as 1 and all the other cantons as 0, as done also by Fiechter (2010).

However, language is but a crude proxy for culture, for what the Swiss case uniquely offers, is to use the degree of citizen's consent in specific referenda over the last 160 years as an indicator of federal political culture. Referenda results since 1848 by cantons are available through the BFS; since 1871 district-data are also available (Linder et al. 2008). There are three reasons for the inclusion of this measure. First, referenda are single issue- and not party- or person-based. In contrast to surveys, one can thus observe not just hypothetical opinions and expectations, but *actual* behaviour and *attested* decisions on a wide range of issues. This increases the internal validity. Second, federal referenda are held nationwide, so they apply the same 'treatment' to all cantons at the same time; hence a greater reliability than the language measure. Third, the tradition of aggregating individual votes to the canton level is, itself, part and parcel of the constitutional amendment process, which asks for a double majority of citizens *and* cantons (counted as the majority of individual votes per canton: external validity). The following six questions, voted between 1874 and 2010, all relate to the 'orientations toward the role of component units' (Duchacek 1987: 341) in the Swiss federal system:

1. Popular vote no. 12 of April 1874 on the total revision of the Federal Constitution of 1848, which marked a clear step towards centralisation, accepted by 63 per cent of the electorate and 15 (12 3/2) cantons (Linder *et al*. 2010: 34–7).
2. Popular vote no. 43 of November 1894 on a fixed share of duty revenues to be allocated to the cantons, initiated by the 'Federalists and Bernese Conservatives' but rejected by 71 per cent and 15 (12 3/2) cantons (Linder *et al*. 2010: 80–1).
3. Popular vote no. 59 of November 1902 on federal support for primary education, accepted by 76 per cent and all but one (half-)canton, Appenzell Inner-Rhodes (Linder *et al*. 2010: 99–100).
4. Popular vote no. 453 of April 1999 on a new Federal Constitution, claimed as being a cosmetic remake but with centralist implications, e.g. through explicitly guaranteeing communal autonomy or prescribing certain social policy goals, accepted by 60 per cent and 14 (12 2/2) cantons (Linder *et al*. 2010: 575–7).
5. Popular vote no. 532 of June 2008 on 'democratic naturalisation procedures', a right-wing initiative aimed at guaranteeing that communes autonomously decide on the procedure for naturalisations, rejected by 64 per cent and all but one canton, Schwyz (BK 2012).
6. Popular vote no. 553 of November 2010 on 'fair taxes for all', a left-wing initiative aimed at homogenising the income tax system and thereby reducing cantonal tax autonomy; rejected by 59 per cent and 22 cantons (BK 2012).

A factor analysis (Field 2005) confirms that all six measure the same 'thing': Cantons in favour of centrally prescribing fair taxes also approved the Federal Constitutions of 1874 and 1999 and federal support for primary education; and they were against a cantonal share of duties and objected to communal democracy as a vehicle for naturalisation procedures. Applied to our 26 cases, Figure 5.1 ranks the cantons along my 'Federal Political Culture Index' [FPC].[4] Although the two are correlated,[5] I do not combine language with FPC but keep them separate to see which one better correlates with cantonal decentralisation.

---

4. Extraction method: principal component analysis. KMO = .705, Bartlett's test of Sphericity significant at p < .001, N = 26. Pre-1978 data for Jura = district aggregates. Source: Linder *et al*. 2008. The resulting Cronbach's alpha is a high .842.
5. Independent sample t-test for the Latin dummy: t(24) = 2.657, p < .05 (two-tailed).

Figure 5.1: Federal political culture index (FPC)

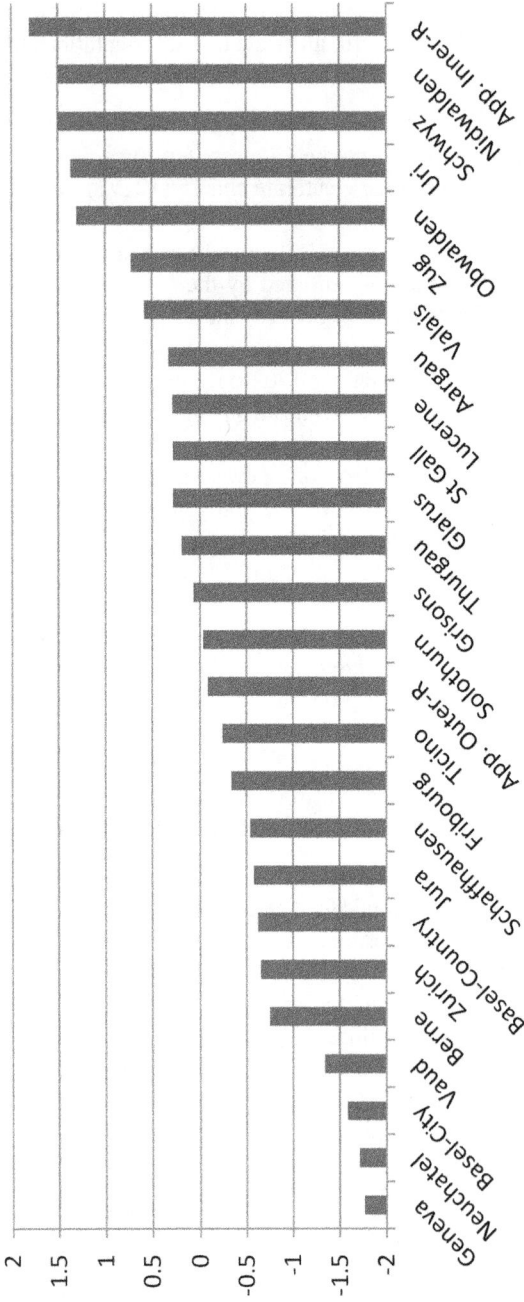

In this index, the historic 'founding cantons', without exception, plus Appenzell Inner-Rhodes, are all on the extreme subsidiarity side, while most of the 'newer' cantons (post-1803) and those with dominant cities occupy places on the wanting-to-centralise-side of the axis. Federal political culture in that sense is retrospective, static, and hence essentially conservative (Dürrenmatt 1942: 292; Vatter *et al.* 1996: 25).

Structural indicators

For area, both Hooghe and Marks (2013) and Treisman (2006: 292) propose a logarithmic measure ($\log_{10}$ of area in 1,000 km^2), while Rühli (2012: 177) simply suggests to divide cantonal area in km^2 by 1,000. Applied to the Swiss cantons, I will use the log-values of area measured in km^2 [*Area*] because in this way both skewness and kurtosis are brought closer to zero (-.375 and .458, respectively), making the distribution normal. The same for cantonal population [*Pop*], where, again in keeping with Hooghe and Marks (2013) and Treisman (2006: 293), I use the log-values of cantonal population as estimated for 2010 (skewness: -.292, kurtosis: -.639). Population size was not tested for by either Rühli (2012) or Fiechter (2010). Data for both variables comes from the BFS (2012). Figure 5.2 plots them both, immediately revealing the positive and significant correlation (Pearson's r = .536, p < .01).

Next up is the task to find a measure of 'monocephality', i.e. the dominance expressed by the biggest city. Rokkan and Urwin (1983: 39) propose 'primacy scores' [*PS*], calculated by taking 'the size of the largest city as a ratio of the sum of the next four largest'. Hence, '[i]f the first-size city is larger than this sum, we have a case of primacy; if it is smaller, the distribution is more polycephalic (1983: 11). Applying this admittedly 'crude' measure (1983: 40) to the Swiss cantons, the ranking displayed in Figure 5.3 results. Drawing the borderline at 1 (first city = next four cities together), only five cantons can unequivocally be described as monocephalic (Basel-City, Zurich, Geneva, Schaffhausen and Vaud). Five others straddle the border (Ticino, St. Gall, Lucerne, Grisons and Aargau) and all others are clearly polycephalic. Primacy scores are negatively and significantly correlated with area (Pearson's r = -.470, p < .05), but this effect is entirely due to Basel-City. Once this canton is excluded, city primacy however is positively and significantly correlated with *population* (r = .401, p < .05), in turn.

The fourth structural variable is topography, which as I have argued in Chapter Two, deserves to be measured separately from both area and population size. A first option is to use Rühli's (2012: 177) 'dummy for mountain cantons', in which Appenzell Inner-Rhodes, Glarus, Grisons, Obwalden, Uri and Valais are coded as 1; Appenzell Outer-Rhodes, Berne, Lucerne, Nidwalden, St. Gall, Schwyz and Ticino as .5; Jura and Neuchâtel as .25; and the other eleven cantons (the 'base category' when it comes to linear regression) as 0 [*mountain1*]. However, as with the Latin variable, I will also test a dummy variable as explained below [*mountain2*].

Figure 5.2: Cantonal population by cantonal area

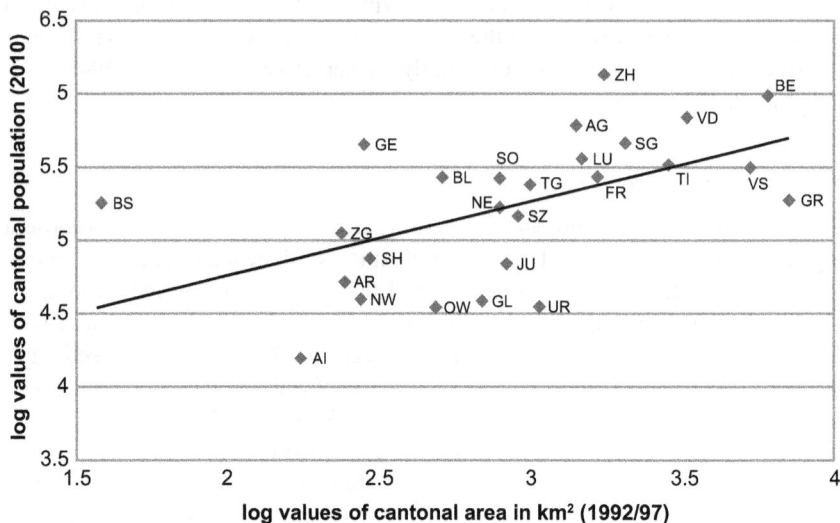

A second option is to rely on the four indicators used by the federal fiscal equalisation scheme, where one of the three pots of money is distributed to the cantons to equalise their 'geo-topographic burdens' and for 'socio-demographic cost compensation' (EFV 2012). To calculate the former, four factors are taken into account (EFV: 2012):

1. The proportion of the cantonal resident population living at 800 meters above sea level or higher.
2. The median height of the cantonal productive area.
3. The proportion of residents living in communes with less than 200 inhabitants.
4. The inverse density of a canton, in hectares per inhabitants.

All four factors are positively and significantly correlated with each other, so I summarise their standardised values into an 'index of geo-topographical fragmentation' [*GTF*], displayed as Figure 5.4.[6]

This index correlates strongly with Rühli's (2012) 'mountain dummy'.[7] But the GTF index is, in fact, better able to capture variation because it is a continuous, 'objective' measure based on data that actually has an impact on

---

6. Bivariate correlation coefficients (Pearson's r) between .483 (p < .05) and .868 (p < .01). Extraction method: principal component analysis. KMO = .664, Bartlett's test of Sphericity significant at p < .001, N = 26. The resulting Cronbach's alpha is a high .855.

7. A liner correlation results in Pearson's r = .861 (p < .001), a comparison of means – more adequate since the mountain variable is categorical – in Eta = .881 (p < .001).

Figure 5.3: Cantonal primacy scores (PS)

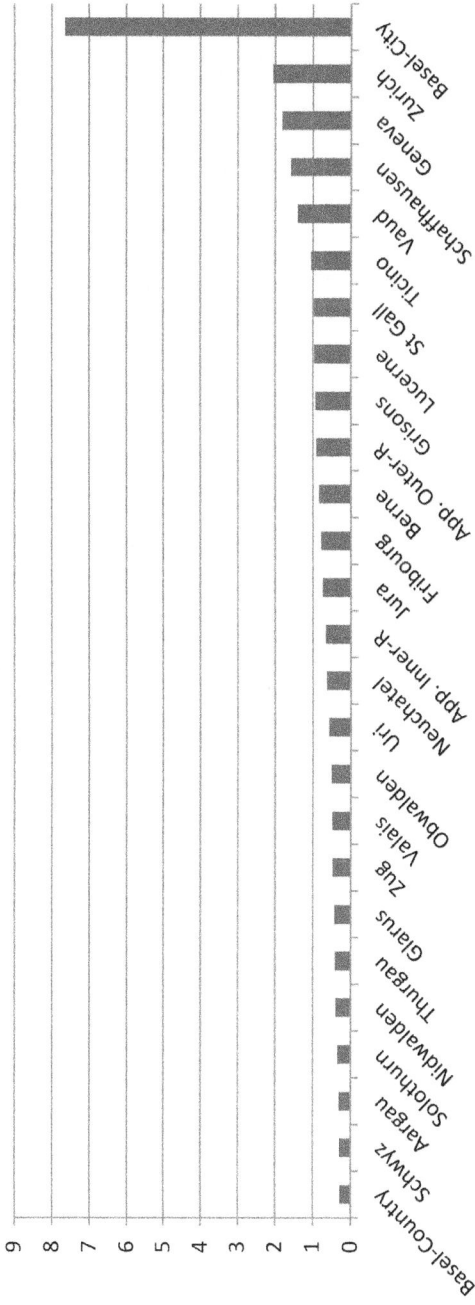

Figure 5.4: Geo-topographical fragmentation index (GTF)

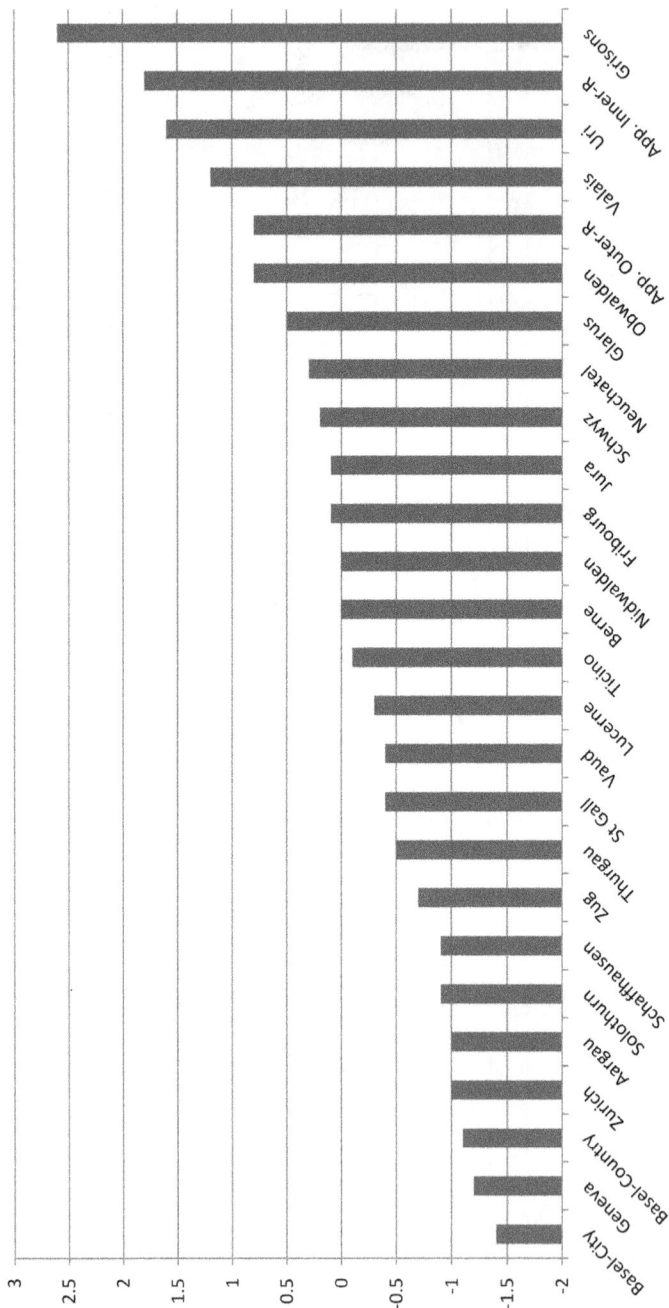

a sizeable portion of vertical redistribution – that is, based on factors that both politicians and the Swiss electorate have, since 2008, found important enough to be made a crucial element of Swiss (fiscal) federalism. More importantly, it relates closely to inaccessibility, distance and therefore – according to H6 – to decentralisation. As proof of that, Rühli (2012: 74) expected mountain cantons to be more decentralised because of distance, but found a negative correlation, i.e. lower (expenditure) decentralisation in mountain cantons. I retain both my topographical index and Rühli's mountain dummy for the moment, but because of collinearity issues will later be forced to include only one at the time.

The final aspect of structure is distance from the centre. As argued above, what matters is the accessibility of the cantonal capital, which I here calculate as the journey time using public transport from the village that is furthest away, or, if there are two that are equally far away and the difference is below ten minutes, the mean of the two [*Dist*].[8] Table 5.3 shows these results.

While it takes more than three hours to reach Chur from Samnaun and also over two hours in cantons Berne and Valais, less than half an hour is needed in Schaffhausen and Zug, and barely 20 minutes in Basel-City. Naturally, this measure of distance correlates positively with area (Pearson's $r = .700$, $p < .001$), my geo-topographical fragmentation index ($r = .621$, $p < .01$) and Rühli's mountain variable ($r = .486$, $p < .05$). More or less the same results obtain when excluding Basel-City.

Political indicators

Turning to political indicators, a first measure of a society's degree of progressiveness is the strength of left-wing political parties. I measure this by adding the proportion of seats occupied by them in a cantonal parliament. Left-wing parties, for that matter, include the cantonal Socialist Parties (SP) and the Greens; I repeat the addition for 2010 and 2011 (BADAC 2012) and average the results into the variable called *LEFT*. For comparative purposes, I also calculate the mean proportion of seats occupied by the major right-wing party, the Swiss People's Party (SVP), for 2010 and 2011 [*RIGHT*]. However, the correlation between the two measures is negative, as expected, but small and far from statistical significance (Pearson's $r = .147$, $p = .484$), and displayed in Figure 5.5. Swiss cantons appear split into four groups, if we take the means (of the means) as borderlines: six cantons with polarised party systems (upper right quadrant), six where centrist parties dominate (lower left), seven centre-left (upper left) and finally six centre-right cantons (lower right).

A first advantage offered by a sub-national research design is that these are really *the same* parties. But a second and even more important advantage

8. Like contemporary Swiss residents and visitors, I rely on the search engine of the Swiss Federal Railway here: http://www.fahrplan.sbb.ch (last accessed 20 May 2012). For each journey I have specified to depart on Monday 4 June 2012, 8am.

is, as with federal political culture, given by the possibility to tap citizen's preferences directly using referenda results. The following ten referenda have been the most important on the left-right cleavage over the last ten years (BFS 2012):

1. Popular vote no. 554 of February 2011 on the 'protection of small arms violence', rejected by 56 per cent of the electorate and 20 cantons.
2. Popular vote no. 552.1 of November 2010 on the 'expulsion of criminal foreigners', initiated by the SVP and accepted by 52 per cent and 20 cantons.
3. Popular vote no. 547 of November 2009 introducing a 'ban on minarets', again initiated by the SVP and accepted by 56 per cent and 22 cantons.
4. Popular vote no. 540 of February 2009 extending the free movement of persons to Romania and Bulgaria, accepted by 60 per cent (and 22 cantons).
5. Popular vote no. 528 of March 2007 on 'a social health insurance', i.e. nationalising health care, rejected by 71 per cent and all but 2 cantons (Neuchâtel and Jura)
6. Popular vote no. 511 of September 2004 on the automatic naturalisation of third-generation foreign residents, rejected by 52 per cent and 19 cantons.
7. Popular vote no. 502 of May 2003 on a 'moratorium over the construction of further nuclear plants', rejected by 58 per cent and all but 2 cantons (Basel-City and Basel-Countryside).

The yes-votes for popular votes 554, 540, 528, 511 and 502 and the no-votes for votes 552.1 and 547 all correlate positively and significantly, so that they can safely be aggregated into a single 'Index of Citizens' Progressiveness' [CPI], displayed as Figure 5.6.[9]

As was to be expected, this CPI correlates strongly with LEFT (Pearson's $r = .760$, $p < .001$) and slightly less with RIGHT ($r = -.549$, $p < .01$). My final variable concerns 'communal patriotism'. The Swiss Electoral Studies (SELECTS 2011) includes two questions that are of direct relevance, while still allowing aggregations to the canton level. The first is about trust in local authorities [LGtrust], the second about attachment to the community [LGattach]. Variation along the attachment dimension (N = 1757), I have recoded to run from 1 ('not at all attached') to 4 ('very attached); local trust levels (N = 1730), on the other hand, run from 0 ('no trust') to 10 ('full trust').

There are only two potential problems with these two variables. The first is lack of variation: both attachment and trust levels are fairly even across the 26 cantons (standard deviations are .794 and 2.257, respectively) and at a very high level (means are 3.19 and 6.53, respectively). The second is lack of discriminatory

---

9. Only the bivariate correlation between yes to free movement of persons and yes to stopping nuclear energy plants from being constructed is insignificant, but only just about and still positive ($r = .330$, $p = .1$). All other coefficients vary between .464 ($p < .05$) and .927 ($p < .001$). Extraction method: principal component analysis. KMO = .754, Bartlett's test of Sphericity significant at $p < .001$, N = 26. The resulting Cronbach's alpha is a high .938.

power: neither local trust nor local attachment takes place at the expense of trust in, or attachment to, *other* governmental levels. Local attachment is positively and significantly correlated with attachment to the cantonal (Pearson's r = .512) and national levels (r = .247), to the linguistic region (r = .250) and even to 'Europe' (r = .098), albeit here only just. The same for local trust, which is positively and significantly correlated with trust in the cantonal government (r = .700), the federal parliament (r = .465) and government (r = .452), and even with trust in national political parties (r = .422), the courts (r = .421) and the police (r = .433). However, trust and attachment seem to measure different things, because the correlation between them is weak and insignificant (r = .337, p = .092), as Figure 5.7 shows.

Table 5.3: Journey times to cantonal capitals

Canton	Capital	Remotest village(s)	Time [min]
GR	Chur	Samnaun	208
BE	Bern	Gadmen & Gsteig bei Gstaad	148
VS	Sion	Oberwald	139
SG	St. Gallen	Pfäfers	112
AI	Appenzell	Reute	104
UR	Altdorf	Realp	99
SO	Solothurn	Kienberg	99
VD	Lausanne	Rougemont	97
SZ	Schwyz	Tuggen	90
JU	Delémont	Les Bois	77
OW	Sarnen	Engelberg	68
FR	Fribourg	Fräschels	68
AG	Aargau	Kaiserstuhl	66
BL	Liestal	Roggenburg	63
LU	Luzern	Marbach & Pfaffnau	62
NE	Neuchâtel	Les Verrières	60
GE	Genève	Chancy	60
ZH	Zürich	Laupen & Flurlingen	56
TI	Bellinzona	Airolo	52
TG	Frauenfeld	Arbon	51
AR	Herisau	Walzenhausen	50
GL	Glarus	Elm	41
NW	Stans	Emmetten	34
SH	Schaffhausen	Buchberg & Stein am Rhein	30
ZG	Zug	Oberägeri	28
BS	Basel	Riehen	18

Figure 5.5: Strength of cantonal left- and right-wing parties

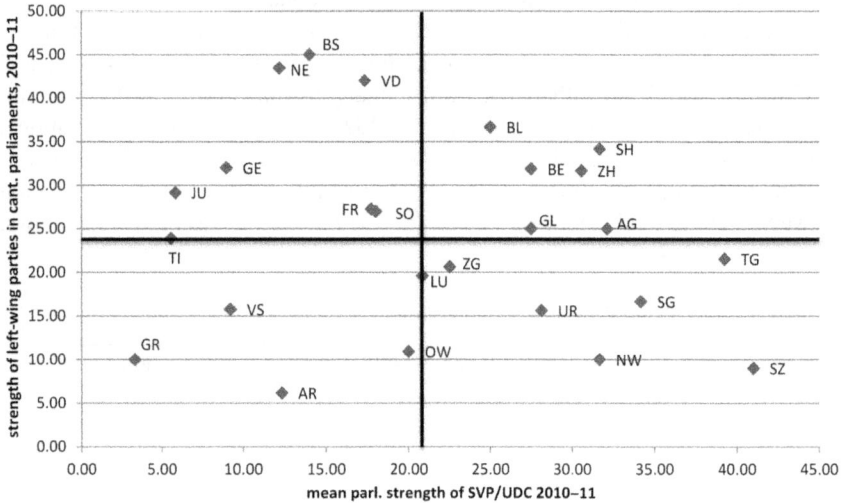

One group of cantons has above average levels of both attachment and trust (upper right quadrant), another has below average of both (lower left) and a third set of cantons has either high local attachment at the expense of local trust (upper left) or the other way round (lower right). I will therefore retain both variables as separate measures of 'local patriotism'. The exact data for these and all the other independent variables are listed in the Data Appendix.

Separate Models

In this section, I first test the socio-cultural, structural and political approaches separately. I then place them alongside each other into a single model. The reason for this procedure is to show that each has its merits, but that without controlling for the factors advocated by the other two, the results are distorted. Only an integrated model can remedy this. I start with the socio-cultural model, the most prominent in the case-specific literature.

A socio-cultural model

Does societal diversity (H1) and/or political culture (H2) determine cantonal decentralisation? Language – indicative of a German-speaking tradition of local self-government (e.g. Fleiner 1986a and 2000) – is the usual explanation offered. But on that observation three questions arise: First, we must enquire whether this correlation is spurious. Maybe other, hidden factors cause decentralisation. So far, cantonal decentralisation lacks a systematic testing of its potential causes. Second, no matter the answer to that first question, we

Figure 5.6: Citizens' progressiveness index

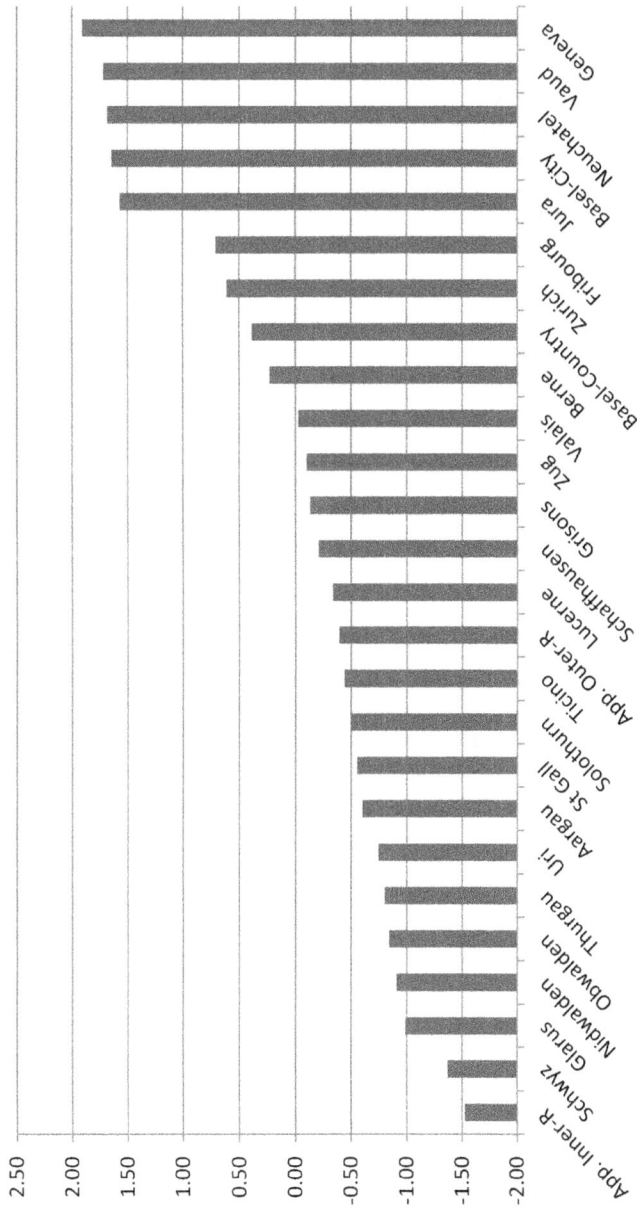

Figure 5.7: Local attachment by local trust

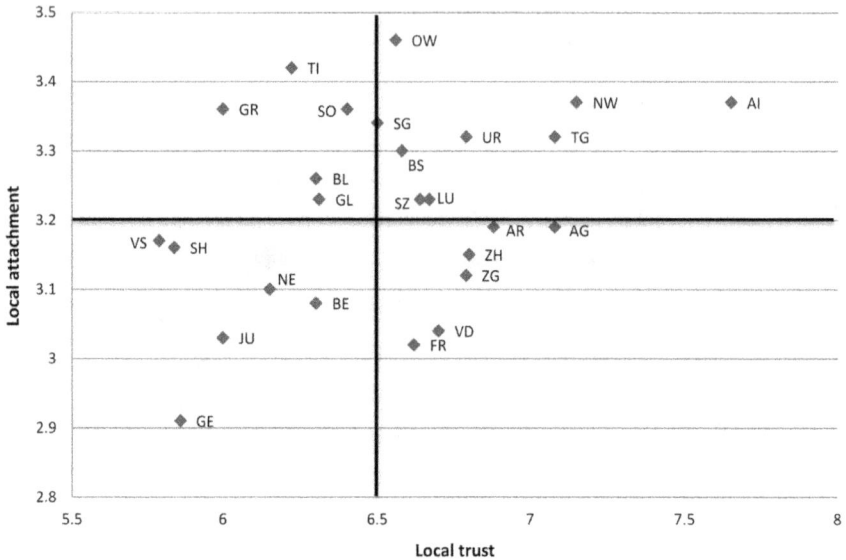

must ask whether there is something 'genetic' about German-speaking Swiss that makes them favour decentralised structures. Or is language itself merely a correlate of a more deep-seated 'specific syndrome of political cultural attitudes' (Inglehart 1988: 1203)? And if so, precisely which cultural elements make for more/less decentralisation? Third, which factors cause different degrees of decentralisation *within* the German-speaking group of cantons? All three considerations mandate – but also caution – us to explain decentralisation using socio-cultural variables. I first consider each independent variable separately and then build them into a socio-cultural linear regression model.

Linguistic diversity. Comparing the 22 monolingual cantons with the four bi- or tri-lingual ones does not result in a significant variation on the dependent variable. Mean cantonal decentralisation is even *lower* in the second group. In other words, linguistically heterogeneous cantons are not significantly more decentralised than linguistically homogeneous ones.[10] We must therefore fail to reject the null hypothesis for H1 of no relationship for linguistic diversity and decentralisation. Even in trilingual Grisons, linguistic diversity is not cited as a reason for decentralisation anymore:

> [Swiss] German is the language of communication, and that's that. When the cantonal parliament discussed the introduction of Romansh Grischun, of the 120 MCPs maybe 40 were actually Rhaeto-Romans. The other 80 simply

10. $t(24) = .525$, p (1-tailed) > .05.

voted on something of which they had no idea. [...] it was decided to introduce Rhaeto-Romansh Grischun simply because to print teaching material in all idioms would be too expensive. (Interview no. 35)[11]

Language may once have had an impact on cantonal structures – but even if it did, it does not have one anymore.

Religious diversity. The same is true for religiously heterogeneous cantons: these 22 are not significantly more decentralised than religiously homogeneous ones.[12] Again, we cannot reject the null hypothesis. The spread for monoconfessional cantons is larger, but their mean cantonal decentralisation is only slightly lower. This fits into what I was told in Fribourg: 'people with different languages and religions have lived for so long in the same area that this is not that great an issue anymore' (Interview no. 14). Religious diversity may also once have been important for structuring politics, but today seems to have lost that relevance, as has linguistic diversity (*see also* Linder *et al.* 2008).

Societal diversity. But could it be that religious and linguistic diversity *together* produce decentralisation, as Stein (1968) suggested? The only canton with diversity in both dimensions is Grisons, which we know to be among the most decentralised. It would make little sense to compare one to all other 25 cantons. When I collapse linguistic and religious diversity into societal diversity [*SocDiv*] as explained above, two more fairly filled groups result: 19 in one, six plus Grisons in the other. Again, however, no significant difference between the two groups exists.[13]

Diversity may thus be less an empirical reason for decentralisation than a normative argument, especially for the conservative right:

There are [communal] mergers that grow from the below and make sense, here I am in favour. What is wrong is for the canton to come and define the number of regions and decree that everyone has to go into one of them. Certain parts of the canton do not belong to any other because of linguistic, cultural diversity; they cannot be mixed together. That would be a problem. (Interview no. 38)

The fiscal federalism literature is replete with such prescriptions, too. I will return to this and similar arguments when considering progressiveness.

Political culture. As for political culture, my first hypothesis was that French-speaking cantons – less exposed to a federal tradition and influenced by the French original of '*La République, une et indivisible*' – were more centralised than German-speaking ones, which can look back upon a centuries-old federal tradition celebrating subsidiarity. Using Rühli's (2012) categorical variable,

---

11. *See* List of Interviews to attribute interview number to interviewee identity.

12. $t(24) = -1.348$, p (1-tailed) $> .05$.

13. $t(24) = -.043$, p (1-tailed) $> .05$.

I find strong evidence for this hypothesis: the most decentralised cantons are exclusively or predominantly German-speaking, while the five most centralised ones are exclusively French- or Italian-speaking. In other words, as the presence of German-speakers decreases, centralisation increases.[14] Nowhere is this more obvious than in Vaud:

> Traditionally, Vaud is rather Jacobin. [...] Our institutions were created under the French influence, that is by Napoleon. This is also why we have prefects. For us, Napoleon is a hero! I am not sure that in Lucerne they would share this opinion, but the French institutions immensely inspired us. Both as regards the prefects and the communes, which until today are much like in France: small and untouched since the 19th century... (Interview no. 17)

What if we turn away from language and look at the relationship between cantonal decentralisation and federal political culture more directly, using the composite index of six referenda results on federal constitutional change towards centralisation at the national level? The results here are equally strong but weaker than when relying on language as a proxy for culture: Figure 5.8 shows the correlation between FPC and cantonal decentralisation (Pearson's $r = .664$, $p < .001$), positive as expected.

The analytical advantages of using this continuous measure are not just increased internal validity, but also a more fine-grained picture. So far, that is without any controls, evidence for H2 leads me to reject the null hypothesis of no relationship. The influence of culture (and history, through this factor) is confirmed also by numerous interviews, for example in Neuchâtel with its unique monarchical legacy of centralisation:

> Our political system of today starts in 1848. [...] still today, the canton sometimes considers the communes as if they were cantonal offices (*services de l'Etat*). Communes have to fight to become acknowledged as public collectivities: when the Government meets the local executive we have to remind them that they are meeting authorities, and not their subordinates (*chefs de service*). They have a general tendency to think that we are subordinated. Our Government is a Prussian King with five heads! We have maintained that idea of a relatively strong Government, in relation both to Parliament and the communes. (Interview no. 23)

In sum, cantonal decentralisation is neither significantly correlated with linguistic or religious diversity individually considered, nor with the presence of both in the form of societal diversity. However, decentralisation is significantly higher in German-speaking cantons and in those with a federal political culture, i.e. a general preference for the subsidiarity principle. When integrating the societal

---

14. Treating this variable as continuous, Pearson's r is a very good $-.724$ ($p < .001$). This does not change in a table of means (that is, regarding the variable as categorical): Eta $= .769$ ($p < .001$).

Figure 5.8: Cantonal decentralisation by federal political culture

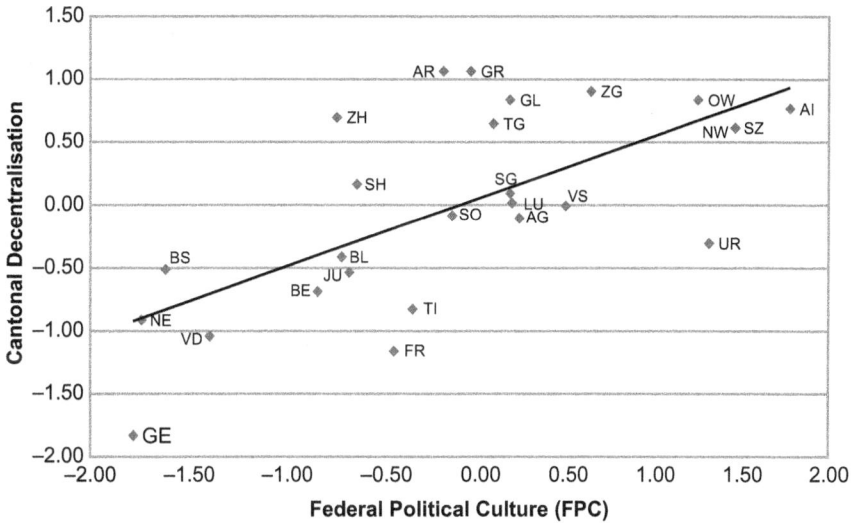

diversity dummy (19 vs. 7), the Latin dummy (also 19 vs. 7) and the continuous measure of federal political culture into a single linear regression model, both political culture and language turn out to have a significant effect (Table 5.4).

For control purposes, I include GNP per capita (in 1,000 CHF) and the absolute number of Local Governments (as of April 2012) per canton (BFS 2012). Both controls exert less influence than either dominant language or political culture, judging by their Beta-coefficients. Collinearity is kept under control (see last two columns) and this socio-cultural model alone is able to explain a very good 65.4 per cent of the variation in cantonal decentralisation. In the direct comparison of federal political culture and language, the latter emerges as both the stronger and more significant predictor of cantonal decentralisation. The sign of the coefficients for both factors points in the hypothesised direction.

A structural model

From a structural point of view, socio-cultural variables are supposed to lose their relevance mainly to the benefit of area (H3) and population (H4); H5 suggested city-structure and H6 distance. As before, I will first test each hypothesis individually and then integrate them into a structural model.

Area. Correlating the logged values of cantonal area with cantonal decentralisation does not result in a significant coefficient and is even negative (Pearson's $r = -.124$, $p = .546$). One could argue that Basel-City represents a special case, having had to let go of its periphery (and area) in 1833 and not even

Table 5.4: The socio-cultural model

Dependent Variable: Cantonal Decentralisation Model summary: R^2 = .654***, Adj. R^2 = .568 (N = 26)					
Independent variables	B	Std. Error	Beta	Tolerance	VIF
Constant	0.263	0.492	–	–	–
Latin (dummy)	−0.851**	0.289	**−0.491**	0.621	1.61
Federal political culture	0.301*	0.144	**0.383**	0.514	1.946
Societal diversity (dummy)	0.119	0.262	0.068	0.756	1.323
No. of Local Governments	−0.001	0.001	−0.137	0.571	1.752
GNP per capita (in 1,000s)	0.001	0.007	0.016	0.648	1.543

Note: *p < .05,**p < .01,***p < .001.

maintaining a separate administration for the actual city of Basel. However, if Basel-City is excluded from the analysis, the correlation remains negative and far from being significant (r = -.230, p = .258); the same if Geneva is also excluded, the other case with extreme values on the dependent variable. Too many small cantons are very decentralised (Appenzell Inner-Rhodes, Appenzell Outer-Rhodes, Zug, Nidwalden, Obwalden) and too many big cantons rather centralised (Vaud, Fribourg, Ticino, Berne). There is thus insufficient evidence to reject the null-hypothesis for H3.

Population. A correlation analysis for the logged values of cantonal population on the whole sample also produces a negative coefficient, contrary to our expectation, and is even significant (Pearson's r = -.453, p < .01). Most small cantons are very decentralised (Appenzell Inner-Rhodes, Obwalden, Glarus, Nidwalden), several big cantons are relatively centralised (Vaud, Berne, Fribourg and Ticino). There is thus strong evidence to reject the null-hypothesis for H4 on the causal influence of population.

Polycephality. Applying Rokkan and Urwin's (1983) measure of polycephality to my sample yields no significant results. As expected, the correlation between logged city primacy scores and cantonal decentralisation is negative, but weak and insignificant (Pearson's r = -.309, p = .125).[15] Moreover, the result appears to be driven by Basel-City, which has extreme values on both variables. That Basel-City, with its economy-dominated focus on its centrality function, is a special case is also expressed in the following remark:

> From an economic point of view, we clearly need larger areas: for us [in Basel-City] this means North West Switzerland. [...] I have always demanded that we centralise as much as possible: merging the Basel-City

---

15. I use the logged values of primacy because the distribution is otherwise not normal. The results for the unlogged values are only slightly different (Pearson's r = -.219, p = .282).

with Basel-Countryside or even the whole economic area no. 31 [Basel-City, Basel-Countryside, and parts of both Solothurn and Aargau]. The economy is for bigger structures because to get four different permissions in, say, life sciences, hinders development and progress. (Interview no. 32)

But even if Basel-City is omitted, the correlation coefficient is still modest and without significance, although negative as expected ($r = -.295$, $p = .152$). There is thus little reason to believe that a monocephalous city structure has a causal influence on cantonal decentralisation (H5).

Topography/Distance. To test H6, I have calculated two measures in addition to Rühli's (2012) 'mountain dummy'. The first is my *index of geo-topographical fragmentation*, which relies on data that filters directly into the federal equalisation scheme. Testing for the whole sample, the measure is positively, but just about not significantly, correlated with cantonal decentralisation (Pearson's $r = .380$, $p = .055$). A special case here seems to be Uri, which is the third most fragmented but still rather centralised. Here, a clear connection between ideology and structure was made on the issue of communal mergers:

The SVP, as matter of principle, wants to change nothing, at best to optimize inter-communal collaboration. [...] The Left, however, favours a more radical solution, like in Glarus: down to three or five municipalities within ten years. For example, [merging] the whole Urserental, then from Göschenen until Erstfeld and finally the rest of the valley. (Interview no. 41)

In other words, as theorised in Chapter Two, topography by itself cannot cause institutions – but as a structural framework, political actors may use it to argue for change in one or the other direction, depending on interests, ideology and/or visions.

My second measure, *distance*, uses the mean duration of a journey by public transport from the remotest village to the cantonal capital on an ordinary Monday morning. The result of a bivariate correlation is very weak and insignificant, though positive, to begin with (Pearson's $r = .038$, $p = .852$).

The cantonal capital may in fact not be the 'centre' as assumed when creating the measure: for example, 'the centre of Appenzell Outer-Rhodes is the city of St. Gall' (Interview no. 11), and not its own cantonal capital, Herisau. Finally, using Rühli's (2012) ordinal variable for *mountain cantons* (ranging from 0 through .25 and .5 to 1 – he wrongly calls it a 'dummy'), at first no significant change between the four groups of cantons obtains, although decentralisation *is* higher in the mountain cantons (Eta = .480, $p = .117$). But when I collapse the fully and partially plain cantons into one group and the partially and fully mountainous cantons into another, there is a significant correlation.[16]

---

16. $t(24) = -2.230$, p (2-tailed) < .05. Treating Rühli's mountain variable with four groups as continuous (which it is, even if only to some extent), a significant and positive correlation coefficient results (Pearson's $r = .422$, p < .05).

In sum, the results for structure are mixed: neither area, polycephality, fragmentation nor distance are significantly correlated with cantonal decentralisation, while there is evidence to suggest that population size and being located in the mountains (i.e. general inaccessibility) influence decentralisation – although this effect seems to be negative, for population. What if these variables are now placed alongside each other, in a linear regression model? Including all six variables at the same time makes them all lose their significance and raises problems both of collinearity and degrees of freedom because of the small sample size (Field 2005: 174). I therefore drop the variables with the weakest bivariate correlation coefficients: distance, area, primacy and GTF. This leaves me with population and the mountain dummy, plus the two controls already deployed in the socio-cultural model. Table 5.5 shows the results of this structural model, which is able to explain only 31.5 per cent of the variation in cantonal decentralisation. This is much less than the socio-structural model above. Moreover, just one of all the coefficients is significant.

A political model

In the political approach, the degree of progressiveness/left-wing orientation in a society matters (H7), on the one hand, and the strength of local/regional attachment (H8), on the other. I, again, discuss the two hypotheses separately and then build them into a single political model.

Progressiveness. The first measure of progressiveness taps the strength of political parties represented in the cantonal parliaments. Correlating LEFT and cantonal decentralisation produces a negative coefficient, as was expected (Pearson's r = -.678, p < .001). Because the strength of left-wing parties in their respective cantonal parliaments is itself correlated with my index of citizens' progressiveness (CPI), I find an equally negative correlation between this latter and cantonal decentralisation: in fact, the association is even slightly stronger (r = -.708, p < .001). This is the strongest bivariate correlation so far, displayed in

Table 5.5: The structural model

Dependent Variable: Cantonal Decentralisation Model summary: $R^2 = .315$, Adj. $R^2 = .184$ (N = 26)					
Independent variables	B	Std. Error	Beta	Tolerance	VIF
Constant	1.476	2.354	–	–	–
Cant. population (log)	−0.399	0.47	**−0.254**	0.362	2.759
Mountain dummy	0.563*	0.317	**0.366**	0.768	1.302
No. of LGs	−0.001	0.002	−0.087	0.369	2.708
GNP per capita (1'000s)	0.007	0.009	0.169	0.782	1.279

Note: *p < .01.

Figure 5.9. Both at the elite and ordinary citizen's level there is thus strong evidence to reject the null-hypothesis for H7. One quotation from Vaud corroborates this finding:

> Over time, all big public policies have been cantonalised, for example social services [...] the canton fixes all the social norms and quotas. We knew it would come more expensive – communes are closer to the citizens so they can keep the costs down – but this really is a question of social equality across the whole canton; in education, health and social policy at least. (Interview no. 17)

Local patriotism. Finally, decentralisation may be a consequence of local patriotism, which I measure through local attachment and local trust. Both attachment and trust yield positive and significant correlation coefficients: Pearson's r is .549 (p < .01) for LG attachment and .401 (p < .05) for LG trust. As with topography and the small German-speaking cantons, however, this variable captures conservatism rather than local patriotism, that is, a general preference for the status quo as against structural reforms. In Schwyz, for example, the electorate refused both to abolish the unique district structure and reform its electoral system (whereby currently every commune has the right to at least one MCP) because of a mixture of conservatism and a general preference for local structures. Both are said to be fostered by the largely agrarian economic socio-structure (Interview no. 1). But only a qualitative study can uncover these myriad micro-relations (*see* Chapter Six).

In sum, the political approach has so far produced the strongest bivariate correlation, that between progressiveness and cantonal decentralisation. Both local

Figure 5.9: Decentralisation by progressiveness

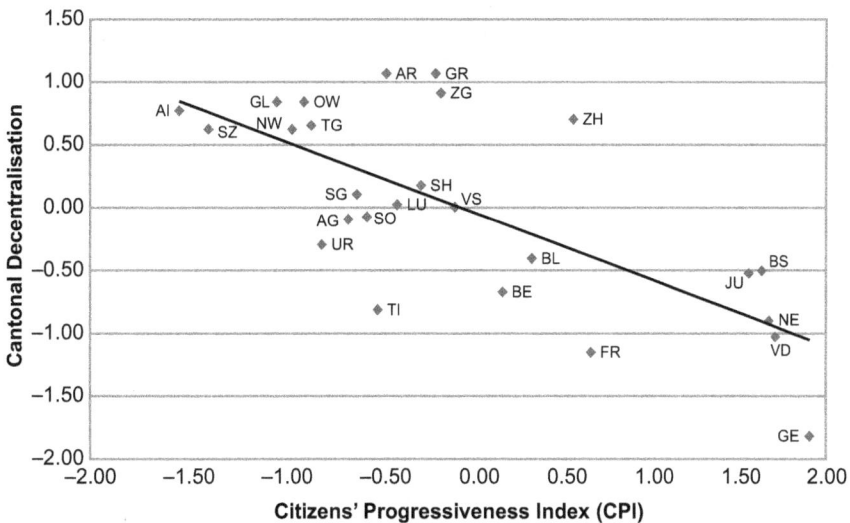

trust and local attachment, on the other hand, have produced only moderate correlations with decentralisation. Placing all four political independent variables alongside, in *a single* linear regression model, produces an overall fit of $R^2 = .643$ (Table 5.6).[17] However, none of the coefficients is significant, although notably left-wing parties are not very far from attaining that level (p = .093). The strength of left-wing parties and the degree of citizens' progressiveness are also the most important predictors, judging by their Beta-values. The model itself is significant at the 99 per cent-level. I now turn to a direct comparison of the three models as well as the synthesis, in line with my theoretical framework (*see* Chapter Two).

Synthesis

Three separate approaches have produced three separate models. Judging solely by their degree of fit, the socio-cultural ($R^2 = .654$ with p < .001; Adj. $R^2 = .568$; *see* Table 5.4) is slightly better than the political model ($R^2 = .643$ with p < .01; Adj. $R^2 = .530$; *see* Table 5.6). The structural model ($R^2 = .315$ with p > .05; Adj. $R^2 = .184$; *see* Table 5.5) comes out as the clear loser. In the Swiss cantons, decentralisation is, therefore, not a technocratic affair as the fiscal federalism literature prescribes. Instead, it is much more a cultural game, as so many of the studies on cantonal-local relations (and other aspects of cantonal politics, for that matter) have amply shown. However, and this really is a revelation, politics also seems to play a role, indeed only slightly second to culture.

But do these patterns continue to hold if tested against each other? To answer this crucial question, I now integrate the three approaches into *a single* linear regression model. This uncovers the independent effect not just of each hypothesised variable, but also of each approach. Including all the independent variables discussed so far plus the two controls, number of LGs and per capita GDP, produces the model shown in Table 5.7, with a wonderful $R^2 = .850$ (p < .05) but also with huge collinearity problems.

Indeed, it is the many and strong inter-correlations that raise the collinearity problem. If tolerance levels below .2 and VIF above 5 are cause for concern (Bahovec 2011: 870), then no less than eight coefficients fall into this category. Thanks to the three separate models developed above, however, I can restrict the choice of variables to those suggested by the theory *and* with a significant coefficient and/or a strong impact in this fully integrated model, because here the variables really have to compete with each other. These independent variables are *language, area* and the *strength of left-wing parties*. A final model with these three predictors, plus the two controls, produces a fit of $R^2 = .744$ (p < .001) and has eliminated collinearity. Its properties are displayed as Table 5.8.

It is this final model that I shall test using qualitative evidence, in the next chapter. To guide my case selection, I next plot the 'the actual scores of the cases',

---

17. In this and in subsequent analyses that include left-wing parties, a value of 0 is included for Appenzell Inner-Rhodes.

Table 5.6: The political model

Independent variables	B	Std. Error	Beta	Tolerance	VIF
Dependent Variable: Cantonal Decentralisation **Model summary: R^2 = .643*, Adj. R^2 = .530 (N = 26)**					
Constant	−0.897	3.932	–	–	–
Progressiveness	−0.335	0.214	**−0.427**	0.254	3.942
Left-wing parties	−0.029	0.016	**−0.437**	0.306	3.264
LG attachment	0.371	1.096	0.066	0.495	2.019
LG trust	−0.072	0.288	−0.041	0.685	1.46
No. of LGs	0	0.001	0.014	0.672	1.488
GNP per capita	0.015	0.008	0.356	0.619	1.615

Note: *p < .01.

Table 5.7: Fully integrated model

Independent Variables	B	Std. Error	Beta	TOL	VIF
Dependent Variable: Cantonal Decentralisation **Model summary: R^2 = .850*, Adj. R^2 = .626 (N = 26)**					
Constant	0.634	4.629	–	–	–
Societal diversity (dummy)	−0.109	0.304	−0.063	0.488	2.049
Latin (ordinal)	−1.11*	0.411	**−0.64**	0.266	3.759
Federal political culture	−0.292	0.366	−0.372	0.069	14.537
Area (logged)	1.035	0.812	**0.696**	0.05	19.955
Population (logged)	−0.426	0.847	−0.272	0.051	19.537
City primacy (logged)	−0.105	0.512	−0.042	0.35	2.858
Distance [min]	−0.008	0.007	−0.45	0.107	9.343
Geo-topogr. fragmentation	0.219	0.431	0.28	0.05	20.2
Mountain (dummy)	−0.664	0.372	−0.432	0.256	3.913
Left-wing parties	−0.064*	0.027	**−0.978**	0.087	11.468
Progressiveness	−0.005	0.366	−0.007	0.069	14.55
Local attachment	0.609	1.173	0.108	0.344	2.904
Local trust	−0.239	0.462	−0.138	0.211	4.73
No. of Local Governments	0	0.003	0.043	0.121	8.286
GNP per capita (in 1'000s)	0.017	0.01	0.394	0.272	3.68

Note: *p < .05, **p < .01.

that is the observed values of cantonal decentralisation, against 'the predicted scores from the statistical estimate' (Lieberman 2005: 439), which are the values predicted by this final model. This is shown in Figure 5.10.

For in-depth study I now select four cases that are more or less 'on the line', i.e. cantons whose degree of decentralisation is 'well predicted' (Lieberman 2005: 44): Vaud, Berne, Schwyz and Grisons.[18] Studying these four should most clearly highlight the causal influence of area, political culture/language and left-wing parties on cantonal decentralisation.

Conclusion

This chapter has tested four different explanations of cantonal decentralisation. In a first comparison, the socio-cultural model (language and political culture) came out as the best predictor, slightly ahead of the political model (left-wing parties, progressiveness, attachment and trust). The structural model (size and topography) came out a distant last. However, an integrated model explains even more of the variation in cantonal decentralisation: 74.4 per cent as opposed to the 65.4 per cent of the socio-cultural and the 64.3 per cent of the political model. Moreover, this final model is significant at the 99.9 per cent probability level and yields three equally strong predictors: 'Latin' language, which captures the difference between German-speaking cantons on the one hand and the French- and Italian- speaking ones on the other, the size of the cantonal area (logged) and the parliamentary strength of left-wing parties (SP and Greens). They are not only able to predict cantonal decentralisation while controlling for the number of LGs and per capita GDP, but also have a stronger influence than either of these two, judging by their Beta-values. Finally, my integrated model also explains 27 per cent more than Rühli's (2012: 177) linear regression, the only existing attempt to predict local autonomy (using the share of local expenditure of total public expenditure in a canton). It is therefore not just culture and structure, but also politics that play an important role in determining cantonal decentralisation. But are these factors really *causes* of decentralisation? And what does it matter? Studying four very diverse cantons, over the next two chapters, will answer this.

---

18. Strictly speaking, all cantons are on the line: statistical outliers are characterised by standardised residuals above |2.5| or |3|; the cantons with the highest standardised residual are UR (-2.048) and GE (-1.987), followed at great length by AR (1.212) and ZH (1.265). The standardised residuals for the selected four cases are -0.387 (SZ), -0.842 (BE), 0.854 (VD) and 0.393 (GR).

Table 5.8: Final model

Independent Variables	B	Std. Error	Beta	TOL	VIF
Dependent Variable: Cantonal Decentralisation **Model summary: R^2 = .744***, Adj. R^2 = .681 (N = 26)**					
Constant	−0.967	1.121	–	–	–
Latin (dummy)	−0.875**	0.239	**−0.505**	0.672	1.488
Area (logged)	0.528	0.327	**0.355**	0.264	3.786
Left-wing parties	−0.03*	0.011	**−0.456**	0.495	2.018
No. of Local Governments	−0.002	0.002	−0.284	0.313	3.197
GNP per capita (in 1'000s)	0.011	0.007	0.243	0.469	2.133

Note: *p < .05, **p < .01, ***p < .001.

Figure 5.10: Actual by predicted decentralisation

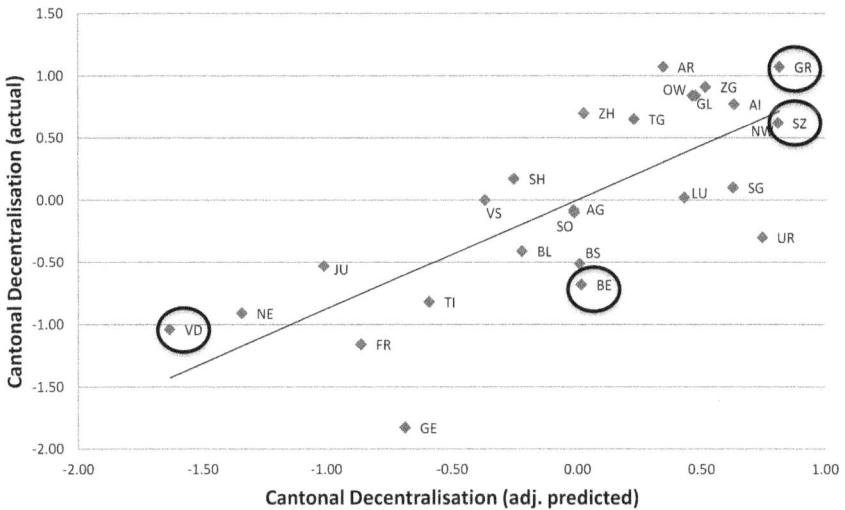

Chapter Six

Tracing Cantonal Decentralisation

After two quantitative chapters that have measured and predicted cantonal decentralisation, it is now time to dedicate an equal amount of space to a more qualitative method. In this and the next chapter, four cantons will be studied in-depth. For in establishing that area, political culture and left-wing parties make a difference to degrees of cantonal decentralisation, two further questions arise.

The first relates to the *effect*: how different are the Swiss cantons really when it comes to decentralisation – are there types of (de)centralisation, in addition to mere degrees? This is the focus of Chapter Seven, where the research goal is to observe the actual workings of (de)centralisation and distil differences as regards its three dimensions. It will be shown that there are also qualitative, not only quantitative differences between centralisation in Vaud; a confederal political system like Grisons; a system with institutional and political (but not so much functional) decentralisation like Schwyz; and one with political (but not so much functional and institutional) centralisation like Berne.

A second question relates to the actual *mechanism*: exactly how do area, culture and parties cause cantonal decentralisation? To answer this question is the purpose of this chapter. The goal here is to study the evolution of centralisation over time through a small-N research framework that enables structured focused comparisons (George and Bennett 2005). Accordingly, this chapter traces how cantonal decentralisation and centralisation have developed over time in four cantons: Vaud, Berne, Schwyz and Grisons, highlighted in Figure 6.1.

Not only does my selection span the East-West dimension, it also includes large and small, centre-left and centre-right, as well as German- and French-speaking cantons. The four cantons have been selected based on their position in Figure 5.10: that they are all on – or at least very close to – the line of fit means that my final quantitative model almost perfectly predicts their degree of cantonal decentralisation. But 'prediction' in this statistical sense, i.e. correlation, is not the same as explanation. This downside of statistical analysis, for all its merits (i.e. avoiding selection bias and omitted variable bias; *see* Landman 2008), can only be overcome by methodological diversification, as argued above.

Before I enter into the history and politics of these four cantons, a brief overview is in order. Table 6.1 lists their location on the centralisation-decentralisation continuum (determined in Chapter Four) and the attributes with correlational relevance (Chapter Five). A first look reveals that Vaud is very centralised despite a *large* area, whereas Schwyz is very decentralised despite a *small* area. This seems to underline the role of political culture (progressive

Figure 6.1: Location of the four case-study cantons

and egalitarian in Vaud vs. conservative and localist in Schwyz) and agency (centre-left in Vaud vs. centre-right in Schwyz) – but if so, how exactly? Grisons and Berne, on the other hand, are both decentralised in line with the expected influence of causal factors: Grisons spreads out over a very large territory and is fragmented into 150 valleys, the cantonal society predominantly German (but with Italian- and Romansh-speaking minorities in certain parts), and, as in Schwyz, with only weak left-wing parties. Berne is similarly spread out, encompassing the Alps, the plains and the Jura mountain chain, and German-speaking with a small French-speaking minority – but, as in Vaud, with a strong left-wing presence in the cantonal parliament. So if the strength of left-wing parties is decisive in making Berne more centralised than other German-speaking cantons, how exactly does this causal process work?

One is led to speculate about the historical evolution of each canton to answer these questions. If we look at the history of canton formation, Grisons was a confederation for most of its past, while in Berne an aristocracy ruled from the city over the countryside until the French invasion of 1798. The capital and other cities still figure prominently in Berne, whereas in Grisons there are barely any that deserve this title in the first place. Has this contributed to today's degrees of cantonal decentralisation? Both Vaud and Grisons are newer additions to the Swiss federation, while Schwyz was among the founding members of the confederal compact and Berne one of the dominant powers in the old 'Confederation of the XIII'. The former two have only been created as cantons some 200 years ago, leading one to suspect different historical legacies. Is path-dependency another

Table 6.1: Attributes of the four case-study cantons

	Vaud (VD)	Berne (BE)	Schwyz (SZ)	Grisons (GR)
Dependent variable*	−1.04	−0.68	0.62	1.07
	Very centralised	Balanced	Very decentralised	Most decentralised
Area [km^2]	3,212	5,959	908	7,105
	Large	Large	Small	Large
Dominant language	French	German (some French)	German	German (some Italian and Romansh)
Left-wing MCPs**	42%	31.8%	9%	10%
Canton since	1803	1353	1291	1803
History	Colony of Berne	Oligarchic city-state –1798	*Landsgemeinde* canton –1848	Independent confederation

Note: *from -2 to +2; **incl. 10% (BE) and 16% Greens (VD) (BADAC 2012).

reason for cantonal decentralisation, or simply a more remote cause, which in turn influences political culture and/or the strength of left-wing parties?

These questions call for qualitative investigation. Chapter Five has left us with clues as to why each of the four cantons possesses the degree of decentralisation it has. The missing piece in the causal puzzle concerns the transformation of clues into evidence. The method I rely on for this is *process tracing*, defined by Bennett and Checkel (2012: 8) as 'the examination of intermediate steps in a process to make inferences about hypotheses on how that process took place and whether and how it generated the outcome of interest'. The outcome of interest is cantonal decentralisation (y); my hypothesis relates to the combined influence of area (x_1), political culture (x_2) and left-wing parties (x_3). The only thing missing at this stage is precisely an understanding of the actual mechanism(s) by which x_{1-3} cause y. In 'combining the historian's craft with the political scientist's commitment to the systematic evaluation of causal claims' (Steinberg 2007: 198), process tracing promises to close that gap. This combination equals treating history as providing evidence that one has to 'read forward', not 'backward', meaning that we have to 'go back [in time] to investigate the foundational moments when democratic institutions were actually created and undertake a thorough analysis of the ideologies, resources and institutional legacies' (Capoccia and Ziblatt 2010: 939). It is striking that the more decentralised a canton, the later this 'foundational moment' in terms of that cantonal constitutional revision with the most lasting impact: 1803 for Vaud, 1830 for Berne, 1848 for Schwyz and 1853 for Grisons.

I thus apply the process-tracing technique to the four case-study cantons through analysing 'the deductive observable implications of hypothesized causal mechanisms within' (Bennett and Checkel 2012: 10) each case. Based on the foregoing clues, I am able to narrow down these causal mechanisms to the following 'prime suspects' (Collier 2011: 1):

1. Although large, Vaud appears to be so centralised because of the influence of an egalitarian *French-inspired political culture*, which has strengthened left-wing parties in their call for cantonal control, power, oversight and service-delivery.
2. Berne is a 'balanced' canton because the centralising influence of *strong left-wing parties* is tempered by the decentralising force of a large area and a conservative, Germanic political culture in the countryside.
3. Schwyz is so decentralised because of its *Germanic political culture* which, despite a small area, significantly weakens left-wing parties.
4. Grisons finally is the most decentralised canton because of its large and fragmented *topography*, which has enabled a conservative political culture to remain rooted within a territorially 'protected' societal diversity, thereby additionally weakening calls by left-wing parties for cantonalisation.

For each canton, I start by outlining the history of 'canton formation' to show how present structures have come about. In particular, I am interested in how the division of local and cantonal powers, as well as the role of regional tiers (plus prefects, in Berne and Vaud), have evolved over time. This is to cover the evolutionary, historical aspect of process tracing. I then focus on recent territorial reforms to trace contemporary political processes. These reforms include a successful territorial rationalisation in both Vaud and Berne; a failed one in Schwyz; and an ongoing regionalisation in Grisons. Cantonal constitutional reform has been *en vogue* since 1965 (Tschäni 1982: 113; Schmitt 2012: 148–50), but what is important here is that looking at these processes allows a categorisation of political actors as to their preferences for more or less cantonal decentralisation (*see* Braun 2009 for an analysis of constitutional reform at the federal level). So if the historical narrative provides background knowledge as well as insights into the temporal embeddedness of present degrees of cantonal decentralisation, studying current reforms validates my 'mechanistic' claim, i.e. the influence of area and culture on decision-making by political actors. Cantons are studied in increasing order of decentralisation.

French political culture in Vaud

The birth of la patrie

The fall of the Old Confederation in 1798 also meant that its multi-tiered membership system of *Stände*, common possessions, allies and external and internal colonies (Oechsli 1988) was over. When the political map of Switzerland was redrawn in the wake of the defeat(s) of the French army, the equality of what were henceforth called 'cantons' prevailed: St. Gall, Aargau, Thurgau, Ticino and

Vaud were elevated, Grisons relegated – because fully incorporated for the first time and thereby deprived of its independence – to that status. It must come as no surprise then that in Vaud, Napoleon is considered 'a great person' (*un grand homme*; Interview no. 17). Napoleon appears as the 'liberator' of Vaud from Berne, of which Vaud had been a possession since 1536, also giving it its first set of 'autonomous' institutions (Bovard 1982: 12). Still today, the cantonal insignia *Liberté et Patrie* ('freedom and fatherland') testify to the admiration for the ideals swept to the fore at Paris in 1789 (Aubert 1983). In fact, in terms of political culture, 'the people of Vaud are the Bernese among the French-speaking Swiss and the French of Switzerland' (Pichard 1978: 34), and I shall, in the rest of this section, show how this has developed over time.

Before 1536, the territory of what is today Vaud was fragmented into Savoyard possessions and dominions of the bishop of Lausanne, who also ruled over the city of Geneva (Rodt 1934: 301–2). The first Savoyard bailiff in Vaud is documented as early as 1290 (Gilliard 1931: 16) but, as Hughes (2006 [1989]: 5) observes: 'The ancient towns, and the many small new towns founded by the counts of Savoy, together give a particular character to Vaud, urbanised as opposed to feudalised, but never communalised.' Unlike in the territory of what is today (a part of) Aargau – another former colony of Berne – local autonomy in pre-BE Vaud had never been very strong. Like in neighbouring France (*see* de Tocqueville 2007 [1856]), localism in medieval Vaud was primarily expressed symbolically, through local attachment and ensuing inter-local jealousies, not in functional, juridical or institutional autonomy. This changed only superficially with the advent of Bernese rule after 1536.

Bernese rule over Vaud was much more unified and coherent than either Bernese rule over Aargau or the prior, Savoyard domination of Vaud. It profited from two factors: the experience acquired, by then, in incorporating subject territories, and the way in which Vaud had come under Bernese rule, which was by military conquest, as opposed to the gradual (and never fully completed) acquisition of rights and jurisdictions over Aargau. Only once, in 1570, did Berne summon the Estates of Vaud (*les Etats de notredit pays de Savoye*), a tribute to their prior existence, to approve a new tax (Feller 1974: 550). However by then the Church representations had disappeared because of the Reformation and the nobility, resentful of its new masters, was replaced by delegates elected in each new bailiwick (Tappy 2006: 77). What the Bernese conquerors did not impose was German: French remained the official language of Vaud throughout this period of external dominance. This was to have significant consequences for the permeability towards political ideas developed in France, such as liberalism, equality and uniformity (Arlettaz 1980: 369).

Probably the best evidence of the thoroughgoing penetration of Vaud by Berne is the ease and speed of the introduction of Protestantism and the complete administrative reorganisation. Rodt (1934: 304) summarises the former: immediately after Berne's troops had marched into Lausanne on 1 April 1536, a *disputatio* between advocates of the old and new faith (amongst them Calvin) was staged in the Cathedral; in October, the authorities allowed the adherents of the latter to burn icons and destroy altars; and by 24 December 1536 already, a 'reformation edict' elevated Protestantism to the status of official religion in the whole of Vaud. The cities, residents and especially the clergy of Vaud only reluctantly embraced the new faith (Maillefer 1903: 227), but Berne was set on imposing it regardless. And so religion became an instrument in the hands of the Bernese aristocracy for the administrative penetration of its new subjects.

The bailiwicks, on the other hand, into which Vaud was divided after the Bernese conquest were Lausanne, Romainmôtier, Moudon, Payerne, Yverdon and Morges, Avenches, Nyon, Vevey and Oron (Encyclopédie 1973: 125). Between 1701 and 1711 Aubonne and Bonmont were added, while Aigle and Gessenay (Saanen-Oesch) had already before been under Berne (Encyclopédie 1973: 129). Orbe/Echallens and Grandson finally were co-ruled with Fribourg and became part of Vaud only in 1803. Figure 6.2 maps these categories of bailiwicks in Vaud for the 18th century.[1]

Together, Protestantism and a more or less uniform but strictly hierarchical district administration distinguished Vaud from other Swiss subject territories, especially from what is today Ticino (Guzzi-Heeb 2004). In Vaud, the paradox was that internal unity was imposed from the outside: on the one hand, 'Bernese domination contributed to the formation of a larger territory, a "fatherland"' (Guzzi-Heeb 2004: 156), because identity was aggrandised from purely local attachments into a proto-cantonal *patrie* – 'proto' because it lacked institutional expression. In coming from the outside, this unity was both imposed and justified from 'above', setting an important cultural precedent for the future. On the other hand, only a protestant worldview was able to legitimise this (emerging) 'state' as a paternalistic caretaker and provider of welfare: aspects which in the Catholic doctrine remained dominions of the Church (Guzzi-Heeb 2004: 160). This caused public institutions – e.g. schools and orphanages – to grow exponentially and fostered a culture of expectations, which in turn strengthened the idea of a *patrie*. In fact, Vaud would probably not have remained part of Berne had it not become protestant; and it would definitely not have become protestant had it not been conquered by Berne:

> The Reformation and the Bernese conquest are the two most important facts of our history. The first profoundly modified the spirit of our people; their intellectual education and morals have received, since then, an entirely new orientation. The conquest decided our political fate. It separated us forever from Savoy; it made us Swiss; but most of all, through uniting under a single domination the different elements of the Vaudois fatherland [*la patrie vaudoise*], it contributed to creating the canton. (Maillefer 1903: 241)

Key to both processes was the bailiff. As elsewhere in Berne, he was appointed by the Bernese Republic from among its own ranks for a period of six years;

---

1. Map by Marco Zanoli/sidonius, at http://www.de.wikipedia.org/wiki/Datei:Bernische-Vogteien-Kanton-Waadt.png (last accessed 26 October 2012).

Figure 6.2: Bernese bailiwicks in Vaud before 1798

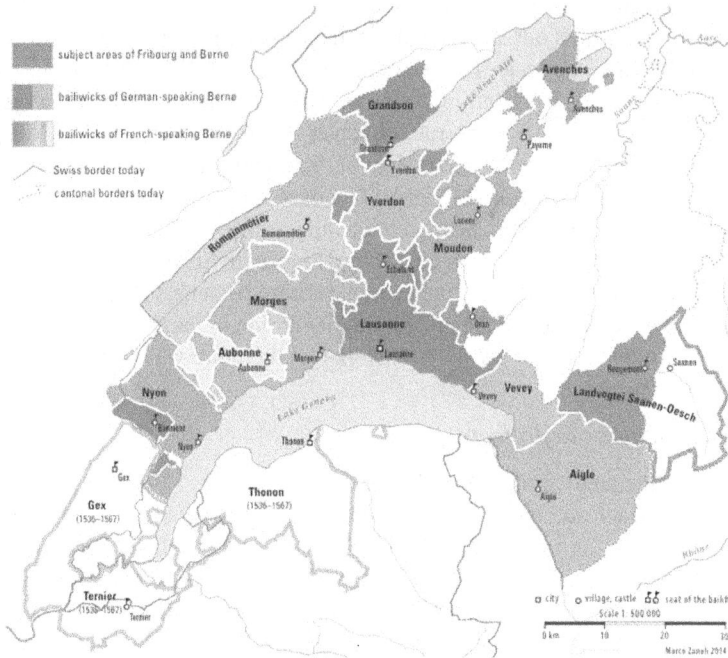

Note: This figure is also available in colour, *see* http://press.ecpr.eu/resources.asp.

his deputy and secretary, however, were chosen from among the residing nobility (Encyclopédie 1973: 127). The bailiff was charged with overseeing the move towards the protestant faith in his district, upholding law and order and collecting (also his own) revenue. Addressed as '*très noble et très magnifique seigneur bailli*' (Maillefer 1903: 307), he was the 'living, palpable and touchable incarnation of sovereign power' (Maillefer 1895: 81) and responsible for administrative, fiscal, military, police (in the largest sense, i.e. including public morals and private life) and judicial matters (Maillefer 1895: 83). But whereas in Berne proper, the Germanic culture was strong enough to bring about the direct election of prefects in the 19th century and, more generally, acted as a powerful check on centralisation, in Vaud the idea of the centralised, strong 'state' (*Etat*) has endured: until today, powerful prefects remain appointed by the cantonal government.

Bernese rule, through the protestant doctrine and a prefectoral administration, may have transformed Vaud into a coherent territory and severed its links with Savoy for good. And yet it did not make it an autonomous polity yet. In fact, such autonomy only came into being through the direct support of France, both militarily and morally. This in turn depended on the close relationships that had developed between Vaud and France thanks to sharing a common language. Most importantly, for all its imposed centralisation, by the end of the 18th century Vaud still lacked its own centre (Hughes 2006 [1989]: 5). The prevailing reaction to this lack of power over their own destiny at the 'cantonal' level was twofold. First, and as already pointed out, an exalted localism (without real powers connected to that); and second, a *de facto* reliance on an outside centre. 'There was no concept of the *Vaudois*, there were only citizens of this or that commune, all subjects of *Leurs Excellences*', that is of Berne, observes Maillefer (1895: 171). Communal authority remained the only expression of 'national authority' (1985: 161) and could, as well, have transformed Vaud into a decentralised polity at the start of the 19th century. But whereas in Berne that century was to bring a shift in the overall centralisation of the political system towards more genuine local power, in Vaud the exact opposite was the case: the cantonal centre became stronger and stronger. By studying the evolution of the prefectoral institution in Vaud in more detail, I will show, in the next section, how the French political culture was key in this process.

From Lieutenants to prefects

Vaud was 'liberated' from Berne by France in January 1798 and 'saved' from again falling back to Berne in October 1802 (Jequier 2005: 89). With its first cantonal constitution of 1803, i.e. Chapter XVII of the Mediation Act granted by Napoleon, the territory of Vaud was divided into 60 'circles' (*cercles*) and many more communes therein (Art. II). By a law of 14 June 1803, the 17 bailiwicks were transformed into 19 districts (Coutaz 2008: 115). With the canton too big to be directed from Lausanne alone, outposts were regarded as a necessity to ensure military defence: the new government proposed eight *Lieutenants du Conseil d'Etat* as its representatives, and the cantonal parliament agreed to that on 20 June 1803 (Coutaz 2008: 115).

But the *Lieutenants* reminded many MCPs of the Bernese bailiffs, and their role remained questioned not least because of financial considerations, until in 1811 their number was reduced to six (Coutaz 2008: 20). *Lieutenants* had to guarantee the execution of decisions by the cantonal government in their area and exercise a number of other functions, such as ensuring security and order and overseeing the mustering of troops. The *Lieutenants* were clearly modelled after the French *préfets*, although their name still differed:

> Before 1803, there was no canton. All institutions were created under French influence, that is by Napoleon. This is why there are prefects. We clearly are part of this tradition. [...] We were of course immensely inspired by the French institutions: prefect but also the communes. The latter were until today very much like the French communes: small and untouched since the 19th century. (Interview no. 17)

Moreover, a strong ideological commitment to centralism appeared. For the father of liberalism in Vaud, Frédéric-César de la Harpe (1754–1838), federalism was equivalent to the *Ancien Régime*; only a centralised system –

both at the national as well as at the cantonal level – could ensure popular sovereignty and freedom of press, conscience, assembly etc. (Meuwly 2011: 202). In 1814, de la Harpe's personal intervention with Tsar Alexander was decisive in securing Vaud's autonomy once and for all (Bastide and Kastl 2003: 93): the ideal of popular sovereignty meant equality of cantons, too. But even if this particular legacy characterises Switzerland as a whole (the very word 'canton' is of French origin), Vaud went much further in its adaptation of French political ideas to its own realities: the ideas of the state, citizenship and political rights, as well as the importance of public finance, figure among the most important influences the French Republic exerted over Vaud (Logoz 2003: 252–5). Of greatest interest here is the territorial organisation, on which I focus in the rest of this section.

Within Vaud as a new canton, 'everything had to be created' (Chavannes 1831: 5). The districts that had been in place for over 250 years, 'a traditional structure of federalist character in some sort, or at least of a particular regionalist spirit' (Encyclopédie 1974: 51), were reorganised according to the French ideals of citizen accessibility and bureaucratic rationality (Logoz 2003: 251). What is also important to highlight is that unlike in other cantons (such as Schwyz or Grisons, see below, where the communes created the canton), the canton created the communes (Haldy 2003: 132; *see also* Haldy 2004). Until 1814, communes only possessed an executing organ, but no deliberative institution or assembly; and even after 1814, tax raising powers and acquisition/alienation of property were subject to cantonal approval (Haldy 2003: 132–3). In other words, 'at the origin of the canton the commune [...] was a police authority whose autonomy was restricted', and still today the 'Jacobin and centralist tradition of the canton is strong' (2003: 135–6). This tradition becomes even more apparent by tracing the further development of the *Lieutenants*.

In 1830, Vaud undertook a constitutional revision, particularly focused on the *Lieutenants*: their powerful, triple status as executive, legislative and judicial agents was heavily criticised in the *Constituante* of 1831 (Meylan 1994: 51). With the *Loi sur les Préfets* of 9 January 1832, they were now called 'prefects' and their number was raised to at least one prefect per district. Henceforth, 19 prefects, plus two for the 'special cases' of Sainte-Croix and Les Ormonts, were nominated to represent the cantonal government (Meylan 1994: 53–4). But neither was the idea challenged that the central government needed the prefects to ensure a uniform applicability of laws throughout the canton, nor were their powers curtailed. In 1857, the cantonal electorate approved the incompatibility of the offices of prefect and MCP (Meylan 1994: 76), but the said law on prefects has been revised only three times so far, in 1920, 1973 (1994: 120) and 2007. Until today, prefects remain appointed by the centre and are not elected in their district (as they are in Berne or Fribourg), although the idea was debated in 1852, 1973 and again in 1990 (Meylan 1994: 123).

The 19 districts, however, were reduced to just ten in 2005 (Vaud 2006). In considering this most recent territorial reform, a final piece of evidence is provided on how political culture has 'caused' centralisation in Vaud. In reflection of the continued population shift towards Lausanne, now the clear economic and political centre,[2] the former bailiwick of Lausanne was divided into three, but seven former bailiwicks in the north aggregated into just two districts. Historical legacies were clearly less important than technocratic criteria of size and accessibility or the cultural ideas of equality between citizens (and districts). For the Government of Vaud, the mismatch between the 'ancient' district structure and where people actually lived was the main reason for the district reform. Because many public services had adapted to the population shift, the old administrative division was no longer adequate:

> The districts are administrative and judicial entities in which the de-concentrated tasks of the canton are exercised. This principle is ancient; for a long time, the basic services have maintained a strong (even if incomplete) link with the structure of districts (civil registry, hospitals and schools). [...] Over time, the link between territorial division and regionalisation of administrative services has weakened. Today, of 61 administrative divisions, only nine correspond entirely to the districts while 20 others comprise several districts. (Vaud 2005: 4)

This observed misfit between actual cantonal service-delivery and the formal district-structure led to fewer but bigger, 'more efficient' and 'modern districts' (Vaud 2005: 4). But the role of the prefect remained unchanged. S/He continues to:

a. represent the central government in the district, watching 'actively' over the implementation of government decisions;
b. be responsible for swearing in local authorities and other district personnel;
c. issue authorisations, permissions, licences, etc.;
d. be an informant for the central government and inspector, if need arises;
e. 'conciliate' in apprenticeship matters;
f. issue and collect fines for contraventions;
g. Act as the president of the district 'commission for tenancy reconciliation' (*commission de conciliation en matière de baux*);
h. offer his 'good services' (*bons offices*) as a mediator to both public and private persons;
i. supervise elections and referenda procedures;
j. maintain law and order and, to this effect, 'dispose' of both cantonal and local police forces;
k. reunite, at least once a year, all district officials of cantonal services as well as all local authorities to examine problems of 'common interest' (*d'intérêt commun*);
l. coordinate with neighbouring districts, cantons and states;

---

2. In 2010, a fifth of the entire cantonal population resided in the capital (BFS 2012).

m.   participate in regional economic development through 'instigating contacts between political, economic, cultural and other associations';

n.   supervise the communes, fractions, communal associations and other inter-communal organisations, specifically by annually examining their activity, management, registry and accounts; and to

o.   encourage and contribute to the relations between communes and mergers between them (*Loi sur les préfets* of 27 March 2007, in force since 1 January 2008, Arts. 16–33).

In short, prefects are representative, mediating, supervisory, information gathering and coordinating agents of the cantonal government. Similar to the bailiffs in 'colonial' Vaud, their competences are wide-ranging and their appointment is done centrally. This situation is diametrically opposed to the one in Berne, where we also find prefects but where they are elected and have fewer powers (*see* below). In sum, Vaud today appears with a triple legacy: a political, but not practical localism, inherited from the Savoyard period; the cantonal unity superimposed by the Bernese Republic; and linguistically, and thus also culturally, close to French political ideas, such as equality and an interventionist state. Naturally, in this environment left-wing parties thrive: their call to oversee the large cantonal area and ensure uniform service-delivery is thus culturally backed up. The prefect – itself the archetype of French centralism (e.g. Garrish 1986: 1) – perfectly embodies all three cultural legacies: in overseeing the many communes and mediating between local jealousies (which date to Savoyard rule) s/he acts as the representative of 'the state' (pioneered by the Berne); and in intervening, if necessary, also in private disputes – especially in housing and apprenticeship matters – s/he ensures equal treatment of the less privileged and works tirelessly towards furthering the 'common interest' (two French ideals).

Left-wing parties in Berne

From the city to the state

Until 1798, and again between 1815 and 1831, Berne was known as the *Stadt und Republik*, i.e. 'city and republic' (Junker and Dubler 2011: 1), but in fact the two were intimately linked (Weyermann 1924: 22). Ever since becoming a member of the Swiss Confederation in 1353, Berne exercised considerable influence over 'Swiss' affairs while maintaining a decidedly westward geopolitical look onto the Duchy of Burgundy (Wälchli 2005) and the County, later also Duchy, of Savoy (Becchia 2012). The history of Berne, however, begins in the city of Berne, founded by the Duke of Zähringen in around 1191. Feller's (1946: 8) *History of Berne* begins with this sentence: 'The birth of a historical entity depends on numerous factors, but always on the ground (*Boden*), which conditions men and their association'. This alludes to the particular location of Berne: on the steep and narrow peninsula surrounded – protected – on three sides by the Aare river (1946: 22). The city has continued to dominate cantonal politics until today and is a key factor in explaining the strength of left-wing parties, which in turn are responsible for the 'balanced' degree of overall cantonal decentralisation, as I will illustrate in this section.

After the foundation of the city, the first wave of territorial expansion took place around 1300 at the expense of the adjacent ecclesiastical parishes (*Kirchspiele*) Bolligen, Vechigen, Stettlen and Muri (Zahnd 2011: 6). Thereafter, the nearby castles of Bremgarten and Belp were destroyed and the fiefdoms over Thun, Laupen and Hasli purchased (Studer Immenhauser 2006: 214). In 1384, Burgdorf was conquered, for the first time with confederal support (Feller 1946: 189–94). By the 15th century, the influence of Burgund and Habsburg was all but eclipsed in Berne's surroundings, the rival city of Fribourg subdued, and the nobility politically dead (1946: 234). In 1415 Aargau, hitherto a Habsburg dominion, was annexed, thereby extending the rule of Berne up to the Rhine in the North (Zahnd 2011: 7). But as with the foundation of the city, territory was not regarded as primarily an economic, but rather as a military resource, and 'to re-establish the unity of the Aare valley had become the guiding principle' for the Bernese oligarchy (Feller 1946: 242). After defeating Charles the Bold of Burgundy at Grandson and in the Battle of Murten, in 1476, further possessions in the West could be added, of which some (Grandson, Murten, Orbe and Echallens) were co-ruled with Fribourg (Maillefer 1903: 307). The conclusion to Berne's extraordinarily successful territorial expansion came in the mid-16th century, with the annexation of Vaud in 1536 (de Capitani 2011: 8) and Gruyères in 1555 (Studer Immenhauser 2006: 444). Within 350 years of its foundation, the city of Berne had thus come to rule over an area extending from Geneva to Zurich and Valais to Basel, controlling important trade routes (Figure 6.3) – and was in desperate need of a political structure to hold it all together.

For lack of alternatives, this structure was provided by the Bernese city oligarchy *in personam*. The various territories 'were linked only to [the city of] Berne, which established all connections and became the centre point [...]. In Berne, the whole came together, and from here it radiated outwards' (Feller 1946: 261). As already stated, Berne's territorial extension remained in place until 1798, but throughout this time it represented primarily a military, and not so much an economic project. This meant that trade was not concentrated in the centre, as in Geneva, Basel and Zurich, but that minor cities in the 'periphery' (such as Burgdorf, Aarau, Zofingen, Thun or Lausanne) were left with considerable economic autonomy in running their own affairs.

Shortly before annexing Vaud, Berne introduced Protestantism throughout its territory – against the resistance especially of peripheral, rural regions (e.g. the Emmental). As in Vaud, the strictly hierarchical organisation of the new 'State Church' (*Landeskirche*) was to prove, together with the system of bailiffs, the most efficient homogenising tool in the hands of the Bernese aristocracy (Oechsli 1922: 149). Inspired by the parallel development of absolutist state building throughout Europe, and fuelled by the upcoming controversies with the Catholic cantons of Central Switzerland, the Bernese authorities were especially concerned to 'transform peasants into Bernese', to paraphrase Weber (1976). Thus, if in Central Switzerland 'the people created the state, in Berne the state created a people'

Figure 6.3: Berne, 13th–16th century

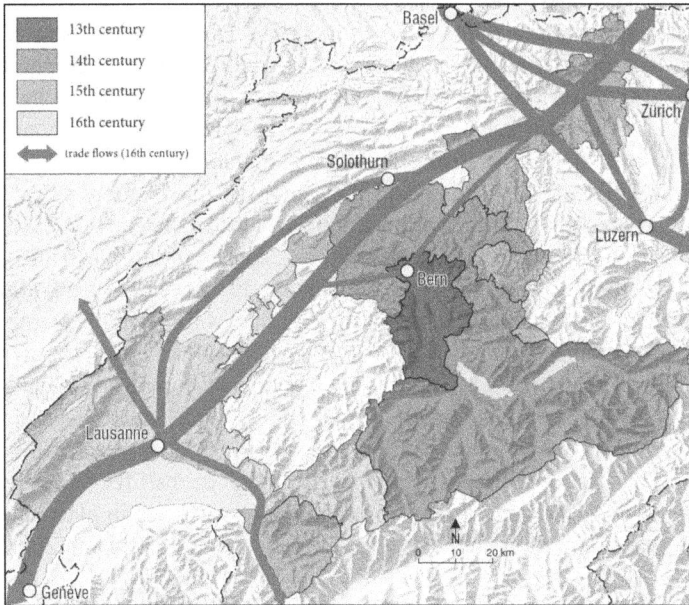

Source: Messerli and Egli 2003: 13.
Note: This figure is also available in colour, *see* http://press.ecpr.eu/resources.asp.

(Feller 1946: 9). Together with the legacy of a multi-cephalous city network, this idea of the state was to provide the cultural bedrock against which left-wing parties were later able to thrive – despite the prevalence of a Germanic and essentially conservative political culture.

What was Berne, then? Hughes (2006 [1988]: 2) rightly calls it the 'canton of the soldier and administrator, the imperial canton […]. Berne is a concept, almost an ideology'. At the heart of this 'ideology' was the city of Berne (Weyermann 1924: 11); its spiritual expression was the Reformation (Feller 1974: 298). A certain territorial fragmentation (Dubler 2008: 447) is expressed in the fact that all four 'municipal cities' (Aarau, Brugg, Lenzburg and Zofingen) managed to emulate the constitution of the city of Berne in that they, too, had their own *Schultheiss* (mayor) and executive council. However, their mayor had to pledge loyalty to the masters in Berne every two years (Weyermann 1924: 19). In other cities, the *Schultheiss* was directly appointed by Berne, and in other parts still the bailiff, in turn, had to defend his rule against much older local, ecclesiastical or noble claims to personal and especially judicial power (e.g. the *Twingherren*; *see* Dubler 1999: 76). Thus, Bernese rule, in Berne proper, was by no means as uniform, established, or unchallenged as it was in Vaud. As a result of peasant emancipation and a pre-existing culture of local autonomy, communes strove to maintain their liberties and often found them guaranteed in the pragmatic, conservative administration, e.g. in the *Berner Oberland* (Bierbrauer 1991: 205).

In all this, the Bernese polity building was neither arbitrary nor unlawful. *Leurs Excellences* in the city attempted to expand their dominion through purchases or exchanges of 'lower' (civil) and 'higher' (criminal) jurisdiction with existing feudal lords, and were keen to observe the 'rule of law' and local customs in their attempts at both centralising the administrative structure and unifying the relationship between themselves and their subjects in the countryside (Bucher 1944). What is more, Berne developed its own idea of statehood very early on: one founded on pragmatism, Protestantism and conservatism (Dürrenmatt 1942). Pragmatism because the subjects in Lenzburg, for example, were allowed to maintain their distinctive local court (*Lenzburger Amtsgericht*): Berne simply turned it into an appeals court, and so it even relieved the city from some of its responsibilities (Bucher 1944: 130). Also, an extensive control system over the bailiffs was developed to ensure they did not 'unduly burden the subject population' with high charges or steal from the Republic (1944: 109). This overall territorial structure with a city dominating its periphery through the bailiffs, and a 'Republic' built from within, upon and around the capital city, remained in place until 1798, when the French invasion put the *Ancien Régime* to rest (Holenstein 2008: 526).

Reforming the district structure

Very much like Vaud, Berne maintained the basic district structure of 1803 for some 200 years. With both Vaud and Aargau gone, the canton was initially divided into 22 *Amtsbezirke* (districts), each headed by an *Oberamtmann* (prefect) nominated for six years by the government of Berne (Junker 1982: 137). After 1815, when the Congress of Vienna attached the Jura region to Berne as compensation for its loss of Vaud and Aargau, five more districts were added, bringing the total number of districts to 27 (Junker 1982: 237; *also* Berne 2006). However, and in stark contrast to Vaud, as early as in 1831 the judicial functions of the *Oberamtmann* were transferred to a newly created district court president, and the prefect was renamed *Regierungsstatthalter* ('government lieutenant'), expressing a much narrower conception of central representation (Flückiger *et al.* 2006: 4). As in Vaud, this reform was a direct consequence of the June Revolution in France and the ensuing triumph of liberalism (Jufer 1960: 20). For Berne, it meant the end of the *Patriziat* and the beginning of the (representational) domination by the countryside over the city (Junker 1990: 38 and 50). However, even the liberals were convinced that the state antedated the people (von Greyerz 1953: 158), and so the prefects remained in place.

In 1893, the popular election of prefects was introduced (Flückiger *et al.* 2006: 11). This democratised the institution by letting the people elect 'their' prefect, and the link with the local electorate was put on an equal if not superior standing over the connection with the central government (2006: 24). Otherwise, and again as in Vaud, the number of districts and prefects remained unchanged until the 21st century. Analysing the very latest effort at reforming the district structure of Berne, in what follows, allows me to show where the different political parties stand and, thus, what the influence of left-wing parties has been as regards cantonal decentralisation.

In 2004, the parliamentary debate to reform the district structure of Berne was introduced by committee chairman and president of the Socialist parliamentary faction, A. Rickenbacher, saying that it was 'high time for a significant reform [...] 200 years after Napoleon forced today's structures upon the people' of Berne (*Tagblatt*, 28 April 2004: 505). The Greens and Liberals, too, supported the reform because

> we have, in our canton, 26 *Amtsbezirke* of which six are smaller than a medium-sized commune with 10,000 inhabitants. [...] The *Seeland* is over-structured: around Lake Bienne alone there are four prefects, each with an elaborate infrastructure, and those on Bienne and Nidau can greet each other through their windows. We need to act now. (D. Lack, *Tagblatt*, 28 April 2004: 527)

C. Stadler mentioned that since 'networks have increased, distances can be overcome much more quickly' (*Tagblatt*, 28 April 2004: 529), and for S. Astier the proximity between prefect and citizens 'can also be negative' (*Tagblatt*, 28 April 2004: 529), meaning larger structures would bring advantages by being less prone to clientelism. In short the Left, supported by the liberal centre, was advocating a modernisation and rationalisation of the 200-year old district structure to ensure equality and professionalism.

Only the conservative right, led by the *Schweizerische Volkspartei* (SVP), was against the reform. A first argument was historical – so for G. Fischer, who asked: 'can something that worked well for over 200 years really be so bad?' Second, reducing the number of districts to only eight would 'create monster entities of the same [demographic] size as medium-sized Swiss cantons [...]. The Berner-Oberland district would be the fifth-largest canton of Switzerland. The direct contact to the citizens as well as to the communes would be lost' (*Tagblatt*, 28 April 2004: 506). His party colleague, W. Aebischer, was even more pronounced: 'We are also against centralisation. The work of the *Regierungsstatthalter* is well acknowledged, close to the citizens and undisputed' (*Tagblatt*, 28 April 2004: 508). R. Bieri – also from the SVP – warned that 'oversized administrative regions are neither efficient nor close to the citizens or the state, and most of all they are not cheap' (*Tagblatt*, 28 April 2004: 509) and numerous other SVP MCPs used similar arguments. In this they were seconded by the EVP, a Christian right-wing party, whose M. Grossen cautioned of 'distances of over one hour journey time' (*Tagblatt*, 28 April 2004: 529). The main worry on this side of parliament, then, were the loss of established, small and citizen-friendly structures with their own identity in favour of impersonal, over-sized, expensive and overly bureaucratic new districts.

Because the SVP was then (and still is today) the largest party in the Bernese parliament, with 67 of 200 seats (33.5 per cent), the debate was protracted. But because the centre-left held a majority (SP: 58 seats; FDP: 36 seats; Greens:

15 seats) of 107 seats (54.5 per cent),[3] the reform eventually passed. When the cantonal Interior Minister argued that the government had tried hard to 'take into account many aspects of our canton, such as area, distance, topography, number of communes and size of the population', his advice to enter the debate was approved by a majority of 98 MCPs against 73 (*Tagblatt*, 28 April 2004: 531). The next day, 99 MCPs voted against 65 in rejecting the SVP's anti-government motion (*Tagblatt*, 29 April 2004: 536). So it was the relative weakness of the SVP, or the relative strength of the SP with centrist support, that enabled the reform to go through.

The detailed debate that then followed was a contest between supporters of four different 'models':

- 'Model 5': division of the canton into five 'administrative regions' (*Verwaltungsregionen*) and abolition of the prefects (one of the two government proposals, also called 'model vision').
- 'Model 5/13': division of the canton into five administrative regions plus 13 'administrative circles' (*Verwaltungskreise*) with, in each, a directly elected prefect (the other government proposal; also called 'model 5+').
- 'Model 4/8+': four administrative regions and at least eight *Verwaltungskreise* with, in each, a directly elected prefect (the model proposed by the committee majority).
- 'Model 5/8+': five administrative regions and at least eight *Verwaltungskreise* with, in each, a directly elected prefect (common proposal by FDP and SP; *Tagblatt*, 29 April 2004: 536–7);

The contest boiled down to one between model 5/8+, favoured by the FDP, the SP and most French-speaking MCPs and model 5/13, favoured by the SVP, EVP and the Greens (*Tagblatt*, 29 April 2004: 544–9). Both models obtained exactly 90 votes, and it needed the president's decisive vote to make 5/8+ triumph (*Tagblatt*, 29 April 2004: 554).[4] The debate continued two years later (*Tagblatt*, 30 January 2006: 142–155; 31 January: 173–188; and 28 March 2006: 526–538). The government proposed five regions and ten districts, while the committee augmented the latter to eleven. The SP, however, demanded a single district for the Seeland region, in line with the original government proposal (*Tagblatt*, 30 January 2006: 153), but a majority of 107 vs. 58 MCPs voted for two separate districts (*Tagblatt*, 31 January 2006: 174). This time, the SP was left in the minority, as the centre-right had its way. For the Mittelland region, the SVP proposed three and the SP again just a single district (*Tagblatt*, 31 January 2006: 176), but a majority voted for the compromise solution of two districts (*Tagblatt*, 31 January 2006: 182–3).

---

3. *See* BFS (2012): '*Kantonale Parlamentswahlen 2009–2012: Mandatsverteilung nach Parteien und Kanton*', table no. je-d-17.02.04.01.03, available at http://www.bfs.admin.ch/bfs/portal/de/index/themen/17/02/blank/key/kantonale_parlemente/mandatsverteilung.html (last accessed 27 September 2012).

4. In fact, a motion by the SVP asking for a nominal vote had been 'forgotten', and the vote had to be repeated. This time, the majority for 5/8+ was even larger: 97 vs. 85 (*Tagblatt*, 29 April 2004: 563).

Finally, another centre-right majority (101 vs. 73 MCPs) followed the government in rejecting an SP-motion to reduce the number of districts in the Oberland region to three (*Tagblatt*, 31 January 2006: 187). What is significant for our purposes here is the centre-right argument in favour of four districts:

> the Oberland makes for 48 per cent of the cantonal area. From Spiez to Saanen you need one hour by car. [...] Such a distance was important for the decision-making of the Government. Topography is also important: in three of the four Oberländer circles we are speaking about valleys. (W. Luginbühl, *Tagblatt*, 31 January 2006: 186)

This shows not just the importance of area but also how different parties interpret this variable.

In all three instances, the SP tried to reduce the number of *Verwaltungskreise*, with the idea that bigger districts enable a better, more professional service delivery. In all three instances, however, they failed to muster a majority. With the votes of the conservative right, parliament eventually settled for five regions and ten districts or 'circles', each with a prefect. What is also significant is that during more than two years of debate, the direct election of prefects was never even mentioned, so widespread was the consensus on its local-democratic effects, pointed out above. The prefect's powers are also much less extensive than in Vaud. Comparing the list of prefectoral powers in Berne (Arts. 9–12 of the *Gesetz über die RegierungsstatthalterInnen* of 28 March 2006) with that mentioned above for Vaud, one is struck by its brevity as well as the absence of the obligation annually to inspect the local accounts; the lack of coordinative duties in general and of the mandate to promote regional economic development in particular; that no mention is made of encouraging communal mergers or swearing in local authorities; and finally, the missing special competencies in tenancy and apprenticeship matters. Prefects are not only regionally elected, but also much weaker in Berne than in Vaud – despite otherwise very similar structures, such as the presence of many small and rural communes in peripheral areas far from the capital in both cantons.

However, while the Germanic political culture may have been instrumental in democratising the prefectoral institution, left-wing parties in turn have contributed to a rationalising and professionalising of the cantonal bureaucracy, and thereby also to centralisation. These parties, and the underlying progressive attitude, draw their strength mainly from the urban areas. In the parliamentary elections of 2010, for example, the SP came first in all the five biggest cantonal cities, Berne, Biel/ Bienne, Burgdorf, Köniz and Thun, reaching vote shares of 28, 31, 27, 25 and 22 per cent, respectively (Berne 2010). But it is the historical fact that the political evolution of Berne has allowed these cities to continue a meaningful existence as economic centres that results in the overall strength of left-wing parties today. This moves the ensuing political culture of Berne closer to that of Vaud – not because of linguistic affinities to France, but because of urbanisation – and distinguishes it from that of other German-speaking cantons, like Schwyz and Grisons, which I discuss next.

Germanic political culture in Schwyz

Schwyz and the Eidgenossenschaft

If the history of the creation of Vaud is largely contained within the history of Berne, that of the creation of Schwyz is intertwined with the history of the *Eidgenossenschaft* as whole. The *Alte Land Schwyz*, the 'old valley community' which today is the district of Schwyz within Schwyz, was one of the signatories of the original 1291/1309 compact, together with Uri and Nidwalden (Bresslau 1895: 6). In the 14th century the community asserted its grazing rights in a dispute with the nearby Einsiedeln monastery (*Marchenstreit* of 1314; Sablonier 2012: 232). However, the most romanticised event of that time is the Battle of Morgarten of 1315, when the Habsburgs were beaten (Sablonier 2012: 233) and which led to a renewal of the confederal defence pact (Castell 1954: 22). Military alliances with the cities of Zurich, Lucerne and Berne, between 1351 and 1353 (Sablonier 2012: 221), and with Glarus and Zug in 1352 (Castell 1954: 26–7), transformed the defence network of sovereign polities into a 'complex and eventually unique federal system.' (Wiget 1991: 167) But like in Berne, territorial expansion lay at the heart of Schwyz's inception.

Indeed, Schwyz could have undergone a similarly successful expansion in the East as Berne in the West, had it not been for rival projects in the near vicinity. Soon after Morgarten, Schwyz replaced the Habsburgs as 'protector' (*Schutzherr*) over Einsiedeln; the March area was integrated by 1436; and Küssnacht joined the emerging polity in 1424. These three territories became 'rural possessions' (*angehörige Landschaften*) of Schwyz (Michel 2011: 1; Landolt 2011: 6). But any further attempts to expand – the occupation of Zug or incorporation of Appenzell – were blocked by Zurich and Lucerne (Wiget 1991: 167–8). The aggrandisement of Schwyz was over as early as 1440, when the *Höfe* Wollerau and Pfäffikon were taken by force from Zurich and turned into a bailiwick or *Vogtei* (Meyer 1926: 163) and when Schwyz, together with Glarus, was given the confederal mandate to rule over Uznach and the Gaster area as *Gemeine Herrschaften* (Castell 1954: 37). Being part of the original group of confederates, Schwyz also received a share in the 'Italian' colonies: in Blenio, Riviera and Bellinzona it ruled with Uri and Nidwalden/Obwalden; in Valmaggia, Locarno, Lugano and Mendrisio with all the other *Stände* (Landolt 2011: 6; Castell 1954: 47–8; Wiget 2012: 168–9). Figure 6.4 maps Schwyz by 1450 plus independent Gersau.

In parallel to the expansion of Berne into what is today Vaud, Schwyz was thus involved in the administration of what are today Ticino and St. Gall; like in the West of Switzerland, here, also, nothing changed until 1798; and similar to the troops of Berne at Neufeld, the defence forces of Schwyz were at least partially successful in fighting the French army (de Capitani 1983: 163–4). Indeed, Dürrenmatt (1942) detects in these two polities conflicting but complementary ideas of the state. That of Berne has already been mentioned: protestant, oligarchic, hierarchical. The confederal idea embodied in the evolution of Schwyz, in turn, 'is completely summarised by the word 'oath-fellowship' [*Eid-Genossenschaft*] [...] to conserve,

Figure 6.4: Territory of Schwyz in 1450

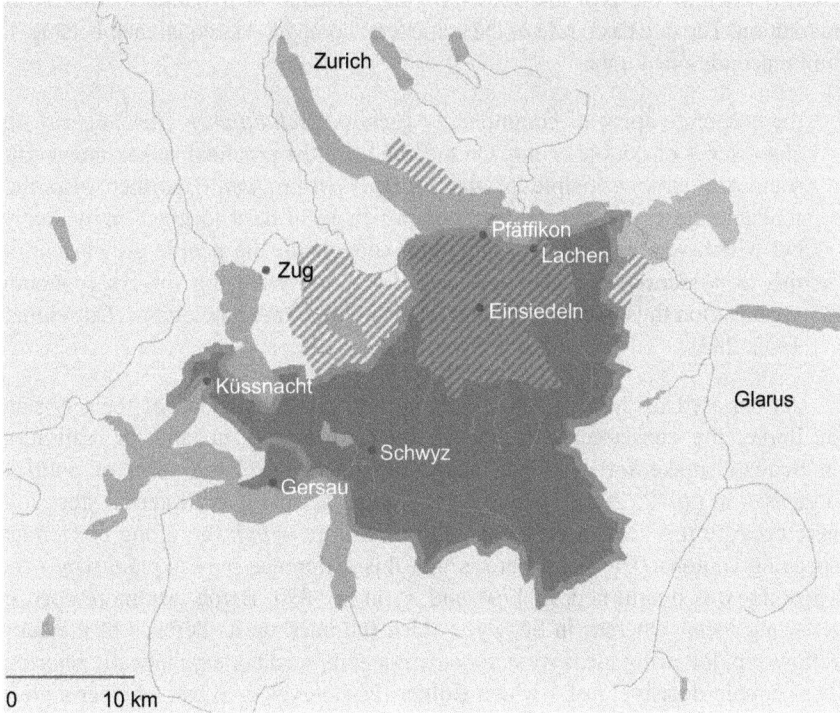

Criminal Law Jurisdiction (*Hochgericht*)
'Altes Land', Küssnacht, Einsiedeln,
March without Reichenburg, and Höfe

Gersau, independet Republic since 1390

Areas with settlement rights (*Landrecht*)
'Altes Land', Einsiedeln (1414), March (1414/37),
Küssnacht (1424), and Höfe (1440)

Areas under the influence of Einsiedeln
Waldstatt Einsiedeln, Höfe, Reichenburg,
parts of the March, Meilen, Männedorf,
stäfa, and Ägeri

Subject territories (*Gemeine Herrschaften*)
Uznach and Gaster (co-ruled with Glarus)

Source: Meyerhans 2012: 31.
Note: This figure is also available in colour, *see* http://press.ecpr.eu/resources.asp.

defend, reject.' (Dürrenmatt 1942: 282) The legitimacy of the alliance between Schwyz, Uri and Nidwalden rested on ancient independence and self-rule: oriented entirely towards the past and thus the polar opposite of dynamic innovation or revolution. The one basic rule of the confederal compact was equal membership, in turn preconditioned upon

> the corporate spirit of commonality [*genossenschaftlicher Gemeingeist*]. Its character is of double origin. On the one hand the practical, sober, uneventful socio-economic principle of the *Markgenossenschaft*. But then also that fundamental conviction of freedom, which is so hard to grasp individually, but which was nevertheless important enough for the people growing up in this *Genossenschaft* to be worth fighting and even dying for. An economic organisation thus becomes a political idea with immediate effect. (Dürrenmatt 1942: 282),

As opposed to the dynamic, evolving and pro-active idea of the city-state of Berne, the conservative nature of the confederal idea, and its realisation in Schwyz, make for a simple, static, organically growing form of political organisation (1942: 282). This contrast matters for the overall causal story told here because it reveals a different political culture *within* the group of German speaking cantons. The point here is that this difference may explain why once oligarchy was overturned, in 1798 and again in 1830, Berne was more open to left-wing ideas, whereas in Schwyz, which fell back on its defence of the oath-fellowship, left-wing ideas were not only not embraced but emphatically rejected. The 'double-decisive' test – which Collier (2011) evokes to test whether a piece of evidence fully confirms a hypothesis while at the same time ruling out all other rivals – here is the Civil War of 1847, pitting rural-conservative confederalism vs. radical-urban centralism. Incidentally, it was the *Landammann* of Schwyz, Alois Reding (son of the *Landammann* who had fought the French troops in 1798), who led the conservative-catholic cantons into a crushing defeat by the progressive, liberal, centralising federal troops, instigated in turn by the Bernese radical, Ulrich Ochsenbein (Bonjour 1948; Feller 1948).

Internally, the organic, popular and conservative idea of the state is best shown through the institution of the *Landsgemeinde* and the way the newly acquired territories were integrated as *angehörige Landschaften*. Decision-making at the *Landsgemeinde* was (and still is) indeed a very simple affair: all men fit for military service met in person to directly decide on their affairs (*see* Art. 21 of the *26 Landespunkte von Schwyz 1701–33*, quoted in Nabholz and Kläui 1940: 158–61; *see also* Vischer 1983; Möckli 1987; Kellenberger 1965). As the assembly of all citizens, it physically embodied the community (*Gemeinde*) of the land in Schwyz as early as in the 13th century. In replacing imperial domination (by the Habsburgs) it became responsible for all judicial, legislative and elective matters (Stadler 2008). Of course, practice did not always comply with this simple idea: by the late 17th century, the *Landsgemeinde* of Schwyz had come to be directed by a few wealthy persons. But its ideal was forcefully upheld and collectively cultivated (Michel 2011: 7): because decision-making was collective, immediate and direct, no elaborate state structures were necessary to transform the will of the people into reality.

The relationship between Schwyz proper and its four subject territories (Küssnacht, March, Höfe and Einsiedeln – Gersau was independent until 1798) equally degenerated from a principle of mutual security guarantee and equality, in the 15th century, into dependency and domination (Lienert 1977: 32–3). Although the territories were permitted to hold their own *Landsgemeinde*, by the end of the 18th century Schwyz symbolically demanded an 'oath of allegiance' (Meyerhans 1998: 6). It was the *Land Schwyz* or *Altschwyz* that embodied the political centre (Meyerhans 2012: 39). However, the subject areas were not prepared to help fight Napoleon's army unless granted full equality with Schwyz proper (Michel 2011: 9 and 13). Although at first giving in, the conservative nature of the oath-fellowship culture resisted this innovation for another 50 years.

As in Berne and Vaud, the old structure ceased to exist in 1798 and was reorganised along 'rational' principles (Auf der Maur *et al.* 1991). But after 1815, Schwyz reverted to its previous asymmetrical relationship with the four subject territories. Moreover, since the Vienna Congress had restored Schwyz 'in its borders of 23 December 1813', this gave Schwyz the legal excuse to annex Gersau by decision of the *Landsgemeinde* of April 1817 (Müller 1982: 154–5; Camenzind 1863: 76; *see also* Müller 1990 and 1996). But the legacy of French ideals lived on in the periphery of the new canton, and the subject territories were no longer prepared to accept inequality. After the *Landsgemeinde* of 1829 had annulled all their previously granted political rights, they formed themselves into the (half)canton *Schwyz, ausseres Land* in 1831 (Michel 1982: 251; Meyerhans 1998: 46–54). Only federal military intervention and the cantonal constitution of 1833 ended the partition and granted all citizens of Schwyz equal political rights, regardless of where they lived (Meyerhans 1998: 55). But not until 1848 did contemporary Schwyz come into being, when Wollerau and Pfäffikon were merged into the Höfe district (Meyerhans 1998: 91). The six districts and 30 communes have remained in place ever since (Suter 2012: 83). The conservative-catholic idea of the organic state has equally persisted, as I show next.

The persistence of districts in Schwyz

In their analysis of political culture in Schwyz, Vatter *et al.* (1996) find that while a typically rural, German-speaking canton, what distinguishes Schwyz are an outright rejection of centralisation at the federal level (Vatter *et al.* 1996: 18) as well as a deep-seated scepticism towards any kind of institutional reform (1996: 25). Together, these two make for an extreme case of 'conservative federalism' (1996: 25), which as I argue here, also works against centralisation at the cantonal level. This is shown using the only attempt ever, in over 700 years of cantonal history, to abolish the districts, which the cantonal electorate overwhelmingly (by 3:2; turnout 48 per cent) rejected in November 2006 (Schwyz 2006).

The *G-Reform* was launched in May 2002, 'G' referring to *Gleichgewicht* ('balance') between tasks, finances, institutions and area (Schwyz 2002: 1). The background report recognised the democratic and economic disadvantages of the convoluted ways of public service-delivery: by the canton, centrally or in a de-concentrated manner; by the districts or the communes, alone or together; inter-communally; or delegated from the canton to the districts, the communes, or to both (Schwyz 2002: 23). The traditional three-tiered structure (Figure 6.5) was regarded as not adequate for present needs anymore. In particular, the report proposed two models that would fundamentally alter this centuries-old territorial structure:

1. '*Bezirke neu*': both modifying and collapsing the six districts into just three, each with a 'legislative assembly' composed of all mayors (Schwyz 2002: 25–26).
2. '*Gemeinden plus*': abolishing all six districts and dividing their tasks (mainly education, health, transport, judicial) between the canton and the 30 communes (2002: 35–36).

Figure 6.5: Districts and communes in Schwyz

Source: Schwyz 2002: 51.
Note: This figure is also available in colour, *see* http://press.ecpr.eu/resources.asp.

For all its visionary content, the report was replete with attempts to 'strengthen proximity' and 'uphold subsidiarity' (two of the nine reform goals; 2002: 25), be fiscally neutral ('no tax increases'; 2002: 30), and to preserve local structures. The existence of communes would have remained untouched in both models. For model 2, the 'protection of cultural, regional and historic characteristics' as well as the 'decentralisation of cantonal tasks' (2002: 37 and 40) was key. The report also deplored a significant 'loss of tradition' (*Traditionsverlust*; Schwyz 2002: 31, 40 and 43); and the 'continuation of existing values and traditions' was another goal of the reform (2002: 25 and 32). The circle that the report tried to square was, then, how to reform without reforming.

This contradiction surfaces in both models. If, as in model 1, the districts are reorganised, Einsiedeln is only slightly enlarged into Einsiedeln-Ybrig, although even in its new form this district would have a significantly smaller population (Schwyz 2002: 27) and be fiscally weaker than the other two (2002: 30). Unlike the technocratic district reform in Vaud, in Schwyz preserving the existing district-structure as much as possible was more important than having equality among them. And if, as in model 2, the districts as supra-local organisations disappear, inter-local collaboration in turn is fostered by enabling the canton to force communes to work together in 'communal groups with a service-centre' (*Gemeindegruppen mit Kompetenzzentrum*), i.e. a single commune paid by others to serve a larger area (Schwyz 2002: 38). In other words, the districts would be abolished but reintroduced in all but name. Preserving local autonomy was also deemed more important than fully cantonalising a task: in model 1, communes would end up with *more* powers than before, e.g. regional hospitals, emergency services and education (2002: 36); model 2 would 'guarantee the continued existence also of the small communes.' (2002: 43) Both models, finally, foresaw an extensive fiscal equalisation scheme between districts and communes (model 1) or only between communes (model 2). In sum, neither in extent nor in depth can either of the two reform proposals be compared to the much more radical reorganisation of state structures in both Vaud and Berne.

After four years of public consultation, the cantonal government recommended model '*Gemeinden plus*', i.e. to fully abolish the districts. The cantonal parliament debated during May and September 2006 (*Verhandlungsprotokoll*, 17 May 2006: 1135–51 and 20 September 2006: 1215–23). Because eventually the cantonal constitution had to be modified – Arts. 22 and 23 CC SZ list all the districts and communes – the electorate was consulted on whether to abolish the districts or not. Before the vote, the parliamentary debate gave parties a chance to position themselves. This is an opportunity to observe differences both of opinion and argumentation between them. In line with my theoretical model (Chapter Two) and the subsequent empirical findings (Chapter Five), I expect a weak SP to advocate change in the name of equality and a strong SVP to insist on the status quo for the mere sake of its preservation.

Indeed, the clearest position was that of the SVP. The party fiercely rejected the reform during both readings, arguing – exactly like in Berne – that a) the three-tiered system had worked well and that b) abolishing the districts would only lead to more centralisation. In the words of their party-spokesperson in this matter, A. Mächler:

> Why should we abolish existing, well-functioning districts that have grown over many years, only to then reconstruct a middle level – which nobody questions is necessary – either through the canton, the communes or, even more complicated: through inter-communal associations? [...] This proposal clearly contradicts SVP-principles. It diminishes direct democracy, lessens popular rights and leads to centralisation. (*Verhandlungsprotokoll*, 20 September 2006: 1216)

A different argumentation, culminating in the same negative verdict, was put forth by R. Urech, also of the SVP:

> The districts are working well; they fulfil their tasks and their purpose. We [would] thus shatter a well-structured organisation and build a new one next to it. If you want to form inter-communal associations, you again have to invest money. The small communes will definitely lose out [...] In the end, we will have a zero-sum game. This is not worth the effort! [...] The population will be hard pressed to see this as a win for them. (Verhandlungsprotokoll, 17 May 2006: 1141)

From the side of the SP, on the other hand, the reform was welcomed in principle, as expected, even if not in its present character. For O. Kümin, SP spokesperson on this, 'it is not really the districts, but the communes that are the problem' (*Verhandlungsprotokoll*, 17 May 2006: 1136), as he set out to demonstrate:

> For many SP members, this proposal heads in the wrong direction. The institutional problem lies insofar with the communes as many small ones are helplessly unable to fulfil their tasks. I mention planning, incoherent settlements [*Zersiedelung*], environment protection, mobility, public transport vs. motorised individual traffic, professional social services etc. One should rather break up the sometimes grotesquely small and unsustainable communal structures, not abolish the districts! (*Verhandlungsprotokoll*, 17 May 2006: 1136)

Nevertheless, the SP as a whole was in favour of the reform. During the second reading, the same MCP outlined that

> One could say that the SP parliamentary group has been thoroughly agitated by the reform wind. A desire has indeed developed for reforming the state structures of Schwyz in the sense of this proposal. [...] it is not just about saving money, for the SP, but [...] the real focus is a structural renewal. (*Verhandlungsprotokoll*, 20 September 2006: 1217)

But the more radical, progressive, long-term goal was not hidden either:

[...] a different way forward, a different goal, would have been better. [...] we should have abolished the communes and strengthened the districts! But if [...] thanks to this *G-Reform* the communes will have learnt to speak to each other, to collaborate, then this could eventually lead to communal mergers, which is still the vision the SP parliamentary group retains. (*Verhandlungsprotokoll*, 20 September 2006: 1217)

Between the SVP, wanting to preserve existing structures and protecting small, rural communes, and the SP, advocating a more radical 'vision' of merging communes into fewer but equal-sized entities of district-size, the FDP and CVP were hesitant about institutional change (as the SVP) but positive about the proposed reform (as the SP). For the CVP – which in 2006 was still the largest party in parliament, with 34 seats (Schwyz 2008) – the districts had outlived themselves (e.g. A. Gmür, *Verhandlungsprotokoll*, 17 May 2006: 1135). Equally so the FDP: although 'in educational matters, the districts have done a good job', what is needed is 'a strengthening of communes in education and a promotion of collaboration' (M. Weber, *Verhandlungsprotokoll*, 17 May 2006: 1138). Both centre-parties made savings one of the key goals of the reform, and 'proximity and reinforced democracy' (P. Beffa, *Verhandlungsprotokoll*, 17 May 2006: 1139) another. In fact, for M. Buchmann from the CVP, proximity and finances are inseparable, especially in the areas of social services and environment protection (*Verhandlungsprotokoll*, 17 May 2006: 1142).

But the centre parties were divided. Thanks to a request by M. Lienert (SVP), a nominal vote at the end of the second reading took place (*Verhandlungsprotokoll*, 20 September 2006: 1221). Hence it is possible to draw an exact picture of party-support for the reform: 53 MCPs voted in favour, 35 against the reform. Of the 35 that rejected the reform, 25 were from the SVP (of a total of 27 SVP MCPs), five (of 24) from the FDP, four (of 34) from the CVP, and one (of 15) from the SP (*Verhandlungsprotokoll*, 20 September 2006: 1221–23). In other words, all parties except the SVP supported the reform, but in the FDP, a fifth and in the CVP, a tenth of the MCPs voted against it. Most of them came from very small, rural communes and had, therefore, voted in line with the concerns expressed above.

The next stage in the reform was the popular vote of November 2006. As already mentioned, the defeat of the proposal was clear. Not only 60 per cent of the electorate, but also a clear majority in all but four of the 30 communes voted against it (Schwyz 2006). Even in the four communes that accepted it, a mere difference of between 23 (Innerthal) and 160 votes (Arth) resulted, while in eight communes the share of the no-votes rose above 70 per cent to reach a record 88 per cent in Ilgau (Schwyz 2006). How do these results correspond to the strength of the SVP? No individual-level data exists, so our analysis must remain at the local level. The correlation between the strength of the SVP in the 2004 elections to the cantonal parliament (mean support over all 30 communes: 27 per cent) and the share of the no-votes in each commune is very weak and insignificant, though positive (Pearson's r = .079, p = .678). Correlating the same outcome with the size of the communal electorate, however, results in a significant and negative coefficient (r = -.392, p < .05). So the size of the commune seems to have been more influential than party affiliation: the bigger a commune, the more supportive of the reform.

However, in the 2012 cantonal parliamentary elections the SVP's mean support across all 30 communes rose to 36 per cent, making it by far the strongest party in parliament, with 35 seats (CVP: 29, FDP: 23, SP: 10, others: 3; Schwyz 2012). Although the correlation between the share of no-votes to the *G-Reform* in November 2006 and SVP performance in 2012 still results in an only weak coefficient (r = .225, p = .231), the association has become much stronger. It thus seems that not only has the SVP's rejection of the *G-Reform* contributed to its failure, since no other party openly campaigned against it. But supporting the existing state structures within Schwyz has also paid off for, or has at least not damaged, the SVP's performance in the subsequent parliamentary elections. Finally, as with left-wing parties in the urban areas of Berne, the extended rural areas of Schwyz reinforce the strength of the conservative right. Hence, both the SVP's electoral performance and the conservative, federalist political culture detected by Vatter *et al.* (1996) have been fuelled by structural conditions like small and rural communes.

In sum, in Schwyz structure and culture together impact on political agency: the SVP was the sole party to wholeheartedly reject the *G-Reform* and embrace the preservation of traditional localism. The one SP MCP, alone in pushing for more radical reforms like the abolition of communes, was left marooned and isolated even within his own party. But even the compromise agreed upon by the (cautious) centre parties failed to clear the popular hurdle. Therefore, the high degree of overall decentralisation in Schwyz can confidently be explained to have its cultural roots in the ancient, Germanic idea of oath-fellowship, which has legitimised minimal state structures, enabled a rural, peasant culture of conservatism, and contributed to the weakness of left-wing ideas and parties. That both districts and communes are centuries-old is thus a necessary, but by itself insufficient factor to explain their continued presence: political agency alone is able to preserve or change them. In turning to Grisons, the third element in the causal story will be highlighted: area, or topography.

The topography of Grisons

The 'Free State of the Three Leagues'

If the history of Schwyz is to a large extent that of the Swiss Confederation, the territorial development of Grisons has long been a more troublesome affair. Like in Schwyz, history begins with a confederal pact – but foreign powers continue to interfere due to Grisons' exposed location; like in Berne, the acquisition of subject territories was a success – but their administration lacked unity and degenerated into malpractice; and like Vaud, Grisons became a canton only in 1803 – but this represented a down-, not an upgrading.

The birth certificate of Grisons is the contract of 23 September 1524 by which the 'judicial communes' (*Gerichtsgemeinden*) of three 'Leagues' (*Bünde*) agreed to form a single organisation: the 'Free State' (*Freistaat*; Liver 1933: 206). Its preamble announced that 'we have decided to renew our previous unions [!] for the purpose of peace, quietude and unity' (quoted in Bundi 2003: 74). Until then, there had not been a single, but several separate, agreements between the Leagues: one signed in 1440 between the *Gotteshausbund* (founded, in turn, in 1367) and the *Oberer Bund* (founded in 1424); another in 1450 between the *Gotteshausbund* and the *Zehngerichtebund* (founded in 1436); and the third in 1474, between the *Oberer Bund* and the *Zehngerichtebund* (Liver 1933: 207). In 1524, then, the 'Free State' was given sole responsibility in foreign affairs – but no other competence – and shared power in defence: no League was allowed to declare war/make peace without approval of the other two (Pieth 1982: 109). Figure 6.6 shows the three Leagues plus subject areas.

Overall, there were 48 judicial communes, each with between one and three (Davos and Chur) votes in the only central organ that existed, the *Bundestag* composed of communal envoys (Pieth 1982: 110). These judicial communes were sovereign in that whichever decision had not been previously sanctioned by them had to be deferred from the Bundestag *ad referendum*, that is back to them for

Figure 6.6: Territorial organisation of Grisons – 1797

Source: NZZ, 25 July 2012: 11.
Note: This figure is also available in colour, *see* http://press.ecpr.eu/resources.asp.

citizen deliberation. This concerned almost everything: only communes could approve, disapprove, modify and initiate policies (Liver 1933: 208). Furthermore, only communes could raise taxes and even the confederal 'army' consisted of communal contingents (1933: 209). In sum, communes alone had 'a state territory, a state people and supreme authority' (Rathgeb 2003: 108). As in Schwyz, this centuries-old cultural legacy continues to live on, only that in Grisons several other elements have reinforced this idea of local sovereignty.

Situated above the judicial communes were the 'higher jurisdictions' (*Hochgerichte*), while the 'neighbourhoods' (*Nachbarschaften*) were smaller units below the communes (Pieth 1982: 114–6). The *Hochgerichte* formed mere administrative districts of their respective League (eight in the Oberer, eleven in the Gotteshaus-, and seven in the Zehngerichtebund). The *Nachbarschaften*, on the other hand, corresponded to the same *Markgenossenschaften* discussed in the context of Schwyz: social collectives organising economic activities like the usage of pastures, alps, forests, rivers and lakes (Pieth 1982: 114–6). For our purposes, what matters most in this five-level structure is not so much the existence of the *Markgenossenschaften* but their liberty. It is here that a first enabling influence of area on agency appears: the acute lack of fertile soil in the mountains made intra- as well as inter-local collaboration a matter of life and death (Liver 1933: 216; *see also* Ostrom 1990).

Feudalism in Grisons ended militarily in 1451 (*Schamserkrieg*; Liver 1933: 225) and legally in 1526 (*Ilanzer Artikel*; Liver 1933: 226), and so, as in Schwyz, the numerous valley communities were free to organise themselves autonomously. After acquiring judicial and electoral competencies, political authority was added (Sablonier 2005: 253–55). So extensive was communal autonomy that it even spilled over into the domination of the subject territories, the area of which made for a good third of the overall size of the polity (*see* Figure 6.6). Chiavenna, Valtellina and Bormio were acquired in 1512, lost to Austria and Spain in 1629, reacquired from France in 1639 (Liver 1933: 237–8) but lost again, this time for good, in 1797 (Rufer 1954). Because each commune was, in turn, entitled to elect its own *commissari* and *podestà* (i.e. bailiffs) for two years (Scaramellini 2007), the sale of colonial offices quickly became the most important income for the communes (Liver 1933: 231 and 240). And because each newly elected representative of Grisons had to recuperate his investments, public office was extensively abused for private profit (Scaramellini 2012). As in Schwyz, communal liberty in Grisons proper thus degenerated into oligarchic corruption, but the idea of local autonomy lived on in the cultural memory (Head 2005: 108; also Head 1995) as much as in legal texts (Rathgeb 2003). This is even more so the case since the medieval-confederal structure of Grisons was permanently altered only in the 19th century, and even then only under pressure from the Swiss federation, which demanded that a simple popular majority be able to modify the cantonal constitution, as opposed to a two-thirds majority of communes (Mueller 2007: 7).

After the forced retreat of the nobility from Grisons, 'communalism' spread in two forms: 'neighbourhoods' and 'judicial communes' (Blickle 2011: 16).

This medieval legacy constitutes one half of the further territorial development of Grisons; the second half stems from French-inspired 'Helvetism' (Rathgeb 2011: 121). Like in every Swiss canton, because of direct democracy such a development can most reliably be traced in comparing constitutional revisions. For Grisons, the main steps in this are the CCs of 1801, 1814 and 1853 (Rathgeb 2011: 123):

1.   In 1801, the canton was unitary-centralised: divided into districts with appointed prefects at their head (like still today in Vaud).
2.   After the fall of Napoleon, Grisons reverted to the confederal end of the decentralisation continuum: Art. 34 of CC 1814 conditioned further constitutional change upon a two-thirds majority of communes (2011: 124).
3.   Between 1851 and 1853, the judicial communes became the 39 *Kreise* and the districts of the Helvetic Republic the 14, later 11 *Bezirke* of today (2011: 125). At the same time, in place of the neighbourhoods, political communes were created that received the bulk of political power that before them had been enjoyed by the judicial communes (2011: 126). With this, 'the ancient political strength of the canton, resting once on the powerful judicial communes, was […] broken' (Metz 2005: 293), and the canton received its contemporary shape – as late as 1853/4.

Since then, attempts to reduce the complexity of communes (political, *bourgoisie*, corporations etc.) and their power *vis-à-vis Kreise*, districts, and the canton have been rejected by the cantonal electorate twice, in 1945 and 1966, because of 'worries about communal autonomy' (Schuler 2011: 137–8), exactly as in Schwyz in 2006. At the intermediate level, the need to coordinate spatial planning and attract (federal) investment led to the creation of 15 'regional planning organisations' and nine 'IHG-regions',[5] respectively (Schuler 2011: 142–3). So unlike in Vaud, where regional economic development was made a core competency of prefects, here communes have freely aggregated into non-binding, single-purpose entities at supra-local level.

What this historical exposé shows, is that '[c]ollectivism, autarky, equality and autonomy, the defining characteristics of the traditional common association' (Barber 1974: 126), set Grisons as much as Schwyz apart from the historical development of Berne and Vaud, where hierarchical, dynamic and representative elements have triumphed. But as opposed as these historical trajectories appear, area and topography played a key role for both. In Grisons in particular, the mountains acted as natural protection of the valley communities. Proof of this is the continued existence of Romansh in various parts of Grisons (Raffestin 1985: 152). For Berne, on the other hand, the open plains enabled territorial extension and acquisitions, for example of Vaud. So area and history

---

5.   'IHG' stands for *Investitionshilfegesetz*, short for *Bundesgesetz über die Investitionshilfe für Berggebiete*, i.e. the Federal Act regulating investments in mountain regions, in force until 2007 and then subsumed within the *Neue Regionalpolitik* (NRP), or 'New Regional Policy'.

both matter for decentralisation today – but as in the other three cantons studied here, exactly how they matter depends on the way they pass through political agency. In the next sub-section I thus study the *Gemeinde- und Gebietsreform*, proposed by the cantonal government in October 2010, and the popular initiative Starke *Gemeinden – Starker Kanton* ('strong communes – strong canton'), launched by the SP Grisons in May 2010. This is to illustrate how political actors make use of area to argue for one or another territorial structure of their canton.

'New regionalism' in Grisons

In its message to the cantonal parliament in October 2010 (Grisons 2010), the government of Grisons outlined a possible, future territorial structure of the canton. Coupled with a reform of the municipalities (*Gemeindereform*) to significantly reduce their number through encouraging especially smaller ones and indeed whole valleys to merge, the canton proposed a *Gebietsreform* ('territorial reform') to create 'between 5 and 8 regions' (Grisons 2010: 592). Similar to the *G-Reform* in Schwyz, this is the first attempt to radically alter the cantonal territorial structures since the middle of the 19th century, when the political communes replaced the former judicial communes as the most important local layer (*see* Rathgeb 2003; Poltéra 1922; Langhard 1977).

There are two main reasons for the *Gebietsreform*. One is the extreme fragmentation of Grisons, which in 2010 was divided into 180 political communes, 115 citizens' communes (*Bürgergemeinden*), 39 circles (*Kreise*), 11 districts (*Bezirke*), 13 regional associations and over 400 inter-communal associations (Grisons 2010: 590) – and all this for a population of barely 190,000 inhabitants. In fact, more than 100 communes had less than 500 inhabitants (2010: 590). As of April 2012, the number of political communes has declined to 176 (BFS 2012) – a sign that at least the communal reform is already working in the desired direction. The second reason is that in a number of policy areas, municipalities are perceived to be too small to function autonomously, and yet the tasks are too diverse to be fully cantonalised. For example, in the field of

Table 6.2: Sub-cantonal levels in Grisons over time

Level	Pre-1798	2010	Post-2020
Regional-2	3 Leagues	11 districts (cantonal)	5–8 regions
Regional-1	26 Hochgerichte	13 regional development associations (public law)	
Local-2	48 Gerichtsgemeinden	39 Kreise	
Local-1	'Neighbourhoods' and citizens communes	180 political and 115 citizens communes	< 50 communes

Sources: Grisons 2010: 591; Rathgeb 2003: 175; Pieth 1982: 109–116.

justice: dealing with bankruptcy, insolvency, or civil registries; in health: the financing of hospitals and home care; in education: primary schools for scarcely populated areas; in social policy: the protection of children and vulnerable adults (e.g. the new KESB, mandated by federal law); and finally in economic policy: regional development and tourism (Grisons 2010: 596–605). Even if all the Swiss cantons have to implement these policies in one way or the other, the topography of Grisons and its societal diversity, especially its trilinguism, represent a unique context.

The proposed cantonal structure would be a simple three-tier one. Through an explicit reference to Grisons as a federal state (*föderalistischer Staat*; Grisons 2010: 610), bigger and stronger communes – possessing 'real autonomy' – are to replace the many small and – especially fiscally – weak ones. The *Kreise*, successors of the once powerful judicial communes (*Gerichtsgemeinden*), would be relieved of service delivery but continue to exist as inter-municipal agencies and constituencies for cantonal parliamentary elections, before eventually being abolished (2010: 670). Finally, the 11 districts, which so far have been territorial divisions of the canton for judicial matters (de-concentration: a legacy of the Helvetic Republic), would be re-organised to coincide with the new 'regions' (*Regionen*). The goal is to have two main governmental levels, cantonal and local, and a regional intermediary for implementing tasks delegated to it from either side (2010: 767).

Table 6.2 lists the number and type of different sub-cantonal levels over three periods, showing how radical the current reform aspires to be. The regions would not only replace the supra-local *Kreise* and comprise the regional development associations, but would also function as de-concentrated districts for cantonal service-delivery. The tasks that the cantonal government envisaged to delegate to these regions were planning, civil registry, social services, economic development, hospitals, waste, music schools, secondary and vocational schools, transport, children and vulnerable adult protection, and or bankruptcy and insolvency (Grisons 2010: 767) – quite an impressive list.

In a first stage, the cantonal parliament was then asked whether a) it agreed *in principle* that this would be the way forward and b) which of the proposed versions – five, six, seven or eight regions – it would favour (Grisons 2010: 677–680). Parliament debated the reform in February 2011 (*Wortlautprotokoll*, 14–16 February 2011: 520–99 and 613–46) in 'basically a special session' just for this reform, as so much time was devoted to it (Marti, in Grisons 2010: 646). Already the committee introducing the project argued for a higher number of regions, proposing 'between eight and eleven regions' (2010: 593). The ensuing debate further clarified three aspects:

1. The demand for an inclusive, bottom-up procedure when actually setting up the regions, that is representatives of communes, regional associations, districts and *Kreise* should all be consulted as to the area, number and functions of the new regions (2010: 617).

2. A definition of regions with only implementing, but neither tax-raising nor legislative powers so as not to rival with the communes (2010: 621).
3. A confirmation of the dual role of these regions, with powers devolved to them not only by the canton but also delegated by the communes (2010: 622).

Two already functioning regional associations with fully developed institutions and para-legal powers are the *Regiun Surselva* and the *Associaziun regiunala Pro Engiadina Bassa*.[6] In the parliamentary debate, representatives from these two organisations argued against restricting membership in the steering committees of the new regions to mayors alone. G. Parolini, MCP and president of the *Associaziun regiunala Pro Engiadina Bassa*, argued that

> one should leave a certain freedom to the [new] regions and not enforce the exact same structures in the whole canton. I am surprised to see such a motion come from the liberal corner. This proposal has really nothing to do with either federalism or local autonomy. On the contrary – this is a centralist diktat from the top! (Grisons 2010: 627)

But in this, as in all other respects, a large parliamentary majority approved the governmental project and, in two cases, also the amendments proposed by the parliamentary committee. The final word in that debate belonged to the president of the cantonal government, who envisaged a decentralisation of powers from the canton to the municipalities if these indeed appeared 'strong enough' (2010: 638). So, far from wanting to centralise, the reform ought to contribute to a meaningful and 'real' decentralisation! In all this, and as in Schwyz and Berne, the only dissent came from the quarters of the SVP.

However, the SVP Grisons is a particular organisation in that it is both new and old. Before 2008, it had been a very strong cantonal party, but with the 'defection' of Federal Councillor Widmer-Schlumpf in 2007, the BDP emerged as a more moderate force (Vatter and Church 2009). This left the rump-SVP with little more than a few local branches, winning only four seats in the 2010 cantonal parliamentary elections, down from 32 in 2006 (BDP: from zero in 2006 to 26 in 2010; Grisons 2010). But those who stayed in the SVP now represent 'the real SVP', i.e. lie closer to the Zurich-line than before (Interviews no. 38 and 43). In fact, on territorial reforms the views expressed are very much the same as by the SVPs of Schwyz and Berne, as this SVP MCP puts it:

> Certain parts of the canton do not belong to any other, because of linguistic, cultural diversity – they cannot be mixed together. That would be a problem! [...] We should allow projects to grow from below, but today many things

---

6. *See also* their respective homepages: http://www.regiun-surselva.ch and http://www.peb-crvm.ch (both sites last accessed 26 October 2012).

are again prescribed: for example the regions, they will be fixed and defined. For me this is already too much, because what you design as template here in Chur may not be ideal for the people on spot. (Interview no. 38)

The same organic principles are upheld by an SVP member of the city parliament of Chur, woven into societal diversity and topographical conditions this time:

The nearly 220 communes in Grisons are a part of the local habitat, the culture and the language, that's extremely important. [...] building regions means that integer and natural areas are unnaturally disrupted. A well-functioning valley community [*Talschaft*] forms part of the culture, on all levels where you govern. No unnatural bonds should be created, although you cannot always avoid them. But the valleys should remain strong and active! (Interview no. 40)

In the cantonal parliament, it was left to E. Nigg (SVP MCP and mayor of Igis-Landquart) to defend communal autonomy against both cantonal and regional encroachments. To him, the governmental report was 'a mere technocratic blueprint by bureaucrats that clearly does not correspond to the political reality'; moreover, 'a [communal] merger always leads to less democracy' (*Wortlautprotokoll*, 14–16 February 2011: 526). Finally, on regions in general: 'we do not want this political level in form of the regions. In fact, what we want are strong communes and the canton: only two levels' (*Wortlautprotokoll*, 14–16 February 2011: 527), and on policy areas in particular: 'currently, civil registries, custodianship and land registries are communal tasks where the canton only exercises supervision. That should remain like that [...] so that there is only a relation between canton and communes' (2011: 635).

However, all 24 questions that the government asked were answered with majorities of up to 104:0 (for question 17: 'do you agree to delegate no more cantonal administrative tasks to the *Kreise*?' (2011: 592). The only questions that caused more substantial opposition were no. 7 on the long-term goal of fewer than 50 communes (60:52; 2011: 561), no. 11 on allowing cross-border local initiatives on communal mergers (62:40; 2011: 570), and no. 22.1 on allowing only elected local executives to sit in the future regional decision-making bodies (66:47; 2011: 633). The government took note and, exactly one year later, proposed to form the eleven regions shown in Figure 6.7. Parliament discussed this much more specific proposal in its session of 11–14 June 2012 and fully approved the eleven regions (*Die Südostschweiz*, 14 June 2012). On 23 September 2012, also the electorate overwhelmingly approved (77.2 per cent and 170 of 176 communes said yes), so the eleven new regions will be implemented by 2013 (NZZ, 24 September 2012: 10).

However, in parallel to this, a popular initiative proposed to even more radically and more quickly simplify the cantonal territorial structure: by reducing the number of communes to around 50. It was the SP that had launched this

Figure 6.7: Eleven new regions for Grisons

Source: Grisons 2012a: 1994.
Note: This figure is also available in colour, see http://press.ecpr.eu/resources.asp.

initiative in May 2010, together with the Business League of Grisons. One year later, they easily submitted the necessary 4,000 signatures (*Die Südostschweiz*, 11 May 2011: 6). The initiative reads as follows:

> The cantonal constitution and legislation are to be amended so that the canton receives a sustainable structure with a division of tasks that makes sense. To that end, an all-encompassing territorial reform is to be undertaken along the following principles:
>
> 1. The canton is structured over three layers: canton, a middle level and communes. Public tasks will in principle be accorded only to these three governmental layers.
> 2. The number of communes shall not be significantly higher than 50.
> 3. Wherever possible and meaningful, the territorial reform shall make use of existing structures. The topographical, linguistic and cultural context is to be taken into account for this.
> 4. Within a maximum of one year after the people of Grisons have accepted this initiative, the [cantonal] government must propose to the [cantonal] parliament a project along these lines.[7]

---

7. See the website of the *'Volksinitiative 'Starke Gemeinden – starker Kanton' (Gebietsreform-Initiative)'* at http://www.gebietsreform-ja.ch (last accessed 10 July 2012).

In May 2012, the cantonal government commented on the initiative, comparing it with its own proposal. In particular, it observed that a) both pursued the same overall goal: creating a unified middle-level to increase public performance; b) on communal mergers, the government strategy approved by parliament in February 2011 was to be preferred because it was 'bottom-up', and not 'top-down' as in the approach of the initiative; and that c) on regions, preparations were already well on their way (Grisons 2012b: 31–32). However, the SP and its ally on this, the Business League, argued as follows:

> What is the purpose of tedious communal mergers, if the resulting new communes run into problems already in medium term? The speed with which things currently happen is much too slow. It would take decades and cost millions until Grisons is sustainably positioned. Our initiative proposes a holistic reform, which restructures all the communes in the whole canton according to the same criteria. (Argumentarium 2010: 2)

The point here is not that the SP advocates a more radical solution and that the SVP defends organic, bottom-up reforms that grow naturally, in full respect of traditional structures, like in the other cantons. Since the breakaway of the BDP in 2008, the SVP Grisons is significantly weakened, so its influence is currently not too high anyway. Rather, the most striking pieces of evidence so far provided for the causal influence of area, are that a) even the SP Grisons is respectful of traditional and topographical structures (point 3 in the text of their initiative), much more than, for example, the SP in Schwyz; that b) although the initiative proposes an egalitarian, 'holistic' approach, no fixed number of communes was prescribed, but a more flexible solution was chosen ('not significantly more than 50'); and that c) even the cantonal government advocates bottom-up solutions out of respect for the territorially anchored societal diversity, unlike the governments of Vaud or Berne.

So not only has polity-building in Grisons been a slowly evolving story of gradual centralisation, still incomplete as regards the elections to the cantonal parliament, which remain a domain of the *Kreise*, and departs from 'a federation with communal statehood [*Bundesstaat mit Gemeindestaatlichkeit*]' (Rathgeb 2003: 213). And not only is policy-making still largely a confederal affair, as will be shown in the next chapter, with shared-solutions being the default option, but also, on top of all this, *all* political actors are federalist in outlook: even the SP initiative's goal is to 'strengthen communes', not to abolish them (Argumentarium 2010: 2; *see also* Grisons 2012b: 31), to build on existing territorial structures and respect societal diversity. The only way this subtle, but important distinction between Schwyz and Grisons can be explained is through area, for both share the same Germanic political culture and have equally weak left-wing parties. The peculiar territorial shape of Grisons has allowed communes to claim 'sovereignty' very early on, protected societal diversity and fostered a localist political culture. This represents a legacy that all political actors have to reckon with.

Conclusion

In line with the empirical model developed before, this chapter has highlighted the causal role of French political culture for centralisation in Vaud; the importance of left-wing parties for a balanced degree of decentralisation in Berne; the key contribution made by the Germanic political culture in maintaining decentralisation in Schwyz; and the effect of topography on intra-cantonal federalism in Grisons. Political agency has been a key element in all four cantons, either through the parties in parliament, referenda or popular initiatives. I will compare these findings more systematically in Chapter Eight. But before that, one last key question must be answered: what is the effect of different degrees of cantonal decentralisation – in other words: what does it matter? This is the topic of Chapter Seven.

Decentralisation – So What?

Let me now briefly concentrate on cantonal decentralisation today. Studying four polities in greater depth not only helps in tracing causal processes leading to cantonal decentralisation (Chapter Six), but a small-N study also allows the observation of differences within the polity-, policy- and politics-dimensions of decentralisation. As shown in Figure 7.1, the ranking of the same four cantons along these components is fairly consistent, with the sole exception of a higher level of politics-centralisation in Berne than in Vaud. But Grisons is the most decentralised canton in all three, Vaud the most centralised in two dimensions.

What does this tell us? (De)centralisation, so the first two chapters of this book have argued, is a three-dimensional continuum. It ranges from the ideal-type of a fully centralised political system in all three dimensions to the other ideal-type: a fully decentralised ('confederal') political system in the polity-, policy- *and* politics-dimension. What matters, then, is how the territorial dimension comes to play when the core functions of a political system are fulfilled: the aggregation and conversion of inputs into collectively binding outputs. Supposedly, differences in decentralisation matter because of the different consequences they have for political actors: the possibilities to influence outputs. To validate that claim, the following needs to be answered: is the political system *in general* really more centralised in Vaud than in Berne, more in Berne than in Schwyz, and more in Schwyz than in Grisons? The short answer is yes: there are two completely different models at work, stemming from two fundamentally different (cultural) expectations towards the canton. But even within the Swiss-German group there are differences. A longer answer, therefore, requires this section to draw on 13 semi-structured interviews conducted over summer 2011 in each of the four cantons, always with cantonal and communal representatives, from the bureaucracy and political parties alike. In this chapter, I thus assess contemporary territorial politics in each of the four cantons. As before, the actual workings of central-local relations are presented according to increasing degrees of overall cantonal decentralisation.

'Political dialogue' in Vaud

Vaud has the highest degrees of polity- and policy-centralisation and the second-highest degree of politics-centralisation of the four cantons studied in-depth. This corresponds to reality also upon closer inspection. As for polity, the one institutional arrangement that sets Vaud apart from all other cantons is the *Plate-forme Canton-Communes*, through which any major policy change that concerns the communes

Figure 7.1: Dimensions of decentralisation in Vaud, Berne, Schwyz and Grisons

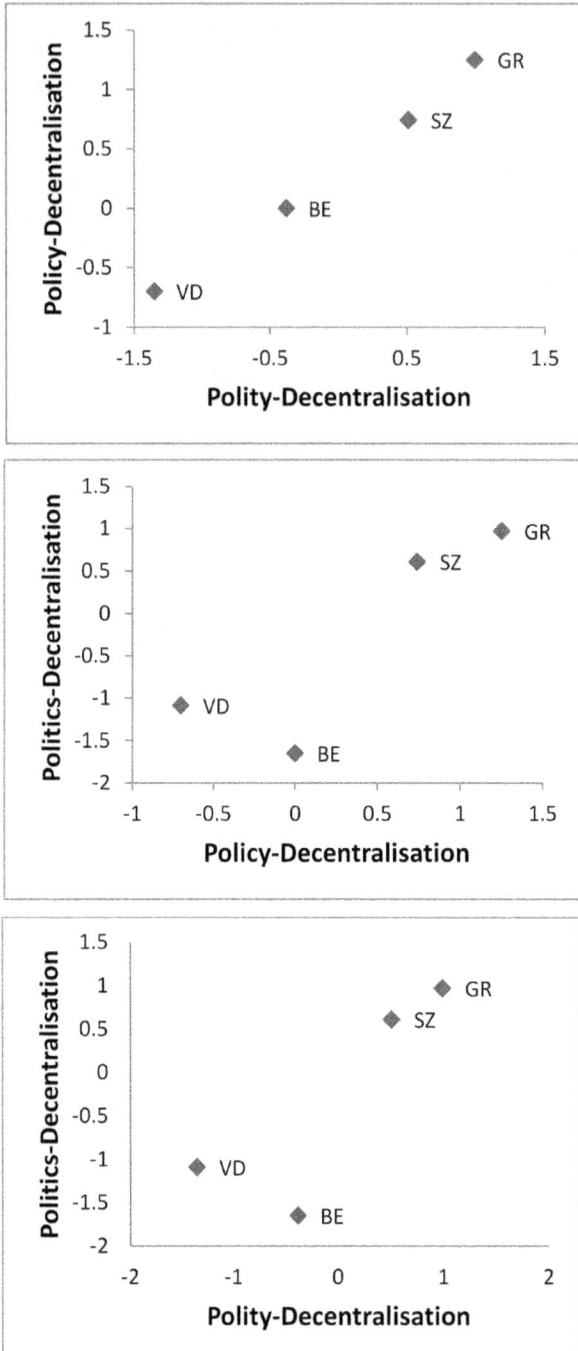

in a significant way has to pass. This 'platform' has its roots in an earlier organ, the *EtatCom* created in 1997 to oversee a disentanglement of cantonal and communal competencies (Horber-Papazian 2004: 80). Back then, it comprised eight working groups to study 199 public functions that could be redistributed either upwards or downwards (2004: 86); eventually, only 34 functions were redistributed in this way (2004: 89). But this model of vertical, intergovernmental cooperation was retained and transformed into the permanent structure of the platform.

Inaugurated in its present form in April 2008, this institution is absent from cantonal legislation and appears to be a purely coordinating organ. It consists of ten members, of whom three are nominated by the cantonal government and the other seven by the two LGAs: five by the *Union des Communes Vaudoises* (UCV), two by the *Association des Communes Vaudoises* (AdCV). For both the canton and each of the two LGAs, one seat is permanent. In 2012, these were occupied by Ph. Leuba, Interior Minister Vaud, Y. Tardy, president of the UCV and J. Y. Thévoz, president of the AdCV.[1] What exactly is the role of this platform?

For the head of the *Service des communes* Vaud – the office within the cantonal bureaucracy in charge of dealing with communes – this platform is 'an eminently political organ. It does not have any legislative power but prepares the projects and discusses them' (Interview no. 17). Agreements found therein still need to be approved by the cantonal government as well as by both LGAs' general assemblies. Recently completed examples of projects discussed in this way are a reform of the police force and a new law on music schools. On police, the platform met nine times between May and December 2008, when finally a 'Protocol on the agreement on the reform of the police forces in Vaud' (*Protocole d'accord pour la réforme de l'organisation policière vaudoise*) was signed that contained the 'strategic and political aspects', subsequently validated by the Government, the UCV and the AdCV (Vaud 2009). On music schools, there were 14 meetings, starting in October 2007, that eventually led to the *Protocole d'accord pour le règlement des bases du financement de l'enseignement de la musique à visée non professionnelle* signed on 7 June 2010 (Vaud 2010b). Only thanks to this platform could agreements be found in both areas, after negotiations had dragged on for several years (Interview no. 17). Two other domains that are being negotiated are public transport on the lake (since November 2010) and out-of-school care (since August 2010), whereas agreements were found for school transports (in May 2011), fiscal equalisation (in December 2009) and social policy (in January 2009). All in all, seven projects have been, or are still being, agreed by communes and the canton using this inter-executive mechanism.

However, there are also downsides to this 'political dialogue', as even the head of the *Service des communes* Vaud is well aware of, since agreements found in this way significantly 'restrict the political manoeuvring space' of the cantonal

1. A. Arn held the seat for the AdCV at the time I conducted my interview with her. *See* the official website of the 'Plate-forme', hosted centrally by the cantonal authorities, at http://www.vd.ch/themes/territoire/communes/plate-forme-canton-communes/ (last accessed September 2012).

parliament (Interview no. 17). In principle, the legislative branch can 'still do whatever it wants', but 'it is difficult to imagine the parliament destroying everything that has been done, since such an important partner as are the communes have been part of the decision-finding process' (Interview no. 17). As with intergovernmental conferences and the role of the unelected Commission in EU matters (Trench 2006), in Vaud a democratic deficit appears in this bypassing of the cantonal parliament. But does this system enable communes to have more influence than in other cantons?

Yes, insofar as direct access to the government is welcomed. Communes in Vaud are appreciative of this inter-executive system. Moreover, it has not only enabled vertical, but also horizontal agreements, i.e. not just between canton and communes but also among communes themselves. As mentioned, one of the first items on the agenda of the platform included a reorganisation of the fiscal equalisation between canton and communes, on which an agreement was finally found on 3 December 2009 (Vaud 2010a). Fiscal equalisation was the reason why the AdCV was formed in the first place – as a breakaway organisation from the UCV to better represent the 'rich communes' (Interview no. 18). But the two LGAs proved to work well together even in the policy area on which they were most divided (Interview no. 18). The significance of the platform can only be grasped in the context of a lack of other means to influence cantonal policies, given that the canton is overall so centralised: there are no instruments of direct democracy that would enable the communes to launch an initiative or a referendum; political competition takes place in constituencies above the local level, at best, and at the cantonal level, at worst; and local representatives in the cantonal parliament feel more attached to their party (and ideology) than to their municipality (and territory). The Greens, for example,

> have two essential criteria in our Charta: diversity and proximity. That means we are rather in favour of decentralisation of power; in principle. We are thus not at all on the same line as, for example, the Socialist Party, who is more in favour of centralisation of power and equal opportunities, for example at the national level. But that does not mean that we are always in favour of local autonomy or of the decentralised regions; that really depends on the topic! (Interview no. 15)

Communes, then, are left with practically no other means than post-hoc legal challenges, for example on the very same question of fiscal equalisation, where the AdCV

> made specific appeals every time we received a bill: every year, every time! Of course, it was the AdCV who made the appeals on behalf of the communes, in a working group together with economists and lawyers […] Many times we went as far as to the Federal Tribunal, but every time we lost. That was really frustrating because we felt the system to be really unjust! In parallel, this platform was created and we put forth our proposal, saying this is what

we want and what we offer: the rich communes will pay, but with the tax rate criterion omitted. And in fact we could agree on a solution – it took six months of negotiations, back and forth, but it worked. Since then, no more appeals! (Interview no. 18)

In this, and like any other interest group, the AdCV acted completely rationally in its calculations. Representing the rich communes, the goal was to pay less; representing a minority, it knew that if it all came down to majority decision, the rich communes would eventually lose:

We did not want to hold a referendum against that [old fiscal equalisation] law because we knew we would lose: the communes who receive are much more numerous – in fact, they made the law in a way that there were less people who had to pay than who received, so in a popular vote it would have been upheld. (Interview no. 18)

The way of doing politics in the platform, i.e. centrally and between cantonal and local executive members, clearly has the advantage of bringing canton and communes together early on in the policy-making process: 'Whenever a problem touches both canton and communes, we negotiate in this platform, and this works rather well.' (Interview no. 18) In fact, this system has significantly improved general governmental relations as well:

Between 2000 and 2005/6, relations between canton and communes were extremely bad because there was little dialogue, and the little there was, was badly organised. As the communes were unable to communicate a clear message, the canton acted and brought a project to the *Grand Conseil* [Parliament], which then cut this project, most often against the communes, although the communes are well represented there. The communes then always cried out 'new attack on communal autonomy' etc. […] The communes always think that the canton wants to burden them with tasks and take away their money without them having to say anything. On our side, we always have the impression that the communes want money, but without the canton having anything to say, in turn […] But now we at least have an official platform […]! (Interview no. 17)

The impression that emerges for Vaud, then, is that communes are less an institutional or policy-making, but rather a political force. Politics is more litigious than in the other three cantons studied here, which seems to be due to the much more confrontational 'French' style of debating. Taking again the example of the police reform, it is worth quoting at length what had been the fragmented situation before and how a rational solution could be found:

the problem has always been that there were two visions: the canton wanted to centralise, the communes wanted to keep their competences. […] we have the cantonal police, the Lausanne police with judicial powers – they also had their own drug squad, on top of the cantonal drug squad: the others had no such competences! – then Morges with more powers in terms of traffic, which Saint-Sulpice did not have, and Ecublens, just beside them, with powers between the former two... [...] the canton would have the means to say: okay, let's just do a unified police, too bad for the communes! But if we had done that, the reaction of communes would have been so strong that it would never have passed the *Grand Conseil*. And even if it did pass, a referendum would have to be held [...] These are political equilibria. I was part of and directed two working groups. We said we had to find a solution, so what we found was a coordinated police: communal police corps remain possible but they all have to have the same competencies – apart from Lausanne – and to have those, they need a certain size. That meant that all those small police corps had no future, as we made them understand, unless they merged with their neighbours to ensure the same service (24/7 and the same formation of police officers). From that moment onwards, the cantonal police would not interfere anymore, unless it was something really important. That was the basis of the solution, with financial details to be negotiated later. I made the cantonal police understand that they would never achieve their unitary position – all they could get was to generally direct the system, but with local representatives. The communes were told that they could continue [to have their own police], but with a much more specific task description as regards formation etc. So it was a compromise, and remains quite complicated: even a little federal! (Interview no. 17)

Several aspects deserve highlighting here. First and foremost, a 'federal compromise' was judged to be the only *politically* viable solution. Although communes are practically weak, in the perception of people localism remains important, especially when connected to traditional institutions such as local planning and the police. Vaud is, after all, significantly less centralised than, for example, Geneva. It was the anticipated political resistance that forced a compromise, not constitutional guarantees of local autonomy or local expenditure or revenue autonomy. Second, the solution found mixed central minimum standards of quality (notably formation and availability) with local discretion in terms of implementation. This is typical of the 'executive federalism' that is also at play in Switzerland as a whole. Third, note the uniqueness of Lausanne as the cantonal capital, which, due to its sheer size and location, necessitates a completely different treatment (e.g. their own drug squad) than the many rural, peripheral, small communes. Hence, the picture that emerges from observing centralisation in Vaud is that

compared with many communes in the German-speaking canton, ours have fewer competences, especially in the big public policy areas, but our communes have fought to maintain their police and have succeeded, so it does not just go in one sense only! (Interview no. 17)

But that it does not go in one sense only is due essentially to the political standing of communes, not because of their polity- or policy-autonomy. The image of political disputes fought out at the inter-executive levels is, nevertheless, very different from the much more cordial, participatory and integrative way of territorial politics in Berne, to which I turn next.

'Corporate lobbying' in Berne

Berne has the second-highest degrees of polity- and policy-centralisation and the highest degree of politics-centralisation of the four cantons studied here. It is the most centralised in the group of 'balanced' cantons (*see* Typology in Chapter Eight,). No 'platform' where communal and cantonal executives meet exists in Berne. There is, however, in the form of the *Verband Bernischer Gemeinden* (VBG), a very strong corporate lobby reuniting all the (political) communes, i.e. not divided into two as in Vaud. Its role is also acknowledged in the cantonal administration:

> Communes are very strong […]. They are included through the normal procedures, i.e. public consultation [*Vernehmlassung*]. They have also a very strong interest group: the VBG is very strong in Berne. […] Because many mayors or members of the communal executive sit in the cantonal parliament, their interests are well represented and taken into account there as well. (Interview no. 16)

The political influence is stronger than in Vaud because it is backed up by policy- and polity-autonomy, but – somewhat paradoxically – also more centralised because of the strength of the VBG. For example, inclusion in public consultations alone would be insufficient for achieving influence – in fact, at that stage it would already be too late to significantly influence policy-making, especially so for the many small communes that often lack professional politicians. As it is argued by the Director General of the VBG:

> We make all our good deals in expert groups, which we either launch ourselves or where the canton approaches us and wants to talk with us. One example: until recently, financing of home care [*Spitex*] was done by communes and canton together. But the communes did not really do anything, they could not steer anything anymore. All the norm costs are predetermined etc. We discussed this in a small group and then invited the section chiefs of the social services, who confirmed this. We communicated this to the canton and this was then eliminated, i.e. this is now financed entirely by the canton. (Interview no. 27)

Strong LGAs, therefore, enable pro-active policy-making, whereas inter-local dissent, as in Vaud, needs to resort to reactive protests. And even when there is an official consultation, in Berne, it is the VBG itself that consults with all of its members first before replying:

On important topics we go out and organise a decentralised event with members of the cantonal government. The next day, all communes receive our opinion in the form of six bullet points and a questionnaire, which we then evaluate. The responses are weighted according to population size, because this makes a difference. That's how we consolidate our attitude: we can then exactly tell to what extent the communes agree. Only once have we received a feedback that was in disagreement with our opinion. Communes know this and trust us. (Interview no. 27)

In comparison with the divided nature of LG associations in Vaud, the VBG is able to speak with *one* voice and on behalf of *all* communes. The paradox is that in this way, the LGA contributes to what it had set out to impede, i.e. centralisation, even if not at the cantonal but at the inter-local, association level. The VGB is aware of this delicate act of balance:

Of course, every association means centralisation, but only of positioning. [As a commune] You have two options: you can either say that the VBG takes a wrong position, [or] that it is too much biased in favour of the big communes and the cities. We are, on the other hand, not guided by differences, but by those interests that all communes have in common. Here we have an incredible power if we steer in a centralised manner! (Interview no. 27)

Consultation with stakeholders is indeed a key characteristic not just of cantonal, but also of Swiss policy making in general (Reich 1975: 119). On the creation of 'regional conferences' (*see* Mueller and Dardanelli 2012), the canton was adamant to achieve local input very early on:

The whole process of setting the boundaries [of the regional conferences] was participatory. First there was a background report, which was sent into public consultation; then the draft law, again sent into public consultation; and finally the government decree, again consultation. Everything was very participatory, together with the regions. Not that the canton would have taken the map and drawn a boundary somewhere. Anyway, this would never have passed. All regions could at least co-decide, for example for the Seeland-Jura bernois region the canton initially proposed to create two regional conferences. But in the public consultation, everybody there wanted a single regional conference, and this was then taken on board. (Interview no. 16)

Only if neither involvement in expert committees nor inputs during consultation phases are successful, does the VBG resort to influencing the cantonal parliament directly:

We have a strong lobby. Through our steering committee we are directly connected to the parliamentary factions – politics is obviously not done in the plenary, but in the factions. This is very important for us. When we get into parliament, it is most often too late for us. We use our influence in a different way: here a lunch, a working group, there a small comment [...] Today we sent a letter to all MCPs because we disagree on something. If something gets into a [parliamentary] committee, we also send all of their members a letter, then we are usually invited to appear before them. If it gets into the plenary, we lobby through our people in the parliamentary factions, so they influence the preparatory work. Finally, when it comes to the showdown, we write all our 400 member communes a letter with the standard argument: invite your MCP, because s/he gets elected with *you* and not here, so go and tell them that they should not go to Berne and do this or that [...] But this is really rare. (Interview no. 27)

Although electoral districts in Berne are equally supra-local as in Vaud, left-wing parties are of broadly similar strength, and although there are as many small, rural and peripheral communes, at least in the perception of the LGA, in Berne the local dimension is more successfully – because 'centrally' – activated than in Vaud. But communes are also practically more important in Berne than in Vaud, with more powers and constitutionally guaranteed local autonomy. As shown in the previous chapter, this latter distinction is representative of French vs. German-speaking cantons at large and has deeper, cultural reasons. What matters here is to observe how the VBG pragmatically searches for alliances with different political parties. Because left-wing parties in Berne are in favour of a more professional service delivery, they often prefer the cantonalisation of a task, especially as regards health or education. Right-wing parties, on the other hand, favour a minimal state and tend to encourage inter-local competition. Caught in-between, the VBG must play its cards wisely:

On the protection of children and vulnerable adults [*Kindes- und Erwachsenenschutzbehörde*], we thought this could be well organised locally, even if in larger areas. We would hire professionals that worked part-time in a psychiatric facility or something like that. [...] the canton wanted to make this a purely cantonal task. Here, the SVP was our ally – simply out of the reflex that everything that is central is bad. On the tax reform, on the other hand, it was the SP that we allied with, so that really depends. The conservatives have an image of the world where everything is like 200 years ago. [...] But with the SP, I and even the SP members in the VBG have the problem that they think dogmatically: the more professional, the better! [...] The Left has the reflex to take the guardianship away from the communes, to professionalise, and hope that everything will be better. (Interview no. 27)

One last aspect that characterises territorial politics in Berne is the French-speaking minority. Different preferences and indeed a different political culture, which as we saw exists in Vaud as a whole, are attributes also of this territorially concentrated minority within Berne, which is both Bernese and French-speaking:

you can observe the francophone influence very clearly; in education policy for example they are very much oriented towards the *Arc jurassien*, with education agreement with Neuchâtel and Jura. Their attitude is at times very different in terms of preferences and services. [...] we introduced a merit-rating system to punish social services that worked badly [...]. The *Romands* nearly freaked out, they found this completely wrong. For them, *solidarité* comes before everything else! [...] Their culture is simply different; they are much more state-oriented [*etatistisch*], simply because they lie closer to France. (Interview no. 27)

This finding is again in line with my expectations, both those developed in the theoretical framework, whereby culture in general exerts a causal influence over (de)centralisation, as well as those derived from the ensuing contextual model, according to which French-speaking cantons are more centralised.

In sum, what this section has shown is that in Berne, underneath a cultural commitment to local autonomy, a certain degree of centralisation permeates both policy-making and the polity-dimension. Politically, even the cantonal LGA is quite centralised in the way it takes its positions and influences cantonal politics, with a professional secretariat located in the centre of Berne city. The middle position of Berne in the overall ranking of cantonal decentralisation, then, can be well observed as a combination of policy- and polity-*de*centralisation with politics-*central*isation. I now observe two cases of overall decentralisation, Schwyz and Grisons, in the final two sections of this chapter.

'Network governance' in Schwyz

Schwyz has the second-highest degrees of decentralisation in all three dimensions, when comparing the four cantons studied here. Institutionally, the mere presence of districts *and* communes, each with significant tax and policy autonomy, makes politics in Schwyz a three-tiered affair. In 2002, the districts' main duties were the management of specific segments in education (*Orientierungsschulen*) and health (regional hospitals), both of which as mandatory tasks, i.e. prescribed by cantonal law (Schwyz 2002: 13). But the districts – which once were the dominant sub-cantonal polities – have, since 1876, constantly lost out both to the communes and the canton (Wiget 2002: 61), although their outright abolition was rejected in 2006 (see above). The overall tendency in Schwyz is to conserve, whether that regards existing structures at cantonal or federal level. What centralisation has occurred at the cantonal level was forced upon it from the outside – the exact opposite of Vaud, where centralisation at canton level was a conscious choice despite the fact that service-delivery would then cost more.

In Schwyz, the reorganisation of the protection of children and vulnerable adults (*Kindes- und Erwachsenenschutzbehörde*, KESB) is an example of such forced cantonalisation. Previously organised communally on a part-time basis, the KESB's were federally mandated to enter into force on 1 January 2013, but cantons were free to decide how exactly they wanted to organise them.

The government of Schwyz initially proposed a 'canton-communes' model, i.e. overall responsibility with the canton and implementation through the communes (Schwyz 2011: 1). This would have ensured institutional continuity, even if under a different name. However, a majority in the parliamentary committee argued for the districts, and a minority for the canton, to be exclusively responsible for both oversight and implementation (2011:1). The cantonal parliament only reluctantly opted for the cantonal solution, that is, to involve neither the districts nor the communes, because a) the districts were too small and diverse and b) the communes seemed unable to guarantee the kind of professionalism demanded by federal law (*Verhandlungsprotokoll*, 14 September 2011: 1461). Outvoted 52:39, only the SVP argued for the pure district-solution to ensure both proximity and cheaper solutions (2011: 1454). However, without such standards set externally – that is by the federation – the local structures would have remained in place. But apart from polity and policy, the decentralised nature of the canton is evident also in its politics-dimension.

For the president of the cantonal LGA, the *Verband Schwyzer Gemeinden und Bezirke* (VSZGB), it is indeed rare that the cantonal parliament votes for cantonal solutions. On the example of data registration: 'When that came to the cantonal parliament, they rejected the creation of a single post. Every commune has to see for itself. […] So we now have 30 people doing exactly the same, that could really have been solved better centrally!' (Interview no. 1). But the conservative majority under SVP-lead refused to make this a cantonal power. The same for emergency services and water patrols: communes are fully responsible for these tasks simply because the canton would not want to participate in their financing, and subsidiarity would dictate this to be a local power (Interview no. 1). This general reluctance to cantonalise also influences the way in which the VSZGB itself works internally:

> One of our main activities really is to maintain the network between the communes in all domains. We constantly try and find out which commune can collaborate with which other, that's really important. In fact, this is our biggest task; at least we from the VSZGB regard it as such: to work towards a network between communes and districts that enables flexible solutions in certain policy areas. (Interview no. 1)

Whereas on this the LGA Schwyz is perfectly in line with the activities of the LGA in Berne and the two LGAs in Vaud, its functions stop here. Unlike the VBG in Berne or the AdCV in Vaud, the VSZGB does not additionally organise corporate lobbying, fights no political battles, coordinates no legal challenges and undertakes no proactive policy-making. It is a purely functional organisation with no political ambitions, for three reasons. The first is that although 'the canton is not always the easiest partner', there is generally 'a collegial partnership' (Interview no. 1). The canton respects the place and role of both districts and LGs, and there is no need to constantly remind it of the local and regional dimensions. All MCPs are elected with the communes as constituencies, so the link is a most direct one;

also, all parties have local sections that choose their candidates free from cantonal influence, unlike in Berne or Vaud where district parties fulfil that role.

The second reason is internal and concerns pressure from the SVP, the largest cantonal party, not to become entangled in party-politics:

> We try to remain an association that mainly delivers services to our members. We have had some problems in the beginning, when some circles, especially members of the SVP, claimed that our association would become exploited. This is why we always act on the level of orientation only, because of course we also have SVP people in our steering committee. (Interview no. 1)

The third and final reason for this exclusive network function is divergence of interests not just among communes, like in Vaud, but also between communes and districts, which additionally complicates decision-making processes within the VSZGB. On the former, a good example concerns water patrols (*Seewacht*): trying to make this task a cantonal one 'was one of my first political projects. But in the end we were forced to acknowledge that it would be impossible. Especially the interests of the *Ausserschwyz* are completely different: if they need to purchase a new boat for 200,000 CHF, that's peanuts for them! But for us, this is a lot of money...' (Interview no. 1) The *Ausserschwyz* is that part of the canton on the shores of Lake Zurich, topographically separated by the core area of Schwyz and more prosperous and progressive. The other example, which shows a conflict between a district and communes therein, concerns debt enforcement agencies. Here,

> the district of Schwyz jumped ahead, without consulting the communes, and wanted to absorb [the local agencies]. And this although among communes, we had organised ourselves in a way that we were already in a position to handle those 2,500 to 3,000 enforcements per year which you need to be working efficiently. We have already built adequate structures. [...] If in the Höfe district the three communes want to work together, that's fine for us, we don't care what they do, that's even okay. But in our district of Schwyz, where we have several communes and where this is shared between several of them, we don't want that structures built over the last 10 years get shattered. (Interview no. 1)

In this as in the previous example, it is striking how often the keywords 'proximity' and 'subsidiarity' are mentioned. The conviction that services are best delivered locally is widespread – so widespread that it is best described as a cultural attribute (Linder and Steffen 2006). Moreover, whoever delivers the service should be fully responsible for both paying for and making decisions on the level at which it is delivered ('fiscal equivalence'; *see* Dafflon 2007 and Stauffer 2001). Although conservative at heart, this is not a static principle but is rather applied and re-applied as policies evolve. A third and final example, which also allows observing actual processes, combines education and social services (*Schulsozialarbeit*). Again, the district of Schwyz started to work, without informing us, by inserting a position into its budget that would finance three employees. We also recognised that there was a problem, on both the higher and lower school levels, but here in Ingenbohl we prefer to allocate that to the social services, and not the schools. [...] The communes of Arth and Schwyz think in the same manner, and now we have to find a solution with the district. [...] I still hope for some common sense in the *Bezirksrat*, i.e. that they say: yes, the communes should organise this because of this or that reason, and that we can then place everything on a reasonable basis through a collaboration contract district-communes (Interview no. 1)

These 'reasonable' forms of collaboration are the ultimate expression of local autonomy, enabling communes to formally retain power while in actual fact delegating the implementation of a task to an inter-local organisation. Schwyz is replete with those kinds of arrangements (Interview no. 1).

In sum, what emerges from, albeit only briefly, observing territorial politics in this particular canton is that overall politics in Schwyz is indeed very decentralised. The polity itself is already quite decentralised, with the canton, 30 communes and three/six districts[2] situated between canton and communes but not hierarchically subordinate to either of the former two. Numerous types of vertical and horizontal collaboration forms between the three 'levels' express the decentralised nature of policy-making. Finally, both citizens and most political parties (i.e. the centre-right, which is dominant with 89 per cent of parliamentary seats) favour traditional structures and familiar, established ways of policy-making. Due to the canton's history, these in turn are based on strong local and district autonomy. In contrast to Grisons, however, the small area is often used as an argument for rationalisation, professionalisation and, therefore, full cantonalisation, e.g. in the case of the KESB's, when the SVP was outvoted. Even if both Grisons and Schwyz are very decentralised, Schwyz's small area and a generally high accessibility (with a few exceptions, e.g. Einsiedeln or Muotathal) help explain a lower degree of overall decentralisation than in Grisons, despite a similarly conservative and federalist political culture and an accordingly structured (centre-right) party system. But before a more systematic comparison is undertaken, in Chapter Eight, decentralisation – or rather: intra-cantonal federalism – in Grisons is observed first.

'Intra-cantonal federalism' in Grisons

Grisons has the highest degrees of polity-, politics- and policy-decentralisation of all four cantons studied here. But what kind of canton is Grisons really? The cantonal civil servant responsible for overseeing communal mergers puts it quite bluntly:

2. There are six districts in total, but three are also communes, at the same time: the so called *Eingemeindebezirke* ('single-commune districts') Küssnacht, Gersau and Einsiedeln.

Federalism is not an alien concept for us because of many reasons. Grisons is territorially, culturally and sociologically so heterogeneous that we have grown accustomed to it somehow by necessity [...]. We have a long tradition of federalism – it is not just a buzzword to us, but we really try to implement it, although today it has become very difficult to make sure that local institutions can actually fulfil their tasks. (Interview no. 9)

Structural factors such as the size of the area, topography and the economic orientation of different cantonal regions, as well as societal diversity, are argued to be the main reasons for a high degree of decentralisation. Without assessing this causal claim again here (*see* Chapter Six), what is clear is that communal autonomy is historically and culturally entrenched. This is also shown by the way in which general politics works:

This is often a political debate: if you introduce a new tasks – and there have been plenty in the last 100 years – it always boils down to who will pay for that. If you want that the task is really publicly delivered, then you only stand a political chance if canton and communes do it together. This then makes for hybrid solutions, where the task is not per se decentralised, but where communes still have a certain degree of influence on a decentralised implementation. (Interview no. 9)

So what in Vaud was justified as 'a little federal compromise' is here the norm: canton and communes together finance, decide and implement most public tasks. A good example to make the difference with Vaud even clearer is the organisation of elections. In Vaud, all local elections throughout the canton are held on the same day, with results published by the canton. In Grisons, on the other hand, not only can communes organise local elections whenever they want, but also the elections to the *cantonal* parliament are organised in the supra-local *Kreise*, with *Kreis*-parties presenting candidates and the canton unable to even calculate the overall turnout. The polity-autonomy of local structures thus extends to a key aspect of the organisation of politics. As for the influence of communes at the cantonal level, there are two ways, formal and informal. But the former is the stronger way:

Communes can launch a communal initiative, I think 20 per cent or 10 per cent [of all communes] or something like that. They can bring their influence to bear through elections to the cantonal parliament – some mayors are also MCPs. These are the official channels. But there is no real interest group for communes in Grisons. There is one for the smallest communes [*IG Kleinstgemeinden*], but politically they are not very strong; rather an information platform for smaller communes. [...] Communes have more influence if they approach the cantonal government as a group and directly demand certain things, e.g. the communes from the Oberengadin: they are an economic, a political power! If a commune from the Bündner Rheintal approaches the government or the bureaucracy, they have certain leverage. There is also a partial group, we call it the 'Puma

Group': the mayors of the biggest communes in Grisons. But this is again a loose group, they only get together on certain topics. [...] Political influence takes place most of all informally, through the cantonal parliament and *ad hoc* on specific issues. Compared to other big cantons, Grisons is rather small, despite its area, with 190,000 inhabitants. Everybody knows everybody and the bureaucracy remains accessible. (Interview no. 9: 84–5)

In all cantons, local autonomy is important – in Grisons, however, it is sacrosanct. Every attempt, real or perceived, to undermine it is fiercely fought off through petitions and postulates, motions and requests from inside parliament. A selection of the most relevant of these in the last decade includes the following:

- Petition of 10 January 2011 by all mayors and MCPs from the *Kreise* Rhäzuns and Trins to form 'their own region' (*see Wortlautprotokoll*, 16 February 2011: 646–7).
- *Anfrage Candinas* of 19 October 2010 on 'public jobs in the different regions of the canton', i.e. the degree of personnel decentralisation.
- *Auftrag Nick* of 9 December 2009 'on the governmental strategy to deal with peripheral spaces', i.e. the canton's response to the federal *Neue Regionalpolitik* (NRP), a federal development scheme for investments.
- *Anfrage Keller* of 22 April 2009 'on the withdrawal from peripheral regions', a direct reaction to an NZZ interview in which a senior cantonal civil servant had mentioned that 'theoretically, letting valleys with unfavourable development prospects die out is an option'.
- *Anfrage Tenchio* of 21 April 2009 'on the dismantling of post offices', asking the government for its strategy to deal with the continued closure of post offices especially in the peripheral communes.
- *Fraktionsauftrag CVP* of 11 February 2009 on 'the future of supra-regional demand for service-public in peripheral regions' and the government's current and future subsidies in this regard.
- *Postulat Pfenninger* of 25 March 2003 'on the concentration and decentralisation of the cantonal bureaucracy', asking the government to de-concentrate cantonal offices away from the cantonal capital, Chur (*see* the respective years of the *Wortlautprotokolle*).

These motions have come from various parties and regions, they touch upon various aspects and policy areas – but what they all have in common is a general thrust towards maintaining a strong local level. As in Schwyz, LGs do not need to organise into efficient lobby groups à la VBG in Berne; inter-communal divides are also not as strong as to bring about a fundamental split in the local landscape, à la UCV and AdCV in Vaud on fiscal equalisation. Despite all their differences, cantonal, as well as local, civil servants and politicians agree on the fundamental character of Grisons as a federal political system. Direct sub-cantonal influence is strongest on specific projects, as when all MCPs from a certain region vote for investments in their area, no matter which party they belong to, for example from the Unterengadin:

The main task of the MCPs is not to work for their region, but for the whole. However, on this [subsidies for a street to Samnaun, on the Austrian border] for sure all MCPs from the Unterengadin were in favour, even the guy from the SP! When I was mayor, he was in the opposition, really tough. Now he is mayor and sees things differently – has a different attitude to things that are important for the commune. Previously, he was always sceptical and hesitant about every elevator etc. But now, as a mayor, he simply had no choice but to fully embrace this project! (Interview no. 35)

In matters with a regional dimension, territorial allegiance thus eclipses party ideology; again in polar opposition to politics in Vaud, where LGs only very rarely work through parliament because party ties are so dominant there. So although, in Grisons, the impression is that even municipal representatives in the cantonal parliament generally strive for a well-balanced perspective on cantonal-local matters, clearly 'they are elected in their [local] constituency, and if they decide something which goes radically against their municipality, they would have to fear for their seat' (Interview no. 9). This underlines the importance of the localist electoral system – which the cantonal electorate has upheld in not less than six popular votes so far (NZZ, 23 October 2012: p. 11). And even when, in some regions, the differences between communes are too wide to bring them all on board, instead of organising them around a specific project, a general defence of local autonomy, in the abstract, is mounted (Interview no. 43). Besides regional alliances, there are also coordination efforts of similarly structured communes, e.g. the mentioned 'Puma Group':

We have an annual conference of mayors from the five biggest communes: Chur, Davos, Igis-Landquart, St. Moritz and Domat-Ems. Of course we have certain interests that we defend together – 'elephants', they call us... We meet once a year. But the influence of our group is less through parliament than directly onto the administration. One often underestimates this: a mayor of a big municipality makes politics rather with the administration than through parliament. This way things go much faster: you simply approach them directly! After all, whatever they produce in Chur comes from the bureaucracy. We have an advantage here, as a big municipality. (Interview no. 43)

Unlike Berne and Vaud, Grisons has a large territory but a much smaller population; this facilitates direct contacts. Finally, emotions ran high when the government in 2010 announced it would form 'between five and eight regions'. In reaction to this, the already mentioned petition from two *Kreise*, Rhäzuns and Trins, demanded to have 'their' district, Imboden, transformed into a region. Several other petitions and opinions expressed by parties, communes, interest groups and individuals eventually made the government realise that 'there is no majority to form fewer than eight regions' (Grisons 2012a: 1988). A direct intervention to maintain 'their' regional structure is described also by the secretary general of the *Region Mittelbünden*, also MCP for the CVP:

We have voiced our intention twice so far: the steering committee of our region[al association] has made it clear that we want to stay within the current regional borders, and we have also invited the responsible [cantonal] Interior Minister to come to our regional assembly, where a unanimous decision was taken to the same effect. But all this is only symbolical, nothing else: 'against a forced merger with Viamala' [...] Maybe we repeat this in the next two months. But more we can't do, for we have no influence. [...] Our steering committee also held a meeting with all MCPs from our region where it was decided that all MCPs would support this and that we would fight for it. That was a cross-party decision – here, regional interests really come before those of the party! (Interview no. 39)

A final point on the decentralised nature of policy-making in Grisons concerns coordinated responses in public consultation phases. This too is regionally organised, not centrally as in Berne and Vaud. Particularly in Mittelbünden, the regional association usually takes the lead:

We are involved in practically everything, because there is not really a domain which the communes are not concerned by. The communes are very thankful for that, because if a small commune is not able to [write a reply], there is not going to be any. It also gives us a certain weight: I know of regional secretary generals that I am sure will come and ask me for a template, once I have drafted one. Up to one third of [all communes in] the whole canton can send back the same reply! This is very positive, because [...] the government can then not simply ignore us. [...] It is at least something if 21 communes act in a united fashion – but of course, as the only region against all others, we stand no chance... (Interview no. 39)

The picture that emerges from this description, then, is that not only is Grisons the most decentralised in its polity-dimension, with communes, *Kreisen* and regional associations, but that also policy-making and political channels function in a very decentralised way. Political actors, too, seem to demand a communal involvement and 'strong communes'. As in Schwyz, a cultural consensus thus exists:

In Grisons, with its 150 valleys – imagine if everything was centralised: the Unterengadin, Tschamut and the Puschlav are much too far away from the centre! The topography is so essential. [...] If you directed everything from Chur, that would not work. It is about proximity to the citizens [*Bürgernähe*], that has to be organised in one way or the other. Also, jobs have to be decentralised, not simply everything centrally. (Interview no. 35)

In sum, Grisons is as close to a (federal) Switzerland *en miniature* as it can possibly get. This analogy is made even in the cantonal bureaucracy:

If you take the [Swiss] Confederation and the cantons, you realise that the cantons have real autonomy in certain areas. It would only make sense to pass this autonomy on in a meaningful way. Why should someone in Chur decide what is to be built in the Münstertal? Let them decide for themselves! This is real, living and breathing communal autonomy: to give as many real powers to the communes because we live in a federal state. (Interview no. 9)

Conclusion

This chapter's purpose was to provide a qualitative illustration of cantonal decentralisation. This has confirmed the location of cantons on the decentralisation continuum: Vaud, with its centralised *plateforme* and litigious but divided LGAs, is the most centralised; next is Berne, where the LGA is structured centrally but policy and polity operate in a rather decentralised fashion. This matters when trying to influence MCPs through the mayors in their respective constituencies. In Schwyz, only a weak and service-oriented LGA exists, but both communes and districts fulfil important roles regardless. A single, general-purpose LGA is absent altogether in Grisons but communes, regional associations and sometimes (e.g. for cantonal parliamentary elections) even the *Kreise* fulfil important roles, making this a quasi-federal Swiss canton. All this confirms the scale of cantonal decentralisation developed in Chapter Four.

Apart from this gradual difference there is also a qualitative gap between the French-speaking Vaud and the three (fully or predominantly) German-speaking Berne, Schwyz and Grisons. All important public policies are centralised at the cantonal level in Vaud, both LGAs have agreed to compromises which go towards uniformity, e.g. in police reform or on music schools, and communes do not work through parliament at all because of being crushed by party struggles. In the other three cantons, by contrast, the cantonal-local 'shared' variant is the default option. MCPs do not generally vote against communes (in Grisons and Schwyz) or, at the very least, are susceptible to coordination from the LGA (in Berne). Thus the a priori presumption is for cantonal solutions in Vaud but for LG involvement in Berne, Schwyz and Grisons.

This chapter has also provided further evidence that the factors identified earlier, indeed, have causal relevance. Corporate lobbying in Berne was mentioned to strategically ally with left-wing parties in tax reform, but with right-wing parties in the social sector to maintain local autonomy. But although left-wing parties are as strong in Berne as in Vaud and although both cantons span a large territory, territorial politics is more participative and inclusive in Berne than it is in Vaud. Here, many a solution could be found only in a political dialogue between the cantonal executive and the leaders of the two LGAs. That Vaud is more centralised than Berne is due also to the influence of *French political culture*; that Berne is less decentralised than the other two German-speaking cantons is due also to the influence of *left-wing parties*.

On the other hand, the lack of centralised LGAs with a political purpose in both Schwyz and Grisons points to the widely shared, deeply engrained and hardly questioned, i.e. cultural, appraisal of local autonomy by all political actors, from the (very weak) left to the (much stronger) centre-right. Communes are cherished to a much higher degree in these two cantons because they have many competencies and powers, despite not being centrally included (as in Vaud with its *plateforme*) and despite the absence of strong corporate lobbying (as in Berne). The LGA of Schwyz, which also comprises the districts, explicitly defies a political purpose – and yet both sub-cantonal layers figure prominently in the political discourse. Decentralisation in Schwyz is all the more puzzling given that the cantonal area is much smaller than in Grisons, which has equally weak left-wing parties and an equally conservative political culture. That Schwyz is so decentralised, then, must be due to the influence of *Germanic political culture*, which is strong enough to offset constraints towards centralisation (arising from a small area) and, in turn, reinforces centre-right parties in preserving existing structures.

In Grisons, finally, all hypothesised causes of decentralisation are present in extreme form: topographical fragmentation, large area, very weak left-wing parties, and a conservative, Germanic political culture. On top of this there is societal diversity, both linguistic and religious. However, in a historical perspective, it was the peculiar *topographical* character of Grisons that enabled both local autonomy to strive and minorities to remain territorially concentrated. I now proceed to discuss the empirical findings of this and the previous chapters more systematically.

Chapter Eight

Comparative Perspectives

This chapter has three purposes, all of them comparative. The first is to compare *across* the four case studies and verify the causal mechanism of cantonal decentralisation; the second, to bring the within-case evidence (of Chapters Six and Seven) to bear on the cross-case findings of Chapter Five and, thus, explain decentralisation in *all* Swiss cantons; and the third, to let both types of empirical data speak to the theoretical framework presented at the outset of this book and, thereby, make inferences for political systems *in general*. The chapter is structured accordingly.

Case-study findings

The purpose of the four case studies was to verify whether the variables significantly correlated with cantonal decentralisation in the quantitative model have, indeed, causal power. There were three such variables, each figuring prominently in one of the 'classic' attempts to explain (de)centralisation:

1. *Area*, standing for the structural approach.
2. *Political culture*, the flagship of the socio-cultural perspective.
3. *Left-wing parties*, purported to matter most by the actor-centred, ideological approach to territorial politics.

As socio-economic controls, I have used per capita GDP and the number of municipalities. In the previous chapter, I have discussed the four cases 'vertically': case after case, highlighting in each canton one causal factor – albeit, according to the model, *all three* factors matter. In this section, I thus compare horizontally, that is, proceeding by causal factor. I start with the influence of cantonal area, continue with the crucial distinction between French- and German-speaking cantons and end with the significance of the strength of Socialist and Green MCPs. Moreover, because it is the *interaction* of area with culture and agency that produces cantonal decentralisation, section two of this chapter builds these case-study findings into an explanatory typology.

The influence of cantonal area

In all four cantons, area was in one way or another mentioned as a reason for justifying a certain territorial structure of the polity. First and foremost, area and topography appear as fundamental features of the cantonal identity in Grisons. The slogan 'canton of 150 valleys' is more than a mere description of facts: it gives expression both to the inaccessibility of remote villages and entire valleys as well as to the societal diversity embodied in territorially grouped Romansh and Italian speaking minorities. Decentralisation, then, becomes a means to protect these minorities in three ways: by guaranteeing that services are also offered in the minority language (e.g. Italian in the courts of Poschiavo), contributing to upholding peripheral infrastructure (especially schools and roads) and enhancing the importance of local politics. The *Kreise* still exist, with parties organised (also) at this level and parliamentary elections taking place in them as constituencies. Grisons undeniably is so decentralised *also* because of the structure of its territory, which goes to say that area is a necessary but, by itself, an insufficient cause. This insight is confirmed by the other three case studies.

In Schwyz, area was also used as an argument for decentralisation, but in a different way. Given that the canton belongs to the group of smaller sized ones, a solution as in Glarus (with only three strong communes; *see also* Kronenberg 2011) or Geneva (extreme centralisation; *see also* Reiser 1998) would not be unthinkable. But, historically, polity formation in Schwyz was fundamentally different from these two cantons and, in fact, resembles more that of cantons like Zurich, Berne, or Lucerne, where territorial expansion was dominated by the capital city – just that in Schwyz this 'capital' was itself a rural community. The struggle for political equality of the subject territories (Höfe, Küssnacht and Gaster) culminated in the secession of 1831–33; the autonomy of Einsiedeln has always been backed up by the religious authority of its monastery; and the once independent Gersau only 'joined' Schwyz after the Vienna Congress. All this contributes to a strong sense of territorial diversity, embodied also in the archaic district structure. But this legacy is powerful only because it is filtered through a political culture that values tradition more than innovation; conservation more than change; and subsidiarity more than uniformity. The only time a simplification of territorial structures was attempted, through the *G-Reform*, the electorate overwhelmingly rejected it under the political lead of the conservative right-wing SVP. The existence of traditional territorial structures was thus used politically to argue against change.

Berne and Vaud, on the other hand, resemble each other very much in terms of territorial structures: both are very large, divided into ten districts, with cantonal prefects and over 300 communes. But the two cantons diverge in the way these structures are given political meaning. Both cantons can be described as entities radiating outwards from the cantonal capital; both have quite a few medium-sized cities: Nyon, Morges, Yverdon and Montreux in Vaud; Biel/Bienne, Thun, Burgdorf and Köniz in Berne. Consequently, it is the sheer size of the cantonal area that is cited in both cantons as the main reason for having ten districts: all political parties agreed on that in the recent reforms, and both electorates accepted the reforms. However, the rationale for districts is bottom-up, in Berne, with the prefects elected and having few competences delegated to them by the canton. In Vaud, prefects continue to be appointed by the cantonal government and enjoy judicial, administrative, as well as police functions. They represent the Jacobin legacy of French rationalism and are the result of centuries of cultural diffusion of political ideas, notably those of equality and uniformity, which they have to ensure. In Berne, on the other hand, the influence of 19th century liberalism was decisive in rendering prefects elected by the district population as early as 1893. A historical legacy is thus not something written in stone: political actors are well able to change the nature of territorial institutions if they see fit. In Vaud, this was done when the originally eight, later only six, *Lieutenants du Conseil d'Etat* were replaced with one prefect per district. That the evolution of the prefectoral institution did not follow the one in Berne can, therefore, not be explained by area alone, but must have other reasons.

In sum, area emerges as a two-edged sword: a condition, that is, and not so much a direct cause. In a very large, fragmented and diverse canton like Grisons, it justifies strong local *and* regional structures. But the same outcome can obtain in small areas, if there is territorial diversity and a political will to maintain this, as the case of Schwyz shows. In very large territories with a clear centre, like Vaud and Berne, size justifies maintaining a certain control under the heading of cantonal cohesion and coherence. For both centralisation and decentralisation, political actors are key in deciding how to make use of these structural conditions: as an argument for strong oversight, in Vaud, or for regionally legitimated prefects, in Berne; or as part of the historical legacy of district identity, in Schwyz, or to protect societal diversity, in Grisons. This brings me to consider the causal role of political culture.

French vs. Germanic political culture

In Switzerland, the main cultural divide separates French- and German-speaking cantons. Numerous studies have shown how in socio-economic, left-right issues, the majority German-speaking parts of Switzerland are pitted against a minority of French- and Italian speaking cantons, while in terms of international openness and progressiveness, the *Romandie* alone succumbs to the other two linguistic blocs (Linder *et al.* 2008: 43). The four case studies have contributed to this insight with data on cantonal territorial structures.

In Vaud, not only is local politics more representative than direct-democratic (Ladner and Fiechter 2008), but two centuries of 'French unitary culture' have also maintained the many small communes in a relationship of dependency towards the cantonal centre. It is the cantonal level that provides most services, with the prefects as central agents in the districts, supervising the communes and ensuring that the same quality standards are upheld across the territory. Today's prefects in Vaud can be traced back to at least 1536, when Berne imposed the Reformation at the same time as its rule. The two have reinforced each other, contributing to a high degree of religious and legal uniformity. This has bequeathed a centralist legacy which Lausanne, capital only since 1803, has made use of in creating the new canton (Meuwly 1990: 31). Several communal mergers and the district reform of 2006 were orchestrated by the cantonal centre and explicitly based on the ideas of equality, justice and progressiveness. The lack of communes, other than the 'political' one, can also be attributed to the Napoleonic innovation of *la municipalité*, which puts residents on an equal footing regardless of their 'local citizenship' – the *Bürgergemeinden*, on the other hand, continue to exist in Berne, Schwyz and Grisons (plus also in several other German-speaking cantons). Finally, both the cantonal insignia *Liberté et Patrie* and the political discourse on *l'Etat* ('the state') testify to the different, more active and prominent role ascribed to the canton in Vaud (and French-speaking Switzerland in general; *see* Eugster *et al.* 2011: F427–30).

In this political culture spectrum, Schwyz clearly lies at the opposite end. With a myriad of district- and local-level public entities, each proudly and effectively claiming a centuries-old legacy, inequality and pragmatism are culturally ingrained. If the modern-type municipality was imposed by the Helvetic Republic throughout Switzerland, in the German-speaking cantons of Schwyz, Berne and Grisons it never achieved the same exclusiveness as communes in Vaud. In Schwyz in particular, local governments continue to compete with the much older districts. The orientation towards pragmatic problem-solving (rather than action guided by abstract principles, as in Vaud) finds expression in several inter-local, inter-district and local-district agreements. The history of these districts as living, breathing entities shows the influence of political culture: they are legitimate not because they are efficient (in fact, they are *not*), but because they have always been there. Their presence is itself a reason for maintaining the very decentralised structure: since they exist, they might as well fulfil some functions! In Vaud, on the other hand, cantonal identity supersedes local identity, both as regards diffuse attachment and specific policy expectations, e.g. in education, health or social care. These areas have all been cantonalised despite the fact that service delivery then became more expensive – in Schwyz, on the other hand, the expected costs of the district reform itself were enough to make it fail. So while in Schwyz the price even of achieving a little less inequality (for even by abolishing the districts, the thirty 'unequal' communes would have remained untouched) was judged as too high, in Vaud the goal of ensuring equality was pursued *despite* higher costs.

The same Germanic, essentially conservative political culture can be detected in Grisons, even if to a lesser extent. Here, too, the *Kreise* have so far survived, but only just about. Their legacy has clearly outlived itself at the expense of the projected regions, which are meant to combine the de-concentrated districts with regional development associations into a symmetrically arranged, functionally efficient but still locally legitimated territorial structure. This is a compromise between radical change à la Vaud (where the number of districts was halved from nineteen to ten) and outright maintenance à la Schwyz. The territorial reform in Grisons goes some way towards rationalising the territorial structure, but keeps with the culturally valued idea of traditional 'living spaces' (*Lebensräume*), to which even the popular initiative launched by the Socialists pays tribute. Note how in Vaud even the centre-right has argued for centralisation, while in Grisons even the Left respects (meaningful) local autonomy, although through significantly fewer communes. There is thus widespread agreement in Grisons that the canton ought to continue and even strengthen decentralisation in a 'federal' way.

The political culture of Berne, finally, appears to be mixed in the sense of combining a desire for equality of service delivery with a decidedly localist way of actually implementing policies. Due to the strong influence of the Bernese LGA – itself centralised with a permanent, professional secretariat situated at the heart of Berne city – local autonomy is higher than in Vaud, but weaker than in Schwyz or Grisons. For centuries, it was in the capital city that all the strings were pulled; an extreme form of oligarchic centralisation. If this historical legacy sits uneasily with the localist, Germanic political culture, then the position of Berne in the overall ranking of cantonal decentralisation is its correct expression. What sets Berne apart from other large and German-speaking cantons such as Zurich, Solothurn, Aargau, St. Gall or Thurgau are polycephality and strong left-wing parties, the latter comparable in strength to those in Vaud. While the idea of a strong and dynamic state has been developed very early on, it was a minimal, military state that left minor economic centres intact as long as they paid tribute to their new masters. Such is the ambivalence of Berne: rural but with many strong, urban mini-centres; with prefects, but regionally elected ones that continue to embody the past of Berne as a City-Republic, not least by residing in the very same castles that once were occupied by the bailiffs. As it was put aptly by one interviewee: 'it is not always clear which canton is speaking, whether it is the turbo-canton that pushes communes to merge, or the canton that supports even the smallest ones through extensive fiscal equalisation mechanisms' (Interview no. 16). This neatly leads to the relevance of left-wing parties for cantonal centralisation, a factor that I discuss next.

The impact of left-wing MCPs

The final factor identified by the quantitative model and verified in each case study concerns political actors. Intuitively, it is to them that one ought to turn in searching for an answer to the question of why exactly certain polities are more (de)centralised than others. The hypothesis that cantons are more centralised (also) because of strong left-wing parties was confirmed in all four cases: they are weakest in the two most decentralised cantons Grisons and Schwyz and strongest in balanced (but Germanic) Berne and centralised Vaud. However, single parties only rarely command a majority in the consensual Swiss cantons (Vatter 2002). To achieve policy success, one needs to muster the support of at least one other party. What makes the Swiss case even more peculiar is the threat (or opportunity) of direct democracy. Thus, to make a parliamentary decision 'referendum-proof' (*referendumssicher*), oftentimes more than simply one other party needs to be brought on board. This was again shown for all cantons.

In Berne, it was a Liberal-Socialist agreement that allowed the territorial reform to pass both the parliamentary and referendum stage: against the resistance only of the SVP, the number of districts was reduced. But against the will of the Socialists, the reduction turned out to be less drastic – notably the districts of Obersimmental-Saanen, Frutigen-Niedersimmental and Interlaken-Oberhasli were kept apart. If for the Liberals the argument of more efficient and, eventually, cheaper public service delivery counted most, the Socialists mainly argued for the need to ensure professionalism, equal access and opportunities across the entire cantonal area. For them, bigger structures meant better quality. For the SVP, in turn, bigger structures implied more bureaucracy, higher costs and a detachment from ordinary citizens, both as regards practical service-delivery (e.g. the time needed to travel from one's residence to where a service is delivered) and, as in Schwyz, the 'identity' of the region, district, area or commune.

The same was true for Schwyz, only that here a) the SVP was significantly stronger than in both Berne and Grisons (where after 2008 the BDP had replaced it as the dominant party in parliament); b) the Socialists, in turn, were much weaker than in both Vaud and Berne, and the Greens non-existent; and where c) the cantonal electorate eventually voted against the proposal supported by all the parties bar the SVP. It was this constellation of political forces, coupled with the financial might and campaign experience of the SVP machinery, which doomed the *G-Reform*. When the SP did propose a territorial reform, it amounted to a much more radical measure: abolishing the 30 communes instead of the six districts and fully reshaping the landscape based on 'objective' factors like area and population size. But the parliamentary wing of the SP was so weak that not even a debate on this took place.

In both Vaud and Grisons the territorial reforms were less politicised, even if for different reasons. In Vaud, the groundwork was laid in a special assembly charged with drafting the new cantonal constitution. In this model, ordinary citizens do all the work; this de-ideologises debates. Even if the parties had held significantly different opinions on the matter, they would have found a way to express themselves. That they did not do so shows that, in principle, all of them agreed that the canton needed to be modernised and that more contemporary and equitable district structures had to be created. In Grisons, in turn, both the SVP and the SP are only very weakly represented in the cantonal parliament. Both need to resort to extra-parliamentary means to try and make themselves heard, for example the SP with the mentioned popular initiative on reducing the number of communes to 'not significantly more than 50'. The result of this double weakness 'at the edges' is the dominance of cantonal politics by the Liberals and Christian-Democrats, which together represent a comfortable 60 per cent of MCPs (BADAC 2012). This crowding of the centre – if one adds the BDP's 27 seats (=22 per cent) – explains why the territorial reform in Grisons is much less a left-right affair than in Schwyz, where the SVP was (and still is) dominant, or in Berne, where both the SP and Greens, as well as the SVP, were (and still are) very strong.

This concludes my review of the role(s) played by the three causal factors in each of the four case studies. The question that now warrants answering is how the evidence drawn from these four cantons fits into the broader purpose of explaining decentralisation in *all* Swiss cantons. Such is the purpose of the next section, where the now both quantitatively and qualitatively confirmed theoretical model is extended into an explanatory typology.

Explanatory typology

To show the *interaction* among causal factors, I now develop an 'explanatory typology' of cantonal decentralisation. In combining the numerical measure of cantonal decentralisation with a contextual explanation of the causal process at play in each canton, such a typology draws on the best of each method. Explanatory typologies are 'multidimensional conceptual classifications based on an explicitly stated theory [...] [where] the descriptive function follows the conventional usage, but in a way that is heavily modified by its theoretical purposes' (Elman 2005: 296). Applied to my focus here, the *theory* is the one stated in Chapter Two; the *purpose* is to explain cantonal decentralisation as measured in Chapter Four and tested in Chapters Five to Seven. The ensuing *classification* encompasses three types: ten decentralised (Appenzell Outer-Rhodes, Grisons, Zug, Glarus, Obwalden, Appenzell Inner-Rhodes, Zurich, Thurgau, Nidwalden and Schwyz), five centralised (Geneva, Fribourg, Vaud, Neuchâtel and Ticino) and eleven balanced cantons (Schaffhausen, St. Gall, Lucerne, Valais, Solothurn, Aargau, Uri, Basel-Countryside, Basel-City, Jura and Berne) (*see* Figure 4.9: Swiss cantons by their degree of decentralisation). I discuss each type in turn.

The decentralised cantons

Ten cantons are of this decentralised type. The quantitatively most significant independent variable, area, can be used to divide them into two groups: the large cantons Grisons, Zurich and Thurgau, on the one hand, and the small Appenzell Outer-Rhodes, Zug, Glarus, Obwalden, Appenzell Inner-Rhodes, Nidwalden and Schwyz on the other. All of them are German speaking and predominantly conservative.

D1 – Three large & Germanic cantons with a conservative periphery: GR, ZH and TG

We have already seen how in Grisons political culture, in wanting to preserve territorially grouped social diversity, was an important factor in causing decentralisation – even labelled 'cantonal federalism', by some. Moreover, the large and topographically fragmented area is not dominated by a single city – instead, each region has its own mini-capital (e.g. Davos, St. Moritz, Igis-Landquart, or Thusis), necessitating a decentralised polity-structure to be maintained over two sub-cantonal levels: regional (districts and regional development associations, at present) and local (*Kreise* and communes). How does this generalise to the other cantons in this group?

The canton most resembling Grisons on all three independent variables is Thurgau. Spread over a large area, the rural and Germanic political culture results in an equally conservative attitude to politics. This reflects in a very high degree of overall cantonal decentralisation. When in 2009 the canton undertook a modest reform of the districts, reducing their number from eight to five, only the

SVP campaigned against it (NZZ, 18 November 2009: 15). Although the party is by far the largest political force in the cantonal parliament (with 39 per cent of the seats; *see* BADAC 2012), the electorate approved the reform with more than 60 per cent of the votes (NZZ, 30 November 2009: 10). Nevertheless, only two months before, the cantonal electorate had rejected the creation of a single civil registry out of the eight district-level ones (NZZ, 30 November 2009: 10). Most other cantonal services are equally organised at district-level – e.g. land registry, bankruptcy offices, justices of the peace and notary's offices – but the canton respects the wishes of the communes in their delimitation (Interview no. 5). Equality is perceived less as a good to be attained, than a dangerous road to bland uniformity: communal autonomy in particular 'is important because in this way, the citizens can directly decide about what should happen in our village. [...] The beautiful thing about communal autonomy is that we don't have unitary pabulum [*Einheitsbrei*]!' (Interview no. 5)

The only other canton in D1, Zurich, is also spread out over a large area and has a Germanic political culture, but historically the canton emerged as a polity around a dominant city. Unlike in Grisons and Thurgau, and much more like in Vaud and Berne, there *is* a single centre. However, owing to the conservative outlook of the surrounding countryside, centralisation attempts were blocked early on, or have never really been attempted. Thus culture and agency together are decisive for the overall degrees of decentralisation in Zurich. This becomes visible in the strength of the SVP, defender of communal autonomy at all costs: in May 2011, the party gained 30 per cent of all parliamentary seats, providing 54 of 180 MCPs (BADAC 2012). Leaving aside the two cities of Zurich and Winterthur, Zurich is predominantly a rural canton with many small and medium-sized towns and villages (Interview no. 13). But unlike in Berne, the capital city often joins the rural communes in resisting cantonal encroachments upon communal autonomy (Interview no. 5). The cantonal LGA, the *Gemeindepräsidentenverband Zürich* (GPVZH), is the main instrument in this resistance, animated by the very same conviction also voiced in Grisons – but organised much more effectively – that 'federalism not only refers to the Confederation and the cantons, but also to the canton and its communes. [...] Each layer has its own competencies – such is the fundamental feature of our state – [its own] tasks, powers and rights.' (Interview no. 12) Communal mergers should 'come from below' (no. 12), and 'even the simple talk of regions is a no-go in Zurich' (Interview no. 13). A good example of this localist way of policy-making is the introduction of 'offices for the protection of children and vulnerable adults' (*Kindes- und Erwachsenenschutzbehörde*, KESB; *see also* case-study of Schwyz above). When the canton wanted to regionalise them at the district level, the resistance of the SVP *and* the GPVZH was strong enough to let communes freely organise themselves (NZZ, 5 July 2011: 13, 16 September 2011: 19 and 17 December 2011: 19). As for the other two cantons in this group, a large area and a conservative, Germanic political culture together determine the preservation of a high degree of cantonal decentralisation.

D2 – seven small, Germanic and rural-conservative cantons: AR, ZG, GL, OW, AI, NW and SZ

A second group of decentralised cantons, D2, has the same characteristics as the first one, save that the cantonal area is, on average, very small. Inducing from the detailed study of Schwyz, cantons in this group share the following characteristics: they are very or rather small, German is the only official language, their political culture is largely conservative – and, consequently, they are very decentralised. But why do culture and politics triumph over area in determining overall decentralisation? After all, small areas could equally well, if not better, be organised in a more centralised manner. But these cantons are so decentralised because area needs to pass through the cultural filter to enter politics, as I now show for each canton.

In Glarus, the communal amalgamation decided by the *Landsgemeinde* in 2006, confirmed in 2007 and in force since 1 January 2011, has strengthened local autonomy: primary schools, for instance, are now an exclusively communal matter (Interview no. 24; *see also* Glarus 2012: 16). The *Landsgemeinde* of Appenzell Inner-Rhodes, on the other hand, has just recently rejected a reform of the local structures, albeit by the slightest of margins possible (NZZ, 30 April 2012: 9). The reform proposal did not include school communes (NZZ, 29 September 2009: 10) or the *Feuerschaugemeinde* (a unique, single-purpose entity at local level; Interview no. 10) and was thus more conservative in character than the solution arrived at in Glarus. But the point is not the success of reform in Glarus and its failure in Appenzell Inner-Rhodes; what matters is that in both cantons, the *Landsgemeinde* as the assembly of all citizens has to sanction every modification of the internal territorial structure; parties (where they exist, as in Glarus) may be important in channelling preferences but do not have the last say. This distinguishes Glarus and Appenzell Inner-Rhodes from the other cantons in this group. Hence the overall framework is validated, and even more directly so than in any other canton, because cantonal area is given causal leverage through an eminently political process only: the three new communes of Glarus correspond to the three 'natural areas' of the valley (South, North and Centre); and Oberegg as an exclave of Appenzell Inner-Rhodes (surrounded by Appenzell Outer-Rhodes and St. Gall) was untouched by the reform proposal. Thus, area is given a political meaning through a conservative perception of history, where what already exists (the communes, in Appenzell Inner-Rhodes, or the 'natural areas', in Glarus) is preferred over what is yet to be created (fewer communes, in Appenzell Inner-Rhodes, or no communes, as was briefly debated in Glarus in 2007).

In Obwalden, the Christian-Democrats (CVP) are, with 36 per cent of the seats, the largest party in parliament, followed by the SVP with 20 per cent and the Liberals (FDP) with 18 per cent; the Socialist Party comes last with only 10 per cent. Very similar proportions exist in Zug (29 per cent CVP, 25 per cent FDP, 24 per cent SVP, 10 per cent SP) and Appenzell Outer-Rhodes (40 per cent FDP, 12 per cent SVP, 6 per cent SP, 5 per cent CVP) (*see* BADAC 2012).

That is, a large centre-right block can easily outvote the SP in all three cantons, exactly as in Schwyz. This means that despite a small cantonal area, structures are not centralised. Even a central office dealing with communal affairs is missing. Another consequence is that not a single project on communal mergers is being undertaken in any of these cantons because it would be perceived as undermining local autonomy. Instead, inter-communal cooperation flourishes, for example in Appenzell Outer-Rhodes:

> The communes fight for their existence as small entities by defending that they are needed. Collaboration where needed, but no forced territorial mergers. The justification is often – and I also think this ensures quality – that proximity to the citizens is an advantage, in cantonal as much as in communal politics: short ways, immediacy of the bureaucracy, and everybody knows everybody. [...] Of course, there are also disadvantages [...] but this background contributes to the maintenance of structures. There is consensus on that. (Interview no. 11)

Culturally, then, the traditional structures are valued as efficient, small and cheap institutions, for example also in Zug:

> Whoever is in favour of communal mergers argues that larger entities are more efficient. But for the identity of the residents it is important to feel at home. [...] Of course there are also financial reasons: if there is no need, then you simply do not merge and can influence things much more directly than in a city-canton with 125,000 inhabitants. (Interview no. 30)

In Obwalden, too, the most important governmental level would really be the communal tier:

> [Most of the] daily life takes place in the municipality. Some people would say that this does not matter. But if you have an important issue, you go to the municipality. Social care goes through us, all that concerns construction – these are the most important areas. (Interview no. 8)

Nidwalden finally is small and compact like the other cantons in this group, stretching over barely 276 km^2. The SVP with 19 seats (32 per cent), the CVP with 18 (30 per cent) and the FDP with 17 (28 per cent) of a total of 60 seats in the *Landrat* dominate cantonal politics. The SP with a single seat is virtually non-existent – however, the Greens are surprisingly strong for a canton at the heart of conservative-minded Central Switzerland: they currently hold 5 seats (8 per cent) (BADAC 2012). Possibly because of the vicinity of the city of Lucerne – from Stans barely 15 minutes by car – a slightly more progressive, pragmatic way of doing politics is present in Nidwalden, evidenced also in this story:

> The conference of mayors [*Gemeindepräsidentenkonferenz*] lobbies for all things that are important for the communes [...]. This can produce a great effect, for example on the financing of foster care, in force since 1 January

2011: so far, it had been the communes that had to pay for home care. On the occasion of a public consultation, however, the communes agreed to give this to the canton, since the competency for hospitals was already at that level anyway. This increases the probability that the service is delivered where it is cheapest. [...] Such things seemed reasonable for us: that you don't artificially separate functions and say they had 'historically grown' [...]. (Interview no. 7)

Nor do such issue-based solutions stop at cantonal borders:

In the area of data protection, there is a single officer for the three cantons [Obwalden, Nidwalden, Schwyz]. IT is also shared across Nidwalden and Obwalden; we have a central data processing centre in Sarnen, the ILZ. [...] These are tasks in which you would have a fake autonomy if every commune had its own software. [...] Nidwalden encouraged this move; before there was chaos. The canton financed the communes: if all chose the same programme, it paid 50% of the costs. Everything goes through finances – if the canton had not paid, we would now have 11 different IT providers. (Interview no. 7)

Location close to Lucerne, then, helps understand why Nidwalden is slightly more progressive than its German political culture would suggest: together with small size, location makes for less decentralisation than in neighbouring Obwalden, but still more than in all the cantons of the balanced type. In sum, in all the seven cantons of group D2, local government is consciously upheld as a political institution with a meaning, a purpose, and an identity. The conviction that local autonomy is an indispensable element of cantonal decentralisation is a key component of the political culture in these cantons and expressed either indirectly, through parties, or directly, at the *Landsgemeinden* or in referenda.

The centralised cantons

Among the five most centralised cantons (group C), four exclusively or predominantly French speaking cantons, Geneva, Vaud, Fribourg and Neuchâtel, as well as the Italian-speaking Ticino can be identified. As it was discussed when studying Vaud, it is the French political culture that, in prioritising equality and uniformity, is the decisive factor in causing centralisation: the existence of a large and fragmented area was regarded as a reason to cantonalise all major public policies, although that proved to be more expensive. But the extreme scores on the dependent variables are obtained by Geneva, by far the most centralised Swiss canton.

Geneva is a city-canton with a small surrounding area, exclusively French speaking, with a very progressive political culture and the highest level of cantonal centralisation. Unlike Basel-City with only two *Landgemeinden*, Rousseau's canton has 44 municipalities in addition to Geneva city and is, with an area of 282 km^2, more than seven times larger than the city-canton on the Rhine. But the progressive, French-inspired political culture compensates for that.

The new cantonal constitution of 2012, replacing that of 1847, best expresses this progressiveness which, by aspiring for equality and uniformity, is co-responsible for centralisation: it enshrines solidarity (Art. 1.1 CC GE 2012), religious neutrality (Art. 3), sustainable development (Art. 10), equality (Art. 15), a 'right to live in a healthy environment' (Art. 19) as well as a housing right (Art. 38) as basic elements of Geneva.[1] The territorial organisation was not an object of major debates in the constituent assembly, although various other models were discussed for a while (NZZ, 31 May 2012: 13). In the end, however, none of the political actors was in favour of changing anything in the 'historical tradition of centralisation' (Interview no. 22). Finally, even in the few areas where communes are competent, centralisation through association takes place: the LGA of Geneva, with headquarters in Carouge, is directly responsible for IT, rubbish collection and extra-school care to ensure equal services for all (Interview no. 22).

The same is true for the other two French-speaking cantons in this group. In Neuchâtel, Liberal-Socialist progressiveness is backed up by the medium size of the cantonal area and the dominance of two cities, Neuchâtel and La Chaux-de-Fonds. The cantonal government recently proposed massive investments into public transport to bring the two parts of the canton, mountains and lakeside, closer together into a single metropolitan region of 120,000 inhabitants (NZZ, 31 January 2012: 10; *see also* RUN 2012), but the electorate narrowly rejected the project (NZZ, 24 September 2012: 10). The tendency to 'think cantonally' becomes evident also in a statement by the president of the LGA of Neuchâtel:

> still today the canton sometimes considers the communes as if they were cantonal offices (*des services de l'Etat*). Communes often have to fight to be acknowledged as public collectivities, e.g. when the Government meets the local executive, we have to remind them that they are meeting authorities, and not department chiefs (*chefs de service*). They have a general tendency to think that we are subordinated. Our Government is a Prussian King with five heads! We have maintained the idea of a relatively strong Government, in relation both to Parliament and the communes. (Interview no. 23)

Although socially very different from Neuchâtel, Fribourg with its sizeable German-speaking minority and Catholic predominance is structured very similarly. With a historical past much like that of Berne, and prefects as powerful as in Vaud, a recent example of the centralist mindset in Fribourg is the 'Law on the promotion of communal mergers'. Approved by the cantonal electorate in May 2011, it charges the seven prefects (elected like in Berne) to consult with all the communes in their districts and incentivise mergers, if and where appropriate (Interview no. 14). Unlike in Vaud, in Fribourg a district reform failed because of

---

1.   The new CC GE was approved on 14 October 2012 by 54% (turnout: 31.9%) and will enter into force on 1 June 2013 (NZZ, 15 October 2012: 7).

popular resistance (NZZ, 30 November 2010: 14), but services are as centralised as in the neighbouring French-speaking cantons:

> Education is fully cantonalised, even inter-cantonal by now, with HARMOS and all that. There is a school organization [*organisation scolaire*], but that remains relative. The commune is just an implementing organ, it has constantly to report to the DICS [*Direction de l'Instruction Publique, de la Culture et du Sport*]. […] there are so many restrictions that the commune cannot really decide anything, at the end of the day. Autonomy remains relative and theoretical. There is budgetary autonomy, e.g. for culture, where we decide and then pay for that. This is a legal autonomy, in the sense that the commune is competent, but this autonomy can also be restricted very easily. (Interview no. 20)

Ticino finally is as Catholic as Fribourg and politically centrist, with FDP and CVP together reaching 47 per cent of MCPs and the two left-wing parties together only 23 per cent. Communal mergers in Ticino have repeatedly failed to clear the referendum because *campanilismo*, a mixture of local identity and jealousy, persists (NZZ, 21 January 2010: 15). Moreover, as in the rest of Switzerland, financial constraints are an important factor in determining the overall degree of decentralisation:

> We were told to strengthen local autonomy, and we have done this. Also that we had to apply the subsidiarity principle, because our democracy only lives thanks to these small communes or even micro-communes. We have to strengthen them, and we do this also by giving them tasks. If we take the tasks away, eventually the commune has no reason to exist anymore: then all the public services are cantonalised. But behind every task there are constraints, both in terms of resources and financially […]. (Interview no. 19)

In other words, even if a stronger political commitment to local autonomy exists than in neighbouring Italy, overall decentralisation is much smaller than in the German-speaking cantons because of the cultural idea that it is still the canton that ought to be responsible for most things – even for strengthening the subsidiarity principle by having an ambitious (and expensive) merger strategy. The result is that Ticino lies considerably closer to the French-speaking cantons than it would probably want to – but only just about, for Ticino is the least centralised of the centralised cantons. This concludes my review of the two extreme classes; the next sub-section is devoted to the in-between cantons.

The balanced cantons

There are eleven cantons in the intermediate class, 'balanced' in the sense of being neither as decentralised as D1 or D2, nor as centralised as C. As with the decentralised cantons, I further divide this class into two groups. The first comprises large, the second small cantons.

B1 – seven large, centre-right cantons: SG, LU, VS, SO, AG, UR and BE

The case study canton for this group was Berne, which is very large and predominantly Germanic but, due to the urban dots on its map and the (historical) centrality of Berne city, with a parliament that is one third progressive in outlook. Five other German-speaking cantons are St. Gall, Lucerne, Solothurn, Aargau and Uri while Valais is predominantly French-speaking but with a strong German-speaking minority. All stretch over quite an extensive area, some with a high degree of topographical fragmentation due to their location in the Alps, others situated in the plains. What explains the balanced nature of these large cantons?

In Lucerne, the CVP and the SVP together represent 54 per cent of all MCPs, with the FDP coming third (19 per cent), the SP fourth (13 per cent) and the Greens last (8 per cent) (BADAC 2012). The same is true for St. Gall: SVP and CVP together represent 62 per cent, the FDP 19 per cent, the SP 13 per cent and the Greens 3 per cent of all MCPs. In both cantons the district structure has recently been abolished, fully in St. Gall and very nearly so in Lucerne. Both cantons have their capital cities oddly situated in one corner, with parts of their area oriented towards different cantons, e.g. Rapperswil-Jona towards Zurich and the Sarganserland towards Grisons, or with strong autonomist thinking present in them, e.g. the Entlebuch in Lucerne (NZZ, 15 September 2010: 17) or Werdenberg in St. Gall (Interview no. 2). In both cantons, a myriad of local and inter-local organisations still exists. In St. Gall: next to the 85 political communes there are 70 school communes, around 100 single-issue 'corporations' plus some 20 'citizen's corporations' (*ortsbürgerliche Korporationen*) (Interview no. 3). Blocked by centre-periphery cleavages, neither of the two capital cities was able to expand into a metropolitan region (*Stadtregion Luzern* and *Metropolitanraum St. Gallen*). But the countryside was still unable to resist the so-called 'creeping centralisation', e.g. in the education domain in Lucerne, where inter-local associations are the rule and not the exception, and where the canton finances 25 per cent of the teachers' salaries (Interview no. 6). In sum, the Germanic political culture is tempered by the influence of the progressively minded capital cities in the interpretation of area for determining only moderate levels of cantonal decentralisation.

In Solothurn, the strength of political parties is perfectly balanced: 27 per cent of MCPs are Liberals, 25 per cent Christian-Democrats, 21 per cent Socialists (plus 6 per cent Greens) and only 18 per cent come from the SVP (BDAC 2012). Together with Ticino, the only Catholic canton that did not join the losing side in the civil war of 1847, Solothurn industrialised very early on. The canton also did not have to re-invent itself after the defeat of the French army but could largely retain its borders of 1481, when it joined the Swiss Confederation. Solothurn is a traditional, centrist canton with only moderately strong parties at either end of the ideological spectrum. The asymmetrical territorial structure is further proof of that: in 2011, the 250,000 inhabitants were organised into 121 political communes (of which 29 had absorbed their citizen communes), 99 standalone citizen communes, 101 ecclesiastical communes and some 120 inter-communal associations (Schönholzer 2011: 2). This kind of historically rooted decentralisation is not perceived as a backward element, but contributes to overall citizen satisfaction and identity:

> What gives you the feeling of home? For sure it's not the canton! As an instrument, I really like the communal assembly, even if people sometimes ridicule it. But here the citizen is able to directly intervene, if he does not like something. And the mayors have to appear twice every year; and you bet they are not always told what is not good in a diplomatic way [...] This is our strength and we know that it contributes to the satisfaction of citizens. I am not being nostalgic [...] but my home is my commune and Switzerland, and certainly not the canton. (Interview no. 28)

Uri is also a centre-right canton where left-wing parties barely make up for 16 per cent of MCPs (BADAC 2012). The topographical peculiarity of this canton is its confinement to a single valley, rising from the lake up to the Gotthard pass. But if Uri is a CVP-dominated canton, in Aargau the SVP is by far the strongest parliamentary group: with 32 per cent of all MCPs it has double the size of the next party, the SP with 16 per cent, as the most recent elections have confirmed (NZZ, 22 October 2012: 7). Nevertheless, together with the 9 per cent Greens, left-wing parties in Aargau are stronger than in Uri. On the other hand, Aargau has no real centre – the canton was formed only in 1803 from various 'leftovers', although by now economic differences have become more important than historical identity (Interview no. 26). Rather than a single centre, Aargau has, like Grisons and Thurgau, many medium-sized cities, whereas Uri has neither. Consequently, the small area and topographical unity of Uri are conducive for central delivery – but this is done inter-locally, by the 20 communes together, e.g. in the inter-communal associations for rubbish collection (*ZAKU*) and wastewater (*Abwasser Uri*) (Interview no. 41).

Valais, finally, is the only non-German speaking canton in this group, but a sizeable German-speaking minority is concentrated in the upper parts of the valley (*Oberwallis*). Valais is a veritable Catholic stronghold: the German- and French-speaking sections of the Christian-Democrats alone amount to over 52 per cent of MCPs, followed at great length by the FDP with 21 per cent (BADAC 2012). The fact that in Valais – as also in Lucerne and St. Gall – the canton actively pursues a strategy of communal mergers is perhaps the best illustration of the middle position of this canton: a large and topographically fragmented area lends itself to decentralisation, but political actors have so far failed to agree on how best to implement this idea, which is also a cultural desire. Thus, it is less because of a cantonal desire for power, and more because of the way local structures are fragmented into many small, rural communes that centralisation, almost accidentally, has taken place over the last decades (*schleichende Zentralisierung*). This counts for Valais as much as for Aargau, Uri, Solothurn, St. Gall, Lucerne and Berne.

B2 – four small cantons: SH, BL, BS and JU

In this second group of balanced cantons we find Jura, a French speaking canton with a strong Christian-Democrat presence; Schaffhausen and Basel-Countryside, which are both German speaking, territorially small and with equilibrated political forces, and the city-canton of Basel-City. At first sight, this group is the most heterogeneous. What unites them are middle degrees of decentralisation, so each canton can be approached as a variation from either extreme:

1. Jura, which was part of Berne for 164 years, represents the rural-Catholic version of equally French-speaking, but much more centralised, Neuchâtel.
2. Schaffhausen resembles centralised Geneva in its superficial territorial structure but is German-speaking.
3. Basel-Countryside and Basel-City formed a single entity until 1833 and lack the local autonomy tradition of the decentralised cantons, although being German-speaking.

The size of these four cantons goes some way towards explaining their moderate degrees of decentralisation. But judging by its French language and small size, one would expect a greater centralisation for Jura than is currently the case. The CVP is the largest party in parliament, with 32 per cent of all MCPs, but SP and Greens together amount to 33 per cent; Liberals reach only 13 per cent and the SVP comes last with 7 per cent (BADAC 2012). Why, then, is Jura less centralised than Neuchâtel, Fribourg or Vaud? One reason is the dire state of cantonal finances:

> For hospitals, in 1995 a *Centre de gestion hospitalière* was created, so there was already a will to centralize. We then merely continued on that path. Communes withdrew from financing through incurring debt, they ended up covering only running costs, and eventually the canton overtook the whole thing. The argument was that one entity alone would be better able to manage hospitals than 80 communes plus the canton together. Now there are other tasks, like education, which could be centralised, but that is probably not ripe yet. There are still school committees and circles – we're just not there yet! (Interview no. 28)

Another reason is the only recently begun process of cantonal 'state building', in turn influenced by more than 150 years of Bernese bureaucracy:

> They tried, in the beginning of our young canton, to decentralise services to the communes, but it quickly led to problems and obstacles. Today, we have problems in making people understand; they often say 'the canton has decided etc.'; that is shocking for me, because the canton, after all, that's us! Participatory democracy, that's us! But the people often have the impression of being dominated by the bureaucracy. Communal autonomy, from a philosophical or human perspective, is extremely important. But as regards

fiscal and economic autonomy, we are extremely limited. If we look at the process which concerns only normal charges, 75% of our expenses are fixed. Then there are other expenses, like salaries etc. that are bound – so what is actually left is an autonomy of between 8% and 10% for a commune like us, with a budget of 2.8 Mio. We have in fact ridiculous sums at our disposal to come up with a strategy or a political vision [...]. (Interview no. 42)

Although French-speaking, then, Jura is culturally more localist in orientation than the centralised cantons, much like Berne. Nevertheless, the desire for equal services – in health care or education – permeates policy-making; together this accounts for the balanced outcome. This leaves us with Basel-Countryside, Basel-City and Schaffhausen. Both Basel-Countryside and Schaffhausen are German speaking, rather small (in terms of area) and with balanced party systems: 36 per cent left-wing, 28 per cent centrist and 32 per cent right-wing MCPs in Schaffhausen; and 37 per cent left-wing, 33 per cent centrist and 27 per cent right-wing MCPs in Basel-Countryside (BADAC 2012). The peculiarity of Schaffhausen is the position of the city of Schaffhausen:

All transport streams flow towards the city – like in a valley where everybody has to get out in the front: that's similar here. [...] By necessity everything is centralised towards the bridgehead at the Rhine; that was also historically very important. The small communes around could never really develop, but remained agricultural communities. That is, [Schaffhausen is] *de facto* centralised, but politically decentralised. (Interview no. 4)

This 'political decentralisation' became evident when the canton launched an initiative to reduce the number of communes to just seven (*see* 'sh.auf' 2004). But local resistance was too strong, for the same reason as evoked also in Grisons:

it is not possible that communal mergers are ordered from the top. That has to come from the bottom. We are open for mergers if a neighbouring commune approaches us. [...] Mergers only make sense if a small municipality and its population want to get together and can identify, otherwise it won't work. [...] There mustn't be any coercion; you have to enjoy that process! The details – commune of origin, flag etc. are not important, but it must never be dictated from the top! (Interview no. 36)

As with the bigger cantons in this group, in Schaffhausen there *is* a policy on communal mergers, but it has yet to enable communes to become stronger. Basel-Countryside, on the other hand, is again – like Aargau or Thurgau – an example of a centre-less canton: 'Freedom was conquered in 1833, but it almost seems as if, until today, nobody has really known what to do with it.' (NZZ, 11 January 2011: 11) Even from within the cantonal administration this impression is confirmed:

There it was, the canton, in 1833, totally broke and without a centre, and had to organise itself. [...] Communal administration was built centrally, by the canton. Decentralisation took place through the districts, which were cantonal. But this was merely in terms of location, as everything remained with the canton. [...] Therein lies the reason why so much is centralised, e.g. construction permits or also, a classic example, secondary schools. (Interview no. 33)

Moreover, the centre-periphery cleavage is perpetuated, although Basel-Countryside 'shook off its masters' (Interview no. 33), as became obvious in the popular vote on whether to subsidise the theatre of Basel-City with 4 million CHF per year: all those communes close to Basel-City approved, some with yes-shares of 67 per cent, whereas further away from the city the same proportions rejected this cross-cantonal subsidy (NZZ, 14 February 2011: 8). This caused cross-local tensions to rise to dangerous levels:

The affluent suburbs of Basel-City, the so-called *Speckgürtel*, regularly use the theatre and were ready to subsidise it. But the 'hip' of the canton – where also the war between city and countryside had taken place – was against it and outvoted us. The municipalities in the *Speckgürtel* cried out loud and threatened to henceforth pay 60 million CHF directly to the theatre, and not into the inter-communal fiscal equalisation [anymore]. Others then came up with an even more radical idea, namely to let the other cantonal citizens pay for their village pub and their village theatre directly, or [even] fully join Basel-City. (Interview no. 33)

The other city canton in this group, then, is even more special: although Basel-City is German-speaking, an extreme degree of urbanisation introduces the same kind of progressiveness that in the larger cantons (Zurich, Berne, Lucerne) is outweighed by a conservative hinterland. Left-wing parties occupy almost half the seats in the cantonal parliament. Moreover, since the secession of Basel-Countryside in 1832–33, Basel-City is all but devoid of a periphery, to an extent that communes have often been 'forgotten' (Raith 1984: 303). The two other communes, Riehen and Bettigen, together elect only twelve MCPs, with the remaining 88 coming from Basel city (*see Der Grosse Rat des Kantons Basel-Stadt* 2012). However, unlike in Geneva (and Ticino) where the whole canton forms a single constituency, here even the city itself is further subdivided to ensure sub-local, neighbourhood representation (like, also, the city of Zurich). The character of Basel-City as a progressive, left-oriented polity with at least some cultural legacy of local autonomy is also responsible for the failure of reunification attempts:

In Basel-Countryside, the Left wants the [cantonal] merger, but the Right is rather sceptical; in Basel-City, the Left is sceptical and the Right wants the unification. In Basel-Countryside the SP and Greens hope that state services will be lifted to the level of the city, and the Right fears exactly the same and that this will cost much more. In the city, the left-wing parties fear that the high level of salaries and state services will be lowered, and the Right says that this would finally bring a healthy mixture, make the state less expensive and more moderate. (Interview no. 32)

Basel-City is thus unique but not an anomaly, and this is explained very well by the model. In sum, both in Schaffhausen and Basel-Countryside, centre-periphery issues are reflected in the political landscape, which is balanced between the left-, the centre and the right-wing poles. The Germanic political culture is thus tempered by urban progressiveness within the canton, in Schaffhausen, or next door, in Basel-Countryside. Together with a small area, this explains lower degrees of decentralisation than in other German-speaking cantons. Jura, on the other hand, is caught between a Bernese tradition of local autonomy and cultural demands for equality, while in Basel-City, urban progressiveness tempers the Germanic political culture without, however, fully eclipsing it. Where does all this leave us for explaining (de)decentralisation *in general*?

Theoretical implications

It is now time to review the theoretical framework presented in Chapter Two (*see* Figure 2.2: Explanatory model) in light of the empirical evidence provided. Direct causal influence was accorded to political actors, be they parties, the electorate, or interest groups. Indirect causal influence, on the other hand, was argued to be related both to socio-cultural (political culture and societal diversity) and structural factors (size and centre-periphery structure). After having travelled across space and time in sub-national Switzerland, what implications can be drawn from this for explaining (de)centralisation in general?

Provided that two assumptions of comparability hold, there is much to learn from this cantonal comparison. The first is that political systems, *qua* systems, produce outputs through interaction and the processing of inputs; because they are *political*, these outputs are collectively binding upon people residing in a given jurisdiction (*see* Easton 1968 [1953]). The second assumption supposes that in democratic systems of a certain size (say, above neighbourhood level), the need arises for institutions – an elected or citizens' assembly and an executive – as well as for intermediary organisations, such as parties and interest groups (e.g. LGAs). Following Vatter (2002) and other cantonal comparativists, the 26 Swiss cantons can indeed be described as 'democracies' in this sense, with autonomy over many areas that, in other states, are a national domain, such as education, police, health, or social care. One could even term the cantons *federal* political systems (in the sense of Watts 1998), because local self-rule is constitutionally enshrined and extensive (formal and informal) and provisions for shared rule exist, too. Be that as it may, what has this revealed that we did not already know?

First and foremost, there is *political culture*. This comparative analysis of the Swiss cantons has clearly shown the causal power of historical legacies: 'ways of doing things', deeply engrained expectations and ensuing patterns of behaviour. Of course, in studying Switzerland one profits from the convenience of being able to compare political behaviour (and not simply opinions or attitudes, as in surveys) across a range of frequent and issue-specific popular votes over a long time, detached from the plebiscitary (and thus distorting) character such events take on when they are rare and/or politicised. Granted, also, that political culture may exert such a strong influence in Switzerland exactly because of the nature of its direct-democratic (national, cantonal and local) politics, which tightens the link between electorate and outputs. But that does not mean that political culture is important only in the Swiss context. Controlling for several other factors, instead, culture has been shown to drive politics by providing an important 'default option' on which to fall back when making decisions: prioritising equality, uniformity and change (and centralisation) in one, subsidiarity, diversity and status quo (and decentralisation) in another context.

Or, to turn things around: simply because political culture is more difficult to measure elsewhere does not mean that it does not have causal power. As my initial literature review has outlined, a legacy of French civil law and Spanish or Portuguese colonialism is positively correlated with centralisation (Treisman 2006; Stegarescu 2005; Arzaghi and Henderson 2005). In Europe, too, in the 'Napoleonic' countries local autonomy is significantly smaller than in the Germanic, Nordic and English-speaking ones (Loughlin 2001a; Loughlin and Delcamp 2003; Hesse and Sharpe 1991) – at least as regards the polity- and policy-dimensions, even if not so much the politics-aspect of lobbying and the *cumul des mandats* (e.g. Tarrow 1974 and 1977). Political culture – and history, which is implied in the definition of culture as long-established, enduring behavioural patterns – thus drives (de)centralisation. But, of course, political culture is not alone in this.

My second finding, the influence of *area* (and size, more generally) on (de)centralisation, is an important reminder of the limited nature of both socio-cultural and political factors. Territory is a crucial element in political discourses because it is the only aspect of the state-triad of area, government, and people that is both visible and tangible: in the form of place (Storey 2012: 25). Moreover, territoriality, the deliberate use of area for social control (Sack 1986), is an integral part of politics as 'the art of association' (Althusius 1995 [1614]). So when political actors invoke the physical boundaries of their homeland, nation or nationality, as in Scotland, Québec or the Basque Country, they are not just driven by the rational desire to gain the next election. Instead, it is because there is something archaic, primordial hidden beneath it, so that relying on territory bestows solidity, indisputability, as well as security (e.g. Herz 1957: 474).

It may seem a truism that territorial governance depends on territory – however, there is a myriad of ways in which area can be given social meaning, with accordingly different consequences for its political organisation: from unitary-centralised to confederal. In this process, different political cultures influence territory-building differently by providing a different frame through which area is given social meaning. Territories once (re)defined, in turn, influence the further cultural evolution through continued nation- and/or state-building. It is thus no coincidence that my analysis, as well as most other studies of (fiscal) decentralisation, regional authority, or federalism, has found a strong, significant and positive influence of area (Treisman 2006; Panizza 1999; Arzaghi and Henderson 2005; Stegarescu 2005 – but *see* Hooghe and Marks 2013; Wallis and Oates 1988 and Timofeev 2003). Area simply is the most obvious point of reference for the political organisation of people and space.

However, the relationship between culture and area must itself pass through political agency to produce decisions. I found that, thirdly, *left-wing parties* are causally related to centralisation. This is again in line with other studies, in which regionalist parties (Hooghe and Marks 2013) or left-wing governments (Stegarescu 2005; Steunenberg and Mol 1997) were shown to correlate with territorial governance. Advocating equal opportunities, uniformity and professional service delivery is more a matter of left-wing/progressive than of right-wing/conservative thinking. Naturally, whether and what kind of reform is advocated also depends on the conditions of departure: 200 years ago, most Swiss cantons were very decentralised, as was confederal Switzerland. It has been the weakness of left-wing ideas in some cantons (and Switzerland as a whole) that has impeded (further) centralisation. The question then becomes: why are left-wing parties stronger in some polities than in others? If the progressive, egalitarian culture of French-speaking areas is one part of the story, the other is that Socialists and Greens thrive in the urban, educated, better paid, cosmopolitan, young and dynamic electorate. Therefore, area and culture both have an impact on politics, but only politics is able to act and change the state structures towards either more centralisation (e.g. by reining in regional borrowing powers in Spain) or more decentralisation (e.g. announcing a referendum on more fiscal autonomy in Catalonia). This political aspect is undertheorised by both the socio-cultural and structural approaches to territorial governance and deserves much closer attention than it has hitherto been given.

The fourth and final implication, then, concerns the *interaction* between the causal variables. If centralisation is the outcome of uniform policy solutions that are preferred by left-wing parties, and if these are strong enough, then policies will eventually be delivered in a centralised polity where sub-system entities have no, or only little, discretion to deviate and where, consequently, political forces and processes adapt accordingly. The strength of left-wing parties, and therefore the likelihood that their demands are met, rises proportionally to the diffusion of an egalitarian, progressive political culture – which is also to say, that a conservative culture can dampen the impact of left-wing ideas. It is from here that potential institutional change comes: since area remains constant and political culture – by definition – changes only slowly, only an interaction between these two (e.g. through urbanisation, migration, economic development and education) can cause a change in political forces. Thus, neither a small, nor a large, area alone can account for (de)centralisation. Only together with strong left-wing parties is area able to legitimise uniform policy solutions – and only if a third condition is met, that is if a political culture exists which accepts or demands such uniformity.

Thus, depending on the cultural frame, even a large area can be made a reason to centralise so that uniformity and equality can be ensured (the case of Vaud – or France). Conversely, even in a small area can decentralisation be advocated to guarantee diversity, if it is culturally desirable to maintain such diversity (Schwyz – or Switzerland). Obviously centralisation is highest where all three factors point in the same direction: a small area, a unitary political culture and strong-left-wing parties (Geneva – or Luxembourg); or a large area, a federal political culture and weak left-wing parties (Grisons – or the United States). Moreover, once achieved, a certain degree of (de)centralisation feeds back on political culture through 'output legitimacy' (Scharpf 2000), thus further fostering pre-existing expectations and behaviour. So where both left-wing parties and an egalitarian political culture are absent, even a small area cannot cause centralisation; and where both right-wing-parties and a federal political culture are missing, even a large area cannot cause decentralisation.

In a hierarchy of *proximate* causes, then, political agency comes out first, political culture second, and area third. As regards their *long-term* effect, however, it is political culture that comes out first, area second, and politics – the most susceptible to change – third. Area is placed second in both causal rankings because although, in principle, immutable, the social meaning given to it depends on both culture and politics. In other words, even if political actors decide on actual degrees of (de)centralisation (through policy-making, constitutional change or the way they organise themselves), they act under cultural influence (expectations by the public, their own preferences, and the push-and-pull by other actors like functional or territorial interest groups) and are constrained by 'objective' factors – such as, first and foremost, the size of their polity. (De)centralisation is caused by an interaction of these factors. Exactly what kind of research agenda can be deduced from this is illustrated next.

Research implications

Where does all this leave us with regard to the state of the art of the current literature(s)? The answer to this obviously depends on which literature we are talking about. For *federal and regional studies*, the major shortcoming identified here was the lack of attention given to political actors. Both socio-cultural and structural approaches to territorial governance under-appreciate the role of ultimate decision-makers. Broschek (2014) goes some way towards bringing actors back into play, but even he prioritises institutional legacies over actual decisions (*see also* Benz & Broschek 2013). Equally laudable are the efforts by Bolleyer *et al.* (2014a) as well as Braun and Trein (2013). The former attempt to better understand

> how governments within multi-level systems coordinate on issues of mutual concern and the extent to which such processes of intergovernmental coordination have been shaped by party-political dynamics [...]. (Bolleyer *et al.* 2014b: 368)

But focusing on governments alone is insufficient if we also want to understand the dynamics *within* sub-national units, which in turn may cause the very (in) action of regional governments. Centralising pressures exerted by left-wing parties *not* in government in Australia and Canada is another case in point (Turgeon and Simeon 2015). The same counts for Braun and Trein, who centre on the impact of the economic crisis on (de)centralisation, but their 'federal actors' (2013: 361) remain monolithic and impenetrable: all the regions vs. the central government. Yet as the case of Spain shows, regions need not always have the same interests as regards (re)centralisation (*see* Máiz and Losada 2013). So the concept of political actors needs to be both deepened (governments, parliaments, parties with and without office etc.) and broadened (richer vs. poorer, larger vs. smaller, central vs. peripheral regions etc.) if we are to grasp why exactly more or less centralisation is advocated and implemented.

For *local government studies*, on the other hand, a different research agenda can be sketched. Here, individual actors and their associations have long occupied a central place (e.g. Callanan and Tatham 2014; Lidström 2013), but given the focus on unitary states as the predominant units of analysis (e.g. Page and Goldsmith 1987; Swianiewicz 2010), the number of cases that can be compared is limited, so more analytical attempts are understandably lacking. One avenue for further research would thus be to focus on local-regional relations, that is countries where the power over local governments is regional, e.g. in the US, Canada, Australia, Germany (*see* Steytler 2009), or also Scotland (Keating 2009a: 18). This would increase the number of cases to be studied and allow for more reliable explanations. Regional studies, too, should be interested in a 'local authority index', modelled along the RAI (Hooghe *et al.* 2008 and 2010), that would list the extent of local autonomy and allow for analyses of cause and effect.

A second avenue for further local government research is mapped out by Goldsmith and Page (2010: 8–9), mentioning the European Union as a new territorial actor. This complicates the network of horizontal and vertical inter-governmental relations even further, but makes that field also a much richer area to study. After all, regions deal not only with the EU, their own nation-states, or other regions; they are also acting increasingly across state borders as well as 'downwards', with a view on local governments. Especially where local entities are anything but small and weak, as in the case of cities, many different dynamics can be expected to develop that may have important consequences not only for that particular region but, in a more distant future perhaps, also the very idea of how politics should be structured (*see* Barber 2013 for an idea). If such polities then also act 'upwards', for example at EU level (*see* Piattoni 2014; Tatham and Thau 2014), then the circle comes to a full closure and scholars are left to explore the multiple ways and arenas in which collectively binding decisions are taken, from the local through the regional and national, to the European and even global level, as well as in all sorts of interaction.

Conclusions

The research question posed at the beginning of this book was how political science could explain the occurrence of different (or similar) degrees of centralisation in otherwise similar (or different) polities. After surveying the literature(s), I have developed an innovative theoretical framework that draws on three different approaches: socio-cultural, structural and party-political. I have shown that each approach has, as its merits, precisely those aspects which are the downsides of the other two: in emphasising societal factors, one brushes over the actor dimension and relativises structure; in focusing on 'territorial ideologies' such as localism, federalism, regionalism and centralism, structural conditions and societal embeddedness are neglected; and in centring on 'objective' variables alone, one forgets that culture cannot act by itself, but needs to be acted upon to become consequential for politics. Because I regard the three approaches as complementary, I integrated them into a single framework. Using the Swiss cantons as a comparative template, I subsequently tested this model in both a quantitative and a qualitative manner.

The evidence provided has confirmed that political culture and size influence – but do not determine – political parties when deciding on (de)centralisation: even left-wing parties in Grisons have advocated strong local autonomy and professed respect for societal diversity; and even right-wing parties in Vaud have been keen on centralising. What makes the study of (de)centralisation worthwhile is that it forces one to go back in time and reconsider the basic elements of the state: territory, power, population. Variables expressing properties of each have proven relevant in explaining (de)centralisation: area, as the physical extension of territory; socio-cultural differences linked, in the Swiss case at least, to the dominant language of the resident population; and the importance of political parties for gauging how and in which policy areas actors push for more or less power for either the central or the local level.

In developing an explanatory typology of cantonal decentralisation, this book has contributed to the study of cantonal-local relations in Switzerland and offered a theoretical model with wider applicability. Differences mainly between the French- and German-speaking cantons have been systematically highlighted, discussed, measured and tested for their statistical and, later, also 'real' causal power. That the former are more centralised is nothing new – on the contrary. But precisely because this observation has turned into a commonplace in the study of Swiss politics, it was necessary to apply the why-question more thoroughly. Five groups of cantons have emerged from this:

1. *Three decentralised and large cantons*, where a conservative periphery (Zurich) or lack of any progressive centre (Grisons and Thurgau) reinforces the Germanic political culture in preserving 'communal sovereignty'.

2. *Seven decentralised and small cantons* (Appenzell Inner-Rhodes & Appenzell Outer-Rhodes, Glarus, Schwyz, Obwalden & Nidwalden, Zug), where the absence of dominant cities combines with a conservative cultural tradition in preserving strongly autonomous local structures.

3. *Seven balanced and large cantons* (Berne, Lucerne, St. Gall, Aargau, Uri, Solothurn, Valais), where area combines with alternating centre-right and centre-left majorities in either reinforcing or tempering a predominantly Germanic political culture.

4. *Four balanced and small cantons*, where area is so small and culture so progressive that single solutions are pragmatically preferred, although a Germanic political culture would tend otherwise (Basel-City); where an egalitarian French political culture is tempered by a Germanic tradition of local autonomy (Jura); or where a dominant centre (within the canton, in Schaffhausen, or next door, in Basel-Countryside) creates centre-periphery tensions that weaken local autonomy despite a cultural propensity for it.

5. *Five centralised cantons*, where area, no matter how small (Geneva), medium-sized (Neuchâtel, Fribourg) or large (Vaud, Ticino), combines with a French-inspired egalitarian culture into demanding and obtaining centralisation.

What does this mean for the study of territorial politics in general? At the time of writing these conclusions, Scotland is (still) demanding independence; in France, attempts at curbing the *cumul des mandats* are under way; Spain's regions have had to ask for money from the central government; the Austrian and German *Länder* are experimenting with direct democracy; and Italy has just announced a provincial reform where area and population are used as 'objective criteria'. In drawing two types of lessons, this book contributes to wider attempts at better understanding territorial governance:

1. The *conceptual lesson* is that (de)centralisation has three dimensions, one relating to institutions, a second capturing the policies delivered by different levels, and a third pointing to how political actors operate such a multi-level system.

2. The *theoretical lesson* is that (de)centralisation is best explained through the enduring strength of left-wing parties, which in turn depends on both cultural and structural conditions such as conservativeness and size.

For the Swiss cantons, these three factors – together with the number of LGs and per capita GDP – were able to predict 68 per cent of the variation of cantonal decentralisation thus understood (*see* Table 5.8: Final model). However, only further, refined testing – modelling, for example, an interaction term – in different contexts – e.g. the EU Member States – can confirm whether through integrating the three different approaches, and refining the dependent variable to take into account its multi-faceted nature, we are able to lower our ignorance about the wider world we live in, and not simply Swiss cantonal democracies.

Finally, if the purpose of theorising is to better understand our reality, then we must do so neither over- nor sub-consciously, as Sartori (1970: 1033) put it – but self-consciously. This includes questioning our questions. One question asked in the Introduction, implied also by the title of this book, was why it was worth studying (de)centralisation in the first place. At this concluding point, three answers can be offered. Firstly, as this comparative analysis of cantonal decentralisation has shown, important *cultural expectations* lie beneath political decisions. Degrees of (de)centralisation mirror a societal balance between state interventionism and private initiatives, between the desire for egalitarianism and the acceptance of diversity, and between different political traditions: those where the state plays a more prominent role vs. others in which 'local sovereignty' is a good not to be forsaken too easily. Although throughout Switzerland small-scale proximity, the virtue of political compromises, proportional representation and even a basic level of communal autonomy are undisputed elements, the differences in the way these 'goods' are implemented in a canton principally depend on whether its political culture is predominantly 'Latin' (French and Italian) or Germanic.

Secondly, however, cultural predispositions alone are insufficient to bring about political outcomes. Political culture can only make certain decisions more likely, but not impose or determine them. Even among the French-speaking cantons there are differences in the degree of centralisation, Geneva being the most and Jura the least centralised. The same applies to the group of German-speaking cantons: some are very decentralised, like Grisons and Appenzell Outer-Rhodes, while others, notably Berne, are more centralised – without however reaching the centralisation levels of 'pure' Latin cantons. This is causally connected to the strength of left-wing parties in some cantons and their weakness in others, as well as size. The study of (de)centralisation is thus also one of *political processes* and the way 'objective' factors like area, centre-periphery structures, the number of local governments, or financial considerations impact on them, alongside an underlying political culture.

Thirdly, analysing these processes from a particularly territorial perspective has revealed different *kinds* of policy-making, e.g. the pragmatism of (cheaper) inter-local, inter-district and district-local solutions in Schwyz vs. the (more expensive) desire for uniformity in health and education in Vaud. The study of (de)centralisation thus uncovers differences in political structures and their *consequences*, e.g. 'centralised' corporate lobbying in Berne vs. intra-cantonal federalism in Grisons. In sum, territory is an important structuring variable of politics, a key element when deciding on policy, and a defining aspect of polity. And so the study of (de)centralisation leads us far beyond territorial governance, providing important structural, economic, cultural, and political insights.

Appendices

Databases

BADAC (2012) *Banque de données des cantons et des villes Suisses* [Database of Swiss cantons and cities]. At http://www.badac.ch (last accessed October 2012).

BFS (2012) *Bundesamt für Statistik* [Federal Office for Statistics], http://www.statistik.admin.ch (last accessed October 2012).

BK (2012) *Bundeskanzlei* [Federal State Chancellery], http://www.bk.admin.ch (last accessed October 2012).

BZ (2008) Betriebszählung [Business Census], http://www.bz.bfs.admin.ch (data obtained through e-mail correspondance in October 2012).

Cantonal and Swiss Constitutions and Laws, accessible through http://www.lexfind.ch.

EFV (2012) *Eidgenössische Finanzverwaltung* [Federal Finance Administration], http://www.efv.admin.ch (last accessed October 2012).

GSB (1994, 2005 and 2009) *Gemeindeschreiberbefragungen* [Surveys among local secretaries]. At http://www.andreasladner.ch (last accessed October 2012).

PARLINE (2012) Database on national parliaments, International Parliamentary Union (ed.). At http://www.ipu.org/parline-e/parlinesearch.asp (last accessed October 2012).

SELECTS (2011) Swiss Electoral Study. At http://www.forscenter.ch/en/our-surveys/selects (last accessed 7 March 2015).

World Factbook (2012) At https://www.cia.gov/library/publications/the-world-factbook (last accessed October 2012).

Newspapers

Die Südostschweiz, ed. in Chur and Glarus, at http://www.diesuedostschweiz.ch.

NZZ – Neue Zürcher Zeitung, ed. in Zürich, at http://www.nzz.ch.

Tages-Anzeiger, ed. in Zurich, at http://www.tagi.ch.

List of interviews

No.	Surname	Name	Organisation/function (as of summer 2011)
1	Joller-Kirstein	Martina	Geschäftsführerin Verband Schwyzer Gemeinden und Bezirke (vszgb)
	Auf Der Maur	Albert	Gemeindepräsident Brunnen and Präsident vszgb; FDP SZ
2	Tinner	Beat	Präsident Vereinigung der St. Galler Gemeindepräsidenten (VSGP) and MCP FDP SG
3	Schaible	Bruno	Gemeindereformer, Amt für Gemeinden SG
4	Jenni	Andreas	Chef Amt für Justiz und Gemeinden SH
5	Kuttruff	Roland	Landammann, Präsident Verband Thurgauer Gemeinden (VTG) and MCP CVP TG
	Marty	Reto	Geschäftsleiter VTG
6	Lauber	Judith	Leiterin Amt für Gemeinden LU
7	Hess	Klaus	Leiter Geschäftsstelle Gemeindepräsidentenkonferenz NW
8	Siegrist	Michael	Gemeindepräsident Alpnach and Präsident Gemeindepräsidentenkonferenz; CVP OW
9	Theus	Simon	Stv. Leiter Amt für Gemeinden, Gemeindereformer GR
10	Hörler-Koller	Lydia	Frau Bezirkshauptmann von Appenzell and MCP AI
11	Müller	Alex	Geschäftsführer der Gemeindepräsidentenkonferenz AR
12	Hulliger	Hans-Peter	Gemeindepräsident Bärestwil and Präsident des Gemeindepräsidentenverband Kanton Zürich (GPVZ); FDP ZH
	Harris	Martin	Geschäftsführer GPVZ
13	Helbling	Arthur	Leiter Gemeindeamt ZH
14	Schmid	Roland	Juristischer Berater, Amt für Gemeinden FR
	Leiser	Brigitte	Finanzen, Amt für Gemeinden FR
15	Mahaim	Raphael	MCP Verts VD

List of interviews (continued)

No.	Surname	Name	Organisation/function (as of summer 2011)
16	Hunyady	Katalin	Amt für Gemeinden und Raumordnung BE
17	Golaz	Eric	Chef du Service des communes et des relations institutionnelles VD
18	Arn	Andrea	Présidente de l'Association des communes vaudoises (AdCV)
19	Gasser	Francis	Chef des finances communales VS
20	Guerry	Micheline	Secrétaire générale de l'Association des Communes Fribourgeoises (ACF)
21	Lattion	Antoine	Préfet de Monthey (VS), président de l'Association des préfets and ancien président de commune
22	Rütsche	Alain	Directeur général de l'Association des Communes Genevoises (ACG)
	Penet	Anne	Directrice adjointe de l'ACG
23	Comte	Raphaël	Président de l'Association des communes neuchâteloises (ACN) and Conseiller aux Etats; FDP NE
24	Kundert	Urs	Leiter Fachstelle Gemeinden GL
25	Genazzi	Elio	Caposezione della Sezione degli enti locali TI
26	Mischler	Walter	Leiter Gemeindeabteilung AG
27	Arn	Daniel	Geschäftsführer des Verbandes Bernischer Gemeinden (VBG/ACB)
28	Ryser	Marcel	Directeur du Service des communes JU
	Bersier	Pierre	Service des communes JU, section finances
29	Bucher	Ulrich	Geschäftsführer Verband Solothurner Einwohnergemeinden (VSEG) and MCP SP SO
30	Derrer Pape	Sylvia	Gemeindeschreiberin Unterägeri and Sekretärin Gemeindepräsidentenkonferenz ZG
31	Marti	Christian	Gemeindepräsident von Glarus and MCP FDP GL
32	Burckhardt	Andreas	ehem. Grossratspräsident; LDP BS

List of interviews (continued)

No.	Surname	Name	Organisation/function (as of summer 2011)
33	Schwörer	Daniel	Leiter Stabsstelle Gemeinden BL; FDP
	Schweighauser	Willi	Gemeindeverwalter Bottmingen BL
34	Zuccolini	Silvio	Pressechef FDP GR
35	Plouda	Jon	Ehem. Gemeindepräsident von Ftan and ehem. Grossrat; BDP GR
36	Hostettmann	Franz	Stadtpräsident Stein am Rhein, Präsident Gemeindepräsidentenkonferenz SH and MCP SVP
37	Blumer	Kasper	Young SVP GL
38	Koch	Jan	MCP SVP GR
39	Caluori	Ludwig	Geschäftsführer Region Mittelbünden and MCP CVP GR
40	Durisch	Christian	Stadtrat Chur; SVP GR
41	Jörg	Beat	Präsident Gemeindeverband Uri and Gemeindepräsident Gurtnellen; CVP
42	Schaffter	Claude	Maire de Montfaucon JU and président de l'Association des maires du district des Franches-Montagnes; indépendant
43	Nigg	Ernst	Gemeindepräsident Igis-Landquart and MCP SVP GR
44	Menzi	Ruedi	Gemeinderat Glarus Nord; SVP GL
45	Grigioni	Roland	Gemeinderat Domat-Ems; SVP GR
	Blum	Hans	Parteipräsident SVP Domat-Ems (GR)
46	Peyer	Ludwig	Geschäftsführer Verband Luzerner Gemeinden (VLG) and MCP CVP LU

Cantonal policy documents

'sh.auf' (2004) *Kräfte bündeln für einen starken Kanton, eine starke Stadt und starke Gemeinden: Schlussbericht des Steuerungsausschusses*, Schaffhausen, 15 December 2004.

Argumentarium (2010) *Volksinitiative, "Starke Gemeinden – starker Kanton" (Gebietsreform-Initiative)*, Chur, 9 May 2010. At http://www. gebietsreform-ja.ch/argumentarium (last accessed October 2012).

Berne (2005) *Gemeinsamer Antrag des Regierungsrates und der Kommission: Reform der dezentralen kantonalen Verwaltung*, Berne, 14 December 2005.

— (2006) *Kantonale Volksabstimmung vom 24. September 2006*, Botschaft des Grossen Rates des Kantons Bern.

— (2010) *Kantonale Wahlen 2010 – Grosser Rat*. Detailed results per constituency, administrative region and municipality, at http://www. wahlarchiv.sites.be.ch/wahlen2010/index.html (last accessed 27 September 2012).

Bulletin de l'Assemblée Constituante du Canton de Vaud. At http://www.archives. vd.ch/constituante.

Der Grosse Rat des Kantons Basel-Stadt: Amtsdauer 2009–2013, Basel, 8 February 2012. At http://www.grosserrat.bs.ch/broschuere (last accessed 10 September 2012).

Glarus (2012) *Wirksamkeitsbericht über die Aufgabenentflechtung zwischen Kanton und Gemeinden im Kanton Glarus – Schlussbericht*. BSS Volkswirtschaftliche Beratung, Basel 27 August 2012.

Grisons (2010) *Botschaft der Regierung an den Grossen Rat – Bericht und Botschaft über die Gemeinde- und Gebietsreform*. Heft Nr. 8/2010–2011. Chur, 26 October 2010.

— (2012a) *Botschaft der Regierung an den Grossen Rat – Teilrevision der Kantonsverfassung (Gebietsreform)*. Heft Nr. 18/2011–2012. Chur, 28 February 2012.

— (2012b) *Botschaft der Regierung an den Grossen Rat – Kantonale Volksinitiative 'Starke Gemeinden – starker Kanton'*. Heft Nr. 2/2012– 2013. Chur, 8 May 2012.

RUN (2012) *Projet d'Agglomération Réseau Urbain Neuchâtelois, deuxième génération, volet 'transports et urbanisation': Rapport final*. La Chaux-de-Fonds, June 2012. At http://www.agglorun.ch (last accessed 10 September 2012).

Schwyz (2002) *Grundlagenbericht G-Reform: Gleichgewicht von Aufgaben, Finanzen, Institutionen und Gebieten. Projekt-Steuerungsteam*. Schwyz, 24 May 2002.

— 2006. *Ergebnis der kantonalen Volksabstimmung vom 26. November 2006 betreffend die Teilrevision der Kantonsverfassung über die G-Reform*. Schwyz, 26 November 2006.

— (2008) *Resultate der Kantonsratswahlen* 1976–2008. Staatskanzlei Schwyz, 26 February 2008. At http://www.sz.ch/xml_1/internet/de/application/d999/d547/d462/p465.cfm.

— (2011) *Umsetzung des neuen Vormundschaftsrechts (Erwachsenenschutz, Personen- und Kindesrecht) – Stellungnahme zu den Ergebnissen der Kommissionsberatung. Beschluss Nr. 799/2011.* Schwyz, 9 August 2011.

— (2012) *Resultate der Kantonsratswahlen* 2012. At http://www.sz.ch/xml_1/internet/de/application/d999/d547/d462/p27309.cfm.

Tagblatt des Grossen Rates des Kantons Bern. At http://www.gr.be.ch/gr/de/index/sessionen/sessionen.html.

Vaud (2005) *Nouveau découpage territorial – consultation publique de juillet à septembre 2005*, Secrétariat général du Département des infrastructures. Lausanne, July 2005.

— (2009) *Exposé des motifs et projet de décret ordonnant la convocation des électeurs pour se prononcer sur l'initiative populaire 'Pour une police unifiée et plus efficace'*, Lausanne, March 2009.

— (2010a) *Exposé des motifs et projet de loi sur les péréquations intercommunales*, Lausanne, February 2010.

— (2010b) *Exposé des motifs et projet de loi sur les écoles de musique*, Lausanne, 30 June 2010.

Verhandlungsprotokolle des Kantonsrates des Kantons Schwyz. At http://www.sz.ch/xml_1/internet/de/application/d999/d960/d31/f40.cfm.

Wortlautprotokolle des Grossen Rates des Kantons Graubünden. At http://www.gr.ch/DE/institutionen/parlament/protokolle/Seiten/Protokolle2012.aspx.

Data Appendix

Dependent Variables

Final index and component indices

	Overall	Cantonal Decentralisation		
		Polity-Dec*	Policy-Dec*	Politics-Dec*
ZH	.70	.61	1.80	−.32
BE	−.68	−.38	.00	−1.65
LU	.02	−.46	1.21	−.70
UR	−.30	.18	−1.27	.18
SZ	.62	.51	.74	.61
OW	.84	1.31	.18	1.03
NW	.62	1.00	−.01	.87
GL	.84	.75	−.57	2.35
ZG	.91	1.54	.49	.71
FR	−1.16	−1.39	−1.39	−.71
SO	−.08	−.43	.56	−.37
BS	−.51	.31	−1.91	.07
BL	−.41	−.58	−.86	.21
SH	.17	.02	.70	−.22
AR	1.07	1.06	1.24	.91
AI	.77	.81	−.52	2.01
SG	.10	−.22	1.04	−.51
GR	1.07	.99	1.25	.97
AG	−.10	.57	−.64	−.23
TG	.65	1.26	.73	−.04
TI	−.82	−.81	−.61	−1.05
VD	−1.04	−1.35	−.70	−1.09
VS	.00	−.41	1.08	−.66
NE	−.91	−1.80	−.33	−.60
GE	−1.83	−2.02	−1.58	−1.88
JU	−.53	−1.06	−.63	.10

Note: *standardised values; *see* Chapter Four for explanation of dimensions.

Perceived LG autonomy

	GSB 1994			GSB 2005			GSB 2009		
	Mean	N	SD	Mean	N	SD	Mean	N	SD
ZH	5.39	115	1.55	5.32	133	1.74	4.52	114	1.62
BE	4.62	216	1.63	4.78	321	1.64	4.58	225	1.69
LU	4.1	62	1.42	4.55	76	1.45	5.02	47	1.73
UR	5.44	9	1.94	5.56	16	1.59	5.56	16	1.86
SZ	4.61	18	1.34	5.31	26	1.62	4.84	19	1.5
OW	6	3	2.65	5.83	6	1.94	6.6	5	1.52
NW	5.5	10	1.43	6.5	10	2.01	5	5	2
GL	5.64	22	1.47	5.24	21	2.07	5	5	1.23
ZG	6	6	2.00	6.2	10	2.10	7.29	7	1.38
FR	4.19	118	1.73	4.36	123	1.58	4.13	86	1.38
SO	4.91	65	1.59	4.73	86	1.64	4.13	61	1.87
BS	5.5	2	2.12	4.67	3	1.16	7	2	1.41
BL	4.35	43	1.34	4.69	72	1.79	4.04	27	1.26
SH	6.13	16	0.89	5	29	1.91	4.69	13	1.55
AR	5.77	13	1.36	6.21	14	1.76	6.09	11	1.81
AI	5	5	1.00	4.4	5	1.95	6	4	1.83
SG	4.88	59	1.70	4.83	65	1.68	5.02	49	1.61
GR	5.75	122	1.76	5.43	145	1.93	5.78	82	1.7
AG	4.91	140	1.57	5.4	181	1.74	4.74	127	1.70
TG	5.94	53	1.38	6.15	61	1.71	6.13	30	1.72
TI	4.29	132	1.81	3.97	133	1.84	3.78	72	1.85
VD	4.73	164	1.70	4.01	232	1.71	4.13	167	1.6
VS	5.51	68	1.63	5.83	100	1.90	5.8	59	1.7
NE	3.71	31	1.76	3.26	42	1.29	3.82	28	1.52
GE	3.18	17	1.55	3.37	30	1.19	3.23	22	0.81
JU	3.97	40	1.79	3.33	63	1.24	3.59	34	1.33
Total	*4.83*	*1549*	*1.73*	*4.78*	*2003*	*1.84*	*4.62*	*1317*	*1.77*

Elements of cantonal politics-decentralisation

	Reg.	LMCP1	Quotas	LGAs	Party dec.	Constit.	DDem
ZH	1	6.27	0	3.5	2.8	3	2
BE	2	5.29	4	4	2.8	1	0
LU	0	13.8	0	3.25	3.3	1	1
UR	2	0	0	2.5	3.5	4	0
SZ	4	4.33	0	3	4	4	0
OW	2	8.05	0	1	4	4	2
NW	2	5.38	0	1	4	4	1
GL	2	52.5	0	0	4	4	4
ZG	2	5.17	0	1	3.8	4	0
FR	1	12.04	0	4	3	2	0
SO	0	8.22	0	4	3.5	2	4
BS	2	0	0	0	1.3	4	0
BL	2	9.1	0	3	2.8	3	4
SH	2	12.38	0	1.25	2.8	1	0
AR	2	22.88	0	1	3.3	4	0
AI	2	46.77	0	1	4	4	4
SG	2	3.44	0	2	3	1	0
GR	4	13.6	0	3	4	3	4
AG	1	8.9	0	2	3.3	2	0
TG	2	26.25	0	3	3	2	0
TI	2	6.65	0	3	1.5	0	3
VD	0	7	0	3.5	3	1	0
VS	2	5.87	2	3	3.4	2	0
NE	2	2.76	0	3	2.7	2	0
GE	2	1.61	0	3.5	0.5	0	0
JU	2	4.84	0	3	3.5	2	4

Note: See second section of Chapter Four for explanation of variables.

Independent Variables

Used for final regression model (Table 5.8)

	No. of LGs (April 2012)	GNP/capita [CHF]*	Left-wing MCPs (ø 2010–11)	Area [km²]+	'Latin'-dummy++
ZH	171	68,804	31.7	1,729	0 (83)
BE	382	45,644	31.9	5,959	0 (84)
LU	87	43,910	20.8	1,493	0 (89)
UR	20	45,712	15.6	1,077	0 (94)
SZ	30	50,170	9.0	908	0 (90)
OW	7	39,646	10.9	491	0 (92)
NW	11	73,286	10.0	276	0 (93)
GL	3	73,236	25.0	685	0 (86)
ZG	11	93,753	18.8	239	0 (85)
FR	165	39,559	29.1	1,671	1 (29)
SO	120	46,844	27.0	790	0 (88)
BS	3	115,178	45.0	37	0 (79)
BL	86	53,502	36.7	518	0 (87)
SH	27	55,126	36.7	298	0 (88)
AR	20	44,215	6.2	243	0 (91)
AI	6	45,936	*n.a.***	173	0 (93)
SG	85	44,866	16.7	2,026	0 (88)
GR	176	49,355	10.0	7,105	0 (68)
AG	219	49,209	25.0	1,404	0 (87)
TG	80	44,918	21.5	991	0 (89)
TI	147	41,335	23.3	2,812	1 (8)
VD	326	52,901	42.0	3,212	1 (5)
VS	141	38,385	14.6	5,224	1 (28)
NE	53	49,775	43.5	803	1 (4)
GE	45	62,839	32.0	282	1 (4)
JU	64	38,070	33.3	839	1 (4)

Notes: *in 1,000s in all regressions; **'0' in final regression model; +logged values in all regressions; ++% German-speakers in 2010 bracketed.

Other independent variables

	FPC	Pop*	PS	GTF	DIST	RIGHT	CPI	LGattach	LGtrust
ZH	−0.65	6.14	2.06	−1.03	56	30.56	0.61	3.15	6.8
BE	−0.75	5.99	0.84	0.00	148	27.5	0.23	3.08	6.3
LU	0.29	5.58	0.97	−0.32	62	20.84	−0.34	3.23	6.67
UR	1.36	4.55	0.58	1.64	99	28.13	−0.75	3.32	6.79
SZ	1.5	5.17	0.3	0.16	90	41	−1.37	3.23	6.64
OW	1.3	4.55	0.51	0.80	68	20	−0.84	3.46	6.56
NW	1.5	4.61	0.4	0.03	34	31.67	−0.91	3.37	7.15
GL	0.28	4.59	0.43	0.46	41	27.5	−0.99	3.23	6.31
ZG	0.72	5.05	0.48	−0.67	28	22.5	−0.10	3.12	6.79
FR	−0.34	5.44	0.79	0.10	68	17.73	0.71	3.02	6.62
SO	−0.03	5.41	0.35	−0.90	99	18	−0.50	3.36	6.4
BS	−1.58	5.27	7.65	−1.40	18	14	1.64	3.3	6.58
BL	−0.62	5.44	0.29	−1.06	63	25	0.39	3.26	6.3
SH	−0.54	4.88	1.59	−0.89	30	31.67	−0.21	3.16	5.84
AR	−0.08	4.72	0.91	0.78	50	12.31	−0.39	3.19	6.88
AI	1.8	4.2	0.66	1.77	104	*n.a.*	−1.52	3.37	7.65
SG	0.28	5.68	0.98	−0.36	112	34.17	−0.55	3.34	6.5
GR	0.07	5.28	0.94	2.62	208	3.33	−0.13	3.36	6
AG	0.33	5.79	0.31	−1.00	66	32.14	−0.60	3.19	7.08
TG	0.19	5.4	0.42	−0.54	51	39.23	−0.80	3.32	7.08
TI	−0.24	5.52	1.05	−0.11	52	5.56	−0.44	3.42	6.22
VD	−1.34	5.85	1.41	−0.45	97	17.33	1.72	3.04	6.7
VS	0.58	5.5	0.49	1.16	139	9.23	−0.03	3.17	5.79
NE	−1.71	5.24	0.63	0.26	60	12.17	1.68	3.1	6.15
GE	−1.76	5.66	1.82	−1.20	60	9	1.91	2.91	5.86
JU	−0.58	4.85	0.74	0.13	77	5.84	1.57	3.03	6

Note: *logged values; *see* Chapter Five for explanation of variables.

Bibliography

Achen, C. H. (1982) *Interpreting and Using Regression*, Beverly Hills, CA: Sage.

Adcock, R. and Collier, D. (2001) 'Measurement validity: a shared standard for qualitative and quantitative research', *American Political Science Review* 95(3): 529–45.

Agranoff, R. (ed.) (1999) *Accommodating Diversity: Asymmetry in federal states*, Baden-Baden: Nomos-Verlag.

Albert, C. D. (2012) 'Defining our terms: bringing rigour to ethnic studies', *Political Studies* 32(2): 70–6.

Albonico, R. (1979) *Nebenamtlich-Nebenbei? Selbstverwaltung in kleinen Gemeinden. Eine Untersuchung über Möglichkeiten und Grenzen des Milizsystems auf der Gemeindeebene in Graubünden*, Hausen a.A.: Pro Vita Alpina-Verlag.

Alesina, A. and Spolaore, E. (2003) *The Size of Nations*, Cambridge: MIT Press.

Alesina, A., Baqir, R. and Easterly, W. (1999) 'Public goods and ethnic division', *The Quarterly Journal of Economics* 114(4): 1243–1284.

Allemann, F. R. (1977) *25mal die Schweiz*, 3rd edn, Munich: R. Piper and Co.

Allen, J. (2004) 'The whereabouts of power: politics, government and space', *Geografiska Annaler* 86B(1): 19–32.

Almond, G. A. (1956) 'Comparative political systems', *The Journal of Politics* 18(3): 391–409.

Almond, G. A. and Verba, S. (1965) *The Civic Culture: Political attitudes and democracy in five nations*, Boston, MA: Little, Brown and Company.

Alonso, S. (2010) 'Incentives to devolve: electoral geography and the peripheral party threat', Paper presented at the 106th Annual Meeting of the American Political Science Association, Washington (DC), 2–5 September.

—— (2012) *Challenging the State: Devolution and the battle for partisan credibility – A comparison of Belgium, Italy, Spain and the United Kingdom*, Oxford: Oxford University Press.

Altenburger, D. (1988) *Der Oberamtmann im Kanton Solothurn. Unter vergleichender Berücksichtigung der Kantone Aargau, Bern, Freiburg, Luzern, Waadt und Zürich*. Berne: Peter Lang.

Althaus, R. (1949) *Die Unterabteilungen der Gemeinden im schweizerischen Recht. Unter besonderer Berücksichtigung des Berner, Bündner, Zürcher, St. Galler und Waadtländer Gemeinderechts*, PhD Diss, Uni Berne, Berne: Stämpfli and Cie.

Althusius, J. (1995 [1614]) *Politica Methodica Digesta*, Abridged trans. F. S. Carney, Indianapolis: Liberty Fund Inc.

Amin, A. (2004) 'Regions unbound: towards a new politics of place', *Geografiska Annaler* 86B(1): 33–44.

Ammon, G., Fischer, M., Hickmann, T. and Stemmermann, K. (eds) (1996) *Föderalismus und Zentralismus: Europas Zukunft zwischen dem deutschen und dem französischen Modell*, Baden-Baden: Nomos Verlagsgesellschaft.

Amoretti, U. M. and Bermeo, N. (eds) (2004) *Federalism and Territorial Cleavages*, Baltimore: Johns Hopkins University Press.

Anderson, G. (2008) *Federalism: An introduction*, Don Mills, Ontario: Oxford University Press.

Ansell, C. K. (2004) 'Restructuring Authority and Territoriality', in C. K. Ansell and G. Di Palma (eds) *Restructuring Territoriality: Europe and the United States compared*, Cambridge: Cambridge University Press, pp. 3–18.

Ardrey, R. (1975 [1966]) *The Territorial Imperative: A personal inquiry into the animal origins of property and nations*, 7th edn, Glasgow: Fontana/Collins.

Arlettaz, G. (1980) *Libéralisme et société dans le Canton de Vaud 1803–1845*, Lausanne: Bibliothèque historique vaudoise.

Arzaghi, M. and Henderson, J. V. (2005) 'Why countries are fiscally decentralizing', *Journal of Public Economics* 89(7): 1157–1189.

Ashford, D. (1978) 'French pragmatism and British idealism: financial aspects of local reorganization', *Comparative Political Studies* 11(1): 231–254.

Aubert, J.-F. (1983) *Petit histoire constitutionnelle de la Suisse*, 4th edn, Berne: Francke.

Auf der Maur, F. *et al.* (1991) *Vom Alten Land zum Bezirk Schwyz: Festgabe des Alten Landes Schwyz an seine Bürgerinnen und Bürger aus Anlass der 700-Jahrfeier der Eidgenossenschaft*, Schwyz: Historischer Verein des Kantons Schwyz.

Bache, I. and Flinders, M. (eds) (2004) *Multi-Level Governance*, Oxford: Oxford University Press.

Bahovec, V. (2011) 'Multicollinearity', in M. Jovric (ed.) *International Encyclopedia of Statistical Science*, Berlin Heidelberg: Springer-Verlag, pp. 869–60.

Baker, J. W. (1993) 'The covenental basis for the development of Swiss political federalism: 1291–1818', *Publius: The Journal of Federalism* 23(2): 19–41.

— (2000) 'Faces of federalism: from Bullinger to Jefferson', *Publius: The Journal of Federalism* 30(4): 25–41.

Baldersheim, H. and Rose, L. E. (2010) 'Territorial choice: Rescaling Governance in European States' in H. Baldersheim and L. E. Rose (eds) *Territorial Choice*, Palgrave Macmillan, pp.1–20.

Bancroft, A. (2000) ''No interest in land': legal and spatial enclosure of gypsy-travellers in Britain', *Space and Polity* 4(1): 41–56.

Bapst, E. (2000) 'The Autonomy of the Swiss Communes: A pleading federalism without autonomous communes? Impossible!' in L. R. Basta Fleiner and T. Fleiner (eds) *Federalism and Multiethnic States: The case of Switzerland*, Basel, Geneva, Munich: Helbing and Lichtenhahn, pp. 213–229.

Barber, B. (1974) *The Death of Communal Liberty: A history of freedom in a Swiss mountain canton*, Princeton, NJ: Princeton University Press.

— (1988) 'Participation and Swiss democracy', *Government and Opposition* 23(1): 31–50.

— (2013) *If Mayors Ruled the World: Dysfunctional nations, rising cities*, New Haven & London: Yale University Press.

Bartolini, S. (2004) 'Old and New Peripheries in the Processes of European Territorial Integration', in C. K. Ansell and G. Di Palma (eds) *Restructuring Territoriality: Europe and the United States compared*, Cambridge: Cambridge University Press, pp. 19–44.

Bassand, M. (2004) *La métropolisation de la Suisse*, Lausanne: Presses Polytechniques et Universitaires Romandes.

Basta Fleiner, L. R. (2000) 'Minority and Legitimacy of a Federal State: An outsider perception of the Swiss model' in L. R. Basta Fleiner and T. Fleiner (eds) *Federalism and Multiethnic States: The case of Switzerland*, Basel, Geneva and Munich: Helbing and Lichtenhahn, pp. 75–102.

Bastide, P. and Kastl, E. (2003) 'Frédéric-César Laharpe et la fin de la République helvétique une et indivisible' in F. Jequier (ed.) *Le Canton de Vaud de la tutelle à l'indépendence (1798–1815): Regards nouveaux sur léconomie et les finances, les Bourla-Papey et la contre-révolution*, Lausanne: Centre Patronal, pp. 93–97.

Becchia, A. (2012) 'Savoyen: Von 1559 bis 1813', *Historisches Lexikon der Schweiz*, http://www.hls-dhs-dss.ch/textes/d/D6641.php.

Bennett, A. (2002) 'Where the Model Frequently Meets the Road: Combining Statistical, Formal and Case Study Methods', Paper presented at the Annual Meeting of the American Political Science Association, Boston.

— (2008) 'Process Tracing: A Bayesian approach', in J. Box-Steffensmeier, H. Brady and D. Collier (eds) *The Oxford Handbook of Political Methodology*, Oxford: OUP, pp. 702–721.

Bennett, A. and Checkel, J. T. (2012) 'Process tracing: from philosophical roots to best practices', *Simons Papers in Security and Development*, 21 (June).

Benz, A. (2009) *Politik in Mehrebenensystemen*, Wiesbaden: VS Verlag für Sozialwis–senschaften.

Benz, A. and Broschek, J. (eds) (2013) *Federal Dynamics: Continuity, change and the varieties of federalism*, Oxford: Oxford University Press.

Beramendi, P. (2009) 'Federalism' in C. Boix and S. C. Stoker (eds) *The Oxford Handbook of Comparative Politics*, Oxford: OUP, pp. 752–781.

Berman, D. R. (2009) 'State-Local Relations; Authority and Finance', in International City Managers' Association (ed.) *Municipal Yearbook*, Chicago, Illinois, pp. 53–65.

Berman, D. R. and Martin, L. L. (1988) 'State-local relations: an examination of local discretion', *Public Administration Review* 48: 637–41.

Bierbrauer, P. (1991) *Freiheit und Gemeinde im Berner Oberland 1300–1700*. Archiv des Historischen Vereins des Kantons Bern, 74. Band. Berne: Stämpfli and Cie AG.

Bird, R. M. and Tarasov, A. V. (2004) 'Closing the gap: fiscal imbalances and intergovernmental transfers in developed federations', *Environment and Planning C: Government and Policy* 22: 77–102.

Bjørna, H. and Jenssen, S. (2006) 'Prefectoral systems and central-local government relations in Scandinavia', *Scandinavian Political Studies* 29(4): 308–332.

Blalock, H. Jr. (1982) *Conceptualization and Measurement in the Social Sciences*, Beverly Hills, CA: Sage.

Blatter, J. and Blume, T. (2008) 'In search of co-variance, causal mechanisms or congruence? Towards a plural understanding of case studies', *Swiss Political Science Review* 14(2): 315–356.

Blickle, P. (2011) 'Kommunalismus und Republikanismus revisited. Graubünden als pradigmatischer Fall', in F. Hitz, C. Rathgeb and M. Risi (eds) *Gemeinden und Verfassung. Bündner Politik und Gebietsstruktur gestern, heute und morgen*, Chur/Glarus: Südostschweiz Buchverlag, pp. 13–34.

Blöchliger, H. (2005) *Baustelle Föderalismus. Metropolitanregionen versus Kantone: Untersuchungen und Vorschläge für eine Revitalisierung der Schweiz*, Avenir Suisse (ed.) [think tank for economic and social issues], Zurich: Verlag NZZ.

Blondel, J. (1995) *Comparative Government: An introduction*, 2nd edn, London, New York, Toronto: Prentice Hall/Harvester Wheatsheaf.

BMZ (2008) *Dezentralisierung und lokale Selbstverwaltung Dezentralisierung in der deutschen Entwicklungszusammenarbeit*, Bundesministerium für wirtschaftliche Zusammenarbeit und Entwicklung (ed.) Bonn. At http://www.bmz.de/de/publikationen/index.html (last accessed March 2011).

Bochsler, D. (2009) 'Neighbours or friends? When Swiss cantonal governments co-operate with each other', *Regional and Federal Studies* 19(3): 349–370.

Bochsler, D., Koller, C., Sciarini, P., Traimond, S. and Trippolini, I. (2004) *Die Schweizer Kantone unter der Lupe – Behörden, Personal, Finanzen*, Berne, Stuttgart, Vienna: Haupt Verlag.

Boeckenfoerde, M., Dann, P. and Wiesner, V. (2007) *Max Planck Manual on Different Forms of Decentralisation*, Heidelberg: Max Planck Institute for Comparative Public Law and International Law.

Bogdanor, V. (1988) 'Federalism in Switzerland', *Government and Opposition* 23(1): 69–90.

— (2001) *Devolution in the United Kingdom*, Oxford: Oxford University Press.

Bolleyer, N. (2009) *Intergovernmental Cooperation: Rational choice in federal systems and beyond*, Oxford: Oxford University Press.

Bolleyer, N., Swenden, W. and McEwen, N. (2014a) *The Dynamics of Multi-Level Systems*, special issue of *Comparative European Politics*, 12(4–5) July/September.

— (2014b) 'A theoretical perspective on multi-level systems in Europe: constitutional power and partisan conflict', *Comparative European Politics* 12(4/5): 367–383.

Bonjour, E. (1948) *Die Gründung des Schweizerischen Bundesstaates*, Basel: Benno Schwab and Co. Verlag.

Bovard, P. -A. (1982) *Le Gouvernement Vaudois de 1803 à 1962 – Récit et Portraits*, Morges: Éditions de Peyrollaz.

Bowie, R. R. and Friedrich, C. J. (eds) (1954) *Studies in Federalism*, Boston, Toronto: Little, Brown and Company.

Bowman, A. O'M. and Kearney, R. C. (2011) 'Second-order devolution: data and doubt', *Publius* 41(4): 563–585.

Braaker, C. (2000) 'Die Gemeindeautonomie', in T. Fleiner *et al.* (eds) *Die neue schweizerische Bundesverfassung. Föderalismus, Grundrechte, Wirtschaftsrecht und Staatstruktur*, Basel, Geneva and Munich: Helbing and Lichtenhahn, pp. 225–249.

Bradbury, J. (2006) '"Territory and power" revisited: theorising territorial politics in the United Kingdom after devolution', *Political Studies* 54: 559–582.

— (2010) 'Devolution in Wales 1997–2010: Interpreting the process and the neofunctionalist method', Paper presented at UK Political Studies Association annual conference, Edinburgh, April.

Bradbury, J. and John, P. (2010) 'Territory and power: critiques and reassessments of a classic work', *Government and Opposition* 45(3): 295–317.

Brady, H. E. (2008) 'Causation and Explanation in Social Science', in J. Box-Steffensmeier, H. Brady and D. Collier (eds) *The Oxford Handbook of Political Methodology*, Oxford: OUP, pp. 217–70.

Brady, H. E. and Collier, D. (eds) (2004) *Rethinking Social Inquiry: Diverse Tools, Shared Standards*, Berkeley, CA: Rowman and Littlefield and Berkeley Public Policy Press.

Brancati, D. (2006) 'Decentralization: fueling or dampening the flames of ethnic conflict and secessionism', *International Organization* 60(3): 651–685.

Braun, D. (1997) *Bringing State Structures Back in: The Significance of Political Arena's in Political Decision-Making*, Travaux de science politique no. 12, Université de Lausanne.

— (2009) 'Constitutional change in Switzerland', *Publius* 39(2): 314–340.

Braun, D. and Trein, P. (2013) 'Economics Crisis and Federal Dynamics', in A. Benz and J. Broschek (eds) *Federal Dynamics: Continuity, change and varieties of federalism*, Oxford: Oxford University Press, pp. 343–365.

Brenner, N. (1998) 'Global cities, glocal states: global city formation and state territorial restructuring in contemporary Europe', *Review of International Political Economy* 5(1): 1–37.

Brenner, N., Jessop, B., Jones, M. and Macleod, G. (eds) (2003) *State/Space: A reader*, Malden, Oxford, Victoria and Berlin: Blackwell Publishers Ltd.

Bresslau, H. (1895) 'Das älteste Bündnis der Schweizer Urkantone', *Jahrbuch für schweizerische Geschichte* 20: 1–36.

Brighenti, A. M. (2010) 'On territorology: towards a general science of territory theory', *Culture & Society* 27(1): 52–72.

Broschek, J. (2011) 'Historischer Institutionalismus und Vergleichende Föderalismusforschung: Fragestellungen und Analyseperspektiven', *Swiss Political Science Review* 17(1): 27–50.

— (2014) 'Pathways of federal reform: Australia, Canada, Germany and Switzerland', *Publius: The Journal of Federalism*, advance online access, doi:10.1093/publius/pju030.

Brown, A. J. (2013) 'From Intuition to Reality: Measuring Federal Political Culture in Australia', *Publius: The Journal of Federalism* 43(2): 297–314.

Brusis, M. (2002) 'Between EU-requirements, competitive politics and national traditions: re-creating regions in the accession countries of Central and Eastern Europe', *Governance: An International Journal of Policy, Administration and Institutions* 15(4): 531–539.

— (2003) 'Regionalisation in the Czech and Slovak Republics: comparing the influence of the European Union', in M. Keating and J. Hughes (eds) *The Regional Challenge in Central and Eastern Europe, Territorial Restructuring and European Integration*, Paris: Presses interuniversitaires européennes/Peter Lang, pp. 89–105.

Bucher, E. (1944) 'Die bernischen Landvogteien im Aargau', *Argovia: Jahresschrift der Historischen Gesellschaft des Kantons Aargau* 56: 1–191.

Bulpitt, J. (1983) *Territory and Power in the United Kingdom: An interpretation*, Manchester: Manchester University Press.

— (2009) 'Central-Local Relations', in I. McLean and A. McMillan (eds) *The Concise Oxford Dictionary of Politics*, 3rd edn, Oxford: Oxford University Press, pp. 68–69.

Bundi, M. (2003) 'Der Freistaat der Drei Bünde im Urteil von in- und ausländischen Kommentatoren', in M. Bundi and C. Rathgeb (eds) *Die Staatsverfassung Graubündens: Zur Entwicklung der Verfassung im Freistaat der Drei Bünde und im Kanton Graubünden*, Chur: Verlag Rüegger, pp. 35–101.

Burgess, M. (1993) 'Federalism as Political Ideology: Interests, benefits and beneficiaris in federalism and federation, in M. Burgess and A. -G. Gagnon (eds) *Comparative Federalism and Federation: Competing traditions and future directions*, New York: Harvester Wheatsheaf, pp. 102–114.

— (2000) *Federalism and European Union: The building of Europe, 1950–2000*, London: Routledge.

— (2006a) *Comparative Federalism: Theory and practice*, London/New York: Routledge.

— (2006b) 'Territoriality and Federalism in the Governance of the European Union', in M. Burgess and H. Vollaard (eds) *State Territoriality and European Integration: Territoriality and federalism in EU governance*, London: Routledge, pp. 100–119.

— (2009) 'Federal Political Culture Revisited: Creating and Sustaining Federal Political Systems', Paper presented at the Annual Conference of the International Association of Centres for Federal Studies (IACFS), 17–19 September 2009, Canterbury/UK.

— (2012) *In Search of the Federal Spirit: New comparative empirical and theoretical perspectives*, Oxford: Oxford University Press.

Burgess, M. and Pinder, J. (eds) (2007) *Multinational Federations*, Abingdon/ Oxon and New York: Routledge.

Buser, D. (2004) *Kantonales Staatsrecht. Eine Einführung für Studium und Praxis*, Basel, Geneva, Munich: Helbing and Lichtenhahn.

Bütikofer, G. (1950) *Die Rechtssetzungsbefugnis der Gemeinden. Ein Beitrag zur Lehre von der Gemeindeautonomie unter besonderer Berücksichtigung des zürcherischen Rechts*, Zurich: Polygraphischer Verlag AG.

Calhoun, J. C. (2003 [1851]) *A Disquisition on Government and A Discourse on the Constitution and Government of the United States*, The Papers of John C. Calhoun, Vol. XXVIII, R. K. Crallé (ed.), Published under the direction of the General Assembly of the State of South Carolina, University of South Carolina Press.

Callanan, M. and Tatham, M. (2014) 'Territorial interest representation in the European Union: actors, objectives and strategies', *Journal of European Public Policy* 21(2): 188–210.

Camenzind, D. (1863) 'Geschichte der Republik Gersau', *Der Geschichtsfreund: Mitteilungen des Historischen Vereins Zentralschweiz* 19: 1–92.

Capoccia, G. and Kelemen, R. D. (2007) 'The study of critical junctures: theory, narrative and counterfactuals in historical institutionalism', *World Politics* 59(3): 341–369.

Capoccia, G. and Ziblatt, D. (2010) 'The historical turn in democratization studies: a new research agenda for Europe and beyond', *Comparative Political Studies* 43(8/9): 931–68.

Carrillo, E. (1997) 'Local government and strategies for decentralization in the 'state of the autonomies', *Publius: The Journal of Federalism* 27(4): 39–63.

Carty, R. K. (2004) 'Parties as franchise systems: the stratarchical organizational imperative', *Party Politics* 10: 5–24.

Castell, A. (1954) *Geschichte des Landes Schwyz*, Zürich: Benziger Verlag Einsiedeln.

Chandler, J. A. (2009) *Local Government Today*, Manchester: Manchester University Press.

Chandler, W. M. (1987) 'Federalism and Political Parties', in H. Bakvis and W. M. Chandler (eds) *Federalism and the Role of the State*, Toronto, London, Buffalo: University of Toronto Press, pp.149–170.

Chattopadhyay, R. (2011) 'Why Metropolitan Regions Matter' in *The Governance of Metropolitan Regions – European and Global Experiences*, Forum of Federations and Committee of the Regions, Brussels, June 2012, pp. 21–27.

Chavannes, D.-A. (1831) *De l'administration publique du canton de Vaud dès 1803 à 1831*, Lausanne: Imprimerie des Frères Blanchard.

Chhibber, P. K. and Kollman, K. (2004) *The Formation of National Party Systems: Federalism and party competition in Canada, Great Britain, India and the United States*, Princeton, NJ: Princeton University Press.

Christin, T. and Hug, S. (2006) 'Federalism, the Geographic Location of Groups and Conflict', *CIS Working Paper no. 26*, http://www.isn.ethz.ch (last accessed 17 December 2011).

Clark, G. L. (1984) 'A theory of local autonomy', *Annals of the Association of American Geographers* 74(2): 195–208.

Clark, T. N. (1974) 'Community autonomy in the national system: federalism, localism and decentralization', in *Comparative Community Politics*, T. N. Clark (ed.) New York: Sage Publications, pp. 21–45.

Coakley, J. (2005) 'Conclusion: Towards a Solution?' in J. Coakley (ed.) *The Territorial Management of Ethnic Conflict*, 2nd edn, Taylor & Francis e-library, pp. 285–307.

Cockburn, C. (1977) *The Local State: Management of cities and people*, London: Pluto Press.

Cole, R. L. and Kincaid, J. (2006) 'Public opinion on US federal and intergovernmental issues in 2006: continuity and change', *Publius* 36(3): 443–59.

Collier, D. (2011) 'Understanding process tracing', *Political Science and Politics* 44(4): 823–30.

Collier, D., Laporte, J. and Seawright, J. (2008) 'Typologies: Forming concepts and creating categorical variables', in J. Box-Steffensmeier, H. Brady and D. Collier (eds) *The Oxford Handbook of Political Methodology*, Oxford: OUP, pp. 152–173.

Coutaz, G. (2008) *Histoire de l'administration cantonale vaudoise: pouvoir exécutif et administratif, 1998–2007. Suivie du bilan de deux cents ans d'histoire de l'administration cantonale vaudoise, 1803–2007*, Chavannes-près-Renens: Archives cantonales vaudoises.

Cox, K. R. (1979) *Location and Public Problems: A political geography of the contemporary world*, Oxford: Basil Blackwell.

Crotty, W. J. (ed.) (1968) *Approaches to the Study of Party Organization*, Boston: Allyn and Bacon, Inc.

Dabla-Norris, E. and Wade, P. (2002) The Challenge of Fiscal Decentralization in Transition Countries. IMF Working Paper WP/02/103. At http://www.imf.org/external/pubs/ft/wp/2002/wp02103.pdf (last accessed March 2011).

Dafflon, B. (1992a) 'L'autonomie fiscale communale: le cas de Fribourg', in E. Weibel (ed.) *L'avenir de l'autonomie communale à l'aube du troisième millénaire*, Publications de l'Institut du Fédéralisme Fribourg, Etudes et Colloques no 5, Editions universitaires, Fribourg, pp 25–43.

—   (1992b) 'The assignment of functions to decentralized government: from theory to practice', *Environment and Planning C: Government and Policy* 10: 283–298.

—   (2007) 'Accommodating Diversity through Pragmatism: An overview of Swiss fiscal federalism', in R. M. Bird and R. M. Ebel (eds) *Fiscal Fragmentation in Decentralized Countries: Subsidiarity, solidarity and asymmetry*, Cheltenham and Northampton: IBRD and World Bank, pp. 114–165.

Dafflon, B. and Tóth, K. (2003) 'Local Fiscal Equalisation in Switzerland: The case of the canton Fribourg, in G. Färber and N. Otter (eds) *Reforms of Local Fiscal Equalisation in Europe*, Speyerer Forschungsberichte 2003/232, Forschungsinstitut für Öffentliche Verwaltung: Speyer/ Germany, pp. 1–20.

Dahl, R. A. and Tufte, E. R. (1973) *Size and Democracy*, London: Oxford University Press.

Dardanelli, P. (2005) *Between Two Unions: Europeanisation and Scottish Devolution*, Manchester: Manchester University Press.

de Capitani, F. (1983) 'Beharren und Umsturz (1648–1815)', in U. Im Hof (ed.) *Geschichte der Schweiz – und der Schweizer,* vol. 2, Basel and Frankfurt a.M.: Helbing and Lichtenhahn, pp. 97–175.

—   (2011) 'Bern (Kanton) – Das Regiment im Inneren', *Historisches Lexikon der Schweiz*, http://www.hls-dhs-dss.ch/textes/d/D7383.php.

de Reynold, G. (1982) *Cités et Pays suisses*, Lausanne: Edition L'Age d'Homme.

de Spindler, J. (1998) *FOCJ: Ein Konzept zur Neuordnung der Zusammenarbeit öffentlich-rechtlicher Gebietskörperschaften,* PhD Diss University of Zurich; Berne, Stuttgart, Vienna: Verlag Paul Haupt.

de Tocqueville, A. (2007 [1856]) *L'Ancien Régime et la Révolution*, J.-M. Tremblay (ed.) 'Les classiques des sciences sociales', at http://classiques. uqac.ca (last accessed May 2012).

—   (2010 [1835]) *Democracy in America*, Historical-Critical Edition of De la démocratie en Amérique, 4. vols., E. Nolla (ed.), trans. J. T. Schleifer, Indianapolis: Liberty Fund.

de Vries, M. S. (2000) 'The rise and fall of decentralization: a comparative analysis of arguments and practices in European countries', *European Journal of Political Research* 38(2): 193–224.

de Winter, L., Gómez-Reino, M. and Lynch, P. (eds) (2006) *Autonomist Parties in Europe: Identity politics and the revival of the territorial cleavage*, 2 vols., Barcelona: Institut de Ciències Polítiques i Socials.

Debarbieux, B. and Rudaz, G. (2008) 'Linking mountain identities throughout the world: the experience of Swiss communities', *Cultural Geographies* 15: 497–517.

Delaney, D. (2005) *Territory: A short introduction*, Malden, Oxford and Victoria: Blackwell Publishing Ltd.

della Santa, M. (1996) *Dalla collaborazione alla fusione: analisi degli aspetti economici, istituzionali e sociologici del commune*, PhD Diss University of Fribourg (CH); Vico Morcote, CH: Tipografia Tipo-Offset Aurora S.A. di Lugano-Canobbio.

Delley, J.-D. and Auer, A. (1986) 'Structures politiques des cantons', in R. Germann and E. Weibel (eds) *Handbuch Politisches System der Schweiz,* vol. 3, *Föderalismus*, Berne: Haupt Verlag, pp. 85–105.

Denters, B. and Rose, L. E. (eds) (2005) *Comparing Local Governance: Trends and Developments*, Basingstoke: Palgrave Macmillan.

Deschouwer, K. (2003) 'Political parties in multi-layered systems', *European Urban and Regional Studies* 10: 213–26.

— (2006) 'Political Parties as Multi-Level Organizations', in R. S. Katz and W. J. Crotty (eds) *Handbook of Party Politics*, London: Sage Publications, pp. 291–300.

Detterbeck, K. and Hepburn, E. (2010) 'Party Politics in Multi-level Systems: party responses to new challenges in European democracies', in J. Erk and W. Swenden (eds) *New Directions in Federalism Studies*, London and NY: Routledge, pp. 106–125.

Deutsch, K. *et al.* (1968 [1957]) *Political Community and the North Atlantic Area: International organization in the light of historical experience*, Princeton, NJ: Press. Princeton University Press.

Dion, D. (1998) 'Evidence and inference in the comparative case study', *Comparative Politics* 30(2): 127–145.

Dubler, A.-M. (1999) 'Berns Herrschaft über den Oberaargau', *Jahrbuch des Oberaargaus* 42: 69–94.

— (2008) 'Herrschen und verwalten auf dem Land: Vogteien und Gemeinden', in A. Holenstein (ed.) *Berns goldene Zeit: das 18. Jahrhundert neu entdeckt*, Bern: Stämpfli Verlag, pp. 446–52.

Duchacek, I. (1987 [1970]) *Comparative Federalism: The territorial dimension of politics*, Lanham, New York, London: University Press of America.

Dürrenmatt, P. (1942) 'Über den bernischen und den eidgenössischen Staatsgedanken', *Schweizer Monatshefte: Zeitschrift für Politik, Wirtschaft, Kultur* 22(6): 279–295.

Duverger, M. (1959 [1951]) *Political Parties: Their organization and activity in the modern state*, trans. B. and R. North, London: Methuen and Co. Ltd.

Dyson, K. (1980) *State Tradition in Western Europe: A study of an idea and institution*, Oxford: Oxford University Press.

Easton, D. (1965) *A Framework for Political Analysis*, Englewood Cliffs, NJ: Prentice-Hall Inc.

— (1968 [1953]) *The Political System: An inquiry into the state of political science*, 9th edn, New York: Alfred A. Knopf Inc.

Eaton, K. and Tyles Dickovick, J. (2004) 'The politics of re-centralization in Argentina and Brazil', *Latin American Research Review* 39(1): 90–122.

Ebel, R. D. and Yilmaz, S. (2002) 'Concept of Fiscal Decentralization and Worldwide Overview', World Bank Institute. A http://www.desequilibrefiscal.gouv.qc.ca/en/pdf/ebel.pdf (last accessed Feb 2011).

Eckstein, H. (1980) *The Natural History of Congruence Theory*, Monograph Series in World Affairs, vol. 18, book 2, Denver, Colorado: Graduate School of International Studies, University of Denver.

— (2000) 'Case Study and Theory in Political Science', in, R. Gomm, M. Hammersley and P. Foster (eds), *Case Study Method*, London: Sage, pp. 119–164.

Eckstein, H. and Gurr, T. R. (1975) *Patterns of Authority: A structural basis for political inquiry*, New York, London, Sydney, Toronto: John Wiley and Sons.

Ecoplan (2009) *Evaluation Gemeindefusionsgesetz: Schlussbericht*, Bern, 18th February.

Edney, J. J. (1974) 'Human Territoriality', *Psychological Bulletin* 81: 959–75.

Elazar, D. J. (1966) *American Federalism: A view from the States*. New York: Crowell.

— (1976) 'Federalism vs. decentralization: the drift from authenticity', *Publius: The Journal of Federalism* 6(4): 9–19.

— (1987) *Exploring Federalism*, Tuscaloosa, AL: University of Alabama Press.

— (1993) 'Communal democracy and liberal democracy: an outside friend's look at the Swiss political tradition, *Publius: The Journal of Federalism* 23(2): 2–18.

— (1995–1999) *The Covenant Tradition in Politics*, IV Volumes, Rutgers University, NJ: Transaction Publishers.

— (1997) 'Contrasting unitary and federal systems', *International Political Science Review Revue internationale de science politique* 18(3): 237–251.

— (1999) 'Political science, geography and the spatial dimension of politics', *Political Geography* 18: 875–886.

— (ed.) (2001) *Commonwealth: The other road to democracy, the Swiss model of democratic self-government*, Lanham, Boulder, New York, Oxford: Lexington Books.

Elkins, D. J. and Simeon, R. (1979) 'A cause in search of an effect, or what does political culture explain?, *Comparative Politics* 11(2): 127–45.

Elman, C. (2005) 'Explanatory typologies in qualitative studies of international politics', *International Organization* 59(2): 293–326.

Emery, G. (1986) *Districts, régions et préfets dans le canton de Fribourg*, Fribourg: Imprimerie Saint-Paul.

Encyclopédie Illustrée du Pays de Vaud (1973) Vol. 4: *L'histoire vaudoise*, Lausanne: Éditions 24 Heures.

— (1974) Vol. 5: *Les Institutions ou Le Pouvoir chez les Vaudois*, Lausanne: Éditions 24 Heures.

Epstein, L. D. (1967) *Political Parties in Western Democracies*, London: Pall Mall Press.

Erk, J. (2003) 'Swiss federalism and congruence', *Nationalism and Ethnic Politics* 9(2): 50–74.

— (2008) *Explaining Federalism: State, society and congruence in Austria, Belgium, Canada, Germany and Switzerland*, London and New York: Routledge.

Erk, J. and Koning, E. (2010) 'New structuralism and institutional change: federalism between centralization and decentralization', *Comparative Political Studies* 43(3): 353–378.

Erk, J. and Swenden, W. (2010) 'The new wave of federalism studies', in J. Erk and W. Swenden (eds) *New Directions in Federalism Studies*, London, New York: Routledge, pp. 1–15.

Eugster, B., Lalive, R., Steinhauer, A. and Zweimüller, J. (2011) 'The demand for social insurance: does culture matter?, *The Economic Journal* 121: F413–F448.

Eurostat (2009) *Eurostat Regional Yearbook 2009*, Luxembourg: Publications Office of the European Union.

Fabre, E. (2008) 'Party organization in a multi-level system: party organizational change in Spain and the UK', *Regional and Federal Studies* 18(4): 309–29.

— (2011) 'Measuring party organization: the vertical dimension of the multi-level organization of state-wide parties in Spain and the UK', *Party Politics* 17(3): 343–363.

Fagagnini, H. P. (1974) *Kanton und Gemeinden vor ihrer Erneuerung – Eine Interdisziplinäre Studie zum inneren Aufbau des Kantons St. Gallen*, Vol 2, St. Galler Studien zur Politikwissenschaft, Stuttgart and Berne: Verlag Paul Haupt.

Falleti, T. G. (2005) 'A sequential theory of decentralization: Latin American cases in comparative perspective', *The American Political Science Review* 99(3): 327–346.

— (2010) *Decentralization and Subnational Politics in Latin America*, Cambridge, New York: Cambridge University Press.

Falleti, T. G. and Lynch, J. (2009) 'Context and causation in political analysis', *Comparative Political Studies* 49(9): 1143–66.

Fargion, V., Morlino, L. and Profeti, S. (2006) 'Europeanisation and territorial representation in Italy', *West European Politics* 29(4): 757–83.

Fearon, J. D. (2003) 'Ethnic structure and cultural diversity by country', *Journal of Economic Growth* 8(2): 195–222.

Fearon, J. and van Houten, P. (2002) 'The Politicization of Cultural and Economic Difference – A Return to the Theory of Regional Autonomy Movements', Paper presented at the 5th Meeting of the Laboratory in Comparative Ethnic Processes, University of Stanford, 10–11 May.

Federalist Papers (1787–88) J. Manis (ed.) Faculty Editor, Pennsylvania State University, Electronic Classics Series, Hazleton, PA.

Feller, R. (1946) 'Geschichte Berns. Von den Anfängen bis 1516', *Archiv des Historischen Vereins des Kantons Bern* 28(2): 1–574.

— (1948) *Berns Verfassungskämpfe 1846,* Berne: Verlag Herbert Lang & Cie.

— (1974) *Geschichte Berns. Von der Reformation bis zum Bauernkrieg, 1516 bis 1653,* Bern and Frankfurt a.M: Verlag Herbert Lang.

Fesler, J. W. (1965) 'Approaches to the understanding of decentralization', *The Journal of Politics* 27(3): 536–566.

— (1968) 'Centralization and Decentralization', in D. L. Sills (ed.) *International Encyclopedia of the Social Sciences*, Vol.2, New York: The Macmillan Company and The Free Press, pp. 370–78.

Fetz, U. (2009) *Gemeindefusion – unter besonderer Berücksichtigung des Kantons Graubünden*, PhD Diss University of Zurich; Zurich, Basel, Geneva: Schulthess Juristische Medien AG.

Fiechter, J. (2010) *Politische Gemeinden und lokale Autonomie in der Schweiz. Eine Studie zur normativen Bedeutung und empirischen Erfassung der Gemeindeautonomie und ihrer Ausprägung im kantonalen und lokalen Vergleich*, Cahiers de l'IDHEAP, no. 251, Lausanne, Switzerland.

Field, A. (2005) *Discovering Statistic Using SPSS*, 2nd edn, London, Thousand Oaks, New Delhi: Sage Publications.

Filippov, M., Ordeshook, P. C. and Shvetsova, O. V. (2004) *Designing Federalism: A theory of self-sustainable federal institutions*, Cambridge: Cambridge University Press.

Fivaz, J. and Schwarz, D. (1999) *Gemeindereformen im Kanton Aargau: Rahmenbedingungen und Einstellungen der Bevölkerung zu Fusionen und Kooperationen anhand einer Fallstudie in den Gemeinden Endingen und Unterendingen*, Berne: Institut für Politikwissenschaft.

Fleiner, T. (1986a) *Die Autonomie der Luzerner Gemeinde im System der schweizerischen Gemeindeautonomie*, Speech at the Annual Congress of the Association of Communal Presidents [Gemeindeammänner-Verband] Canton Lucerne in Sempach, 31 October.

— (1986b) 'Die Gebietshoheit der Kantone', in R. E. Germann and E. Weibel (eds) *Handbuch Politisches System der Schweiz*, vol. 3: *Föderalismus*, Berne: Verlag Paul Haupt, pp. 55–81.

— (2000) 'Switzerland: Constitution of the Federal State and the Cantons', in L. R. Basta Fleiner and T. Fleiner (eds) *Federalism and Multiethnic States: The Case of Switzerland*, Basel, Geneva and Munich: Helbing and Lichtenhahn, pp. 103–144.

— (2002) 'Recent developments in Swiss federalism', *Publius* 32(2): 97–123.

Fleiner, T. and Basta Fleiner, L. R. (2000) 'Federalism, Federal States and Decentralization, in L. R. Basta Fleiner and T. Fleiner (eds) *Federalism and Multiethnic States: The case of Switzerland*, Basel, Geneva and Munich: Helbing and Lichtenhahn, pp. 1–40.

Fleiner-Gerster, T. (1992) 'L'autonomie communale a-t-elle un avenir?' in T. Fleiner-Gerster (ed.) *L'avenir de l'autonomie communale à l'aube du troisième millénaire*, Fribourg: Institut du Fédéralisme, pp. 1–8.

Fleurke, F. and Willemse, R. (2004) 'Approaches to decentralization and local autonomy: a critical appraisal', *Administrative Theory and Praxis* 26(4): 523–544.

Flora, P., Kuhnle, S. and Urwin, D. (eds) (1999) *State Formation, Nation-Building and Mass Politics in Europe: The theory of Stein Rokkan*, Oxford: Oxford University Press.

Flückiger, D., Steffen, B. and Pfister, C. (2006) 'Repräsentanten der Obrigkeit – volksnahe Vermittler. 200 Jahre Regierungsstatthalter im Kanton Bern', *Berner Zeitschrift für Geschichte* 68(2): 1–62.

Forsberg, T. (1996) 'Beyond sovereignty, within territoriality: mapping the space of late-modern (geo)politics', *Cooperation and Conflict* 31(4): 363–364.

Forster, P. (2000) 'Eigenständigkeit der Kantone, Vorrang und Einhaltung des Bundesrechts und Bundesgarantien', in T. Fleiner at al. (eds) *Die neue schweizerische Bundesverfassung: Föderalismus, Grundrechte, Wirtschaftsrecht und Staatsstruktur*, Basel, Geneva, Munich: Helbing and Lichtenhahn, pp. 131–147.

Forsyth, M. G. (1981) *Unions of States: The theory and practice of confederation*, Leicester: Leicester University Press.

Fortunato, V. (1974) *Die Eingemeindungsfrage im Kanton Graubünden*, PhD Diss. University of Zurich.

Franzese, R. J. (2006) 'Multicausality, Context-Conditionality and Endogeneity', in C. Boix, S. C. Stokes and J. S. Saden (eds) *The Oxford Handbook of Comparative Politics*, Oxford: Oxford University Press, pp. 27–72.

Freitag, M. (2006) 'Bowling the state back in: political institutions and the creation of social capital', *European Journal of Political Research* 45: 123–152.

Freitag, M. and Vatter, A. (2008) 'Decentralization and fiscal discipline in subnational governments: evidence from the Swiss federal system', *Publius: The Journal of Federalism* 38(2): 272–294.

Frenkel, M. (1993) 'The communal basis of Swiss liberty', *Publius: The Journal of Federalism* 23(2): 61–70.

Frey, R. L. (1977) *Zwischen Föderalismus und Zentralismus. Ein volkswirtschaftliches Konzept des schweizerischen Bundesstaates*, Bern and Frankfurt/M.: Herbert Lang.

Friedrich, C. J. (1968) *Trends of Federalism in Theory and Practice*, London: Pall Mall Press.

Friedrich, U. (1999) 'Aufgaben', in D. Arn, U. Friedrich, P. Friedli *et al.* (eds) *Kommentar zum Gemeindegesetz des Kantons Bern*, Bern: Stämpfli Verlag, pp. 449–533.

Friedrich, U., Arn, D. and Wichtermann, J. (1998) *Neubildung politischer Gemeinden im Kanton Schaffhausen. Überlegungen zu einer optimalen Gemeindegrösse und zu Vor- und Nachteilen von Gemeindefusionen*, Bern.

Furniss, N. (1974) 'The practical significance of decentralization', *The Journal of Politics* 36(4): 958–982.

Gamble, A. (2006) 'The constitutional revolution in the United Kingdom', *Publius: The Journal of Federalism* 36(1): 19–35.

Gamper, A. and Palermo, F. (2011) 'Federalism, local government and policymaking', *Federal Governance* 8(3): 1–4.

Garrett, G. and Rodden, J. (2003) 'Globalization and fiscal decentralization', in M. Kahler and D. Lake (eds) *Governance in a Global Economy: Political authority in transition*, Princeton: Princeton University Press, pp. 87–109.

Garrish, S. (1986) *Centralisation and Decentralisation in England and France*, Bristol: University of Bristol, School of Advanced Urban Studies.

Gasser, A. (1943) *Gemeindefreiheit als Rettung Europas. Grundlinien einer ethischen Geschichtsauffassung*, Basel: Verlag 'Bücherfreunde'.

— (1952) 'Die direkte Gemeindedemokratie in der Schweiz', in M. Bridel (ed.) *La démocratie directe dans les communes suisses / Die direkte Gemeindedemokratie in der Schweiz*, Recueil de travaux publié par l'Institut de science politique de l'Université de Lausanne, Zurich: Polygraphischer Verlag AG, pp. 50–66.

— (1976) *Staatlicher Grossraum und autonome Kleinräume. Gemeindeautonomie und Partizipation (ausgewählte Aufsätze)*, Basel: Social Strategies Publishers Co-operative Society and University of Basel Press.

Gassmann, J.-L. (2009) 'Jura: La nouvelle loi-cadre sur la gestion des eaux combattue par les communes', *Newsletter of the Institute of Federalism* 1/2009, http://www.federalism.ch (last accessed 22 August 2012).

Gassmann, J.-L. and Mueller, S. (2011) 'Préfet élu, préfet perdu?', Paper presented at the Conference on 'Figures du préfet – une comparaison européenne', Science Po Toulouse, 17–18 November.

Geddes, B. (2007) *Paradigms and Sand Castles: Theory building and research design in comparative politics*, 4th edn, Ann Arbor: The University of Michigan Press.

Geertz, C. (1973) 'Thick Description: Toward an interpretive theory of culture', in C. Geertz (ed.) *The Interpretation of Cultures*, New York: Basic Books, pp. 3–30.

George, A. L. and Bennett, A. (2005) *Case Studies and Theory Development in the Social Sciences*, Cambridge, Mass: MIT Press.

Germann, R. E. and Weibel, E. (1986) 'Einführung', in R. E. Germann and E. Weibel (eds) *Handbuch Politisches System der Schweiz*, vol. 3, *Föderalismus*, Berne: Verlag Paul Haupt, pp. 11–28.

Gerring, J. (2004) 'What is a case study and what is it good for?' *American Political Science Review* 98(2): 341–354.

— (2007) *Case Study Research: Principles and practices*, Cambridge: Cambridge University Press.

Geser, H. (1981) *Bevölkerungsgrösse und Staatsorganisation. Kleine Kantone im Lichte ihrer öffentlichen Budgetstruktur, Verwaltung und Rechtsetzung*, Berne: Peter Lang.

— (1996) *Die Beziehungen der Gemeinde zur kantonalen Ebene*. At http://www.socio.ch/gem/t_hgeser6.htm (last accessed Sept 2010).

— (1997a) 'Zwischen Aufgabenzuwachs und Autonomieverlust: Neue Selbstbehauptungsstrategien der Gemeinden im Zeitalter "vertikaler Politikverflechtung"'. At http://www.socio.ch/gem/t_hgeser5.htm (last accessed Sept 2010).

— (1997b) *Die politisch-administrative Organisation der Schweizer Gemeinden*. At http://www.socio.ch/gem/t_hgeser2.htm (accessed: Sept 2010).

— (2004) 'The Communes in Switzerland', in U. Klöti, P. Knoepfel and H. Kriesi *et al.* (eds) *Handbook of Swiss Politics*, Zurich: Neue Zürcher Zeitung Publishing, pp. 350–391.

Geser, H., Höpflinger, F., Ladner, A. and Meuli, U. (1996) *Die Schweizer Gemeinden im Kräftefeld des gesellschaftlichen und politisch-administrativen Wandels*, Final report of the Swiss National Foundation project no. 12–32586.92, 'Aktuelle Wandlungstendenzen und Leistungsgrenzen der Gemeindeorganisation der Schweiz'. Zurich: Soziologisches Institut.

Giacometti, Z. (1941) *Das Staatsrecht der schweizerischen Kantone*, Zurich: Polygraphischer Verlag AG.

Giacometti, Z. (1952) 'Die rechtliche Stellung der Gemeinden in der Schweiz', in M. Bridel (ed.) *La démocratie directe dans les communes suisses / Die direkte Gemeindedemokratie in der Schweiz*, Recueil de travaux publié par l'Institut de science politique de l'Université de Lausanne, Zurich: Polygraphischer Verlag AG, pp. 11–49.

Gilliard, C. (1931) 'Les baillis de Vaud', *Revue historique vaudoise* 39: 15–21.

Giordano, B. (2000) 'Italian regionalism or "Padanian" nationalism – the political project of the Lega Nord in Italian politics', *Political Geography* 19: 445–471.

— (2001) 'The contrasting geographies of "Padania": the case of the Lega Nord in Northern Italy', *Area* 33(1): 27–37.

Giordano, B. and Roller, E. (2004) Té para todos? A comparison of the processes of devolution in Spain and the UK, *Environment and Planning* A 36: 2163–2181.

Glaus, P. (1984) *Konzeption der Gemeindeautonomie mit besonderer Darstellung der Autonomie der sanktgallischen Gemeinde*, PhD Diss University of Zurich; Zurich: Schulthess Polygraphischer Verlag AG.

Goertz, G. (2006) *Social Science Concepts: A user's guide*, Woodstock: Princeton University Press.

Goldsmith, M. (1990) 'Local Autonomy: Theory and practice', in D. S. King and J. Pierre (eds) *Challenges to Local Government*, London: Sage, pp. 15–36.

— (1995) 'Autonomy and City Limits', in D. Judge, G. Stoker and H. Wolman (eds) *Theories of Urban Politics*, London: Sage, pp. 228–252.

— (2006) 'From Community to Power and Back Again?', in H. Baldersheim and H. Wollmann (eds) *The Comparative Study of Local Government and Politics: Overview and Synthesis*, Opladen and Farmington Hills: Barbara Budrich Publishers, pp. 11–31.

Goldsmith, M. J. and Page, E. C. (2010) 'Introduction', in M. J. Goldsmith and E. C. Page (eds) *Changing Government Relations in Europe: From localism to intergovernmentalism*, London: Routledge, pp. 1–13.

Gottmann, J. (1952) *La Politiques des États et leur Géographie*, Paris: Librairie Armand Colin.

— (1969) 'The Renewal of the Geographic Environment', An Inaugural Lecture delivered before the University of Oxford on 11 February 1969, Oxford: Clarendon Press.

— (1973) *The Significance of Territory*, Charlottesvile: The University Press of Virginia.

— (ed.) (1980) *Centre and Periphery: Spatial Variation in Politics*, Beverly Hills, London: Sage Publication.

Gourevitch, P. A. (1977) 'The reform of local government: a political analysis', *Comparative Politics* 10(1): 69–88.

— (1980) *Paris and the Provinces: The politics of local government reform in France*, London, Sydney: George Allen and Unwin.

Greenwood, R. and Stewart, J.D. (1986) 'The institutional and organizational capabilities of local government', *Public Administration* 64(1): 35–50.

Greer, S. L. (2006a) 'Introduction', in S. L. Greer (ed.) *Territory, Democracy and Justice*, Houndmills, Basingstoke, Hampshire and New York: Palgrave Macmillan, pp. 1–17.

— (2006b) 'Conclusion: Territorial politics today', in S. L. Greer (ed.) *Territory, Democracy and Justice*, Houndmills, Basingstoke, Hampshire and New York: Palgrave Macmillan, pp. 257–274.

Grodecki, S. (2007) 'Les compétences communales – Comparaison intercantonale', in T. Tanquerel and F. Bellanger (eds) *L'avenir juridique des communes*, Geneva, Zurich, Basel: Schulthess Médias Juridiques SA, pp. 15–78.

Grodzins, M. (1963) 'Centralization and Decentralization in the American Federal System', in. R. A. Goldwin (ed.) *A Nation of States,* Chicago: Rand McNally and Co, pp. 1–23.

— (1967 [1960]) 'American Political Parties and the American System', in A. Wildavsky (ed.) *American Federalism in Perspective*, Boston: Little, Brown and Company, pp. 109–143. [Originally published in *Western Political Quarterly* 13(4): 974–998.]

Gruner, E. (1977) *Die Parteien in der Schweiz*, 2nd edn, Berne: Francke Verlag.

Gurr, T. R. and King, D. S. (1987) *The State and the City*, London: Macmillan.

Guzzi-Heeb, S. (2004) 'Évolution de la société et transformation du pouvoir: Tessin et Vaud, de l'Ancien Régime à la souveraineté cantonale', *Revue historique vaudoise* 112: 153–168.

Hadley, C. D., Morass, M. and Nick, R. (1989) 'Federalism and party interaction in West Germany, Switzerland and Austria', *Publius* 19(4): 81–97.

Haldy, J. (2003) 'L'autonomie communale du XIXe siècle à nos jours', in O. Meuwly (ed.) *Les constitutions vaudoises, 1803–2003: miroir des idées politiques*, Lausanne: Bibliothèque historique vaudoise, pp. 131–7.

— (2004) 'L'organisation territoriale et les communes', in P. Moor (ed.) *La Constitution vaudoise du 14 avril 2003*, Berne: Staempfli Editions SA, pp. 291–310.

Hall, P. A. (2013) 'Tracing the progress of process tracing', *European Political Science* 12(1): 20–30.

Hall, P. A. and Taylor, R. C. R. (1996) 'Political science and the three new institutionalisms', *Political Studies* XLIV: 936–957.

Handbuch Politisches System der Schweiz, R. E. Germann and E. Weibel (eds) vol. 3, *Föderalismus*, Berne: Verlag Paul Haupt, pp. 85–105.

Hayek, F. (2011 [1960]) *The Constitution of Liberty*, Chicago: University of Chicago Press.

Head, R. C. (1995) *Early Modern Democracy in the Grisons: Social order and political language in a Swiss mountain canton 1470–1620*, Cambridge: Cambridge University Press.

— (2005) 'Die Bündner Staatsbildung im 16. Jahrhundert: zwischen Gemeinde und Oligarchie', in *Handbuch der Bündner Geschichte*, Vol. II, 2nd edn, Chur: Verlag Bündner Monatsblatt, pp. 85–112.

Hechter, M. (1975) *Internal Colonialism: The Celtic fringe in British national development, 1536–1966*, Berkeley and LA: University of California Press.

Heer, A. (1944) *Das glarnerische Kantons- und Gemeindebürgerrecht und dessen spezieller Inhalt*, PhD Diss University of Zurich; Glarus: Tschudi and Co.

Henderson, A. (2004) 'Regional political cultures in Canada', *Canadian Journal of Political Science / Revue canadienne de science politique* 37(3): 595–615.

Hendriks, F. (2001) 'Luxembourg: Change and continuities in the local state', in . J. Loughlin (ed.) *Subnational Democracy in the European Union: Challenges and opportunities*, Oxford: Oxford University Press, pp. 173–181.

Hepburn, E. (2011) '"Citizens of the region": Party conceptions of regional citizenship and immigrant integration', *European Journal of Political Research* 50(4): 504–529.

Herz, J. H. (1957) 'Rise and demise of the territorial state', *World Politics* 9(4): 473–493.

Hesse, J. J. and Sharpe, L. J. (1991) 'Local Government in International Perspective: Some comparative observations', in J. J. Hesse (ed.) *Local Government and Urban Affairs in International Perspective*, Baden-Baden: Nomos Verlagsgesellschaft, pp. 603–621.

Hesse, K. (1962) *Der unitarische Bundesstaat*, Karlsruhe: Verlag C. F. Müller.

Heywood, A. (2000) *Key Concepts in Politics*, Houndmills, Basingstoke: Palgrave.

Hix, S. and Høyland, B. (2011) *The Political System of the European Union*, 3rd edn, Basingstoke: Palgrave Macmillan.

Hoffmann, S. (1959) 'The Areal Division of Powers in the Writings of French Political Thinkers', in A. Maass (ed.) *Area and Power: A theory of local government*, Glencoe, Illinois: The Free Press, pp. 113–49.

Holenstein, A. (2008) '"Untergang" und Helvetische Revolution im kollektiven Gedächtnis Berns', in A. Holenstein (ed.) *Berns goldene Zeit: das 18. Jahrhundert neu entdeckt*, Bern: Stämpfli Verlag, pp. 526–31.

Honey, R. (1976) 'Conflicting problems in the political organization of space', *The Annals of Regional Science* 10(1): 45–60

Hooghe, L. and Marks, G. (2001) *Multi-level Governance and European Integration*, Lanham, MD and Oxford: Rowman and Littlefield.

— (2003) 'Unraveling the Central State, but how? Types of multi-level governance', *American Political Science Review*, 97(2): 233–43.

— (2013) 'Beyond federalism: estimating and explaining the territorial structure of government', *Publius: The Journal of Federalism* 43(2): 179–204.

Hooghe, L., Marks, G. and Schakel, A. H. (2008) 'Regional authority in 42 democracies, 1950–2006: a measure and five hypotheses', *Regional and Federal Studies* 18(2–3): 111–302 (double special issue).

— (2010) *The Rise of Regional Authority: A comparative study of 42 democracies (1950–2006)*, London: Routledge.

Hopkin, J. (2009) 'Party matters: devolution and party politics in Britain and Spain', *Party Politics* 15(2): 179–198.

Hopkin, J. and van Houten, P. (2009) 'Decentralization and state-wide parties: introduction', *Party Politics* 15(2): 131–135.

Horber-Papazian, K. (2004) *L'intervention des communes dans les politiques publiques,* PhD Diss École Polytechnique Fédérale de Lausanne; Lausanne, Switzerland.

— (2006) 'Les communes', in U. Klöti *et al.* (eds) *Handbuch der Schweizer Politik*, 4th edn, Zurich: Neue Zürcher Zeitung Publishing, pp. 233–258.

Horber-Papazian, K. and Jacot-Descombes, C. (2014) 'Les communes', in P. Knoepfel, Y. Papadopoulos, P. Sciarini, A. Vatter and S. Häusermann (eds) *Handbuch der Schweizer Politik*, 5th edn, Zurich: Neue Zürcher Zeitung Publishing, pp. 275–305.

Horber-Papazian, K. and Soguel, N. (1996) 'La répartition des tâches cantons-communes ou le rendez-vouz manqué des réformes', *Swiss Political Science Review* 2(2): 143–164.

Hough, D. and Jeffery, C. (2006) *Devolution and Electoral Politics,* Manchester: Manchester University Press.

Hrbek, R. (ed.) (2004) *Political Parties and Federalism: An international comparison,* Baden-Baden: Nomos Verlag.

Hueglin, T. O. (1998) 'Das Westfälische System aus der Föderalismus-Perspektive des Althusius', University of St. Gallen, working paper no. 270.

Hueglin, T. O. and Fenna, A. (2006) *Comparative Federalism: A systematic inquiry,* Peterborough, ON: Broadview Press.

Hughes, C. (1963) *Confederacies,* Leicester: Leicester University Press.

— (2006 [1944]) *A History of the Cantons* – Chapter Fourteen, 'The Other Cantons (Appenzell, Glarus and Zug; Fribourg; Geneva; and Grischun'). Fragment, http://www.kent.ac.uk/politics/cfs/csp/hughes.html (last accessed 22 August 2012).

— (2006 [1988]) *A History of the Cantons* – Chapter Two, 'Berne'. Fragment, http://www.kent.ac.uk/politics/cfs/csp/hughes.html (last accessed 22 August 2012).

— (2006 [1989]) *A History of the Cantons* – Chapter Twelve, 'Vaud'. Fragment, http://www.kent.ac.uk/politics/cfs/csp/hughes.html (last accessed 22 August 2012).

— (2006 [n.d.]) *A History of the Cantons* – Chapter Five, 'Schwyz', Fragment, http://www.kent.ac.uk/politics/cfs/csp/hughes.html (last accessed 22 August 2012).

Humes, S. (1991) *Local Governance and National Power: A worldwide comparison of tradition and change in local government,* New York: Harvester Wheatsheaf.

Huntington, S. P. (1959) 'The Founding Fathers and the Division of Powers', in A. Maass (ed.) *Area and Power: A theory of local government*, Glencoe, Illinois: The Free Press, pp. 150–205.

Hutchcroft, P. D. (2001) 'Centralization and decentralization in administration and politics: assessing territorial dimensions of authority and power', *Governance: An International Journal of Policy and Administration* 14(1): 23–53.

Huwyler, F. (2009) *Gemeindeorganisation des Kantons* Schwyz, *Gesetz mit Begleiterlassen, Wegleitung*, Rickenbach/Schwyz: Verband Schwyzer Gemeinden und Bezirke.

Inglehart, R. (1977) *The Silent Revolution: Changing values and political styles among western publics,* Princeton, NJ: Princeton University Press.

— (1988) 'The renaissance of political culture', *The American Political Science Review* 82(4): 1203–1230.

Jackman, R. W. and Miller, R. A. (1996) 'A Renaissance of Political Culture?' *American Journal of Political Science* 40: 632–59.

Jackman, S. (2008) 'Measurement', in J. Box-Steffensmeier, H. Brady and D. Collier (eds) *The Oxford Handbook of Political Methodology*, Oxford: OUP, pp. 119–51.

Jagmetti, R. (1972) 'Die Stellung der Gemeinden', *Zeitschrift für schweizerisches Recht* 91(2): 221–400.

Janda, K. (1980) 'Political Parties: A cross-national survey', New York: New Press. Accessible at http://janda.org/ICPP/ICPP1980/index.htm, last accessed 27 Feb 2011.

Jeffery, C. (1996) 'Sub-national authorities and "European Domestic Policy"', *Regional and Federal Studies* 6: 204–19.

— (2000) 'Sub-national mobilization and European integration: does it make any difference?', *Journal of Common Market Studies* 38(1): 1–23.

— (2006) 'Devolution and local government', *Publius: The Journal of Federalism* 36(1): 57–73.

— (2008) 'The challenge of territorial politics', *Policy and Politics* 36(4): 545–557.

Jequier, F. (2005) 'Le Canton de Vaud (du Léman) "sauvé" par l'Acte de Médiation', in A. -J. Czouz-Tornare (ed.) *Quand Napoléon Bonapartere créa la Suisse*, Paris: Paris: Société des études robespierristes, pp. 83–96.

John, P. (2001) *Local Governance in Western Europe*, London: Sage Publications.

Johnston, R. (2001) 'Out of the moribund: territory and territoriality in political geography', *Political Geography* 20(6): 677–693.

Jones, R. (1999) 'The mechanics of medieval state formation: observations from Wales', *Space and Polity* 3(1): 85–99.

Jufer, P. (1960) 'Die Bernische Bezirksverwaltung gestern und heute', *Jahrbuch des Oberaargaus* 3: 16–28.

Junker, B. (1982) *Geschichte des Kantons Bern seit 1798, Band I: Helvetik, Mediation, Restauration 1798–1830*, Historischer Verein des Kantons Bern, Berne: Stämpfli.

— (1990) *Geschichte des Kantons Bern seit 1798, Band II: Die Entstehung des demokratischen Volksstaates 1831–1880*, Historischer Verein des Kantons Bern, Berne: Stämpfli.

Junker, B. and Dubler, A. -M. (2011) 'Bern (Kanton)', *Historisches Lexikon der Schweiz*, http://www.hls-dhs-dss.ch/textes/d/D7383.php (last accessed 17 February 2015).

Katz, R. and Mair, P. (1994) *How Parties Organize: Change and adaptation in party organizations in Western democracies*, London: Sage Publications.

Kauzya, J.-M. (2005) 'Decentralization: Prospects for Peace, Democracy and Development', UN Division for Public Administration and Development Management Discussion paper. At http://unpan1.un.org/intradoc/groups/public/documents/un/unpan021510.pdf (last accessed March 2011).

Kavanagh, D. (1972) *Political Culture*, London: The Macmillan Press Ltd.

Kay, A. (2005) 'Territorial justice and devolution', *BJPIR* 7: 544–560.

Keating, M. (1998) *The New Regionalism in Western Europe: Territorial restructuring and political change*, Cheltenham, UK and Northampton, MA, USA: Edward Elgar.

— (2003) 'Regionalization in Central and Eastern Europe: The diffusion of a Western model?' in M. Keating and J. Hughes (eds) *The Regional Challenge in Central and Eastern Europe: Territorial restructuring and European integration*, Brussels: Presses interuniversitaires européennes/ Peter Lang, pp. 51–68.

— (ed.) (2004) *Regions and Regionalism in Europe*, The International Library of Comparative Public Policy, vol. 16, Cheltenham, UK and Northampton, MA, USA: Edward Elgar Publishing.

— (2008) 'Thirty years of territorial politics', *West European Politics* 31(1): 60–81.

— (2009a) *The Independence of Scotland: Self-Government and Shifting Politics of Union*, Oxford: OUP.

— (2009b) 'Rescaling Europe', *Perspectives on European Politics and Society* 10(1): 34–50.

—   (2013) *Rescaling the European State: The making of territory and the rise of the meso*, Oxford: Oxford University Press.

Keating, M. and Wilson, A. (2010) 'Federalism and Decentralisation in Italy', Paper presented at the PSA Conference, Edinburgh, March-April.

Kellenberger, M. (1965) *Die Landsgemeinden der schweizerischen Kantone. Ein verfassungsgeschichtlicher Überblick seit 1900*. Winterthur: Verlag P. G. Keller.

Kelsen, H. (1961) *General Theory of Law and State*, trans. A. Wedberg, New York: Russell and Russell.

Kennel, A. (1989) *Die Autonomie der Gemeinden und Bezirke im Kanton Schwyz*, Diss iur., University of Fribourg (CH).

Kincaid, J. (1982) *Political Culture, Public Policy and the American States*, Philadelphia: Institute for the Study of Human Issues.

King, D. S. and Pierre, J. (eds) (1990) *Challenges to Local Government*, London: SAGE Publications.

King, G., Keohane, R. and Verba, S. (1994) *Designing Social Inquiry*, Princeton: Princeton University Press.

King, J. (1994) 'Political culture, registration laws and voter turnout among the American states', *Publius: The Journal of Federalism* 24: 115–27.

King, P. (1982) *Federalism and Federation*, Baltimore, Maryland: The Johns Hopkins University Press.

Kirchgässner, G. and Guptara, P. (2006) 'Sustainable Public Finances with Sub-Federal Fiscal Autonomy: The case of Switzerland', in R. Blindenbacher and A. Ostien Karos (eds) *Dialogs on the Practice of Fiscal Federalism: Comparative perspectives*, Montreal: McGill-Queen's University Press, pp. 34–36.

Klöti, U. and Kübler, D. (eds) (2004) *Lokalpolitik zwischen Autonomie, Demokratie und Effizient. Ergebnisse eines Forschungsseminars*, Studien zur Politikwissenschaft 323, Zurich: Institut für Politikwissenschaft.

Knapp, B. (1986) 'Etapes du fédéralisme suisse', in R. E. Germann and E. Weibel (eds) *Handbuch Politisches System der Schweiz*, vol. 3: *Föderalismus*, Berne: Verlag Paul Haupt, pp. 31–53.

Kochen, M. and Deutsch, K. W. (1973) 'Decentralization by function and location', *Management Science* 19(8): 841–856.

Kolers, A. (2009) *Land, Conflict and Justice: A political theory of territory*, Cambridge: Cambridge University Press.

Kollman, K. (2013) *The Perils of Centralization: Lessons from church, state and corporation*, Cambridge: Cambridge University Press.

Kölz, A. (2004) *Neuere Schweizerische Verfassungsgeschichte. Ihre Grundlinien in Bund und Kantonen seit 1848*, Berne: Stämpfli Verlag AG.

Krane, D., Rigos, P. N. and Hills, M. B. Jr. (2001) *Home Rule in America: A fifty state handbook*, Washington, D.C.: Congressional Quarterly Press.

Kratochwil, F. (1986) 'Of systems, boundaries and territoriality', *World Politics* 39(1): 27–52.

Kronenberg, R. (2011) *Die Gemeindestrukturreform im Kanton Glarus*, Zurich, Basel, Geneva: Schulthess Juristische Medien AG.

Krueger, S. and Bernick, E. M. (2009) 'State rules and local governance choices', *Publius: The Journal of Federalism* 40(4): 697–718.

Kübler, D. and Schwab, B. (2007) 'New regionalism in five Swiss metropolitan areas: an assessment of inclusiveness, deliberation and democratic accountability', *European Journal of Political Research* 46: 473–502.

Ladner, A. (1991) *Politische Gemeinden, kommunale Parteien und lokale Politik*, Zürich: Seismo.

— (1994) 'Finanzkompetenzen der Gemeinden – ein Überblick über die Praxis', in F. Eng, A. Glatthard and B. H. König (eds) *Finanzen der öffentlichen Hand 5 'Finanzföderalismus'*, Emissionszentrale der Schweizer Gemeinden, pp. 65–85.

— (2004) *Stabilität und Wandel von Parteien und Parteiensystemen. Eine vergleichende Analyse von Konfliktlinien, Parteien und Parteiensystemen in den Schweizer Kantonen*, Wiesbaden: VS Verlag für Sozialwissenschaften.

— (2005) 'Switzerland: Reforming small autonomous municipalities', in B. Denters and L. E. Rose (eds) *Comparing Local Governance: Trends and developments*, Basingstoke/New York: Palgrave Macmillan, pp. 139–154.

— (2007) *Local Government and Metropolitan Regions: Switzerland*, Working paper IDHEAP 2/2007. Chavannes-Lausanne: Institut de hautes études en administration publique.

— (2008) *Die Schweizer Gemeinden im Wandel: Politische Institutionen und lokale Politik*. Cahier de l'IDHEAP 237. Chavannes-Lausanne: Institut de hautes études en administration publique.

— (2009) 'Swiss Confederation', in N. Steytler (ed.) *Local Government and Metropolitan Regions in Federal Systems: A Global Dialogue on Federalism,* Vol. 6, Montreal, Kingston, London and Ithaca: McGill-Queen's University Press, pp. 329–362.

Ladner, A. and Fiechter, J. (2008) 'L'état des communes dans le canton de Vaud', *Cahier de l'IDHEAP 238*, Lausanne: Swiss Graduate School of Public Administration.

Ladner, A. and Steiner, R. (eds) (2005) *Schweizer Kantone und Gemeinden im Wandel*, Berne: Verlag Paul Haupt.

Landman, T. (2008) *Issues and Methods in Comparative Politics: An introduction*, 3rd edn, New York: Routledge.

Landolt, O. (2011) 'Schwyz (Kanton) – Herrschaft und Politik vom Hochmittelalter bis zum Ende des 18. Jh'. *Historisches Lexikon der Schweiz*, http://www.hls-dhs-dss.ch/textes/d/D7385.php (last accessed 17 February 2015).

Lane, J. E. and Ersson, S. (2005) *Culture and Politics: A comparative approach*, Aldershot: Ashgate Publishing Company.

Langhard, K. (1977) *Die Organisation der politischen Gemeinden des Kantons Graubünden im Spiegel der neueren kantonalen und kommunalen*

Rechtssetzung, PhD Diss University of Zurich; Zurich: Juris Druck + Verlag.

Lapid, Y. (1999) 'Where should we begin?', *Political Geography* 18(8): 895–900.

Larkins, J. (2009) *From Hierarchy to Anarchy: Territory and politics before Westphalia*, New York: Palgrave Macmillan.

Lavander, V. (2010) 'Institutional Approach', in D. Marsh and G. Stoker (eds) *Theory and Methods in Political Science*, Basingstoke: Palgrave Macmillan, pp. 60–79.

Le Galès, P. (1995) 'Du gouvernement des villes à la gouvernance urbaine', *Revue française de science politique* 45(1): 57–95.

— (2002) *European Cities: Social conflicts and governance*, Oxford: Oxford University Press.

Leech, B. L. (2002) 'Asking questions: techniques for semistructured interviews', *PS: Political Science and Politics* 35(4): 665–668.

Lehmbruch, G. (1993) 'Consociational democracy and corporatism in Switzerland', *Publius: The Journal of Federalism* 23(2): 43–60.

Leresche, J.-P. and Joye, D. (1993) *Les transformations du pouvoir local en Suisse*, Travaux de Science Politique 7, Laussane: Université de Lausanne.

Leresche, J.-P. (1992) 'Les communes Suisse face aux nouveaux espaces européens', *Die Stadt – les villes* 5: 16- 19.

Levy, J. S. (2008) 'Counterfactuals and Case Studies', in *The Oxford Handbook of Political Methodology*, J. Box-Steffensmeier, H. Brady and D. Collier (eds) Oxford: OUP, pp. 627–644.

Lidström, A. (2013) 'Local Government Associations Worldwide: Promoting democratic local governance', in G. Shabbir Sheema (ed.) *Democratic Local Governance: Reforms and innovations in Asia*, Tokyo: United Nations University Press, pp. 73–88.

Lieberman, E. S. (2005) 'Nested analysis as a mixed-method strategy for comparative research', *The American Political Science Review* 99(3): 435–452.

Lienert, K. R. (1977) *Der Kanton Schwyz: Herausgegeben im Auftrag der Kulturkommission des Kantons Schwyz*, Einsiedeln and Zurich: Benziger Verlag.

Lieske, J. (1993) 'Regional subcultures of the United States', *Journal of Politics* 55: 888–913.

Lijphart, A. (1971) 'Comparative politics and the comparative method', *American Political Science Review* 65: 682–693.

— (1975) 'The comparable cases strategy in comparative research', *Comparative Political Studies* 8: 158–177.

— (1979) 'Religious vs. linguistic vs. class voting: the "crucial experiment" of comparing Belgium, Canada, South Africa and Switzerland', *The American Political Science Review* 73(2): 442–458.

— (1999) *Patterns of Democracy*, New Haven: Yale University Press.

— (2002) 'Preface', in A. Vatter (ed.) *Kantonale Demokratien im Vergleich*, Opladen: Leske + Budrich, pp. 13–15.

Linder, W. (1996. Schweizerische Politikwissenschaft: Entwicklungen der Disziplin und ihrer Literatur. *Swiss Political Science Review* 2(4): 1–98.

— (1999) *Schweizerische Demokratie: Insitutionen, Prozesse, Perspektiven*, Berne, Stuttgart, Vienna: Haupt Verlag.

— (2010) *Swiss Democracy: Possible solutions to conflict in multicultural societies*, Basingstoke: Palgrave Macmillan.

Linder, W. and Steffen, I. (2006) 'Politische Kultur', in U. Klöti *et al.* (eds) *Handbuch der Schweizer Politik*, 4th edn, Zurich: Neue Zürcher Zeitung Publishing, pp. 15–34.

Linder, W., Bolliger, C. and Rielle, Y. (2010) *Handbuch der eidgenössichen Volksabstimmungen 1848–2007*, Bern, Stuttgart, Wien: Haupt Verlag.

Linder, W., Zürcher, R. and Bolliger, C. (2008) *Gespaltene Schweiz – geeinte Schweiz. Gesellschaftliche Spaltung und Konkordanz bei den Volksabstimmungen seit 1874*. Baden: hier + jetzt.

Lipset, S. M. and Rokkan, S. (1990 [1967]) 'Cleavage Structures, Party Systems and Voter Alignments', in P. Mair (ed.) *The West European Party System*, Oxford: OUP, pp. 91–138.

Little, D. (1998) *Microfoundations, Method and Causation: On the philosophy of the social sciences*, New Brunswick: Transaction Publishers.

Litvack, J.and Seddon, J. (eds) (1999) *Decentralization Briefing Notes*, World Bank Institute Working Papers, Washington, D.C. At http://siteresources.worldbank.org/WBI/Resources/wbi37142.pdf (downloaded in March 2011).

Liver, P. (1933) 'Die staatliche Entwicklung im alten Graubünden', *Zeitschrift für schweizerische Geschichte* 13(2): 206–248.

Livingston, W. S. (1952) 'A note on the nature of federalism', *Political Science Quarterly* 67(1): 81–95.

— (1956) *Federalism and Constitutional Change*, Oxford: Clarendon Press.

Lluch, J. (2012) 'Autonomism and federalism', *Publius* 42(1): 134–161.

Locke, R. M. and Thelen, K. (1995) 'Apples and oranges revisited: contextualized comparisons and the study of comparative labor politics', *Politics and Society* 23(3): 337–367.

Logoz, R.-C. (2003) 'La Constitution de l'An I et son influence sur les constitutions vaudoises. L'importance et le destin d'un mythe', in O. Meuwly (ed.) *Les constitutions vaudoises, 1803–2003: miroir des idées politiques*, Lausanne: Bibliothèque historique vaudoise, pp. 249–76.

Loughlin, J. (2000) 'Regional autonomy and state paradigm shifts in Western Europe', *Regional and Federal Studies* 10(2): 10–34.

— (2001a) 'Introduction: The transformation of the democratic state in Western Europe', in J. Loughlin (ed.) *Subnational Democracy in the European Union: Challenges and opportunities*, Oxford: Oxford University Press, pp. 1–33.

— (2001b) 'Portugal: The difficulties of regionalization', in J. Loughlin (ed.) *Subnational Democracy in the European Union: Challenges and Opportunities*, Oxford: Oxford University Press, pp. 255–270.

—   (2001c) 'Greece: Between "henosis" and decentralization', in J. Loughlin
        (ed.) *Subnational Democracy in the European Union: Challenges and
        Opportunities*, Oxford: Oxford University Press, pp. 271–287.

—   (2007a) *Subnational Government: The French Experience*, Houndmills,
        Basingstoke and New York: Palgrave Macmillan.

—   (2007b) 'Federalism, regionalism and local government: comparative
        perspectives on transforming the nation-state', *European Political
        Science* 7: 472–482.

Loughlin, J. and Delcamp, A. (eds) (2003) *La décentralisation dans les Etats de
        l'Union européenne*, 2nd edn, Paris: La Documentation Française.

Loughlin, J. and Seiler, D.-L. (2001) 'France: Between centralization and
        fragmentation: the difficulties of regionalization', in J. Loughlin (ed.)
        *Subnational Democracy in the European Union: Challenges and
        Opportunities*, Oxford: Oxford University Press, pp. 185–210.

Luchsinger, K. (1941) *Der Tagwen im Rahmen des glarnerischen Gemeindewesens*,
        PhD Diss University of Berne; Glarus: Tschudi and Co.

Lutz, G. and Strohmann, D. (1998) *Wahl- und Abstimmungsrecht in den Kantonen/
        Droits politiques dans les cantons*, Bern/Stuttgart/Wien: Verlag Paul
        Haupt.

Maass, A. (1959) 'Division of Powers: An areal analysis', in A. Maass (ed.) *Area
        and Power: A Theory of Local Government*, Glencoe, Illinois: The Free
        Press, pp. 9–26.

MacDougall, T. (2001) *Towards Political Inclusiveness: The changing role of local
        government in Japan*, World Bank Institute Working Paper. Washington.
        DC.

Magin, R. and Eder, C. (2008) 'Kommunale Selbstverwaltung und
        Dezentralisierung', in M. Freitag and A. Vatter (eds) *Die Demokratien
        der deutschen Bundesländer*, Opladen: Verlag Barbara Budrich,
        pp. 195–220.

Maillefer, P. (1895) 'Le Pays de Vaud sous le regime bernois', *Revue historique
        vaudoise* 3(1): 13–23; 3(2): 47–57; 3(3): 74–87; 3(4): 108–118; and 3(6):
        161–171.

Maillefer, P. (1903) *Histoire du Canton de Vaud dès les origines*, Lausanne: Payot
        and Cie.

Máiz, R. and Losada, A. (2013) 'The Erosion of Regional Powers in the Spanish
        "State of Autonomies"', in F. Requejo and K. -J. Nagel (eds) *Federalism
        beyond Federations: Asymmetry and processes of resymmetrisation in
        Europe*, Farnham, UK: Ashgate, pp. 81–108.

Majone, G. (2006) 'Federation, Confederation and Mixed Government: A EU-
        US comparison', in A. Menon and M. A. Schain (eds) *Comparative
        Federalism: The European Union and the United States in comparative
        perspective*, Oxford: Oxford University Press, pp. 121–146.

Mamadouh, V. (2001) 'The territoriality of European integration and the territorial
        features of the European Union: the first 50 years', *Tijdschrift voor
        Economische en Sociale Geografie* 92(4): 420–436.

Mann, M. (1997) 'The Autonomous Power of the State', in J. Agnew (ed.) *Political Geography: A reader*, London: Arnold, pp. 58–81. [Originally published in *European Journal of Sociology* 25 (1984): 185–213.]

Mansuri, G. and Vijayendra, R. (2012) 'Can Participation be Induced? Some evidence from developing countries', *World Bank Policy Research*, working paper no. WPS 6139.

Marbach, J. R., Katz, E. and Smith, T. E. (eds) (2006) *Federalism in America: An encyclopedia*, Vol. 1, Westport, CT: Greenwood Press.

Mathias, J. (2004) *Regional Interests and Regional Actors: Wales and Saxony as modern regions in Europe*, Abingdon/Oxon and New York: Routledge.

Mayntz, R. and Scharpf, F. W. (1995) 'Der Ansatz des akteurzentrierten Institutionalismus', in R. Mayntz and F. W. Scharpf (eds) *Gesellschaftliche Selbstregelung und politische Steuerung*, Frankfurt a.M.: Campus, pp. 39–72.

McDonnell, D. (2006) 'A weekend in Padania: regionalist populism and the Lega Nord', *Politics* 26(2): 126–132.

McKay, D. (2001) *Designing Europe: Comparative lessons from the federal experience*, Oxford: Oxford University Press.

McLean, I. and McMillan, A. (eds) (2009) *The Concise Oxford Dictionary of Politics*, 3rd edn, Oxford: Oxford University Press.

Meguid, B. (2008) *Party Competition between Unequals*, Cambridge: Cambridge University Press.

Mény, Y. and Wright, V. (1985) 'General Introduction', in Y. Mény and V. Wright (eds) *Centre-Periphery Relations in Western Europe*, London: George Allen and Unwin, pp. 1–9.

Mermoud, J.-C. (2005) 'La répartition des tâches entre cantons et communes: L'exemple du projet de réforme du Canton de Vaud', in B. Waldmann (ed.) *Conférence nationale sur le fédéralisme: le fédéralisme coopératif face à de nouveaux défis*, Basel: Helbing and Lichtenhahn, pp. 223–243.

Messerli, P. and Egli, H. (2003) 'Der Staat Bern – vom grössten Stadtstaat nördlich der Alpen zum Teil des Espace Mittelland', *Geographische Rundschau* 55(9): 12–19.

Metz, P. sen (2005) 'Staat und Verwaltung', in *Handbuch der Bündner Geschichte*, Vol III,. 2nd edn, Chur: Verlag Bündner Monatsblatt, pp. 283–309.

Meuwly, O. (1990) *Histoire des droits politiques dans le canton de Vaud de 1803 à 1885*. PhD Diss, University of Lausanne.

— (2011) 'Frédéric-César de la Harpe fondateur du libéralisme vaudois', in O. Meuwly (ed.) *Frédéric-César de la Harpe: 1754–1838*, Lausanne: Bibliothèque historique vaudoise, pp. 198–210.

Meyer, H. A. (1978) *Wandlungen im Bestande der Gemeinden*, PhD Diss University of Zurich; Belp, CH: Jordi AG.

Meyer, K. (1926) 'Geographische Voraussetzungen der eidgenössischen Territorialbildung', *Mitteilungen des historischen Vereins des Kantons Schwyz* 34: 29–224.

Meyerhans, A. (1998) *Der Kanton Schwyz, 1798–1848: Der Weg in den Bundesstaat,* Schwyz: Verlag Schwyzer Hefte.
— (2012) 'Von der Talgemeinde zum Länderort Schw', in *Geschichte des Kantons Schwyz*, Historischer Verein des Kantons Schwyz (ed.), Vol II, Zurich: Chronos Verlag, pp. 9–63.
Meylan, Ja. (1972) *Problèmes actuels de l'autonomie communale,* Basel: Verlag Helbing + Lichtenhahn.
Meylan, J., Gottraux, M. and Dahinden, P. (1972) *Schweizer Gemeinden und Gemeindeautonomie,* trans. J. Rittmeyer, M. Korn and U. Beck, Studiengruppe für Gemeindeautonomie in der Schweiz, Lausanne: Imprimeries Populaires.
Meylan, Je. (1986) 'Les communes', in R. E. Germann and E. Weibel (eds) *Handbuch politisches System Schweiz,* vol. 3, *Föderalismus,* Berne: Verlag Paul Haupt, pp. 137–170.
— (1987) *Die Schweizer Gemeinden,* Lausanne [Originally published as Les communes suisses. Aspects institutionnels, charactéristiques générales, moyens à disposition. Lausanne: Imprimerie A. Groux.]
Meylan, M. (1994) *Les préfets vaudois, acteurs de leur époque,* Yens-sur-Morges: Edition Cabédita.
Michel, K. (1982) 'Der Halbkanton"' Schwyz, äusseres Land"'. Der *Geschichtsfreund: Mitteilungen des Historischen Vereins Zentralschweiz* 135: 251–256.
— (2011) 'Schwyz (Kanton)', *Historisches Lexikon der Schweiz,* http://www. hls-dhs-dss.ch/textes/d/D7385.php (last accessed 17 February 2015).
Miller, D. Y. (1991) 'The impact of political culture on patterns of state and local government expenditures, *Publius: The Journal of Federalism* 21: 83–100.
Miller, E. F. (2010) *Hayek's, The Constitution of Liberty' – An Account of Its Argument,* London: The Institute of Economic Affairs.
Mitchell, J. (1997) 'Territorial Politics and the Study of the European Union', ECSA Conference Paper, Seattle, June.
Möckli, S. (1987) *Die schweizerischen Landsgemeinde-Demokratien,* Berne: Verlag Paul Haupt.
Montero, A. P. and Samuels, D. J. (2004) 'The Political Determinants of Decentralization in Latin America: Causes and Consequences', in A. P. Montero and D. J. Samuels (eds) *Decentralization and Democracy in Latin America,* Notre Dame, IN: University of Notre Dame Press, pp. 2–39.
Moon, D. S. and Bratberg, O. (2010) 'Conceptualising the multi-level party: two complementary approaches', *Politics* 30(1): 52–60.
Moor, P. (2007) 'L'institution communale: hier, aujourd'hui et demain', in T. Tanquerel and F. Bellanger (eds) *L'avenir juridique des communes,* Geneva, Zurich, Basel: Schulthess Médias Juridiques SA, pp. 9–24.
Moots, G. A. (2009) 'The Covenant Tradition of Federalism: The pioneering studies of Daniel J. Elazar', in A. Ward and L. Ward (eds) *The Ashgate*

Research Companion to Federalism, Surrey: Ashgate Publishing Company, pp. 391–412.

Moreno, L., Arriba, A. and Serrano, A. (1998) 'Multiple identities in decentralized Spain: The case of Catalonia', *Regional and Federal Studies* 8(3): 65–88.

Morgan, D. R. and Watson, S. S. (1991) 'Political culture, political system characteristics and public policies among the American states', *Publius* 21: 31–48.

Mueller, S. (2007) 'Communal Merger in the Canton of Glarus, Switzerland: Democratic but Illegitimate?', Paper presented at the IFF Summer University on 'Federalism, Constitutionalism and Democratic Governance in Multicultural Societies'. Fribourg/CH, 27 August–14 September.

— (2011) 'The politics of local autonomy: measuring cantonal (de)centralisation in Switzerland', *Space and Polity* 15(3): 213–39.

— (2014) 'Shared rule in federal political systems: conceptual lessons from subnational Switzerland', *Publius: The Journal of Federalism* 44(1): 82–108.

Mueller, S. and Dardanelli, P. (2012) 'Localism or Centralism? Exploring 'Macro-Local' Reforms in the Swiss Cantons', Paper presented at the 62nd PSA Annual Conference in Belfast, 3–5 April 2012.

— (2013) 'The parliamentary and executive elections in Switzerland, 2011', *Electoral Studies* 32(1): 197–201.

Müller, A. (1982) '1817 – ein denkwürdiges Jahr für die altfrye Republik Gersau', *Mitteilungen des historischen Vereins des Kantons Schwyz* 65: 147–157.

— (1990) 'Gersau: 3. Juni 1390', *Mitteilungen des historischen Vereins des Kantons Schwyz* 82: 81–87.

— (1996) 'Gersau zur Zeit der Helvetik 1798–1803', *Mitteilungen des historischen Vereins des Kantons Schwyz* 88: 67–78.

Müller, K. (ed.) (1987) *Bausteine der Schweiz. Porträts der 26 Kantone*, Zurich: Verlag NZZ.

Müller, W. C. and Strøm, K. (eds) (1999) *Policy, Office, or Votes? How political parties in Western Europe make hard decisions*, Cambridge: Cambridge University Press.

Munck, G. L. (2010) 'Comparative Politics: Taking Stock and Looking Forward. Committee on Concepts and Methods', *Working Paper no. 30*. At http://www.concepts-methods.org (last accessed November 2011).

Murphy, A. B. (1989) 'Territorial policies in multiethnic states', *Geographical Review* 79(4): 410–421.

— (2002) 'Brussels: division in unity or unity in division?', *Political Geography* 21(5): 695–700.

Musgrave, R. A. (ed.) (1965) *Essays in Fiscal Federalism: Studies of government finance*, Washington DC: The Brookings Institution.

Nabholz, H. and Kläui, P. (eds) (1940) *Quellenbuch zur Verfassungsgeschichte der Schweizerischen Eidgenossenschaft und der Kantone. Von den Anfängen bis zur Gegenwart*, Aarau: Verlag H. R. Sauerländer and Co.

Nawiasky, H. (1946) 'Grundbegriffe der Gemeindeautonomie', in H. Nawiasky (ed.) *Die Gemeindeautonomie*, Einsiedeln, Köln: Verlagsanstalt Benziger and Co. AG, pp. 14–26.

Neidhart, L. (2002) *Die politische Schweiz. Fundamente und Institutionen*, Zurich: NZZ Verlag.

Nettl, J. P. (1968) 'The state as a conceptual variable', *World Politics* 20(4): 559–592.

Newman, D. (ed.) (1999) *Boundaries, Territory and Postmodernity*, London and Portland, Or: Frank Cass.

Niederer, A. (1956) *Gemeinwerk im Wallis*, PhD Diss University of Zurich; Basel: Buchdruckerei G. Krebs Verlagsbuchhandlung AG.

Nordlinger, E. A. (1965) 'Democratic Stability and Instability: The French Case', *World Politics* 18:1, 127–131, 133, 135, 137, 139, 141, 143, 145, 147, 149, 151, 153, 155, 157.

Nüssli, K. (1985) *Föderalismus in der Schweiz. Konzepte, Indikatoren, Daten*, Chur: Rüegger.

Oates, W. E. (1972) *Fiscal Federalism*, New York: Harcourt Brace Jovanovich.

—   (1999) 'An essay on fiscal federalism', *Journal of Economic Literature* 37(3): 1120–1149.

O'Dowd, L., Anderson, J. and Wilson, T. M. (2003) *New Borders for a Changing Europe: Cross-border cooperation and governance'*, Abingdon/Oxon and New York: Routledge.

Oechsli, W. (1922) *History of Switzerland 1499–1914*, Cambridge: University Press.

—   (1988) 'Orte und Zugewandte: eine Studie zur Geschichte des schweizerischen Bundesrechtes', *Jahrbuch für schweizerische Geschichte* 13: 1–497.

O'Neill, K. (2003) 'Decentralization as an electoral strategy', *Comparative Political Studies* 36(9): 1068–91.

Ordeshook, P. C. and Shvetsova, O. V. (1994) 'Ethnic heterogeneity, district magnitude and the number of parties', *American Journal of Political Science* 38(1): 101–123.

Ostrom, E. (1990) *Governing the Commons: The evolution of institutions for collective action*, Cambridge: Cambridge University Press.

Oxford Dictionary of English Language (2005) C. Soanes and A. Stevenson (ed.) 2nd edn, Oxford: Oxford University Press.

Paasi, A. (2002) 'Regional transformation in the European context: notes on regions, boundaries and identity', *Space and Polity* 6(2): 197–201.

Pacella, M. and Mazzoleni, O. (2010) *Aggregazioni comunali: l'esperienza dei cittadini di Acquarossa, Capriasca, Lugano e Maggia*, Documenti statistici 46, Bellinzona: Ufficio di statistica.

Page, E. C. (1991) *Localism and Centralism in Europe: The political and legal bases of local self-government*, Oxford: Oxford University Press.

Page, E. C. and Goldsmith, M. (1987) *Central and Local Government Relations: A comparative analysis of West European unitary states*, London: Sage.

Panebianco, A. (1988) *Political Parties: Organization and power*, trans. M. Silver, Cambridge and New York: Cambridge University Press.

Panizza, U. (1999) 'On the determinants of fiscal centralization: theory and evidence', *Journal of Public Economics* 74(1): 97–139.

Papadopoulos, Y. (1991) *La Suisse: Un 'Sonderfall' pour la théorie politique?*, Travaux de science politique no. 2, Université de Lausanne.

Park, B.-G. (2008) 'Uneven development, inter-scalar tensions and the politics of decentralization in South Korea', *International Journal of Urban and Regional Research* 32(1): 40–59.

Parsons, T. (1967) *Politics and Social Structure*, New York: The Free Press.

Pasquier, R. (2005) '"Cognitive Europeanization" and the territorial effects of multilevel policy transfer: local development in French and Spanish regions', *Regional and Federal Studies* 15(3): 295–310.

Pelinka, A. (2002) 'Die FPÖ in der vergleichenden Parteienforschung. Zur typologischen Einordnung der Freiheitlichen Partei Österreichs', *Österreichische Zeitschrift für Politikwissenschaft* 31(3): 281–290.

Pennings, P., Keman, H. and Kleinnijenhuis, J. (1999) *Doing Research in Political Science: An introduction to comparative methods and statistics*, London: Sage.

Penrose, J. (2002) 'Nations, states and homelands: territory and territoriality in nationalist thought', *Nations and Nationalism* 8(3): 277–297.

Perritaz, S. (2003) *Intercommunalité, agglomération et fusion de communes: l'optimal et le possible dans les zones urbaines suisses*, PhD Diss University of Fribourg, Switzerland.

Pestalozzi, H. U. (1973) *Das Initiativrecht in der Zürcher Gemeinde*, PhD Diss University of Zurich, Switzerland.

Peter, H. (1928) *Zentralisation und Dezentralisation*, Berlin: Verlag von Julius Springer.

Peters, B. G. (1998) *Comparative Politics: Theories and methods*, Basingstoke, UK: Palgrave.

— (1999) *Institutional Theory in Political Science: The 'new institutionalism'*, London, New York: Pinter.

Piattoni, S. (2010) *The Theory of Multi-Level Governance: Conceptual, empirical and normative challenges*, Oxford: Oxford University Press.

— (2014) 'Blurring Political and Functional Representation: Sub-national territorial interests in European multi-level governance', in P. A. Hall, W. Jacoby, J. Levy and S. Meunier (eds) *The Politics of Representation in the Global Age: Identification, mobilization and adjudication*, Cambridge: Cambridge University Press, pp. 155–175.

Pichard, A. (1978) *La Romandie n'existe pas: six portraits politiques: Fribourg, Genève, Jura, Neuchâtel, Valais, Vaud*, Lausanne: Éditions 24 Heures.

Pierre, J. (1990) 'Assessing Local Autonomy', in D. S. King and J. Pierre (eds) *Challenges to Local Government*, London: Sage, pp. 37–54.

Pieth, F. (1982) *Bündnergeschichte*, 2nd edn, Chur: F. Schuler.

Poggi, G. (1978) *The Development of the Modern State: A sociological introduction*, London: Hutchinson and Co Ltd.

Pollock III, P. H. (2008) *The Essentials of Political Analysis*, 3rd edn, Washington, DC: CQ Press.

Polsby, N. W. (1979) 'Preface', in L. J. Sharpe (ed.) *Decentralist trends in Western Democracies*, London and Beverly Hills: Sage Publications, pp. 1–7.

Poltéra, C. (1922) *Die Kreise und ihre Verwaltung nach bündnerischem Staats- und Verwaltungsrecht*, PhD Diss University of Fribourg. N.P., Schossig and Co.

Pratchett, L. (2004) 'Local autonomy, local democracy and the "new localism"', *Political Studies* 52: 358–375.

Proudhon, P. J. (1863) *Du principe fédératif et de la nécessité de reconstituer le parti de la revolution*, Paris: E. Dentu.

Przeworski, A. and Teune, H. (1970) *The Logic of Comparative Social Inquiry*, New York: Wiley.

Putnam, R. D. (1993) *Making Democracy Work: Civic traditions in modern Italy*, Princeton: Princeton University Press.

Pye, L. W. (1968) 'Political Culture', in D. L. Sills (ed.) *International Encyclopedia of the Social Sciences*, Vol. 12, New York: Macmillan, pp. 218–24.

Raffestin, C. (1985) 'Langues et pouvoir en Suisse', *Espace géographique* 2: 151–5.

Ragin, C. (1987) *The Comparative Method: Moving beyond qualitative and quantitative Strategies.* Berkeley and Los Angeles, CA: University of California Press.

Raith, M. (1984) 'Gemeinden', in L. Burckhardt, R. L. Frey, G. Kreis and G. Schmid (eds) *Das politische System Basel-Stadt*, Basel and Frankfurt a.M.: Helbing and Lichtenhahn, pp. 303–318.

Rathgeb, C. (2003) *Die Verfassungsentwicklung Graubündens im 19. Jahrhundert*, PhD Diss University of Zurich; Zurich, Basel, Geneva: Schulthess Juristische Medien AG.

— (2011) 'Bündner Verfassungsentwicklung und Gemeindewesen im 19. Jahrhundert', in F. Hitz, C. Rathgeb and M. Risi (eds) *Gemeinden und Verfassung: Bündner Politik und Gebietsstruktur gestern, heute, morgen*, Chur: Südostchweiz Buchverlag, pp. 121–33.

Reich, R. (1975) 'Notes on the local and cantonal influence in the Swiss federal consultation process', *Publius* 5(2): 117–126.

Reinhardt, V. (2008) *Geschichte der Schweiz*, Munich: Verlag C. H. Beck.

Reiser, C. M. (1998) *Autonomie et démocratie dans les communes genevoises*, Basel, Geneva, Munich: Helbing and Lichtenhahn.

Remak, J. (1993) *A Very Civil War: The Swiss Sonderbund War of 1847*, Boulder, San Francisco, Oxford: Westview Press.

Requejo, F. (2005) *Multinational Federalism and Value Pluralism: The Spanish case*, Abingdon/Oxon and New York: Routledge.

Rezazadeh, R. (1961) 'The concept of centralization and decentralization: an analysis and evaluation', *International Review of Administrative Sciences* 27: 425–430.

Rhodes, R. A. W. (1981) *Control and Power in Central-Local Government Relations*, Westmead, Farnborough, Hants, England: Gower Publishing Company Limited.

Richardson, J. J. Jr., Zimmerman Gough, M. and Puentes, R. (2003) 'Is Home Rule the Answer? Clarifying the Influence of Dillon's Rule on Growth Management', Discussion Paper prepared for the Brookings Institution Center on Urban and Metropolitan Policy.

Riker, W. (1964) *Federalism: Origin, Operation, Significance*, Boston: Little Brown.

—   (1969) Six books in search of a subject or does federalism exist and does it matter', *Comparative Politics* 2(1): 135–46.

—   (1975) 'Federalism', in F. Greenstein and N. Polsby (eds) *Handbook of Political Science*, Vol. 5, Reading, Mass.: Addison-Wesley, pp. 93–172.

Riklin, A. (1992) 'Die Neutralität der Schweiz', in A. Riklin, H. Haug, and R. Probst (eds) *Neues Handbuch der schweizerischen Aussenpolitik*, Bern, Stuttgart, Wien: Verlag Paul Haupt, pp. 191–209.

Riley, P. (1976) 'Three 17th century German theorists of federalism: Althusius, Hugo and Leibniz', *Publius* 6(3): 7–4.

Rodden, J. (2002) 'The dilemma of fiscal federalism: grants and fiscal performance around the world', *American Journal of Political Science* 46(3): 670–687.

—   (2003) 'Reviving Leviathan: Fiscal federalism and the growth of government', *International Organization* 57: 695–729.

—   (2004) 'Comparative federalism and decentralization: on meaning and measurement', *Comparative Politics* 36(4): 481–500.

—   (2006) *Hamilton's Paradox: The promise and peril of fiscal federalism*, Cambridge: Cambridge University Press.

Rodt, E. V. (1934) 'Bern's Besitznahme, Reformation und Organisation der Waadt', *Blätter für bernische Geschichte, Kunst und Altertumskunde* 20(4): 301–305.

Rohlfing, I. (2008), 'What you see and what you get: pitfalls and principles of nested analysis in comparative research', *Comparative Political Studies* 41(11): 1492–1514.

Rokkan, S. and Urwin, D. (eds) (1982) *The Politics of Territorial Identity*, London, Beverly Hills, New Delhi: SAGE Publications.

—   (1983) *Economy, Territory, Identity: Politics of West European peripheries*, London, Beverly Hills, New Delhi: SAGE Publications.

Rossi, M. (1999) 'Decentralisation: Initial experiences and expectations of the SDC', in . Swiss Agency for Development and Cooperation (ed.) *Decentralization and Development*, Berne: SDC Publications on Development, pp. 14–25.

Rubin, H. J. and Rubin, I. S. (1995) *Qualitative Interviewing: The art of hearing*, Thousand Oaks, London and New Delhi: SAGE Publications.

Rufer, A. (1954) 'Die Veltlinerfrage auf dem Rastatter Kongress', *Schweizerische Zeitschrift für Geschichte* 4(3): 321–347.

Ruggie, J. G. (1993) 'Territoriality and beyond: problematizing modernity in international relations', *International Organization* 47(1): 139–174.

Rühli, L. (2012) *Gemeindeautonomie zwischen Illusion und Realität. Gemeindestrukturen und Gemeindestrukturpolitik der Kantone*, Kantonsmonitoring 4, Zurich: Avenir Suisse.

Sablonier, R. (2005) 'Politik und Staatlichkeit im Spätmittelalter', in *Handbuch der Bündner Geschichte*, Vol. 1, 2nd edn, Chur: Verlag Bündner Monatsblatt, pp. 245–94.

Sablonier, R. (2012) 'Politischer Wandel und gesellschaftliche Entwicklung 1200–1350', in Historischer Verein des Kantons Schwyz (ed.) *Geschichte des Kantons Schwyz*, Vol. 1, Zurich: Chronos Verlag, 219–71.

Sack, R. D. (1983) 'Human territoriality: a theory', *Annals of the Association of American Geographers* 73(1): 55–74.

Sack, R. D. (1986) *Human Territoriality: Its theory and history*, Cambridge: Cambridge University Press.

Saltman, M. (ed.) (2002) *Land and Territoriality*, Oxford: Berg.

Sartori, G. (1970) 'Concept misformation in comparative politics', *American Political Science Review* LXIV(4): 1033–1053.

— (2005 [1976]) *Parties and Party Systems: A framework for analysis*, ECPR Press: University of Essex Printing Centre.

Scaramellini, G. (2007) 'Chiavenna', *Historisches Lexikon der Schweiz* http://www.hls-dhs-dss.ch/textes/d/D7043.php (last accessed 17 February 2015).

— (2012) 'Veltlin', *Historisches Lexikon der Schweiz*, http://www.hls-dhs-dss.ch/textes/d/D7135.php (last accessed 17 February 2015).

Schakel, A. H. (2008) 'Validation of the Regional Authority Index', *Regional & Federal Studies* 18(2): 143–166.

Schakel, A. H., Hooghe, L. and Marks, G. (2015) 'Multilevel governance and the state', in S. Leibfried, E. Huber, M. Lange, J. D. Levy, F. Nullmeier and J. D. Stephens (eds) *Oxford Handbook on the Transformation of the State*, Oxford: Oxford University Press, (forthcoming).

Schaltegger, F. (1952) *Die thurgauische Gemeindeautonomie*, PhD Diss University of Zurich; Zurich: Juris-Verlag.

Scharpf, F. W. (1997) *Games Real Actors Play: Actor-centered institutionalism in policy research*, Oxford, Oxford University Press.

— (1995) 'Federal arrangements and multi-party systems', *Australian Journal of Political Science* 30: 27–39.

— (2000) 'Notes Toward a Theory of Multilevel Governing in Europe. MPIfG Paper 2000/5. Accessible at http://www.mpi-fg-koeln.mpg.de/pu/mpifg_dp/dp00–5.pdf (last accessed 13 November 2014).

Schattschneider, E. E. (1942) *Party Government*, New York: Farrar and Rinehart.

Schellenberg, B. (1975) *Die Organisation der Zweckverbände. Unter besonderer Berücksichtigung der Praxis des Kantons Zürich*, PhD Diss University of Zurich; Zurich: Schulthess Polygraphischer Verlag.

Schmidt, M. G. (2004) *Wörterbuch zur Politik*, Stuttgart: Kröner Verlag.

Schmitt, N. (2002) *De l'existence, des fonctions et de l'utilité d'un échelon intermédiaire en Suisse et plus spécialement dans le Canton du Valais*, Etude réalisée par l'Institut du Fédéralisme de l'Université de Fribourg. Granges-Paccot: IFF.

— (2012) 'New Constitutions for All Swiss Cantons: A contemporary challenge, in M. Burgess and G. A. Tarr (eds) *Constitutional Dynamics in Federal Systems: Sub-national perspectives,* Montreal and Kingston, London, Ithaca: Forum of Federations and McGill Queen's University Press, pp. 140–63.

Schmitt, N. and Gassmann, J.-L. (2005) 'Le référendum des communes', *Bulletin de législation* no 3, Institut du fédéralisme, Université de Fribourg.

Schönholzer, L. (2011) *Solothurn*, Presentation held at the "ERFA-Tagung Gemeindereformen" in Emmenbrücke, 24 March 2011.

Schreyer, B. and Schwarzmeier, M. (2000) *Grundkurs Politikwissenschaft: Studium der politischen Systeme. Eine studienorientierte Einführung*, Wiesbaden: Westdeutscher Verlag.

Schuler, F. (2011) 'Die Entwicklung des Bündner Gemeindewesens im 20. Jahrhundert', in F. Hitz, C. Rathgeb and M. Risi (eds) *Gemeinden und Verfassung. Bündner Politik und Gebietsstruktur gestern, heute, morgen*, Chur: Südostschweiz Buchverlag, pp. 135–52.

Schweizer, R. J. (1981) *Verfassung des Kantons Glarus: Kommentar zum Entwurf,* 2 Vols, Kommission für die Vorberatung der Totalrevision der Kantonsverfassung (ed.), Regierungskanzlei des Kantons Glarus.

Schwoerer, D. (1998) 'Bezirke und Gemeinden', in K. Jenny, A. Achermann, S. Mathis and L. Ott (eds) *Staats- und Verwaltungsrecht des Kantons Basel-Landschaft*, Liestal: Verlag des Kantons Basel-Landschaft, pp. 250–272.

Scott, J. C. (1996) 'State Simplifications: Nature, space and people', in. I. Shapiro and R. Hardin (eds) *Political Order*, Nomos: Yearbook of the American Society for Political and Legal Philosophy, vol. XXXVIII: 42–85. New York and London: New York University Press.

Scott, K. (2011) *Federalism: A normative theory and its practical relevance*, New York, London: Continuum.

Selway, J. S. (2011) 'The measurement of cross-cutting cleavages and other multidimensional cleavage structures', *Political Analysis* 19: 48–65 [Advance Access publication January 4, 2011].

Sharpe, L. J. (1970) 'Theories and values of local government', *Political Studies* XVIII(2): 153–174.

— (1979) 'Decentralist trends in Western Democracies: A first appraisal', in L. J. Sharpe (ed.) *Decentralist trends in Western Democracies*, London and Beverly Hills: Sage Publications, pp. 9–79.

— (1993) 'The European Meso: An appraisal', in L. J. Sharpe (ed.) *The Rise of Meso Government in Europe*, London and Newbury Park, CA: Sage Publications, pp. 1–39.

Shugart, M. S. (2005) 'Comparative Electoral Systems Research: The maturation of a field and new challenges ahead', in M. Gallagher and P. Mitchell (eds) *The Politics of Electoral* Systems, Oxford: Oxford University Press, pp. 25–55.

Sidgwick, H. (1903) *The Development of the European Polity*, London: Macmillan and Co.

Siegfried, A. (1948) *La Suisse, démocratie-témoin*, Neuchâtel: A la Baconnière.

Simeon, R. and Elkins, D. J. (1974) 'Regional political cultures in Canada', *Canadian Journal of Political Science / Revue canadienne de science politique* 7(3): 397–437.

Skelcher, C. (2005) 'Jurisdictional integrity, polycentrism and the design of democratic governance', *Governance* 18(1): 89–110.

Slater, D. (1989) 'Territorial power and the peripheral state: the issue of decentralization', *Development and Change* 20(3): 501–531.

Smith, B. C. (1982) 'Measuring Decentralization', in G. Jones (ed.) *New Approaches to the Study of Central-Local Government Relations*, Hants, England: Gower Publishing, pp. 137–151.

— (1985) *Decentralization: The territorial dimension of the state*, London: George Allen and Unwin.

Snyder, R. (2001) 'Scaling down: the subnational comparative method', *Studies in Comparative International Development* 36(1): 93–110.

Somerville, P. (2004) 'State rescaling and democratic transformation', *Space and Polity* 8(2): 137–156.

Sorens, J. (2009) 'The partisan logic of decentralization', *Regional and Federal Studies* 19(2): 255–272.

Stadler, H. (2008) 'Landsgemeinde', *Historisches Lexikon der Schweiz*, http://www.hls-dhs-dss.ch/textes/d/D10239.php (last accessed 17 February 2015).

Stauffer, T. (2001) 'Intergovernmental fiscal relations in fragmented societies: the case of Switzerland', *Environment and Planning C: Government and Policy* 19: 207–222.

Stegarescu, D. (2005) 'Costs, Preferences and Institutions: An Empirical Analysis of the Determinants of Government Decentralization', Mannheim: Centre for European Economic Research.

Stein, M. B. (1968) 'Review: Federal political systems and federal societies', *World Politics* 20(4): 721, 723, 725, 727, 729, 731, 733, 735, 737, 739, 741, 743 and 745–747.

Steinberg, J. (1976) *Why Switzerland?*, Cambridge: Cambridge University Press.

Steinberg, P. F. (2007) 'Causal assessment in Small-N policy studies', *The Policy Studies Journal* 35(2): 181–204.

Steiner, R. (2003) 'The causes, spread and effects of intermunicipal cooperation and municipal mergers in Switzerland', *Public Management Review* 5(4): 551–571.

Steiner, R., Reist, P. and Kettiger, D. (2010) *Gemeindestrukturreform im Kanton Uri: Analyse der Urner Gemeinden und mögliche Handlungsoptionen.*

Bericht im Auftrag des Regierungsrates des Kantons Uri, KPM-Schriftenreihe no. 36, Bern.

Stepan, A. (2001) *Arguing Comparative Politics*, Oxford: Oxford University Press.

Stephens, G. R. (1974) 'Centralization and the erosion of local autonomy', *The Journal of Politics* 36(1): 44–76.

Stephens, G. R. and Wikstrom, N. (2000) *Metropolitan Government and Governance*, New York: Oxford University Press.

Steunenberg, B. and Mol, N. (1997) 'Fiscal and Financial Decentralization: A comparative analysis of six West European countries', in J. -E. Lane (ed.) *Public Sector Reform: Rationale, trends and problems*, London, Thousand Oaks CA: SAGE Publications, pp. 235–256.

Stewart, J. (1983) *Local Government: The conditions of local choice*, London, Boston, Sydney: George Allen and Unwin.

Steytler, N. (ed.) (2009) *Local Government and Metropolitan Regions in Federal Systems: A global dialogue on federalism*, Vol. 6, Montreal, Kingston, London and Ithaca: McGill-Queen's University Press.

Stoker, G. and Marsh, D. (2010) 'Introduction', in D. Marsh and G. Stoker (eds) *Theory and Methods in Political Science*, 3rd edn, Basingstoke: Palgrave Macmillan, pp. 1–12.

Stoll, H. (2008) 'Social cleavages and the number of parties: how the measures you choose affect the answers you get', *Comparative Political Studies* 41(11): 1439–65.

Storey, D. (2012) *Territories: The claiming of space*, 2nd edn, London and New York: Routledge.

Strayer, J. R. (1971) *Medieval Statecraft and the Perspectives of History*, Princeton: Princeton University Press.

Studer Immenhauser, B. K. (2006) *Verwaltung zwischen Innovation und Tradition. Die Stadt Bern und ihr Untertanengebiet 1250–1550*, Ostfildern: Jan Thorbecke Verlag.

Stutzer, A. (1999) 'Demokratieindizes für die Kantone der Schweiz', in *Working Papers of the Institute for Empirical Research in Economics*, Zurich: University of Zurich, Institute for Empirical Research in Economics.

Sutcliffe, J. B. (2007) 'Local government in a multi-level setting: lessons from England and Ontario', *Regional and Federal Studies* 17(2): 253–273.

Suter, M. (2012) 'Die Staatsgeschichte 1798–2008 im Überblick', in Historischer Verein des Kantons Schwyz (ed.) *Geschichte des Kantons Schwyz*, Vol. IV, Zurich: Chronos Verlag, pp. 67–117.

Swenden, W. (2006) *Federalism and Regionalism in Western Europe: A comparative and thematic analysis*, Basingstoke: Palgrave Macmillan.

Swenden, W. and Maddens, B. (2009) 'Introduction: Territorial Party Politics in Western Europe: A framework for analysis', in W. Swenden and B. Maddens (eds) *Territorial Party Politics in Western Europe*, Basingstoke: Palgrave Macmillan, pp. 1–30.

Swianiewicz, P. (2010) 'If territorial fragmentation is a problem, is amalgamation a solution? An East European perspective', *Local Government Studies* 36(2): 183–203.

Sykes, O. and Shaw, D. (2008) 'Investigating territorial positioning by sub-state territories in Europe', *Regional and Federal Studies* 18(1): 55–76.

Taagepera, R. (2003) 'Arend Lijphart's dimensions of democracy: logical connections and institutional design', *Political Studies* 51(1): 1–19.

Tanquerel, T. and Bellanger, F. (eds) (2007) *L'avenir juridique des communes*, Geneva, Zurich, Basel: Schulthess Médias Juridiques SA.

Tappy, D. (2006) 'La conquête bernoise et les Etats de Vaud', in A. Holenstein (ed.) *Berns mächtige Zeit: das 16. und 17. Jahrhundert neu entdeckt*, Bern: Stämpfli Verlag, pp. 76–79.

Tarlton, C. D. (1965) 'Symmetry and asymmetry as elements of federalism: a theoretical speculation', *The Journal of Politics* 27(4): 861–74.

Tarrow, S. (1974) 'Local constraints on regional reform: a comparison of Italy and France', *Comparative Politics* 7: 1–36.

— (1977) *Between Center and Periphery: Grassroots politicians in Italy and France*, New Haven and London: Yale University Press.

— (1995) 'Bridging the quantitative-qualitative divide in political science', *American Political Science Review* 89(2): 471–474.

— (2004) 'Centre-Periphery Alignments and Political Contention in Late-Modern Europe', in C. K. Ansell and G. Di Palma (eds) *Restructuring Territoriality: Europe and the United States Compared*, Cambridge: Cambridge University Press, pp. 45–64.

— (2010) 'The strategy of paired comparison: toward a theory of practice', *Comparative Political Studies* 43(2): 230–259.

Tatham, M. and Thau, M. (2014) 'The more the merrier: accounting for regional paradiplomats in Brussels', *European Union Politics* June 15(2): 255–276.

Teschke, B. (2006) 'The Metamorphoses of European Territoriality: A historical reconstruction', in M. Burgess and H. Vollaard (eds) *State Territoriality and European Integration: Territoriality and Federalism in EU Governance*, London: Routledge, pp. 37–67.

Thelen, K. (1999) 'Historical institutionalism in comparative perspective', *Annual Review of Political Science* 2: 369–404.

— (2002) 'The Explanatory Power of Historical Institutionalism', in R. Mayntz (ed.) *Akteure, Mechanismen, Modelle. Zur Theoriefähigkeit makrosozialer Analysen*, Frankfurt/New York: Campus Verlag, pp. 91–107.

Thoenig, J.-C. (2008) 'Territorial Institutions', in R. A. W. Rhodes, S. A. Binder and B. A. Rockman (eds) *The Oxford Handbook of Political Institutions*, Oxford: OUP, pp. 281–302.

Thorlakson, L. (2007) 'An institutional explanation of party system congruence: evidence from six federations', *European Journal of Political Research* 46: 69–95.

— (2009) 'Patterns of party integration, influence and autonomy in seven federations', *Party Politics* 15(2): 157–177.

— (2010) Party Organizational Strategy in Multi-level Systems', Paper presented at the 2010 Canadian Political Science Association- Annual Conference, Montreal, Quebec, 1–3 June.

Thürer, D. (1986) *Bund und Gemeinden. Eine rechtsvergleichende Untersuchung zu den unmittelbaren Beziehungen zwischen Bund und Gemeinden in der Bundesrepublik Deutschland, den Vereinigten Staaten von Amerika und der Schweiz*, Beiträge zum ausländischen öffentlichen Recht und Völkerrecht, vol 90. Berlin: Springer-Verlag.

Thürer, G. (1946) 'Geschichtliche Entwicklung der Gemeindeautonomie', in H. Nawiasky (ed.) *Die Gemeindeautonomie*, Einsiedeln, Köln: Verlaisanstalt Benziger and Co. AG, pp. 27–40.

Tiebout, C. M. (1956) 'A pure theory of local expenditures', *Journal of Political Economy* 64(5): 416–24.

Tilly, C. (ed.) (1975) *The Formation of National States in Western Europe*, Princeton: Princeton University Press.

Timofeev, A. (2003) 'Determinants of Decentralization within Russian Regions', Budapest: Local Government and Public Service Initiative.

Toonen, T. A. J. and van der Meer, F. M. (2006) 'Area and Administration: A multi-level analysis of a multi-layered phenomenon', in M. Burgess and H. Vollaard (eds) *State Territoriality and European Integration: Territoriality and federalism in EU governance*, London: Routledge, pp. 71–99.

Töpperwien, N. (2004) 'Defining Local Government – Political Constraints and the Question of Boundaries', Paper presented at the VIth World Congress of the IACL in Santiago de Chile.

Trechsel, A. H. and Kriesi, H. (1996) 'Switzerland: the referendum and initiative as a centrepiece of the political system', in M. Gallagher and P. Vincenzo Uleri (eds) *The Referendum Experience in Europe*, London: Macmillan Press Ltd, pp. 185–207.

Treisman, D. (2002) 'Defining and Measuring Decentralization: A Global Perspective', Unpublished paper http://www.sscnet.ucla.edu/polisci/faculty/treisman/Papers/defin.pdf (last accessed 27 February 2011).

— (2006) 'Explaining fiscal decentralisation: geography, colonial history, economic development and political institutions', *Commonwealth and Comparative Politics* 44(3): 289–325.

— (2007) *The Architecture of Government: Rethinking political decentralization*, Cambridge: Cambridge University Press.

Trench, A. (2006) 'Intergovernmental Relations: In search of a theory', in S. L. Greer (ed.) *Territory, Democracy and Justice*, Houndmills, Basingstoke, Hampshire and New York: Palgrave Macmillan, pp. 224–56.

Tschäni, H. (1982) 'Constitutional change in Swiss cantons: an assessment of a recent phenomenon, *Publius* 12(1): 113–130.

Turgeon, L. and Simeon, R. (2015) 'Ideology, Political Economy and Federalism: The welfare state and the evolution of the Australian and Canadian federations', in A. G. Gagnon, S. Keil and S. Mueller (eds) *Understanding Federalism and Federation: Essays in honour of Michael Burgess*, Farnham, UK: Ashgate, (forthcoming).

UN-HABITAT (2009) 'International Guidelines on Decentralisation and Access to Basic Services for all', United Nations Human Settlement Programme (ed.) Nairobi. At http://www.unhabitat.org/pmss/listItemDetails. aspx?publicationID=2613 (last accessed March 2011).

Urio, P. (1986) 'Les administrations cantonales', in R. E. Germann and E. Weibel (eds) *Handbuch Politisches System der Schweiz*, vol. 3, *Föderalismus*, Berne: Verlag Paul Haupt, pp. 107–136.

van Biezen, I. (2003) *Political Parties in New Democracies: Party organization in Southern and East-Central Europe*, London: Palgrave.

Van Evera, S. (1997) *Guide to Methods for Students of Political Science*, Ithaca, NY: Cornell University Press.

Vatter, A. (2002) *Kantonale Demokratien im Vergleich: Entstehungsgründe, Interaktionen und Wirkungen politischer Institutionen in den Schweizer Kantonen*, Opladen: Leske + Budrich.

— (2003) 'Legislative party fragmentation in Swiss cantons: a function of cleavage structures or electoral institutions?', *Party Politics* 9(4): 445–461.

— (2006a) 'Föderalismus', in U. Klöti et al.(eds) *Handbuch der Schweizer Politik*, 4th edn, Zurich: Neue Zürcher Zeitung Publishing, pp. 79–102.

— (2006b) 'Die Kantone', in U. Klöti et al.(eds) *Handbuch der Schweizer Politik*, 4th edn, Zurich: Neue Zürcher Zeitung Publishing, pp. 203–231.

— (2014) 'Kantone', in P. Knoepfel, Y. Papadopoulos, P. Sciarini, A. Vatter and S. Häusermann (eds) *Handbuch der Schweizer Politik/Manuel de la politique Suisse*, Zurich: Verlag NZZ Libro, pp. 245–274.

Vatter, A. and Church, C. (2009) 'Opposition in consensual Switzerland: a short but significant experiment', *Government and Opposition* 44(4): 412–37.

Vatter, A. and Freitag, M. (2002) 'Die Janusköpfigkeit von Verhandlungsdemokratien. Zur Wirkung von Konkordanz, direkter Demokratie und dezentralen Entscheidungsstrukturen auf den öffentlichen Sektor der Schweizer Kantone', *Schweizerische Zeitschrift für Politikwissenschaft* 8(3): 53–80.

— (2007) 'The contradictory effects of consensus democracy on the size of government: evidence from the Swiss cantons', *British Journal of Political Science* 37: 359–367.

Vatter, A., Linder, W. and Farago, P. (1996) 'Determinanten politischer Kultur am Beispiel des Schwyzer Stimmverhaltens', *Swiss Political Science Review* 3(1): 1–63.

Vile, M. J. C. (1961) *The Structure of American Federalism*, London: Oxford University Press.

Vischer, E. (1983) *Heimat und Welt. Studien zur Geschichte einer schweizerischen Landsgemeinde-Demokratie*, Berne: Francke Verlag.

Vollaard, H. (2009a) *Political Territoriality in the European Union. The Challenging Boundaries of Security and Healthcare*, PhD Diss University of Leiden (NL).

— (2009b) 'The logic of political territoriality', *Geopolitics* 14(4): 687–706.

von Greyerz, H. (1953) *Nation und Geschichte im bernischen Denken. Vom Beitrag Berns zum schweizerischen Geschichts- und Nationalbewußtsein*, Bern: Verlag Herbert Lang and Cie.

Vromen, A. (2010) 'Redesigning the Qualitative Approach', in D. Marsh and G. Stoker (eds) *Theory and Methods in Political Science*, Basingstoke: Palgrave Macmillan, pp. 249–266.

Wälchli, K. F. (2005) 'Burgund (Herzogtum)', *Historisches Lexikon der Schweiz*, http://www.hls-dhs-dss.ch/textes/d/D7281.php (last accessed 17 February 2015).

Walker, R. B. J. (1984) 'The territorial state and the theme of Gulliver', *International Journal* 39(3): 529–552.

Wallis, J. J. and Oates, W. E. (1988) 'Decentralization in the public sector: an empirical study and local governments', in H. S. Rosen (ed.) *Fiscal Decentralization: Quantitative studies,* NBER Project Report, Chicago and London: University of Chicago Press, pp. 5–32. Available online at http://www.nber.org/chapters/c7882.pdf (last accessed 13 May 2012).

Watts, R. L. (1996) *Comparaison des régimes fédéraux des années 1990*, Kingston, Ontario: Queen's University Press.

— (1998) 'Federalism, federal political systems and federations', *Annual Review of Political Science* 1(1): 117–137.

— (2006) 'Origins of Cooperative and Competitive Federalism', in S. L. Greer (ed.)*Territory, Democracy and Justice*, Houndmills, Basingstoke, Hampshire and New York: Palgrave Macmillan, pp. 201–223.

— (2008) *Comparing Federal Systems*, 3rd edn, Montreal and Kingston, London, Ithaca: McGill-Queen's University Press.

Weber, E. (1976) *Peasants into Frenchmen: The modernization of rural France, 1870–1914*, Stanford: Stanford University Press.

Weber, M. (1992 [1919]) *Politik als Beruf*, Stuttgart: Philipp Reclam jun.

Weinberg, D. (1983) 'Conflicting political models in a Swiss commune', *Ethnology* 22(1): 17–26.

Wernli, K. (2005) 'Aufgabenteilung Kanton-Gemeinden im Kanton Aargau: Erfahrungen aus dem Projekt', in Institut für Föderalismus (ed.) *1. Nationale Föderalismuskonferenz*, Basel: Helbing & Lichtenhahn, pp. 213–221.

Weyermann, H. (1924) *Der Regierungsstatthalter als Administrativ- und Administrativjustizorgan der bernischen Staatsverwaltung*, PhD Diss University of Berne; Berne: Buchdruckerei Büchler and Co.

Wheare, K. C. (1963) *Federal Government*, London, New York, Toronto: Oxford University Press.

Wiget, J. (1991) 'Schwyz vom späten Mittelalter bis 1798', *Mitteilungen des historischen Vereins des Kantons Schwyz* 83: 167–174.

— (2002) 'Die historische Bedeutung der schwyzerischen Bezirke und deren Entwicklung in der Zeit der alten Eidgenossenschaft', in Projekt-Steuerungsteam (ed.) *Grundlagenbericht G-Reform: Gleichgewicht von Aufgaben, Finanzen, Institutionen und Gebieten*, Beilage 3: 52–69, Schwyz, 24 May 2002.

— (2012) 'Platz dem Landvogt! Die Bedeutung der Untertanengebiete', in Historischer Verein des Kantons Schwyz (ed.) *Geschichte des Kantons Schwyz*, Vol III, Zurich: Chronos Verlag, pp. 165–193.

Wildavsky, A. (1987) 'Choosing preferences by constructing institutions: a cultural theory of preference formation', *American Political Science Review* 81: 3–21.

Williamson, J. (2009) 'Probabilistic Theories of Causality', in H. Beebee, C. Hitchcock and P. Menzies (eds) *The Oxford Handbook of Causation*, Oxford: OUP, pp. 185–212.

Winteler, J. (1961) *Glarus: Geschichte eines ländlichen Hauptortes*, Herausgegeben vom Gemeinderat Glarus zum 100, Gedenktag des Brandes vom 10./11. Mai 1981, Glarus: Verlag Tschudi and Co.

Würgler, A. (2008) 'The League of the Discordant Members or How the Old Swiss Confederation Operated and How it Managed to Survive for so Long', in A. Holenstein, T. Maissen and M. Prak (eds) *The Republican Alternative: The Netherlands and Switzerland compared*, Amsterdam: Amsterdam University Press, pp. 29–50.

Ylvisaker, P. (1959) 'Some Criteria for a 'Proper' Areal Division of Governmental Power', in A. Maass (ed.) *Area and Power: A theory of local government'*, Glencoe, Illinois: The Free Press, pp. 27–49.

Zahnd, U.M. (2011) 'Bern (Kanton) – Kommunale Bewegung und Territorialbildung im Spätmittelalter', *Historisches Lexikon der Schweiz*, http://www.hls-dhs-dss.ch/textes/d/D7383.php (last accessed 17 February 2015).

Zimmerman, J. F. (1994) *State-Local Relations: A partnership approach*, 2nd edn, Westport, Connecticut and London: Praeger.

— (2010) *The Book of the States*, Council of State Governments.

Zürn, M., Enderlein, H. and Wälti, S. (eds) (2010) *Handbook on Multi-Level Governance*, Cheltenham: Edward Elgar.

Zwahlen, H. (1968) 'L'autonomie communale à la lumière de la jurisprudence récente du Tribunal fédéral suisse', in *Mélanges Marcel Bridel: Receuil de travaux publiés par la Faculté de droit*, Lausanne: Imprimeries Réunies S.A., pp. 631–649.

Index

www.ingramcontent.com/pod-product-compliance
Lightning Source LLC
Chambersburg PA
CBHW072054020426
42334CB00017B/1507